A SOUTHERN COMMUNITY IN CRISIS

A SOUTHERN COMMUNITY IN CRISIS

Harrison County, Texas, 1850–1880

By Randolph B. Campbell

Foreword by Andrew J. Torget

With a new preface by the author

Texas State Historical Assocaition

Austin

Library of Congress Cataloging-in-Publication Data

Names: Campbell, Randolph B., 1940– author, writer of introduction. | Torget, Andrew J., 1978– writer of foreword. | Texas State Historical Association, issuing body.
Title: A southern community in crisis : Harrison County, Texas, 1850–1880 / by Randolph B. Campbell ; foreword by Andrew J. Torget ; with a new preface by the author.
Description: Paperback edition. | Austin : Texas State Historical Association, [2016] | Originally published in 1983. | Includes bibliographical references and index.
Identifiers: LCCN 2016033642 | ISBN 9781625110404 (pbk.)
Subjects: LCSH: Harrison County (Tex.)—Politics and government. | Harrison County (Tex.)—Social conditions. | Harrison County (Tex.)—Economic conditions. | Reconstruction (U.S. history, 1865–1877)—Texas—Case studies.

To

Max Lale

and

The Memory of Georgiana

Marshall, Texas

Table of Contents

List of Tables

List of Illustrations

Robert W. Loughery: editor of the *Texas Republican*

N. V. Board: unionist political leader

David Abner: member of the Constitutional Convention of 1875

George W. Whitmore: unionist politician and Republican congressman

"Mimosa Hall": built on the Webster plantation by the family slaves

"Edgemont": the plantation home of Montreville J. Hall

Acknowledgments

The research and writing of a book creates obligations that cannot be adequately acknowledged with a few words. To many of those who have helped me, words are all that I can give. In a larger sense, however, I hope eventually to meet my indebtedness to the historical profession with the same kinds of encouragement and aid that were extended to me.

My friends in Harrison County must be mentioned first. Max and Georgiana Lale offered unfailing kindness and support from the time we first met in 1971. Max's devotion to the study of history is inspiring. And Georgiana, as Bill Moyers of the CBS Evening News said in paying tribute to her at her death in 1982, "carried on a long affair with the past." Citizens like Max and

Georgiana hold together the communities that constitute our nation, and it is to them that this book is dedicated.

Mrs. Inez Hughes, Director of the Harrison County Historical Museum, understood my interest in her community's past and assisted my research in a variety of ways. County Clerk Glenn Link gave me the "run" of his office. Douglass V. Blocker and Mr. and Mrs. John Blocker Ware allowed me to visit their antebellum plantation homes and permitted the use of their family records. Mrs. Eudora C. Hodges of Dallas provided valuable information on the Perry family.

My colleagues at North Texas State University did not laugh as I spent year after year studying thirty years in the history of one East Texas community. The Faculty Research Committee provided four years of financial support for various aspects of the project. Richard Lowe read and criticized the entire manuscript. Don Chipman gave consistent encouragement and even spent several days collecting information on slave prices from probate papers in the Harrison County courthouse. Bill Holmes prepared the map of Harrison County. The staff of our computing center, especially Steve Minnis, provided essential assistance in the handling of quantitative data from the census returns.

The American Council of Learned Societies awarded me a grant for research assistance in 1976. The money was well spent as it (and such other funds as I had for that purpose) went to Ruth Sheehan for her work in collecting the manuscript census samples. Ruth's intelligent and conscientious work helped me avoid many problems in data collection.

I owe a major debt of gratitude to the editors of several historical journals. Professor L. Tuffly Ellis, Director of the Texas State Historical Association and editor of the *Southwestern Historical Quarterly*, believed in this project from the beginning. He has given aid and encouragement in more ways that I can count. Professor Sanford W. Higginbotham, editor of the *Journal of Southern History*, published two of my articles on Harrison County, thereby helping me to believe that the story was worthy of telling. The essentials of the second of those articles, "Population Persistence and Social Change in

Nineteenth-Century Texas: Harrison County, 1850-1880'' (Vol. XLVIII, May 1982, 185-204) are contained in Chapter 14. They are re-stated with the approval of Professor Higginbotham. Professor John T. Hubbell, editor of *Civil War History,* published my account of political life, ''Political Conflict Within the Southern Consensus: Harrison County, Texas, 1850-1880'' (Vol. XXVI, September 1980, 218-239). The essentials of this article appear in Chapter 6 with the approval of the Kent State University Press, publisher of *Civil War History*. Professor Archie McDonald, editor of the *East Texas Historical Journal*, published several of my research findings and has always encouraged my interest in Harrison County.

Finally, there is my family. Landon and Clay have grown up with Harrison County research. They were pre-schoolers when it began, and now they are teenagers. At least we have taken time to go through many soccer, baseball, and basketball games along the way. My wife, Diana, has served as research assistant, literary critic, typist, and proofreader. Through it all she has only occasionally asked why she did not marry wealth rather than someone who only studies it.

Randolph B. Campbell
Denton, Texas
July, 1983

Foreword

When Randolph B. Campbell's *A Southern Community in Crisis* first appeared in 1983, the book embodied some of the most important movements roiling the historical profession during that era. In the wake of the tumultuous social and political upheavals of the 1960s and early 1970s, for example, historians had begun pushing hard to recover the histories of everyday people in hopes of telling the past "from the bottom up" rather than "from the top down." Turning away from sweeping narratives centered on national figures, these scholars increasingly embraced community-focused studies where a ground-level approach could allow them to explore the lives of people who had been largely left out of the traditional American narrative. At that same moment, the emergence of new computing centers on college campuses led a smaller group of historians to begin experimenting with applying statistical methodology to historical records. These "quantifying" scholars also hoped to provide a clearer sense of what was happening on the ground, and they seized upon the power of computers as a means for unlocking and analyzing patterns of everyday life embedded within census records, election returns, tax rolls, and anything else that might provide quantifiable information about prevailing trends within various communities and regions. In both of these approaches, a new generation of historians worked to write a deeper and more granular portrait of the past.

In this work, Campbell brought together those two methods—a community-focused orientation, combined with statistical analysis of surviving records—in order to provide a ground-level history of how the great events of the mid-nineteenth century affected the lives of everyday people in East Texas. The book follows the men and women of Harrison County, Texas, through the tumultuous years spanning the coming, fighting, and aftermath of the U.S. Civil War. The county emerged during the 1850s as a leading edge of the cotton boom in Texas, where Harrison planters held more enslaved people than any other county in the state. When the war came, white residents of the county threw themselves behind the Confederate cause, only to find themselves dismayed when the failure of that cause led to the sudden emancipation of the county's majority black population in 1865. The mighty struggles over labor, citizenship, and power that followed during Reconstruction revealed men and women of every social station struggling to define what new order would emerge from the chaos of the post-war period.

What Campbell finds, ultimately, is that Harrison County was a Southern place, and the "conservative revolution" supported by the county's white residents in 1861 brought tremendous change to the county against their will—most powerfully by ending slavery—but did not, in the end, dislodge the county's overall power structure that concentrated most local wealth and political influence within the hands of white elites at the expense of the black majority. Indeed, Campbell's framing of Harrison County (and, by implication, East Texas) as fundamentally Southern in nature provides the driving framework for the book. One of the central arguments woven throughout the pages is that the economic, political, and social world of Harrison County was indelibly Southern, and the trials and triumphs of the people who lived within the county—both black and white—followed similar paths to those of people elsewhere in the territories that made up the cotton South. Although Campbell does not claim Harrison County to be "typical" or representative of any other place, he does hold up the county as a window into how Southern people experienced those powerful and trying years.

What makes the volume so powerful is the remarkable depth of the research behind it. Much of the evidence was unearthed in the Harrison County courthouse, which Campbell mined for insights that only probate records, court minutes, and deed books can provide, along with extensive work in surviving manuscripts and newspapers. Such traditional sources were paired with innovative use of statistics and quantification, which might feel unfamiliar to the modern reader. Quantification has become less prominent among historians in the years since this book first appeared, and scholars today tend to bury numbers and discussions of methodology within endnotes and appendixes. Yet it would be difficult to deny the raw power of the numbers that Campbell marshals to his cause, which, when combined with a broad array of local records, document in beautiful specificity the evolution of economic, social, and political realities in Harrison County. In short, there are no easy generalizations in *A Southern Community in Crisis.* What the reader encounters instead are exacting insights into what the community's surviving records can tell us.

The methodology and focus that gave *A Southern Community in Crisis* its power would go on to define much of Campbell's later scholarship. The seeds of his groundbreaking work on slavery in Texas, *An Empire for Slavery: The Peculiar Institu-*

tion in Texas, 1861–1865 (LSU Press, 1989), can be found in chapter 5 of this book. A preview of his broadly influential *Grass-Roots Reconstruction in Texas, 1865–1880* (LSU Press, 1997) constitutes the final third of this volume. In those books and other publications, scrupulous research in local records and relentless attention to the experience on the ground allowed Campbell to challenge an enduring misperception that Texas was somehow outside the Southern experience.

Yet for all that came after it, *A Southern Community in Crisis* remains essential reading for anyone who wants to understand life in Texas during the coming, fighting, and aftermath of the Civil War. That Campbell did his job so well—with such rigor in his research, and such humanity in his writing—is the reason the book is still so useful today. Few academic volumes remain timely and relevant more than thirty years after they were first published. This is one of those exceptional books.

Andrew J. Torget
Denton, Texas
July 2016

July 2016 Author's Preface

Writing a new introduction to an old book presents a not-to-be-missed opportunity to offer an apologia, a defense wrapped in an explanation, for the old work. My apologia for *A Southern Community in Crisis: Harrison County, Texas, 1850–1880* begins with the title. Use of the word "community" opened the door for one critic after another to point out that the inhabitants of a county with a population more enslaved than free hardly had the shared interests, attitudes, and goals necessary to fit all standard dictionary definitions of the word. Most dictionaries continue to recognize that "community" can mean simply a physical space, but the word is so freighted with social and political implications that another word meaning "place" would have reduced criticism. Perhaps, of course, the author should have had enough awareness of a potential problem to explain the title in the first place.

Critics also argued that *Southern Community in Crisis* placed too much emphasis on continuity at the expense of change. That could be a valid criticism. After all, the elimination of slavery would appear to have revolutionized the county and outweigh any continuity. Certainly, from the point of view of those who gained freedom, the change was life changing. On the other hand, the same kinds of people, and in many cases the same individuals, who had controlled the county economically, socially, and politically in 1850 retained the same sort of control in 1880. Change cannot be denied, but the extent and fundamental nature of that change can be debated. Whether the study exaggerates the degree of continuity is a matter for each reader to decide.

Southern Community in Crisis relied heavily on quantitative data, especially those gleaned from the United States Census and Texas tax records, and at times employed complicated statistical measures that some deemed inappropriate for a local study. Granted that analytical quantitative history is rarely fun to read, the fact is that questions dealing with very important issues such as the profitability of slavery and the economics of social structure can only be answered through the use of numbers. The book has twenty-eight tables, and even if this edition were a revision rather than a reprint, all would remain.

Finally, the reasons for reprinting this book, regardless of its flaws as addressed in my apologia, remain the same as those for its original publication. Historians have published countless studies of the American Civil War and Reconstruction. Most of those works focus on events and developments at the national or state level, explaining and analyzing the causes of disunion, the course of the war, and the bitter disputes that arose during restoration of the Union. Much less attention has been given to studying how ordinary people experienced the years from 1861 to 1876. There are exceptions, but this generalization largely holds true for Texas, and it leaves a large question:

What did secession, civil war, emancipation, victory for the United States, and the period of reconstruction that followed mean at the local level in Texas; to individuals in the counties and towns where most Texans lived? To be more specific, how did a locality such as Harrison County, a cotton-growing, planter-dominated area with the largest slave population of any county in the state, experience these years of crisis? Providing an answer to that question was the basic purpose of *A Southern Community in Crisis: Harrison County, Texas, 1850–1880,* a book first published by the Texas State Historical Association in 1983 and now reprinted some thirty-three years later.

Randolph B. Campbell
Denton, Texas
March 2016

A SOUTHERN COMMUNITY IN CRISIS

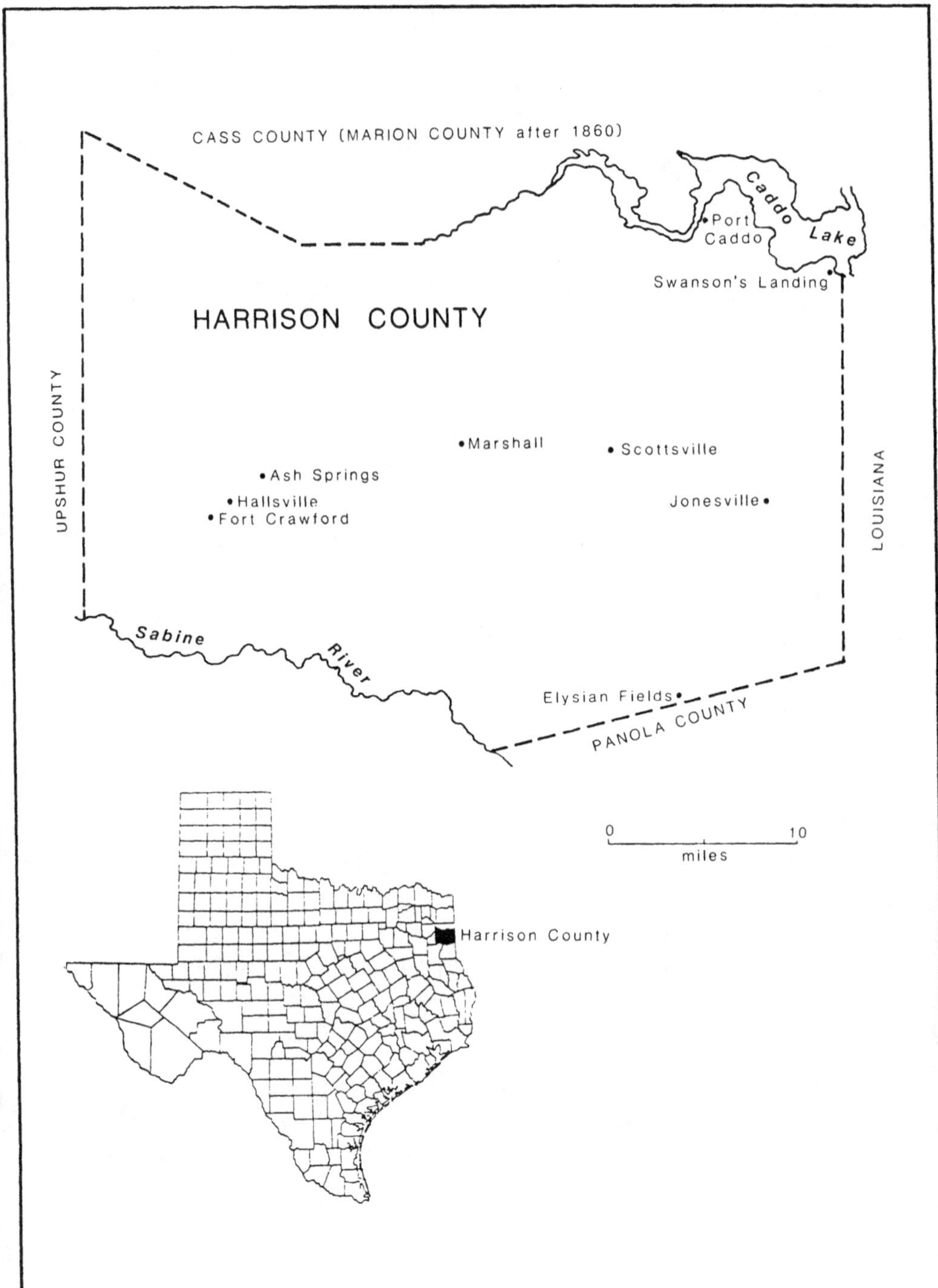

CASS COUNTY (MARION COUNTY after 1860)
Caddo
Lake
Port
Caddo
Swanson's Landing
HARRISON COUNTY
UPSHUR COUNTY
LOUISIANA
Marshall
Scottsville
Ash Springs
Hallsville
Fort Crawford
Jonesville
Sabine
River
Elysian Fields
PANOLA COUNTY
0
10
miles
Harrison County

Introduction

HARRISON COUNTY is located in the East Texas timberlands on the border between the Lone Star State and Louisiana. Edward Smith, a pioneer in the southeastern part of the county, described the area in such glowing terms that one listener decided that his settlement should be called "Elysian Fields."[1] The name stuck. Although some observers may not have agreed that the land was quite so delightful, settlers moved in rapidly. Created in 1839, Harrison grew to become one of the most populous counties in antebellum Texas and the center of cotton plantation agriculture in the northeastern part of the

[1] Walter Prescott Webb, H. Bailey Carroll, and Eldon S. Branda (eds.), *The Handbook of Texas* (3 vols; Austin, 1952, 1976), I, 564, 780-781.

state. By 1860 it had more Negro slaves than any other county in Texas and boasted 145 planters who owned at least twenty slaves each.[2]

In spite of the fact that the majority had migrated to Texas from the states that formed the Confederacy in 1861, many residents of Harrison County were not ultra-southern in their sentiments during the secession crisis, and a few were staunch unionists. When the Lone Star State seceded in 1861, however, the overwhelming majority who voted on the issue supported leaving the United States and joining the Confederate States of America. Four very demanding years of Civil War followed. The community was not invaded, but hundreds of its men fought, and the majority of its people were called upon to make at least some material sacrifice. Federal troops occupied Marshall in 1865, and Reconstruction, first under presidential and then under congressional direction, took five years. Texas returned to the Union in 1870, and Republicans governed the state for four years before conservative white Democrats regained control. In Harrison County, where emancipation and the enfranchisement of Freedmen created a black majority, Republican government continued until November, 1878, The community was then "redeemed" in a spectacularly controversial election and by 1880 was prepared to leave behind the era of Civil War and Reconstruction to become part of the "New South."[3]

During the mid-nineteenth century then, the people of Harrison County lived with institutions and witnessed developments that were critical to American history. They experienced slavery, secession, Civil War, emancipation, and Reconstruction, and one hundred years later we continue to seek

[2]General descriptive information is found in James C. Armstrong, "History of Harrison County, Texas, 1839-1880," (M.A. Thesis, University of Colorado, 1930). Summary census data on population and slave/cotton agriculture for 1860 is found in United States Bureau of the Census, Eighth Census, *Population of the United States in 1860; Compiled from the Original Returns of the Eighth Census* (Washington, 1864), 474-486; and ibid., *Agriculture of the United States in 1860; Compiled from the Original Returns of the Eighth Census* (Washington, 1864), 240-242.

[3]Documentation of these statements concerning Harrison County's history from 1850 to 1880 will be provided in detail throughout this study. Armstrong, "History of Harrison County," provides a general outline based primarily on newspaper sources.

the historical "truth" about that era. How, we ask, could slavery exist, and what was its impact on slaves, slaveholders, and nonslaveholders? What were the basic economic, social, and political arrangements of antebellum society, and why did that society support secession and war? What was the impact of war, emancipation, and Reconstruction on those who experienced those developments? What were the chief characteristics of economic, social, and political life as the postbellum period gave way to the "New South" era of the 1880s? These very large questions, each of which covers a number of lesser and more precise ones, are historical perennials to be interpreted and reinterpreted so long as we continue to seek to understand and learn from our past. In this study, answers are sought in the history of one East Texas community.

The historical experience of the people of Harrison County from 1850 to 1880 also raises an even larger question, one concerning the extent of change and of continuity in our past. Americans generally have little difficulty with the concept of change. After all, the United States was born in revolution, survived a civil war, and lived through a great depression. In the process, it established republicanism, abolished slavery, and adopted several basic welfare-state measures. And all the while, material and technical progress was the rule rather than the exception. Few Americans object when theirs is termed a "revolutionary" nation. But what of continuity? Through all this torrent of change, have we not in many respects remained fundamentally the same? Have we ever revolutionized our economic system or rearranged our social structure? Viewed from the perspective of change, our history seems vital and exciting; but the perspective of continuity may contribute as much or even more to our understanding.

Developments in Harrison County from 1850 to 1880 present strong possibilities for finding both continuity and change. The South, and Harrison County was definitely southern, is famed for its resistance to change.[4] On the other hand, how

[4]See, for example, John Hope Franklin, "The Great Confrontation: The South and the Problem of Change," *Journal of Southern History*, XXXVIII (Feb., 1972), 3-20.

could the region lose a war, see slavery ended, and undergo Reconstruction directed by northern Republicans without experiencing drastic alterations in economic, social, and political arrangements? Exactly how different, we must ask, was the Harrison County that entered the "New South" in 1880 from the Harrison County of the Old South? In the largest sense then, the purpose of this study is to determine the degree of continuity and change over time in every aspect of one southern community's life during the era of Civil War and Reconstruction.

There are a number of potential difficulties inherent in writing community history that must be considered at the outset. First, a distinction should be made between studying the community as a community and examining the community's history as an approach to the past. Anthropologists and sociologists in particular have written on the community as such seeking to discover how people in various cultures relate to their natural surroundings (the community as "ecological system") and to each other (the community as "social system"). These matters are important to the historian too, and they will be examined, especially economic life and social structure. This study will explain how individuals in the community produced goods and services to make a living and how they dealt with each other in a system of hierarchical social relationships. Moreover, it will describe the community's population in terms of demographic characteristics, education, religion, and politics. But this emphasis on the Harrison County community as such, which borrows to some extent from other disciplines, is secondary to an examination of how the major institutions and developments of the years from 1850 to 1880 were experienced in that community. The study is essentially historical.[5]

[5]For a discussion of the problems involved in defining "community," see Ruth E. Sutter, *The Next Place You Come To: A Historical Introduction to Communities in North America* (Englewood Cliffs, N.J., 1973). Robert Redfield, *The Little Community* (Chicago, 1956), is an interesting introduction to community studies from an anthropological point of view. David J. Russo, *Families and Communities: A New View of American History* (Nashville, 1975), emphasizes the historical approach. Mark Friedberger and Janice R. Webster, "Social Structure and State and Local History," *Western Historical Quarterly*, IX (July, 1978), 297-314, contains some very useful suggestions on community studies.

Second, there may be some difficulty involved in defining a county as a community for purposes of historical investigation. After all, a county can be nothing more than an artifical political subdivision, and in the mid-twentieth century, even many rural areas have numerous small communities within a particular county. During the era of Civil War and Reconstruction, however, the people of Harrison county clearly thought of themselves as a community. The county provided the physical limits of their local government; and their economic and social lives, beyond the purely individual activities or contacts in the immediate neighborhood, also were centered within the county. Marshall, the county seat, had a municipal government and was the focal point of community activity, but it was not independent enough of the surrounding area to constitute a community in itself. Instead, important questions concerning, for example, political or economic developments always called for county-wide meetings. Those who lived within the county saw themselves as citizens of "Old Harrison." No definition of the term "community" will be satisfactory to all—at times we even hear references to the "world community"—but it is not uncommon for local histories to define counties as communities, and the concept seems appropriate to this study.[6]

Finally, the historical questions asked in this study are very large. They have both regional and national significance; yet answers are being sought at the local level. Can the examination of one community tell us anything of general importance about slavery, antebellum southern society, secession, Civil War, and Reconstruction? There are several reasons to expect an affirmative answer to this question.

In the first place, mid-nineteenth-century Americans did

[6]Merle Curti, *The Making of An American Community: A Case Study of Democracy in a Frontier County* (Stanford, Cal., 1959), is an outstanding work based on defining a county as a community. It deals with Trempealeau County, Wisconsin, from 1850 to 1880. See also James C. Bonner, *Georgia's Last Frontier: The Development of Carroll County* (Athens, Ga., 1971). Russo, *Families and Communities*, 14, 51, emphasizes towns as "little communities" and argues that people living in rural areas were "outside the framework of community life." I believe, however, that Harrison County planters and farmers would have been surprised to discover that they were outside the community.

not have rapid transportation or instant communication; and extensive federal centralization was well in the future. Residents of Harrison County were fortunate if they could keep fully abreast of what happened in Marshall, let alone developments in Austin and Washington. Granted that the actions of federal and state governments affected them importantly, individuals in Harrison County were concerned most immediately with conditions in their own community. The local economy — how people made a living—was not under normal conditions greatly influenced by government of any sort. Transportation facilities, such as roads and even railroads, were as much matters of local control as of state or national concern, or even more so. The laws and policies of federal and state governments were often filtered through officials elected at the county level before coming home to ordinary citizens. Thus, in the mid-nineteenth century, men's lives depended heavily upon their local community, and we may quite reasonably seek at that level answers to very large historical questions about the era.[7]

Secondly, local history affords an opportunity for depth and richness of detail impossible in a broader study. To be fully understood, the impact of great events such as secession, Civil War, and Reconstruction must be measured at the community level as well as at the state and national level. This is not to say that Harrison County (or any community for that matter) should be considered "typical" and the whole story generalized from its experience or that broad-based studies are somehow less important. The point is only that local history has validity and special value as one way to approach understanding the past.

In some respects this argument for local history is similar to that usually advanced for biography. The stories of individual lives, no matter how important the individual, cannot replace general accounts of whole societies, institutions, and chronological periods. But most historians will agree that biography is one form of their discipline and that it has some

[7]The argument for local history has been developed in detail by Russo, *Families and Communities*. See also Thomas H. Smith, "The Renascence of Local History," *The Historian*, XXXV (Nov., 1972), 1-17.

special values. Biography humanizes history by emphasizing the character and personality as well as the career of its subject. And because biography focuses on one individual, it often reduces the complexity of historical developments thereby making them more vivid and better understood. A biography of George Washington, for example, will not tell the whole story of the American Revolution, but it can hardly fail to inform concerning developments from 1763 to 1789 and to present a vital perspective on these events.[8] The analogy between community history and biography is imperfect, but the justification for seeking answers to large questions in investigations of local areas should be clear. A study of one community during the years from 1850 to 1880 should add another dimension to our understanding of how Americans experienced the great events of the Civil War era.[9]

Community studies, perhaps more frequently than any other type of historical investigation, tend to be hampered by a lack of appropriate research materials. In the case of Harrison County, however, the diversity and richness of historical sources, both traditional and quantitative, is truly impressive. A detailed historiographical-methodological essay is not in order at this point, but readers should by made aware in advance of the nature, uses, and limitations of these materials.

Virtually every historical source traditionally employed in narrative and descriptive accounts is available for Harrison County. These include personal letters, diaries, memoirs, travelers' accounts, plantation journals, newspapers, and the records of state and local government preserved in the state archives and the county courthouse.[10] Furthermore, there are

[8]The chapter entitled "Biography and History" in Allan Nevins, *The Gateway to History* (Garden City, N.Y., 1962), 347-369, provides an excellent introduction to this subject. See also John A. Garraty, *The Nature of Biography* (New York, 1957).

[9]Friedberger and Webster, "Social Structure and State and Local History," 297-298, argue that a community can be portrayed as a "living, changing organism."

[10]Research on Harrison County is greatly facilitated by the availability of local newspapers which are vital in putting together the train of historical events in a community. The Marshall *Texas Republican* was published from 1849 until 1869 under the editorship of Robert W. Loughery. Loughery was an associate editor with Trenton A. Patillo from July until November, 1849, when the latter retired and left full control to

twenty-two slave narratives provided by bondsmen who lived in antebellum Harrison County. These narratives, the result of WPA-directed interviews with aged former slaves conducted during the 1930s, are technically an early venture in oral history, but they have taken on the character of slave memoirs and will be used as such in this study.[11]

The primary quantitative sources for mid-nineteenth-century Harrison County are the manuscript United States censuses of 1850 through 1880 which provide what has been called the "basic scaffolding" for a re-creation of the community's social structure.[12] By linking information from the population schedules with data from the agricultural schedules, it is possible to develop a reasonably detailed view of the status of every

his ultra-southern colleague. Loughery moved to Jefferson, Texas, in 1869 and to Galveston shortly thereafter. He returned to Marshall in 1875, however, and published the *Tri-Weekly Herald* until 1880 before once more moving to Jefferson. Thus, Loughery's newspapers spanned the entire period from 1850 to 1880 with the exception of about six years, and extensive files of both are available. Webb, Carroll, and Branda (eds.), *Handbook of Texas*, II, 84-85, 756.

Relatively large files of two other newspapers from this period are extant also. The *Harrison Flag*, begun in 1856 as a conservative opponent of the *Texas Republican*, suspended publication during the Civil War, but appeared again until 1868 after the conflict. The Marshall *Messenger* was published first in 1877. Several other newspapers appeared during the years from 1850 to 1880. In some cases only scattered copies are extant; in some, not a single issue survives. Although these papers cannot help in explaining the community's history, they were part of it and will be considered in the appropriate places. A listing of Harrison County and Marshall newspapers is found in *Texas Newspapers, 1813-1939: A Union List of Newspaper Files in Offices of Publishers, Libraries, and a Number of Private Collections* (Houston, 1941), 143.

The Texas County Records Inventory Project has since 1973 been publishing inventories of the materials preserved in courthouses across the Lone Star State. Most important for this study is Seth Walton et al., (comp.), *Inventory of County Records: Harrison County* (Austin, 1979). For an example of using local records in a major historical study, see Robert W. Fogel and Stanley L. Engerman, *Time on the Cross: The Economics of American Negro Slavery* (Boston, 1974), II, 24.

[11] Paul D. Escott, *Slavery Remembered: A Record of Twentieth Century Slave Narratives* (Chapel Hill, N.C., 1978), is a detailed statistical and literary analysis of this source. See also John W. Blassingame, "Using the Testimony of Ex-Slaves: Approaches and Problems," *Journal of Southern History*, XLI (Nov., 1975), 473-492; and David Thomas Bailey, "A Divided Prism: Two Sources of Black Testimony on Slavery," *Journal of Southern History*, XLVI (Aug., 1980), 381-404.

[12] Friedberger and Webster, "Social Structure and State and Local History," 298. A good general introduction to the United States census as a historical source is Barnes F. Lathrop, *Migration into East Texas, 1835-1860: A Study from the United States Census* (Austin, 1949), 3-22.

family in the community. Fortunately, since Harrison County had 11,822 people in 1850, 15,001 in 1860, 13,241 in 1870, and 25,172 in 1880 and ranked among the most populous in Texas, it is not necessary to collect data on every person in all four census years to obtain a demographic and economic profile of the community during that era. Population samples provide a more manageable and equally dependable alternative. Unless otherwise indicated, all quantitative descriptions of the Harrison County community in this study are based on samples of households taken from the manuscript censuses of 1850 through 1880.[13]

Researchers who work with the manuscript census returns are aware that at times individuals who were not necessarily members of the same family lived in a given household. Care must be taken, therefore, in all references to "family" and "household" since the two are not perfectly interchangeable. This study sampled the census by household because the intent was to examine the whole community. The main samples for each year, however, were limited to data on the heads of households and their dependents. This virtually amounted to a sample of families because in nearly all households, even if there

[13] Descriptions of the censuses of 1850, 1860, 1870, and 1880 are found in Carroll D. Wright, *The History and Growth of the United States Census* (Washington, 1900), 147-166, 227-229, 234-238, 312-315. The censuses of 1850 and 1860 consisted of six schedules: Schedule 1 (Free Inhabitants), Schedule 2 (Slave Inhabitants), Schedule 3 (Statistics of Mortality), Schedule 4 (Productions of Agriculture), Schedule 5 (Products of Industry), and Schedule 6 (Social Statistics). In 1870, there was no slave schedule, and the population schedule was entitled simply (Inhabitants). Otherwise the census forms were exactly like those used in 1850 and 1860. In 1880, revisions in the law made major revisions in all the forms. The three used in this study were Schedule 1 (Inhabitants), Schedule 2 (Productions of Agriculture), and Schedule 3 (Products of Industry). These manuscript census returns are available on microfilm. Hereinafter they will be cited as Seventh Census, 1850; Eighth Census, 1860; Ninth Census, 1870, and Tenth Census, 1880, with appropriate schedule numbers. Total population statistics for 1850-1880 are from the following: James D. B. DeBow (ed.), *Statistical View of the United States . . . Being a Compendium of the Seventh Census* . . . (Washington, 1854), 314; U.S. Bureau of the Census, *Population of the United States in 1860*, 485; ibid., Ninth Census, *The Statistics of the Population of the United States; Compiled from the Original Returns of the Ninth Census (June 1, 1870)* (Washington, 1872), 64; ibid., Tenth Census, *Statistics of the Population of the United States at the Tenth Census, (June 1, 1880)* (Washington, 1883), 373. Further discussion of the census, sampling procedures, and the reliability of the population samples for 1850-1880 is found in Appendix 1.

were apparently unrelated individuals present, the family head and his dependents were recorded first by the census taker. Any references to "family" in this study are based on the primary samples of 500 heads of households from 1850 and 1860, 964 from 1870, and 1,000 from 1880. Secondarily, data were recorded on non-heads of households; that is, those individuals living in the sample households who were at least eighteen years of age, had an occupation given in the census, and had no obvious dependent relationship to the head of household and his family. This group was not very large and, with notable exceptions, not very stable or influential in the community. They will be considered only briefly in Appendix 2.[14]

Tax rolls constitute a second major quantitative source used in this study. Compiled annually for the purpose of collecting state and county ad valorem property taxes, these rolls provide an alphabetical (at least by the first letter of the surname) listing of all property holders and poll taxpayers in the community at the beginning of each year. For each taxpayer, they include the number of acres and assessed value of every tract of land owned, the number of slaves and their total assessed value, and the numbers and value of horses and other livestock. Money loaned at interest was taxed as was the value of merchandise stocked by store owners. Tax assessors appear to have undervalued property slightly, but the undervaluation also seems to have been consistent.

The tax rolls, although they have no demographic data, are helpful in dealing with individuals as well as providing a measure of the community's wealth. They are the only source, for example, through which the economic status of a single person or family may be checked systematically over the years from 1850 to 1880. The census will not serve this purpose because the value of personal property was not recorded in 1850, and no estimates of wealth were made in 1880. Also, because they were compiled annually, the tax rolls offer more precise evidence

[14] Appendix 2 offers a summary of statistical data on non-heads of household and a few suggestions concerning their significance in the community.

than do the census returns as to the date an individual arrived in or departed the county. In short, while the tax rolls are more limited than the census as a source of quantitative demographic and economic data on the community, they are an important supplement. For a few purposes, they are even superior.[15]

Their richness and diversity notwithstanding, at least one caveat is in order concerning these historical materials. Reliance on traditional sources tends to provide only the perspective of the better-educated and wealthy on events and developments in the community. Members of the middle and lower classes who generally wrote and preserved fewer letters, kept fewer diaries, wrote fewer memoirs, etc., remain inarticulate where the historical record is concerned. Investigations of the past become prisoners of their "elite" sources. This limitation may be overcome to some extent by the use of the censuses and courthouse records in conjunction with more traditional materials. Census data, as noted above, allow a demographic and economic profile of any family regardless of social status. Courthouse records, especially wills and estate inventories preserved among the probate papers, indicate something of the values and life styles of families that left no traditional sources. This is not to claim that census statistics or inventories of property make the inarticulate "speak"; they do not. Quantitative data, however, do reveal the extent of economic-social stratification in the community. And the combination of this information with traditional sources such as the records left by the elite, newspaper accounts, and election results is at least suggestive concerning the "minds and hearts" of the community's common people.

In summary, this study attempts to explain how one southern community experienced the great events of the era of Civil War and Reconstruction. And it seeks to determine the degree of change and continuity in the life of that community

[15]Tax Records for mid-nineteenth-century Texas are available on microfilm on a county-by-county basis. Records of the Comptroller of Public Accounts, Ad Valorem Tax Division, County Real and Personal Property Tax Rolls, 1850-1880, Archives Division, Texas State Library, Austin. Hereinafter these records will be cited as Harrison County Tax Rolls with the appropriate year.

over the thirty years from 1850 to 1880. It is predicated upon the idea that while no single county can be considered "typical" much can be learned in seeking answers to very large historical questions in a limited area. The sources, both traditional and quantitative, are very rich, presenting an opportunity to tell a story that is both descriptive and analytical. The first step is to consider in detail the community as it stood during the 1850s. In the process, major questions concerning slavery and antebellum economic, social, and political life may be answered, and a basis for measuring the extent of change brought to the community by war, emancipation, and Reconstruction will be established.

PART ONE

The Antebellum Community

1

The Land and the People

HARRISON COUNTY in 1850 covered a land area of 570,880 acres centering on the small town of Marshall. From east to west across the county, it was approximately thirty-eight miles from the Louisiana state line to the boundary with Upshur County. The distance from Cass County on the north to Panola County on the south ranged from nineteen to twenty-eight miles. Topographically, the northwestern section of the county had some moderately rough hills while the eastern area, especially the southeast, was comparatively flat. In general, however, the terrain was gently rolling. Drainage from the northern and eastern parts of the county, about two-thirds of the total area, flowed to the Red River in Louisiana via Little

Cypress Creek, Cypress Bayou, and Caddo Lake. The lake provided a water route, navigable by steamboat most of the year, to Shreveport and thence by the Red and Mississippi rivers to New Orleans. In Texas, a frontier state of vast distances, such a transportation link was vital to the development of a community during the antebellum years. The other third of the county was drained by the Sabine River which formed a portion of its southern boundary.[1]

Settlers in Harrison County found two soil types: upland sedimentary, which constituted more than three-quarters of the total, and lowland alluvial. The sedimentary soil, although probably not so rich as the alluvial, was primarily deep sandy loam noted for being loose and easily cultivated. As was the case with the terrain in general, the eastern half of the county seems to have enjoyed an advantage over the west in soil composition and quality. Edward Smith, a traveler through the community in 1849, noted that ten miles west of Marshall land sold for one to two dollars per acre while fourteen miles east of town an acre cost five dollars. Most of the county was heavily timbered with a great variety of soft and hardwoods, especially pine, oak, and cypress. Land had to be cleared before it could be farmed, but it is doubtful that many pioneers found this troublesome since, in the majority, they came from forested areas, and they could use the timber for building, fencing, and fuel. Subsoils in the central and eastern areas of the county also contained plentiful clays that could be fired to make bricks.[2]

Harrison County's climate could probably be best described as mild. Typically, in the lower South this meant hot summers and cool winters. The East Texas Immigration Society provided a nice "booster" description in 1873: "Our summers are long and somewhat enervating. Yet we have no cases of total

[1] Armstrong, "History of Harrison County," 3-5; *An Economic Survey of Harrison County, Prepared for the Texas and Pacific Railway Company* (Austin, 1949), 1.01-1.02. Webb, Carroll, and Branda (eds.), *Handbook of Texas*, I, 266.

[2] Armstrong, "History of Harrison County," 5-8; *Economic Survey of Harrison County*, 2.03-2.05; Edward Smith, *Account of a Journey through Northeastern Texas . . .* (London, 1849), 180.

prostration from the heat. Our winters are always mild. The ice in our ponds is never sufficient to bear up the weight of an ordinary man, and in our running water, ice never forms." Temperatures averaged eighty-three degrees during the summer months and frequently hovered around the one hundred degree mark. But the mean for winter was forty-nine degrees. One resident, a native of the District of Columbia, claimed that spring began in January, a pardonable exaggeration perhaps to those who were familiar with the longer winters even in the upper South. In any case, the growing season was long, and once settlers adjusted to the summer heat and humidity, the climate was much less demanding on the farmer and stockman than was the case in other areas being settled at the same time, such as Iowa and Wisconsin. Rainfall averaged approximately forty-five inches a year. Although there were occasions of overly wet springs or, more commonly, drouth in July and August, rain was usually well distributed throughout the four seasons. Snow was not common.[3] Thus, climate and rainfall were rarely responsible for a general crop failure.

Harrison County must have seemed a hospitable new home to most of the migrants who settled there during the fifteen or twenty years prior to 1850. They were, as we will see, almost all southerners accustomed to living in heavily timbered, well-watered regions characterized by rolling or hilly terrain and a relatively mild climate. It has been observed that American pioneers as they moved west preferred to stay on the same parallel of latitude and find a natural environment as similar as possible to that from which they had removed. Harrison County had numerous settlers from older states of the lower South, especially Alabama and Georgia, who appear to have been doing just that. Those who came from the upper South, notably

[3] "East Texas Immigration Society, Elysian Fields, Texas," in *The Texas Almanac for 1873* (Galveston, 1872), 98 (quotation); Armstrong, "History of Harrison County," 8-10; *Economic Survey of Harrison County*, 2.0101-2.0102. The claim that spring began in January was made by Hobart Key of Marshall. Hobart Key to "Mag.," June 2, 1854, Key Family Papers, property of Hobart Key, Jr., of Marshall. The community certainly was unprepared for severe winter weather. In early January, 1877, an eighteen-inch snowfall collapsed roofs all over town. Marshall *Tri-Weekly Herald*, Jan. 4, 1877.

from Virginia and Tennessee, moved in a more southwesterly direction. Their greatest adjustment, however, was probably to the heat of summer, and that was relatively minor. James C. Quillin, a native of Virginia, informed his brother in 1852 that Harrison County was "a very pleasant country to live in." Only the drinking water, especially water from springs, was inferior to that back home, he said.[4] These pioneers found not only climate, terrain, and vegetation to their liking; they also settled on productive and easily cultivated soil. Thus, they were in an advantageous position to continue without serious modification the agricultural way of life they had known in the older South. For some this meant subsistence farming, but for others it meant the application of slave labor to the production of a cash crop. Encouraged by natural conditions, they made antebellum Harrison County into a slaveholders' community.

The attraction of Harrison County's natural environment for mid-nineteenth-century pioneers to the cotton frontier is borne out by the influx of settlers there. By 1850, although it was by no means the area of earliest Anglo-American settlement in Texas, Harrison ranked first among the state's counties in total population. There were 5,604 whites, 5 free blacks, and 6,213 slaves, making a total of 11,822 residents. By comparison, such population centers of the future as Harris and Bexar counties reported 4,668 and 6,052 residents respectively. Slaves were the majority in Harrison, accounting for 52.6% of the community's people. There were Texas counties with an even greater proportion of bondsmen in their populations, but none had more slaves in absolute numbers. During the next ten years Harrison County's free population grew 10.9% to 6,217 while the number of slaves increased to 8,784, a 41.4% expansion. Although these growth rates by no means matched those for Texas as a whole(173.2% and 213.9% increases in free and slave populations respectively), they kept Harrison first among the

[4]Frank L. Owsley, "The Pattern of Migration and Settlement on the Southern Frontier," *Journal of Southern History*, XI (May, 1945), 147-176; James C. Quillin to Ezekiel Quillin, August 13, 1852 (quotation), Quillin Family File, Harrison County Historical Museum, Marshall.

state's counties in the absolute number of bondsmen and third in total population on the eve of the Civil War.[5]

As would be expected, antebellum Harrison County was overwhelmingly rural. The great majority of its citizens lived on scattered farms and plantations rather than in towns or even around crossroads stores. Yet for a rural area the community's population was not extremely sparse. There were approximately thirteen people for every square mile in 1850 and seventeen in 1860. And it is doubtful that many individuals felt terribly isolated. James C. Quillin, living nine miles west of Marshall in 1852, wrote his brother that his home was on a road so "publick" that anything he had to spare could be sold at his front door. Moreover, there were ten other families within two miles of his house. Other areas of the community to the east were more heavily populated. Harrison County's people lived under rural conditions during the 1850s, but this did not mean social isolation.[6]

Farms throughout the antebellum Harrison County countryside probably looked a great deal less prosperous than they were in fact. The acres of cotton and corn were representative enough, but for the most part these were not neatly arranged into fields divided by clean fence rows. Livestock, especially hogs, often roamed the woodlands and small areas of naturally open range. A critical traveler might think a farmer had no livestock when in fact the woods sheltered a considerable number of hogs fattening on the acorn mast. Winters were generally so mild that barns and out-buildings for livestock were not necessary. One resident warned a friend from Maryland in 1854: "At first you will be much disappointed in this county—all are so who come

[5] DeBow (ed.), *Statistical View of the United States*, 308-319. Matagorda County, for example, had a larger proportion of slaves to whites than did Harrison, but there were only 2,608 people in the whole county. U.S. Bureau of the Census, *Population of the United States in 1860*, 484-486. It might be noted that Harrison County's one free black family disappeared during the 1850s. Immigration was apparently especially heavy during the early years of that decade. The *Caddo Gazette* in 1851 was quoted as reporting immigrants moving through Shreveport in "unprecedented numbers." Marshall *Texas Republican*, December 20, 1851.

[6] Quillin to Ezekiel Quillin, August 13, 1852 (quotation), Quillin Family File.

from farming countries — pastures — meadows — orchards and gardens — but most of these things *can* be had here. . . ." Harrison County farmers could have built a more attractive agricultural landscape, but they were content with cultivating their cleared acres. Furthermore, southern farmers of Anglo-American descent are not known to this day for keeping their fence rows clean, their barns painted, and their machinery out of the weather.[7]

Harrison County had very few "urban" residents during the antebellum years. The only true town was Marshall, the seat of government and the commercial and social center for the larger rural community. Founded in 1839, Marshall became the county seat in 1842. By the summer of 1849, the Marshall *Texas Republican* could boast that "our town" has become "one of the largest and most important places in the state. . . . Quite a number of buildings are in the course of erection, and several others contemplated, which will soon be under way. What better music than the sound of the hammer, the saw, and the trowel?" The Texas legislature first incorporated the town of Marshall in December, 1844. In 1850, the municipality was enlarged to include a one square mile area centering on the courthouse. According to the census taken that year, it had 768 whites and 374 slaves. The town grew larger during the last antebellum decade reaching a population of two to three thousand by 1860. Louise Wigfall Wright, daughter of Louis T. Wigfall, the ultra-southern United States senator from Marshall, remembered it as "not different from a thousand other little country towns throughout the South." But Edward Smith who visited Jefferson, Clarksville, Paris, Bonham, McKinney, and Dallas during a trip across northeastern Texas in 1849 described Marshall to prospective British immigrants as "the most flourishing place through which we travelled. . . .

[7]Hobart Key to "Mag.," June 2, 1854, Key Family Papers. Forrest McDonald and Grady McWhiney, "The South from Self-Sufficiency to Peonage: An Interpretation," *American Historical Review*, 85 (Dec., 1980), 1095-1118, emphasizes the importance of open-range livestock raising to antebellum agriculture. This article also argues that most southern farmers being of Celtic origin tended to work only as hard as they needed to "get by."

An iron casting furnace, two saw mills, and other useful works, with several large hotels, and many stores, testify that enterprise and wealth abound amongst the people." George F. Pierce, a bishop of the Methodist Episcopal Church, South, visited Marshall in 1856 and called it "beautiful and picturesque. . . . The people," Pierce enthused, "are intelligent, social, and public spirited, hospitable and generous on a noble scale."[8]

Marshall, as is typical of Texas county seats, was built around a courthouse square. Pleasant Vickers, a fifteen-year-old who lived there briefly during the 1850s, diagrammed what he called the "Public Square" on September 10, 1854. His sketch shows roads from east, west, north, and south bisecting the "common" and meeting at the courthouse. Stores, shops, and offices surrounded the square. There were also two hotels, the Planters Hotel and the Marshall Hotel, which would soon be joined by the Adkins House in offering hospitality to visitors. Livery stables were connected with the hotels. Vickers noted on his diagram that "Marshall has other streets," and indeed the town had 128 dwellings by 1850. Louise Wigfall Wright remembered sandy streets with houses set behind lawns filled with roses and honeysuckle. The servants' quarters and always necessary woodpiles were in back.[9]

Antebellum Marshall was hardly a city, but in a state that had no urban area with 10,000 people, it had to be recognized as a major center of commercial and professional activity. Probably no other settlement in Harrison County should be called a town, although Port Caddo, located on Caddo Lake in the

[8]Webb, Carroll, and Branda (eds.), *Handbook of Texas*, I, 148; H. P. N. Gammel (comp.), *The Laws of Texas, 1822-1897* (Austin, 1898-1902), II, 1052-1054; III, 770-772; Marshall *Texas Republican*, July 27, 1849 (first and second quotations), November 2, 1850; Louise Wigfall Wright, *A Southern Girl in '61* (New York, 1905), 11 (third quotation); Smith, *Journey Through Northeastern Texas*, 70 (fourth quotation); George Foster Pierce, *Incidents of Western Travel: In a Series of Letters*, ed. by Thomas O. Summers (Nashville, 1859), 102-103 (fifth quotation). It is necessary to estimate Marshall's population in 1860 because there was no census for the town as such. The Marshall *Texas Republican* of November 10, 1860, claimed the town's population was 2,500 to 3,000.

[9]Diary of Pleasant N. Vickers, 1853-1856 (quotation), Harrison County Historical Museum, Marshall, Marshall *Texas Republican*, November 2, 1850; Wright, *Southern Girl in '61*, 11. By 1860, the square had brick pavement. Marshall *Texas Republican*, September 8, 1860.

northeastern area, was next in importance. Established in the late 1830s, Port Caddo served as a port of entry for the Republic of Texas. At least fifty people lived there in 1850 including, as befitted a transshipment point on the way to Shreveport, four merchants, three grocers, and a tavern keeper. During the 1850s, with the building of the county's first railroad, another port on the lake — called Swanson's Landing — was built. The only other settlements in the county that were not purely rural farms or plantations were based on country stores and/or post offices. Elysian Fields in the southeastern part of the county grew around Edward Smith's store established in 1839, and a settlement in the western area originated the same year when William C. Crawford, a pioneer settler, built a fort for protection against Indians. The fort had a post office and a church in 1849. By 1860, there were post offices at Scottsville and Jonesville to the east and Ash Springs to the west of Marshall.[10] None of these settlements, however, amounted to much more than a few houses clustered around a country store or rural post office.

The community's people may be characterized in a variety of general ways as revealed in Table 1, a summary of the demographic and economic characteristics of the sample of 500 household heads taken from the manuscript censuses of 1850 and 1860. An overwhelming majority of those who headed households, more than 90% in both 1850 and 1860, were natives of slaveholding states. In 1850, a majority (52%) were from the upper South originally, but by 1860 individuals born in the lower South were most numerous (47% compared to 43% from the border states). This situation is explained by two factors. Obviously there was an increase in the flow of migrants

[10] Andrew Forest Muir, "The Thirty-Second Parallel Pacific Railroad in Texas to 1872" (Ph.D. Dissertation, University of Texas, 1949), 74; Webb, Carroll, and Branda (eds.), *Handbook of Texas*, I, 564, 758, 929; II, 583; III, 747. The town of Port Caddo was indicated as such in the manuscript census of 1850. Seventh Census, 1850, Schedule 1. In 1870, when the Texas and Pacific Railway crossed a mile north of Fort Crawford, the small settlement moved to the railroad and named itself Hallsville. Eighth Census, 1860, Schedule 1, gives the county's post offices. The community of Ash Springs cannot be precisely located on the basis of existing records.

from the deep South. But secondly, many of the older settlers native to the border states had lived and begun families in the lower South prior to moving to Texas. In both census years, the great majority (at least 60%) of Harrison County's children born in states other than Texas were natives of the lower South. As these children came of age, they added to the proportion of deep southerners heading households in the community. It appears then that Harrison County was settled first by natives of the older border states such as Virginia and Tennessee, and then during the last antebellum decade came increasingly to be controlled by people whose background lay entirely in the lower South, primarily in Alabama and Georgia.[11]

Household heads ranged in age from nineteen to seventy-two in 1850 and sixteen to seventy-four in 1860, but most were neither very young or very old. The average age was thirty-eight in 1850 and forty-one ten years later. Males headed 92% of all households in 1850; females only 8%, including the one free black family in the community. This situation was little different ten years later. The great majority of households (79% in 1850 and 80% in 1860) consisted of a man, his wife, and their children; some were headed by widowers, widows, or individuals who apparently were unmarried. Households were not on the average so large as might be expected, consisting typically of the head and four to five dependents. Approximately two-thirds of all households, however, had a child aged five to seventeen and therefore a prospective student.[12]

Nearly three of every four families in antebellum Harrison County depended directly on farming for a living. The only other occupations involving more than 5% of the working household heads were skilled trades such as blacksmithing and bricklaying (approximately 7.5% of the sample households in both 1850 and 1860) and professions such as the law and

[11] Information on birthplaces is drawn from Seventh Census, 1850, Schedule 1 and Eighth Census, 1860, Schedule 1. The generalization presented here is similar to the conclusion of Lathrop, *Migration into East Texas*, 34-58, although his study does not focus on Harrison County.

[12] Seventh Census, 1850, Schedule 1; Eighth Census, 1860, Schedule 1.

TABLE 1

Demographic and Economic Characteristics of Harrison County's Population, 1850 and 1860 (In Terms of Household Heads)

Characteristic	1850	1860
Mean Age	37.9 years	40.5 years
Male/Female Ratio	92.4/7.6	89.6/10.4
Males with Wives	79.9%	80.9%
Mean Number Dependents	4.4	4.2
Contained School Age Child	66.8%	65.0%
Birthplace		
Upper South	52.0%	43.4%
Lower South	42.0%	47.0%
Free States	4.2%	3.6%
Foreign	1.2%	5.4%
Unknown	.6%	.6%
Occupation		
Farming	72.2%	72.8%
Commerce	2.4%	3.8%
Professions	6.0%	6.6%
Public Office	.6%	.6%
Manufacturing	1.4%	.4%
Skilled Trades	7.6%	7.4%
Unskilled Services	1.4%	2.8%
Overseer	3.4%	1.4%
Miscellaneous	5.0%	4.2%
Proportion Owning Slaves	57.4%	60.8%
Mean Size of Slaveholding*	10.9	13.7
Mean Value of Real Property	$1,452	$3,189
Mean Value of Personal Property	—	$9,585

*These means are based only on the slaveholding households.

medicine (6% in 1850 and 6.6% in 1860). Merchants and manufacturers combined did not head as many as 5% of the households in 1850 or 1860. Antebellum Harrison County then was overwhelmingly agricultural.[13]

Slaveholding was also a dominant characteristic of the community; in fact, a majority of all households in both 1850 (57.4%) and 1860 (60.8%) owned at least one Negro bondsman. This situation contrasted notably with that across the South as a whole where only one family in four owned slaves. Most Harrison County slaveholders during the 1850s were male farmers, but approximately 10% of all slaveowners were women. And nearly one in five had a non-agricultural occupation. Slaves were owned by merchants, doctors, lawyers, teachers, blacksmiths, hotel operators, and even by overseers who made a living supervising other men's plantation labor forces. Slaveholdings ranged in size from a single bondsman up to 103 in 1850 and 104 in 1860. Small slaveowners were most numerous, but the average holding was relatively large, 11 slaves per owner in 1850 and 14 in 1860.[14] All aspects of the "Peculiar Institution" will receive further discussion; suffice it to say here that any visitor to the area could hardly have failed to see that it was a slaveholders' as well as a farmers' world.

Property ownership was widespread in the community. In 1850, approximately two-thirds of all households owned real property, and the mean value was $1,452 per household. It may seem surprising that in an overwhelmingly agricultural area even one-third of the population would be propertyless, but the situation in Harrison County was virtually identical to that for the state as a whole in 1850. This circumstance is explained in part by the presence in frontier areas such as Texas of many recent arrivals who had not yet acquired property. During the 1850s, as Harrison County matured, property ownership there

[13] Ibid.

[14] Seventh Census, 1850, Schedules 1 and 2; Eighth Census, 1860, Schedules 1 and 2. The fact that only one family in four across the South owned slaves is given in many sources. See Kenneth M. Stampp, *The Peculiar Institution, Slavery in the Antebellum South* (New York, 1956), 29-30.

TABLE 2

Distributions of Real and Personal Property in Harrison County, 1850 and 1860

Dollar Values	0	1–249	250–499	500–999	1,000–4,999	5,000–9,999	10,000–19,999	20,000–49,999	50,000+	*Totals*
1850										
Percentage of Population	34.4	6.0	6.0	16.0	31.0	3.8	2.4	.4	0.0	100.0
Percentage of Real Property	0.0	.7	1.5	7.6	45.7	17.2	21.0	6.3	0.0	100.0
Gini Index = .681										
1860										
Percentage of Population	22.2	2.2	5.4	11.8	38.2	12.2	6.2	1.6	.2	100.0
Percentage of Real Property	0.0	.1	.6	2.6	27.1	25.4	24.0	16.9	3.3	100.0
Gini Index = .644										
1860										
Percentage of Population	2.2	12.2	11.0	8.0	20.4	17.0	14.2	12.8	2.2	100.0
Percentage of Personal Property	0.0	.2	.4	.5	5.2	12.7	20.4	41.7	18.9	100.0
Gini Index = .663										

became more widespread than it was statewide. By 1860, nearly 80% of the community's households owned real property and 98% had personal property. The comparable statistics statewide were 67% and 90%. Mean values were greater in Harrison County too; $3,189 in real and $9,585 in personal property compared to $2,699 in real property and $3,692 in personal for households across Texas.[15]

Finally, while property ownership was widespread, property itself was concentrated in the hands of a relatively small minority of households. Put another way, most families in Harrison County owned some property, but a few owned a great deal more than others. Table 2 shows that 2.8% of the population in 1850, the owners of $10,000 or more in real property, controlled 27.3% of all real estate reported in the census. By 1860 however, 8% of all households had $10,000 or more, and they owned nearly half (44.2%) of the county's real property. Personal property showed a similar distribution that year. Owners of $20,000 or more, constituting 15% of the sample households, controlled 60.6% of this form of wealth.

The data in Table 2 demonstrate an unequal distribution of property in antebellum Harrison County, but they do not provide precise comparisons between the distributions for 1850 and 1860 and with property-holding conditions elsewhere in Texas. It is necessary, therefore, to reduce each distribution to a standard measurement called the Gini Index of Concentration. The Gini Index may range from 0 (a state of perfect equality of distribution where every household owned virtually the same value of property) to 1 (perfect inequality where one household owned all property). In Harrison County, the Gini Index for real property was .681 in 1850 and .644 in 1860. Personal property in 1860 had an Index of .663. Antebellum Harrison County thus had a relatively high and stable degree of property concentration. At the same time, however, inequality was not quite so

[15] Seventh Census, 1850, Schedule 1; Eighth Census, 1860, Schedule 1. Information on the whole state is drawn from Randolph B. Campbell and Richard G. Lowe, *Wealth and Power in Antebellum Texas* (College Station, Texas, 1977), 32-47.

great there as it was statewide (Gini Indices of .780 in 1850 and .786 in 1860 for real property and .756 for personal property in 1860).[16]

In summary, if we could create a "typical" antebellum Harrison County household on the basis of these general characteristics, it would be headed by a forty-year-old male from the lower South. There would be a wife and three or four children in addition to the family head. They would live in a rural but not isolated area and support themselves by farming. Five or six Negro bondsmen would perform much of the essential labor, although members of the white family would probably work with them. The family would not be poor; instead it would own approximately $10,000 worth of property. On the other hand, given the concentration of real and personal property in the hands of a relatively few households, the typical family would hardly be wealthy, not even in terms of what constituted wealth in the Texas of that era.

The members of a typical household in antebellum Harrison County appear to have enjoyed a reasonably stable and comfortable life. They lived on the land in a nuclear family headed by a male in early middle age. And they had wealth enough to be at least adequately supplied with the necessities of life. "Typical" families are mythical, however, and not nearly so interesting as the various individuals who were used to form the average. Most of Harrison County's households varied considerably from the mean. Therefore, an equally or perhaps even more revealing way of describing the community's people is to examine them in terms of social or class structure.

[16]The Gini Index of Concentration and the problems of comparing concentrations of property at different times are discussed fully in Randolph B. Campbell, "Planters and Plain Folk: Harrison County, Texas, as a Test Case, 1850-1860," *Journal of Southern History*, XL (Aug., 1974), 383-385. The statement that the degree of concentration was "relatively" high means in relation to the Index itself since 0 would be perfect equality of distribution and 1 would be perfect inequality. Information on property distributions statewide is from Campbell and Lowe, *Wealth and Power in Antebellum Texas*, 40-46. For 1860, it is possible to combine real and personal property values from the census for a more comprehensive measure of wealth. The Gini Index of Concentration for wealth in Harrison County was .638; for Texas, .742.

It is customary to think of the antebellum South as having four distinct economic-social classes: planters who owned large numbers of slaves, usually twenty or more, and produced most of the region's cash crop; yeomen farmers who had few if any slaves and supported themselves on the fringe of the commercial economy; poor whites who owned virtually nothing and lived at a bare subsistence level; and the Negro slaves. Harrison County had each of these classes, but many difficulties arise when we attempt to fit the entire population into one or the other on the basis of precise quantitative measurements. In the first place, most of the dividing lines are arbitrary. What, for example, is the rationale for saying that a man with twenty slaves is a planter and one with nineteen is not? Secondly, it is possible to misjudge the social position of an individual when his property-holding status is the only consideration. The son of a large planter, for example, may appear to have been a small farmer if he was married and on his own, when in fact he stood heir to dozens of slaves and a position in the upper class. Third, a sizable non-agricultural group, primarily townspeople in professions and trades, do not fall within the traditional southern class structure, and a significant proportion of the population, roughly 10% to 20%, simply defies classification on the basis of occupation, slaveholding, wealth, or any of the factors commonly used in determining social class. These limitations and difficulties must be remembered as we re-create the social structure of antebellum Harrison County. The statistical basis for describing each economic-social class is presented in Table 3.

Large planters, the owners of twenty or more slaves, constituted the community's upper class. Only 8.6% of the county's households enjoyed this status in 1850. The proportion rose notably to 14.2% on the eve of the Civil War as a result of the improving status of "old settlers" and the influx of immigrants who brought forces of bondsmen with them. But even with this increase, large planters remained an elite minority in numbers and wealth. Throughout the antebellum decade, they were more than three times as rich as the average household head; they owned nearly three times as many slaves as the

TABLE 3

Demographic and Economic Characteristics of Social Classes in Harrison County, 1850 and 1860 (In Terms of Household Heads)

	Large Planters		Small Planters		Yeomen		Poor Whites		Non-Farmers	
	1850	1860	1850	1860	1850	1860	1850	1860	1850	1860
Proportion of Population*	8.6	14.2	11.0	11.2	33.8	39.8	10.0	7.4	16.2	17.8
Mean Age	41.7	45.2	42.9	46.4	38.3	40.4	33.9	35.6	35.4	37.7
Birthplace										
Upper South	39.5	38.0	43.6	39.3	58.0	49.7	50.0	35.1	54.3	44.9
Lower South	60.5	59.1	49.1	60.7	37.3	45.2	44.0	59.4	29.6	25.8
Free States	—	1.4	5.4	—	3.5	—	4.0	2.7	12.3	10.1
Foreign	—	1.4	—	—	1.2	2.5	—	2.7	3.7	16.9
Unknown	—	—	1.8	—	—	2.5	2.0	—	—	2.3
Mean Number of Dependents	5.2	4.7	4.9	4.6	4.6	4.6	4.0	3.4	3.9	3.7
Mean Value of Real Property (in dollars)	5,451	9,228	3,470	4,444	948	1,059	28	10	978	2,972
Mean Value of Personal Property (in dollars)	—	34,961	—	13,110	—	3,509	—	1,056	—	6,862

Proportion Owning Slaves	100.	100.	100.	100.	55.6	55.3	—	—	49.4	59.6
Mean Size of Slaveholding**	33	37	14	14	5	4	—	—	4	4
Mean Improved Acreage	330	473	131	234	50	67				
Mean Cash Value of Farm (in dollars)	5,203	8,211	2,706	4,160	990	1,629				
Mean Value of Livestock (in dollars)	1,516	2,289	752	1,182	348	535				
Mean Bushels of Corn	1,859	2,192	846	1,118	397	384				
Mean Bales of Cotton	29	93	11	39	3	9				

* This row does not account for the entire sample population because some households did not fall into any of these social classes.

** These means are based only on the slaveholding households.

typical slaveholder; and their plantations were approximately three times as large and productive as the property of the average farmer. By 1860 in Harrison County, it was common for a large planter to hold property worth more than $44,000, including nearly forty slaves and a 1,400 acre plantation producing more than ninety bales of cotton. Wealthholding to this extent truly placed a family in the upper class.[17]

Membership in the large-planter class meant more than wealth, of course; it also meant social leadership, political power, and a style of life for which the Old South was famous. William T. Scott, the largest property holder in the county, provides a good example. Born in Mississippi in 1811, Scott came to East Texas during the 1830s and settled about seven miles east of the future town of Marshall. By 1850 he owned 103 slaves, and he remained throughout the decade the community's only owner of more than 100 bondsmen. Scott served in the last congress of the Republic of Texas and continued his political career through the early statehood period. During the 1850s, he served three terms in the Texas State Senate and was involved in every major development affecting the community.[18] His name will appear frequently in this story.

William T. Scott lived and reared his large family (twelve children) in an unpretensious Louisiana style raised cottage built in 1840. Other large planters were closer to the "Gone with the Wind" ideal in their homes. John J. Webster, a native of Virginia who had worked as a building contractor in Tuscaloosa, Alabama, before moving to Texas during the late 1830s, settled a plantation northeast of Marshall where in 1844 his slaves fired brick and built a classic revival mansion called "Mimosa Hall." With its large windows, high ceilings, and column-lined veranda, Webster's house still stands as a monument to the planter class, as does the nearby C. K. Andrews house which was built by Webster's slaves in 1845. John J. Webster, who had eighty slaves in 1850, died four years later, but his son John B. Webster

[17]All quantitative information on the planter class is drawn from Seventh Census, 1850, Schedules 1, 2, and 4 and Eighth Census, 1860, Schedules 1, 2, and 4.

[18]Webb, Carroll, and Branda, (eds.), *Handbook of Texas*, II, 583.

inherited "Mimosa Hall" and one-third of these bondsmen and maintained a place as a large planter until the Civil War.[19]

Among the Webster's neighbors in the county's northeastern sector were the Perrys, Josiah D. and Dr. Harwood P., who were brothers, and their cousins Joshua and Levin. All four were natives of North Carolina, and all were large planters throughout the last antebellum decade. Letters preserved by Levin Perry's daughter-in-law, Harriet Person Perry, offer a glimpse of their social life. A family friend was married in December, 1859, and according to Perry's daughter Louisa, "Papy" gave a "little party" for the groom. Sixty persons attended at "Spring Hill," Levin Perry's plantation home. "The supper table was very pretty," Louisa wrote. During the Civil War when the Ladies Aid Society of the neighborhood wanted to give a "tableaux" to raise money for the solders they held it at Spring Hill because the house had such a long and large hall. Levin Perry also provides an example of how members of the large-planter class could emphasize the responsibilities that went with their position in the community. Writing in 1849 to his son Theophilus who attended the University of North Carolina and eventually became a lawyer, Perry warned:

> . . . that period of your life "now passing" stamps your future character both in respectability and usefulness and lay not the flattering unction to your soul for a "moment" that in this enlightened day and generation you can assume any high place in society without the indispensable prerequisite of a well cultivated mind.

A less demanding side of the planter life style was pictured by Edmund Key in his remembrance of J. Y. Collier, a North Carolina native who lived a few miles south of Marshall. "I always think of him," Key wrote, "on a fine horse, wearing a

[19]Rebecca Fortson Fitch, "The Use of Native Materials in the Ante Bellum Buildings of Harrison County, Texas" (M.A. Thesis, North Texas State University, 1952), 57-58, 64, 69. For information on John J. and John B. Webster, see Max S. Lale and Randolph B. Campbell, eds., "The Plantation Journal of John B. Webster, February 17, 1858-November 5, 1859," *Southwestern Historical Quarterly,* LXXXIV (July, 1980), 50-57.

big white coat, a hunting horn slung across his shoulder, followed by a pack of twenty deer hounds."[20]

Although John J. Webster, the Perrys, and Collier were exceptions, most large planters were native to the lower South. They were, as might be expected in an upper class, somewhat older than average for heads of households. The great majority were males, but females were a larger proportion of this class than any other. This should not be surprising either. Land and slaves were productive forms of wealth, and a woman who owned them had a source of security and independence. The widow, for example, of a large planter had a far better chance to head her own household supported by slave labor than did the wife of a small yeoman farmer or poor white who died leaving virtually no property and no labor force. This was especially true since most large plantations were managed by overseers anyhow.[21]

Overseers, the men who contracted to manage the slaves and lands of large planters, did not fall into any of the traditional antebellum social classes. Instead, they were an adjunct to the upper class, and as such, their position in the community must be considered briefly at this point.

Overseers generally enjoyed very little prestige and were even looked down on to some extent by the planter class. William K. Scarborough, an authority on the overseer, argued that these men were ostracized by the planters, discouraged from having company, and required to stay on the plantation

[20] Seventh Census, 1850, Schedules 1, 2, and 4: Eighth Census, 1860, Schedules 1, 2, and 4. In 1860, Josiah D. Perry paid taxes on 57 slaves; Dr. Harwood P. Perry on 72; Joshua Perry on 35; and Levin Perry on 79. Harrison County Tax Rolls, 1860. Louisa Perry to Theophilus Perry, January 3, 1860 (first and second quotation); Harriet P. Perry to Sallie Person, February 18, 1863; Levin Perry to Theophilus Perry, June 5, 1849 (third quotation), Person Family Papers, Duke University Library, Durham, North Carolina. Edmund Key, "Memoranda for my Children" (fourth quotation), Key Family Papers.

[21] Seventh Census, 1850, Schedules 1, 2, and 4; Eighth Census, 1860, Schedules 1, 2, and 4. The statement that most large plantations had overseers is based on several types of evidence. First, there were forty-three large planters in the sample of five hundred households from the 1850 census, and thirty-six overseers appeared in the same sample. This does not prove, of course, that there was a one-to-one match of planters and overseers, but it is suggestive. Second, fourteen slaves who had lived on large Harrison County plantations left narratives of their lives, and nine of them made reference to overseers. See George P. Rawick (ed.), *The American Slave: A Composite Autobio-*

nearly all the time. Overseers lived, he wrote, "in almost a social vacuum." This apparently held true for Harrison County. John B. Webster in his plantation journal always referred to his "overseer" rather than to an individual by name. Some overseers preferred to tell the census enumerator that they were farmers or to give no occupation at all. For example, Lucy Thomas, a slave on the William F. Baldwin plantation, remembered a man named Lewis Brantley as the overseer. Brantly appears in the census of 1860 as a member of the Baldwin household, but as a farmer rather than an overseer.[22]

Overseers in antebellum Harrison County did not constitute a stable class dedicated to plantation management as a career. In 1850, only seventeen individuals in a sample of five hundred household heads listed their occupation as overseer. At the same time, the households sampled housed nineteen men who worked as overseers but were not established enough to have homes of their own. Even among those who headed households, the average overseer in 1850 was only twenty-nine years old (far younger than even the average poor white), unmarried, and without any real or personal property. And in virtually all cases, these men had removed from the county by 1860. According to the census that year, only eight households of five hundred sampled were headed by overseers. Most were still young, unmarried men of little wealth.[23] Overseers were essential to the large planters, but their own position in the community does not appear very enviable.

In summary, a statistical profile easily demonstrates that large planters stood at the apex of the antebellum Harrison

graphy (Westport, Conn., 1972), IV, Part 1, 130-132, 191-192; IV, Part 2, 246-248; V, Part 3, 160-161, 177-179, 190-192, 265-267; V, Part 4, 89-91, 235-237.

[22]William Kauffman Scarborough, *The Overseer: Plantation Management in the Old South* (Baton Rouge, 1966), 45, 46 (quotation). Rawick (ed.) *American Slave*, V, Part 4, 89-91; Eighth Census, 1860, Schedule 1. The plantation journal of John B. Webster for the period from February 17, 1858, to November 5, 1859, has been preserved. The original manuscript is the property of Douglass V. Blocker, a descendant of Webster who now lives at "Mimosa Hall." A typed copy edited by Max S. Lale and Randolph B. Campbell is on deposit in the library of East Texas Baptist College at Marshall. Hereinafter this source will be cited as Webster Plantation Journal.

[23]Seventh Census, 1850, Schedule 1; Eighth Census, 1860, Schedule 1.

County's economic structure. Individual cases suggest that this upper class provided general social leadership and dominated political life as well. Obviously, then, detailed discussions of the agricultural economy, social life, and politics will bring us back frequently to the large planters. And certainly any significant changes in the community could be expected to affect this class, perhaps dramatically.

Next on the social scale were small planters who, although defined narrowly as farmers owning ten to nineteen slaves, were as numerous as large planters in antebellum Harrison County (see Table 3). They constituted an upper middle class, distinct from the large planters primarily in that they simply were not as wealthy. Like members of the upper class, small planters were a little older than average for the community, were more likely to be from the lower South, and had a greater percentage of their households headed by females. But they owned less real property, fewer slaves, and smaller farms. By 1860, for example, a typical small planter had less than half the wealth and the number of slaves belonging to the average large planter. (The margin between large and small planters in these areas had increased during the 1850s.) And his farm was only half as large and productive. Small planters were not on a level with their larger counterparts; at the same time, however, they had far too much property and too many slaves to be considered yeomen. It would distort the social structure to include them with either group.[24]

Small planters seem to have been primarily men on the way up the social ladder. Of the fifty-five small planters who were included in the population sample in 1850, twenty-seven remained in the community ten years later. Of this group, four (14.8%) had declined in status, six (22.2%) were still small planters, and seventeen (63%) had risen to the upper class. Individual cases dramatically illustrate this upward trend among small planters. Montreville J. Hall reported a farm of 550 acres worked by fourteen slaves and producing fifteen bales of cotton

[24] Quantitative information on the small planters (Table 3) is drawn from Seventh Census, 1850, Schedules 1, 2, and 4 and Eighth Census, 1860, Schedules 1, 2, and 4.

in 1850. Ten years later, Hall, whose primary occupation was the law, owned thirty-four slaves and a 1,147 acre plantation that produced 104 bales of cotton. He was one of Harrison County's delegates to the secession convention in 1861. Hall's classic revival plantation home "Edgemont" still stands a few miles to the west of Marshall. Thomas W. Winston, a young man from Alabama, increased his slaveholding from fourteen to thirty bondsmen during the last antebellm decade. In 1850, his 150 acres produced no cotton, but by 1860 he owned 1,200 acres and grew 156 bales of cotton. The next year Winston became the captain of a volunteer company, the "Texas Hunters," and served as an officer throughout the war.[25] Many such examples could be cited, but the point is clear: small planters were a numerous, upwardly mobile class. They aspired to join the upper class, and many did become larger planters during the last antebellum decade.

Yeoman farmers constituted the bulk of Harrison County's middle class (see Table 3). Historians have generally overlooked this class while concentrating on the planters and poor whites, but as Frank L. Owsley and his students at Vanderbilt University reminded us thirty years ago, these "plain folk" were the backbone of the community. Slightly more than half of the yeomen were small slaveholders with fewer than ten bondsmen; the remainder were small nonslaveholding farmers. Together they amounted to one-third of the total population in 1850 and increased to 40% by 1860.[26]

Yeomen differed from large and small planters in that they were somewhat younger and much more likely to be natives of the upper South. And since the definition of class is primarily economic, they were notably less wealthy than the groups above them on the social ladder. Even small planters had more than three times as much property in 1850 and 1860. On the eve of the Civil War, the typical yeoman's farm had fewer than 100

[25] Ibid. For a description of Hall's home "Edgemont," see Fitch, "Use of Native Materials in the Ante Bellum Buildings of Harrison County," 60-61. Winston's Civil War career will be documented below in Chapter 8.

[26] Frank Lawrence Owsley, *Plain Folk of the Old South* (Baton Rouge, 1949); Seventh Census, 1850, Schedules 1, 2, and 4; Eighth Census, 1860, Schedules 1, 2, and 4.

improved acres and grew less than ten bales of cotton. It appears too that individuals in this class were somewhat less likely to move higher in the social structure than were the small planters. Of the sixty-four yeomen in the population sample of 1850 who remained in the community ten years later, only 14.5% had risen in status while 79.7% were in the same class.[27]

Yeomen were not wealthy, nor did they share importantly in the commercial economy and rise rapidly, but it would be a mistake to think of them as poor. Their farms produced corn, food crops, and a little cotton, and supported livestock, especially milk cows and hogs. In 1860, the value of their home manufactures surpassed that of any other class. Yeomen farmers might live in "dog run" houses, two-room log or frame constructions joined by an open space, but they did not live in want by the standards of that era. James C. Quillin, a Virginia-born yeoman who migrated to Texas with a stay in Georgia on the way, provides a good example. According to the census of 1850, Quillin, a nonslaveholder, supported his wife and eight children on a 160-acre farm worth $480 (only 30 acres were improved). He grew no cotton, but produced 250 bushels of corn and 50 bushels of sweet potatoes and owned five milk cows, five head of other cattle, and thirty hogs. Quillin was not well-to-do even among yeomen farmers, but in a letter to his brother in 1852 he praised the country highly, spoke of how much milk and butter he had, and even made reference to selling extra produce. N. V. Board, another native of Virginia, stood closer to the top of the middle class. After marrying a woman from Kentucky and beginning his family there, Board came to Texas during the 1840s. By 1850 he had eight children, six Negro slaves, and a farm of 1,080 acres that produced 700 bushels of corn and eighteen bales of cotton. He also had $850 worth of livestock including thirty-six head of cattle and eighty hogs. Ten years later, two of Board's sons had married and established their own farms, most probably on land given to them by their father. But Board himself still had six slaves and 590 acres valued together

[27] Seventh Census, 1850, Schedules 1, 2, and 4; Eighth Census, 1860, Schedules 1, 2, and 4.

at $6,320. His land and labor produced 800 bushels of corn and eleven bales of cotton. Board was thus a substantial member of the yeoman class; a position that apparently helped him gain some recognition in the community during the last antebellum years. Twice, in 1858 and again in 1860, he was elected to the commissioners court, the chief governing body of the county.[28]

Below the yeomen farmers on the social ladder stood the poor whites. Much was made of the utter poverty and degradation of this class by contemporary anti-southern observers, and historians have estimated that as many as a million antebellum southerners fell into it. Quantitative definitions of poor whites are not common, however, in spite of all this attention, and it is doubtful that any will be completely satisfactory. For purposes of this study, the class was limited to households headed by farmers who did not own farms and whose total real property was valued at less than $250. Fifty families (10% of all households) fell into this group in 1850; the number declined to thirty-seven (7.4%) by 1860 (see Table 3). Thus, poor whites were a relatively small and declining class in antebellum Harrison County. Perhaps the definition is too limited, but even if we include other candidates for this lower class such as those who had no occupation listed in the census and those who were unskilled laborers, poor whites would constitute only about 15% of all household heads.[29]

Several characteristics of poor whites are especially striking.

[28] Seventh Census, 1850, Schedules 1, 2, and 4; Eighth Census, 1860, Schedules 1, 2, and 4. Quillin to Ezekiel Quillin, August 13, 1852, Quillin Family File. Board's officeholding is documented in Election Registers, 1846-1880, Records of the Secretary of State, Archives Division, Texas State Library, Austin. The title of this useful source varies slightly over the years, but it will be cited as Election Registers with the dates inclusive for the years of this study.

[29] Seventh Census, 1850, Schedule 1; Eighth Census, 1860, Schedule 1. The most extreme claims concerning poor whites are found in abolitionist works such as John E. Cairnes, *The Slave Power: Its Character, Career and Probable Designs* . . . (London, 1863), 81-83. He claimed that 70% or four million southerners fell into this category. Modern scholars generally agree that the number was somewhere between 500,000 and 1,000,000 or roughly 10% of the white population. See Clement Eaton, *A History of the Old South* (New York, 1966), 408; Monroe Lee Billington, *The American South: A Brief History* (New York, 1971), 78; and Francis Butler Simkins and Charles Pierce Roland, *A History of the South* (New York, 1972), 138.

They were notably younger than family heads in other classes, and they were far less likely to remain in the community for ten years. Only 18% of those present in the county in 1850 remained there until 1860 or beyond. Compared to planters and yeomen, poor whites generally did not move up or hold their own, they simply moved out. Of course, by definition they were poorer than others. In 1850, for example, when the typical household had $1,452 in real property, poor whites averaged $28 per family. They did not own land so they had to rent or support themselves as farm laborers. George Pandrill, for example, a fifty-year-old native of England who appears in the census of 1860 as a landless farmer, worked in 1858-1859 on John B. Webster's plantation, primarily as a ditchdigger. Pandrill had a wife and seven children, and it seems probable that, like most poor white families, bare subsistence was their lot.[30]

Typically, the discussion of antebellum social structure would, at this point, move to the bottom of the ladder and consider the slaves. In Harrison County, however, there was a class of non-farmers nearly equal in numbers to the large and small planters combined. Composed primarily of merchants, professionals, and tradesmen living in Marshall and the smaller settlements, this group amounted to between 15% and 20% of the community's households in both 1850 and 1860 (see Table 3). Demographically, non-farmers differed most notably from other classes in that a far greater proportion of them were not native to the South. Indeed in 1860, more than one quarter were originally from the free states or foreign nations. Economically, this group stood along side or perhaps a little ahead of the yeomen farmers as part of the middle class. By 1860 more than half of them owned slaves, and they were, on the average, nearly twice as wealthy as yeomen. Obviously their subsistence depended on those in the community who worked the land, but apparently most had the wealth to support a comfortable, although not affluent, life. The community was essen-

[30] Seventh Census, 1850, Schedule 1; Eighth Census, 1860, Schedule 1; Webster Plantation Journal.

tially agricultural, but its sizable and thriving non-farming population should not be overlooked.[31]

Harrison County had one other notable group of residents who cannot be placed with certainty in any of the traditional social classes or with the non-farmers either, at least not on the basis of census data. In 1850, the sample popluation included forty-five household heads (9% of the total) who are best called slaveholding farmers without farms in that they gave their occupation as farmer and reported the ownership of slaves but not of farm property. In a few cases, planters and yeomen fell into this class because of inaccurate census enumeration. Most, however, did not belong to the landholding classes, and while as slaveholders they were not exactly poor whites, they seem to have been closer to this lower class than any other. Like the poor whites, they were somewhat younger than average in the community (38.8 years), they were more likely to move away (only 26.7% remained there in 1860), and they constituted a smaller part of the total population in 1860 than in 1850. There were only eight households in this group at the last antebellum census.[32]

Finally, Negro slaves occupied the bottom rung of Harrison County's social ladder during the 1850s. They constituted a massive lower class more numerous than all those above them combined. In 1850, there were 2,671 whites and 3,123 slaves in the five hundred households sampled. Ten years later the number of whites stood at 2,622, a slight decline, but there were 4,174 slaves. The bondsmen, of course, were not evenly distributed among the whites. Instead, a majority lived on large plantations. In 1860, for example, the seventy-one large cotton planters in the sample owned 2,612 bondsmen, 62.6% of the

[31] Seventh Census, 1850, Schedules 1 and 2; Eighth Census, 1860, Schedules 1 and 2.

[32] Ibid. The case of Hugh Y. Hall presents a good example of inaccurate census reporting. Hall appeared in Schedules 1 and 2 of the census of 1850 as a farmer owning thirty-four slaves. No farm could be found for him in Schedule 4, however, in spite of the fact that the Harrison County Tax Rolls for 1850 show him as the owner of more than 500 acres. In 1860, the census reported a 2,150 acre plantation for H. Y. Hall. Clearly he was a planter in 1850 rather than a slaveholding farmer without a farm, but the census confused the situation. Fortunately, cases of this sort were rare.

total. Thus, although there were many small slaveholders, the typical slave lived with at least ten or more of his fellow bondsmen and performed the bulk of the community's agricultural labor, especially in the production of cotton.[33]

The fundamental fact of life for every member of this lower class was existence as a piece of chattel property. Although their humanity was recognized in a variety of ways, slaves were essentially at the disposal of their owners in much the same way as a horse or work animal. They were bought and sold, hired out, mortgaged, and bequeathed to heirs. The job of the majority was to work from before daybreak until sundown five days a week and half a day on Saturday. In return, they generally received a subsistence standard of living. The "Peculiar Institution," as southerners called it, will be analyzed in detail below; the point here is that Harrison County's entire economic-social structure rested on an enslaved lower class. Obviously any change in the status of the Negro majority would shake the community to its very foundations.

[33] Seventh Census, 1850, Schedules 1, 2, and 4; Eighth Census, 1860, Schedules 1, 2, and 4. The distribution of slaves among the slaveholding population will be discussed in detail in Chapter 5 below.

2

The Agricultural Economy

LIFE IN ANTEBELLUM Harrison County revolved around agriculture. Farmers headed three of every four households, and most others were in some way dependent on the agricultural economy. Undoubtedly wherever men met in the community; on country roads, at rural post offices, or on the streets and in the stores of Marshall, they voiced the typical farmers' questions: "Will it rain soon?" "Finished picking cotton yet?" "How are prices at New Orleans?" We have no record of such conversations, but letters written by farmers and planters from the county inevitably turned to agricultural conditions, and local newspapers commented regularly on the weather and crops. These are the constant concerns of an agricultural community.

In their letters, farmers were sometimes optimistic, often pessimistic, and always aware of the uncertainties of nature. Levin Perry, no doubt like many in the county, was enthusiastic about conditions in the summer of 1859. "My prospects for a crop were never so flattering," he informed his son. William T. Scott, however, was not satisfied even in 1859. While admitting that his sons Buckner and Preston had made good crops, his own, he said, were "light." Scott's view notwithstanding, 1859 was a good crop year and so was 1852. But the 1849 cotton crop was ruined by heavy rains and the "bole-worm," and the 1860 crop was cut drastically by drouth. A series of three letters from D. F. McCarty, a small planter who owned ten slaves in 1860, to his brother provides an excellent illustration of the ups and downs of the farmer's life. In March, 1859, McCarty prepared to plant big crops, sixty-five acres of corn and seventy-five acres of cotton in addition to wheat, oats, and rye. The year was a good one, and he made 800 bushels of corn and thirty bales of cotton. The next year also found McCarty optimistic; at least he was in the spring. But then there was a severe drouth in June and July followed by heavy rains in late August and early September, ruining picking conditions for the cotton that had survived. McCarty wrote: "It is almost a total failure of crops in this section and I only made 10 bales of cotton and only corn to do me this present time and it will take all the cotton I have made to pay for provisions for my family and will have to find some expedient to raise the money and in all probability at a heavy interest." To make matters worse, McCarty had contracted in April when prospects were good to buy a number of family tombstones, and now he had to pay. "I as others could not see the result of things," he wrote.[1] Farmers in any place at any

[1] Levin Perry to Theophilus Perry, June 20, 1859 (first quotation), Person Family Papers; William T. Scott to P. R. Rose, October 10, 1859 (second and third quotations), Preston R. Rose Family Papers, Archives, Barker Texas History Collection, University of Texas, Austin; D. F. McCarty to James R. McCarty, March 6, 1859, May 5, 1860, January 31, 1861, (fourth and fifth quotations), McCarty Family File, Harrison County Historical Museum, Marshall. Most planters would have been happy with Scott's "light" crop since by the date of his letter he had picked and ginned 224 bales of cotton. On crops in 1852, see William T. Scott to P. R. Rose, September 22, 1852, Rose Family

time should be able to sympathize with D. F. McCarty of antebellum Harrison County.

Nineteenth-century Texas was famed as an area of plentiful, inexpensive land, and Harrison County was no exception. Farms there were sizable, averaging 530 acres in 1850 and 611 acres in 1860 (see Table 4). Most contained two kinds of acreage designated as "improved" and "unimproved" in the census. Improved land had been cleared and brought under cultivation; unimproved areas were generally forested. Farmers worked regularly to clear "new ground," as they called it, and this moved land from the unimproved to the improved category. The average farm in 1850 had 112 improved acres (21% of the total); ten years later the mean was 184 acres (30.2% of the typical farm's land). As would be expected, large planters had far more acreage than small planters in both 1850 and 1860, and in turn small planters had more than did the yeomen farmers. Moreover, planters' landholdings expanded more rapidly than those of yeomen during the 1850s. For example, small planters averaged 131 improved acres in 1850 and 234 in 1860, an increase of 78.6%, while yeomen's holdings of improved land advanced only from 50 to 67 acres, a 34% gain. Two points concerning the basic agricultural economy thus become clear: first, land was plentiful enough that even the average yeoman farmer had approximately 300 acres, and second, land was by no means equally distributed among the agricultural population.[2]

The average Harrison County farm had a total cash value for its acreage and improvements of $2,022 in 1850 and $3,497

Papers, and James C. Quillin to Ezekiel Quillin, August 13, 1852, Quillin Family File. On crops in 1849, see Marshall *Texas Republican*, August 23, October 18, 1849; John W. Rogers to T. H. Etheridge, September 12, 1849, Rogers Family File, Harrison County Historical Museum, Marshall. On crops in 1860, see D. F. McCarty to James R. McCarty, January 31, 1861, McCarty Family File. Information on the weather in 1860 is from the Marshall *Texas Republican* and from two manuscript ledger books kept by M. J. Hall from 1860 to 1874. Hall's entry for June 23, 1860 read: "Corn nearly dead—the driest time ever known here." These ledgers belong to Mrs. Margaret G. Hudson of Gainesville, Florida.

[2] All the statistics presented in Table 4 are based on the samples of 500 households drawn from the censuses of 1850 and 1860: Seventh Census, 1850, Schedules 1, 2, and 4; and Eighth Census, 1860, Schedules 1, 2, and 4.

TABLE 4

Mean Agricultural Property and Production in Antebellum Harrison County

	All Farmers		Large Planters		Small Planters		Yeomen Farmers	
	1850	1860	1850	1860	1850	1860	1850	1860
Improved Acreage	112	184	330	473	131	234	5 0	67
Unimproved Acreage	419	427	831	932	444	493	306	228
Cash Value of Farms (in dollars)	2,022	3,497	5,203	8,211	2,706	4,160	990	1,629
Value of Farm Implements (in dollars)	161	190	398	439	223	247	81	85
Value of Livestock (in dollars)	619	1,028	1,516	2,289	752	1,182	348	535
Bushels of Corn	725	904	1,859	2,192	846	1,118	397	385
Bushels of Other Grains	15	80	52	234	31	61	1	22
Bales of Cotton	9	32	29	93	11	39	3	9
Bushels of Food Crops	285	187	757	325	361	183	140	138
Pounds of Cheese & Butter	85	129	165	165	111	124	57	118
Value of Home Manufacturers (in dollars)	5	11	8	8	2	8	5	13
Value of Animals Slaughtered (in dollars)	113	225	260	386	127	216	71	170

in 1860 (Table 4). Land alone was generally valued at less than $4 per acre in 1850 and less than $6 ten years later. Property appraisals found in probate case papers reveal the gradually increasing values during the decade. In 1850, for example, Isaac Beck left his widow Nancy 278 acres worth $4 each. James Campbell's 294 acres were valued at $1,470 ($5 each) in 1855. In 1859, appraisers set the value of William J. Blocker's 1,280 acre plantation at $8 per acre. At the same time, Blocker's thirty-seven slaves had an average value of $840 each regardless of age, sex, or condition.[3] There can be no better indication that land was relatively inexpensive and that the agricultural economy of antebellum Harrison County was land-rich and labor-poor.

It should be noted too that while large planters were by far the richest class their land generally was not much more valuable than that worked by smaller farmers. In 1860, for example, the average cash values of farms ranged only from $5.84 per acre among large planters to $5.52 per acre for yeomen.[4] More than likely, planters in the eastern part of the county owned somewhat better land, but the notable differences that might be expected do not appear. The positions of large planters were generally based on their slaves and the size of their acreage, not its value.

Harrison County farmers not only enjoyed inexpensive land; they also found no need for large investments in tools and implements. Most concentrated on the production of corn and cotton, crops that could be cultivated successfully with simple tools and slave labor and that defied sophisticated mechanization well into the twentieth century. Thus, while a modern observer may marvel at how little antebellum Harrison County farmers spent on implements, it should not necessarily be taken as a sign of backward agriculture. Typically, a farmer needed heavy plows for breaking land, harrows to aid in preparing it for

[3]Estates of Isaac Beck, James Campbell, and William J. Blocker, Harrison County Probate Papers, County Clerk's Office, Marshall.

[4]Eighth Census, 1860, Schedules 1, 2, and 4.

planting, light plows for cultivating crops, and wagons for hauling. Of course, he also had to have harness for his work animals. He used hand implements such as axes and hoes and probably had a few basic blacksmith and carpenter tools. Beyond this, a cotton gin was vital, especially for large planters.[5]

During the 1850s, the typical Harrison County farm reported less than $200 worth of equipment. Yeomen farmers did not own $100 worth of implements, and even large planters had no more than five or six hundred dollars invested (Table 4). The estate of John J. Webster provides a good illustration. Webster, a large planter owning seventy-four slaves and 6,177 acres at his death in 1854, had three wagons worth $100, plows valued at $200, carpenter and blacksmith tools listed at $40, thirty-two sets of harness valued at one dollar each, and hand tools such as axes and hoes worth ten dollars. These tools and implements amounted to $382 in an estate assessed at $84,916. Interestingly, the inventory of Webster's property did not list a cotton gin. Almost certainly he and other large planters in the county owned gins, but virtually none of the estate inventories included this key piece of plantation machinery. Apparently gins were seen as part of the farm in general, its land and buildings, and assessed as such. A new gin manufactured by J. S. Alexander in Harrison County during the 1850s cost approximately $250. So even if we assume that Webster owned a gin and add its value to his investment in farm equipment the total would still be around $600. At the same time, a thirty-four year old slave blacksmith named John who was part of Webster's estate in 1854 was valued at $1,800.[6] Clearly the cost of tools

[5]Gavin Wright, *The Political Economy of the Cotton South: Households, Markets, and Wealth in the Nineteenth Century* (New York, 1978), 107-109, notes that the lack of mechanization in southern agriculture does not prove a lack of progress on the part of planters who had slave labor to exploit. He does argue, however, that the lack of mechanization retarded industrial growth because it inhibited the manufacture of agricultural implements.

[6]Estate of John J. Webster, Harrison County Probate Papers. The cost of a gin manufactured in Marshall by J. S. Alexander is suggested by information in Seventh Census, 1850, Schedule 5 — Products of Industry. Alexander reported the manufacture of ten gins valued in total at $2,600.

and implements, like the investment in land, was negligible compared to the costs of labor.

Harrison County was not a center of stock raising in antebellum Texas. Where cattle were concerned, for example, it did not rank among the top twenty counties in the state in either 1850 or 1860. Horses and sheep were not especially numerous in Harrison County either. But its farms were well stocked with animals that were necessary to a slaveholding/-cotton and corn agricultural economy. In 1860, for example, it ranked first in the state in the number of mules (2,590), an important work animal, and second in the number of hogs (30,832), the key meat supplier for the community.[7]

The average Harrison County farm had more than $600 worth of livestock in 1850 and $1,000 in 1860. Values were reasonably steady through the decade so the increase was due primarily to larger livestock holdings by 1860. Mules, depending on their ages, were generally worth $75 to $100, horses were slightly less valuable, and oxen cost $35 to $50 per yoke. Cattle were valued consistently at $5-7 per head; hogs and sheep at $2-3 each. It should be noted that large planters had livestock holdings roughly twice as large as those of small planters, indicating that they did not neglect this aspect of agriculture to focus exclusively on cotton production.[8]

Relatively little attention was given to the care and feeding of livestock. Work animals were kept in lots or pens where they would be readily available; cattle and hogs, marked with their owner's identifying mark or brand, generally ranged through the woods and natural open areas. Once oats were cut and corn harvested (by pulling both the ears and the fodder), these fields served as a sort of pasture. In general, Harrison County farmers

[7] DeBow (ed.), *Statistical View of the United States*, 310-319; U.S. Bureau of the Census, *Agriculture of the United States in 1860*, 140-151.

[8] Statistics of livestock value are presented in Table 4. The estimates of livestock values are based on assessments made during probate and preserved in the Harrison County Probate Papers. A random sample of fourteen such inventories, for example, showed 679 hogs with an average value of $2.62, 337 head of cattle at $6.33 each, 120 sheep at $2.13, 26 yoke of oxen at $54.80 per yoke, 43 mules at $95.47, and 53 horses at $84.52.

bothered very little with feeding their livestock other than the work animals which received corn, oats, and fodder. No hay was produced to feed cattle, and hogs were expected to fatten on the acorn mast.[9]

Harrison County farmers were not stockraisers; instead, like their kinsmen across the lower South, they gave primary allegiance to "King Cotton." The cotton crop of 1849 totalled 4,581 bales and that of 1859 amounted to 21,440 bales, an increase of 368%. This spectacular expansion of cotton production reflected not only the fact that 1859 was a better crop year but also a rise in the number and proportion of Harrison County farmers engaged in cotton culture and in the amount of acreage devoted to it. In 1849, more than one-quarter of the community's farmers (27.7%) grew no cotton, but by 1859 only 15.6% were not involved to some extent. Corn production increased only about 75% during the 1850s (376,620 to 660,043 bushels) as opposed to 368% for cotton. According to the census, productivity per acre remained stable during the decade at 1,000 pounds of seed cotton per acre and twenty to twenty-five bushels of corn per acre, so it seems clear that farmers devoted relatively more land to cotton than to corn as the years passed. Contemporaries noted this trend. As early as 1852, one observer commented that "cotton seems to be the only crop attended to" in Harrison County.[10]

[9]For comments on the treatment of livestock in antebellum Harrison County, see Webster Plantation Journal; Hobart Key to "Mag," June 2, 1854, Key Family Papers; William T. Scott to P. R. Rose, September 22, 1852, Rose Family Papers; and Mary Jo Edwards, "Texas Agriculture as Reflected in Letters to the *Southern Cultivator* Prior to 1861" (M.A. Thesis, East Texas State Teachers College, 1948), 35-36. Harrison County farmers produced no hay in either 1850 or 1860. DeBow (ed.), *Statistical View of the United States*, 317; U.S. Bureau of the Census, *Agriculture of the United States in 1860*, 146.

[10]Summary statistics are from DeBow (ed.), *Statistical View of the United States*, 308-319; U.S. Bureau of the Census, *Agriculture of the United States in 1860*, 140-151. See also Seventh Census, 1850, Schedule 6; Eighth Census, 1860, Schedule 6; letter reprinted in Edwards, "Texas Agriculture," 35-36 (quotation). These sources also reveal that in both census years Harrison County ranked second among Texas counties in the size of its cotton crop. (The 1859 crop for San Augustine County was printed inaccurately as 31,342 bales when it should have been 3,142 bales.) The proportions of farmers who did not grow cotton are drawn from my manuscript samples. Seventh Census, 1850, Schedule 4 and Eight Census, 1860, Schedule 4.

Cotton culture, because it required large amounts of labor, especially at picking time, was dominated by the larger slaveholders. As was shown in Table 4, the crops of planters owning twenty or more slaves were more than twice as large as those of small planters in both 1849 and 1859 and far surpassed those of the yeomen. From another perspective (Table 5), we can see that large planters who constituted only 16% of all farmers in 1849 and 22% in 1859 produced 51% of all cotton reported in the first census year and 62% of that reported in 1860. At the same time, the yeoman farmer majority grew less than one-quarter of the county's cotton. The importance of slave labor is illustrated even more dramatically in the fact that slaveholding farmers produced more than 94% of all cotton grown in the county in both 1849 and 1859 (Table 5). The great majority of farmers, then, cultivated cotton as a cash crop, but the yeomen, especially those who held no slaves, contributed relatively little to this aspect of the agricultural economy. Cer-

TABLE 5

Cotton Production by Antebellum Harrison County Planters and Farmers

	1849			1859		
	Large Planters	Small Planters	Yeomen Farmers	Large Planters	Small Planters	Yeomen Farmers
% of Landholding Farmers	16.1	20.6	63.3	21.8	17.2	61.0
% of Cotton Produced	51.1	25.6	23.3	62.4	20.8	16.8

	1849		1859	
	Slaveholders	Non-slaveholders	Slaveholders	Non-slaveholders
% of Landholding Farmers	71.9	28.1	72.7	27.3
% of Cotton Produced	94.2	5.8	94.6	5.4

tainly they were dwarfed by planters such as William T. Scott, whose 356 bale crop in 1859 was the largest recorded in antebellum Harrison County. Perhaps, as Gavin Wright has suggested, smaller farmers chose deliberately to be sure that they had enough bread and meat before devoting energy to a cash crop. Yeomen were not willing to risk their subsistence on a chance to make more money.[11]

Cotton cultivation began with the bedding of the land in February and March when heavy plows were used to throw up ridges or beds of soil. In early April, shallow furrows were opened along the beds by light plows, and cotton seed, saved from the ginning of previous crops, were dropped by hand into the furrows. The seeds were then covered by harrows and left to germinate in the beds while the lower area between the rows, the "middles" in planter terminology, collected moisture as a precaution against dry weather. Within ten days or so cotton plants began to push through the soil and working the crop began in earnest. The young shoots were thinned to a "stand" of single plants about two feet apart, and grass and weeds had to be plowed from the middles and chopped from the rows regularly through May, June, and into July. On large plantations hardly a day passed that did not see at least a part of the labor force engaged in cotton cultivation.[12]

Cotton plants usually bloomed in early June, and within two months the bolls were open and ready to pick. Small farmers who grew only enough cotton to produce a few bales were able to clean their fields in a relatively short time, even if they had only their wives and older children to supplement their own labor. But on large plantations, the picking season generally began in August and extended into the late fall. At times

[11] Statistical summaries presented here were drawn from Seventh Census, 1850, Schedules 1, 2, and 4 and Eighth Census, 1860, Schedules 1, 2, and 4. Wright, *Political Economy of the Cotton South*, 62-74.

[12] For cotton cultivation in Harrison County, see Webster Plantation Journal and Hall Ledger Books for 1860. For a good discussion of cotton agriculture in Texas, see Abigail Curlee, "A Study of Texas Slave Plantations, 1822-1865" (Ph.D. Dissertation, University of Texas, 1932), 154-174.

the last cotton was not picked until January or February of the following year. Planters sent male and female adult slaves into the fields six days a week, and on some plantations a day was from sunup to sundown with the cotton being weighed in by candlelight. Cotton picking time meant months of sustained tedious labor.[13]

Planters and overseers often bragged about spectacular feats of cotton picking by individual slaves. In 1852, for example. Thomas J. Wells, overseer for A. B. Wright, claimed that four of his hands picked 600 or more pounds of seed cotton each during the same day. The average per hand, however, was probably somewhat less than 200 pounds per day. On John B. Webster's plantation in 1858, a slave named Samuel consistently outpicked all others, and his average over fifty-one working days from August 9 to October 9 was 210.7 pounds. At the height of the picking season on September 15, 1858, Webster had thirty-one male and female hands in the fields, and they averaged only 155 pounds each.[14]

The best land in Harrison County generally yielded about one bale of cotton per acre during the 1850s. Put another way, one acre produced nearly 1,500 pounds of seed cotton which, when the seeds were removed from the fibers by ginning, amounted to 450-500 pounds of lint cotton, enough for one bale. It is doubtful, however, that Harrison County farmers, especially the smaller ones, produced at this level. James C. Quillin, a nonslaveholder living west of Marshall, estimated in 1852 that he would get 500 pounds of lint from every two acres planted. D. F. McCarty, a small planter, planned a seventy-five acre crop in 1859 and reported thirty bales produced for the past crop year in the census of 1860. The *Texas Almanac for 1859* reported 51,708 acres of cotton in Harrison County in 1858. Production figures are not available for that year, but for 1859, when certainly there was no significant decline in cotton acreage, the crop was 21,440 bales. It seems then, that on the

[13] Webster Plantation Journal; Rawick (ed.), *American Slave*, IV, Part 1, 133-136.
[14] Marshall *Texas Republican*, October 23, 1852; Webster Plantation Journal.

average, Harrison County farmers were fortunate to produce one bale of cotton for every two acres planted.[15]

Once picked, the cotton had to be ginned and baled; that is, the fiber or lint had to be separated from the seeds and pressed into bales weighing approximately 500 pounds each. Harrison County planters were fortunate to have J. S. Alexander's gin factory, the largest in the state, located in their community. In 1850, J. F. Rosborough, a large slaveholder located southeast of Marshall, testified in the *Texas Republican* that a seventy-saw gin he had purchased from Alexander was the equal to any that he had ever owned. Rosborough's gin, operating on water power, cleaned enough cotton to average six 500 pound bales per day. William Davenport had a smaller forty-five-saw gin built by Alexander that was powered by two horses and cleaned two bales per day. Gins and presses were too expensive for small farmers who produced only a few bales of cotton so the latter generally used the machinery belonging to their larger neighbors.[16]

Ginning began almost as soon as cotton picking started and continued into the winter. Often the process was not completed and all the baled cotton ready for shipment until the spring of the following year. If a planter survived all the hazards of nature threatening his crop to that point, his financial fate then hinged on the marketing process and prices at New Orleans. This aspect of the agricultural economy will be examined in detail below. Other crops, however, must be considered first.

Cotton as a cash crop was the staple of Harrison County's agricultural economy, but corn, the chief food supplier for

[15]The census reported an average of 1,000 pounds of seed cotton per acre in Harrison County. Seventh Census, 1850, Schedule 6 and Eighth Census, 1860, Schedule 6. James C. Quillin to Ezekiel Quillin, August 13, 1852, Quillin Family File; D. F. McCarty to James R. McCarty, March 6, 1859, McCarty Family File; Eighth Census, 1860, Schedule 4; "Census for the State of Texas for 1858," in *The Texas Almanac for 1859* (Galveston, 1858), 209. In 1858, John B. Webster's slaves picked 307, 289 pounds of seed cotton which produced 176 bales averaging 508.68 pounds each. Thus nearly 1,750 pounds of seed cotton went into each bale, Webster Plantation Journal.

[16]Raymond E. White, "Cotton Ginning in Texas to 1861," *Southwestern Historical Quarterly*, LXI (Oct. 1957), 267; Marshall *Texas Republican*, March 23, 1850.

humans and animals alike, was also a staple in the sense of the chief commodity produced. More than 96% of all farmers in the population samples for both 1850 and 1860 grew at least a few bushels of corn. Many produced large crops, for Harrison County ranked first in the state in corn production in both 1850 (376,620 bushels) and 1860 (660,043 bushels). Large planters grew far more, on the average, than did other farmers, but by 1860, the mean for all farmers was 904 bushels, and even small planters grew more than 1,100 bushels each (see Table 4).[17]

Corn cultivation began in late February once the land was prepared and rows laid off approximately three feet apart. Seeds were dropped, usually by slave women and boys on the larger farms and plantations, into furrows opened along the rows and then covered by plows or harrows. Once the corn came up, conscientious farmers thinned the plants to assure maximum growth and plowed and hoed every week or two through the spring to keep down the grass and weeds. It was possible to get by with less attention to the corn crop once a good "stand" had been assured, but farmers who had the labor or the energy generally continued cultivation into June. By late July under the East Texas sun, the ears of corn were fully mature and the fodder began to turn brown. Farmers then sent their hands into the fields to strip the leaves from the stalks and tie them in bundles to feed the work animals. Ofter the ears of corn still in the shuck remained on the stalks until November and December before they were gathered. The stalks were then knocked down and the land plowed in preparation for next year's crop. Productivity in a normal year ranged from twenty-five to fifty bushels per acre. Edward Smith estimated yields at this level in 1849, and William T. Scott, who seems to have been consistently pessimistic about his prospects, predicted eighteen bushels per acre as a light crop in 1859. If Harrison County planters averaged twenty-five bushels per acre, as apparently they did, they were in line with farmers across the lower South.[18]

[17] Seventh Census, 1850, Schedule 4; Eighth Census, 1860, Schedule 4.

[18] Webster Plantation Journal; Smith, *Journey Through Northeastern Texas*, 24;

Sweet potatoes are commonly considered garden vegetables, but in antebellum Harrison County, they were grown on a scale far beyond that of ordinary gardening. The census of 1860 reported 121,403 bushels grown in the community, by far the largest crop of any Texas county. Planters nurtured buds or slips from mature potatoes in moist, warm "hotbeds" beginning in March and then in late April or early May set out the young plants in bedded rows similar to those used for cotton and corn. Potato patches were cultivated through the summer and the new potatoes were dug up and stored before frost hit the vines in the fall. Some of the sweet potatoes may have been fed to hogs, but most went for human consumption. And they probably were a better food than irish potatoes, being especially rich in vitamins A and C. Harrison county farmers grew relatively large crops of white potatoes too, ranking third in the state in 1860 with 10,037 bushels.[19]

The agricultural censuses also reported large quantities of peas and beans for Harrison County. In 1860, the 23,874 bushel crop ranked second in the state. Almost certainly the census was recording not English garden peas or anything commonly considered beans but instead cowpeas, commonly known across the South as "black-eyed peas." Black-eyed peas are technically a kind of bean, and some historians have argued that they were grown primarily to replenish the soil or to feed to animals. There is direct evidence, however, in the plantation journal of John B. Webster that peas, which were sown by hand and harrowed in during April and May and harvested in October and November, were threshed and used for human consumption.[20] Natives of

William T. Scott to P. R. Rose, October 10, 1859, Rose Family Papers. Census estimates of corn production were twenty-five bushels per acre in 1850 and twenty bushels in 1860. Seventh Census, 1850, Schedule 6 and Eighth Census, 1860, Schedule 6. For productivity across the South, see Lewis Cecil Gray, *History of Agriculture in the Southern United States to 1860* (Washington, 1933), II, 816.

[19] Summary statistics are from U.S. Bureau of the Census, *Agriculture of the United States in 1860*, 140-151. Information on Harrison County sweet potato cultivation is in Webster Plantation Journal. Fogel and Engerman, *Time on the Cross*, I, 113, presents an argument for the nutritional value of sweet potatoes.

[20] U.S. Bureau of the Census, *Agriculture of the United States in 1860*, 140-151;

the rural South, many of whom still eat black-eyed peas, will hardly find this surprising.

Corn, sweet potatoes, and black-eyed peas were the primary food crops of the county's agricultural economy. Wheat, oats, and rye were relatively uncommon; less than half of the farmers in the 1860 census sample grew so much as one bushel of any of these grains. Nevertheless, the community ranked third in the state that year in rye production, with 5,582 bushels, and fifth in oats, with 53,809 bushels. Wheat and rye were of the winter variety, sown in November and December and harvested in June. Oats were planted in January or February and also cut in June. Wheat and rye were used for flour, it seems, while oats were fed to livestock. In all cases, once the fields were harvested, work animals were allowed to graze on the stubble.[21]

Finally, no Harrison County farm or plantation was complete without its garden that produced vegetables such as cabbage, squash, and cucumbers. Of course, smaller farmers who did not have slave forces to feed, grew potatoes, peas, and beans on a garden scale too. Watermelon patches were common as were turnip fields, although not all turnips were used for human consumption. The gardening season ran from March well into the fall, providing a relatively long period when diets heavily dependent on pork and corn could be supplemented by vegetables.[22]

How strong was the agricultural economy of antebellum Harrison County? The community had a backbone of yeomen farmers whose well-being was vital to its social and economic

Webster Plantation Journal; Paul A. David et al., *Reckoning With Slavery: A Critical Study in the Quantitative History of American Negro Slavery* (New York, 1976), 254-255.

[21] Eighth Census, 1860, Schedule 4; U.S. Bureau of the Census, *Agriculture of the United States in 1860*, 140-151; Webster Plantation Journal.

[22] "Horticulture," in *The Texas Almanac for 1857* (Galveston, 1856), 5-29, is a description of Texas garden crops and the monthly cultivation routine common during the 1850s. The Marshall *Texas Republican*, September 1, 1860, commented on the importance of the turnip crop in helping planters "get by" the failure of other crops that drouth year.

health. And apparently, as explained in Chapter 1, the great majority were, at least by the standards of that day, reasonably well supplied with the necessities of life. Most farmers were able to produce and/or acquire adequate food, clothing, and shelter during the 1850s; in fact yeomen expanded their landholdings and increased their output from 1850 to 1860. Thus, there are many indications that basic farming activity served the majority well during the last antebellum decade, and the economy was strong in that respect.

In another sense, however, the true strength and future prospects of the community's agricultural economy depended not on its backbone but on its head, the planter class. Although a minority, the planters who dominated commercial agriculture were the driving force in Harrison County farming. They invested in land and slave labor and sought to cultivate cotton for a profit. They produced a marketable surplus and brought cash returns to spend and invest in the community. Antebellum Harrison County was preeminently a planters' society, and therefore, the productivity, profitability, and self-sufficiency of slave plantations were key measures of the agricultural economy's strength at that time.

The most easily understood measure of productivity on Harrison County plantations is the amount of cotton produced per slave. This is determined from census data simply by dividing the number of bondsmen held by cotton planters into the number of bales they grew in a year. Of course, not all slaves contributed equally to cotton production. Elderly bondsmen, infants, and young children did not work at all, and women were generally less important than prime field hands. All, however, were part of a planters's investment in labor (past, present, and future) and should be considered in the calculation of productivity, especially as it relates to profitability. Moreover, it is far easier to determine bales per slave than to define and count "prime field hands" in the labor force and then calculate productivity on that basis.[23]

[23] The problem of determining productivity per slave and per hand is discussed in

The 1850 census sample included forty-three large planters owning twenty or more slaves and fifty-five small planters holding from ten to nineteen bondsmen. As would be expected, virtually all produced cotton during the 1849-1850 crop year. Only two large planters and six small ones did not. Omitting these non-producers, we see (Table 6) that forty-one large planters owning a total of 1,383 slaves grew 1,229 bales of cotton, an average of .89 bales per slave. The forty-nine small cotton planters produced at an almost identical level. Ten years later there were seventy-one large and fifty-six small planters in the sample populations, and only five (three with twenty or more slaves and two with ten to nineteen bondsmen) did not produce cotton. Productivity per slave had jumped markedly to more than two and one-half bales. Perhaps the planters and their slaves worked more effectively, but more than likely the sharp increase was due to more land being devoted to cotton culture and to the fact that 1859 was a far better crop year than 1849. In any case, these calculations based on census data, when compared to similar investigations of other cotton growing areas, suggest that by the close of the antebellum period, given the necessary natural conditions, Harrison County planters could be at least as productive as those elsewhere in the cotton South.[24]

Productivity was important, but the "bottom line," of course, was profit. How profitable was slave/cotton agriculture in antebellum Harrison County? The rate of return per slave for cotton planters in 1850 and 1860 may be calculated using the formula $r = a + \frac{P(y) - C}{K}$ where a = the percentage of natural increase in the stock of slaves, P = the price of cotton, y = the amount of cotton produced per slave, C = the annual

James D. Foust and Dale E. Swan, "Productivity and Profitability of Antebellum Slave Labor: A Micro-approach," *Agricultural History*, XLIV (Jan. 1970), 41-43.

[24] Seventh Census, 1850, Schedules 1, 2, and 4; Eighth Census, 1860, Schedules 1, 2, and 4. Foust and Swan, "Productivity and Profitability of Antebellum Slave Labor," 53, estimate productivity for the cotton South at 1.59 bales per slave in 1850 (far higher than my Harrsion County estimates) and 2,22 bales per slave in 1860 (very comparable to my Harrison County estimates).

maintenance cost per slave, and K = the total investment cost per slave. At a glance, this formula may seem overly technical, but a brief consideration of the values to be assigned to each of its components will clarify the factors involved. It is impossible to establish the degree of profitability beyond question, but at least we can appreciate the complexity of the problem.[25]

The annual rate of natural increase in the value of the slave force belonging to cotton planters (a) has been set at 2.15%. This estimate, based on the increase in the slave population of the entire South, was developed by several specialists on the profitability of slavery. The number of slaves in Harrison County grew very rapidly during the 1850s, but there is no practical way of determining how many were imported, either with their owners or through the slave trade, and how many were children born to slaves already residing in the community. Thus, the estimate of a 2.15% natural increase is the most satisfactory available.[26]

Cotton prices averaged 10.8 cents per pound at New Orleans for both the 1849 and 1859 crop years. Harrison County planters, of course, had to get their cotton to New Orleans, and once the costs of shipping and handling are subtracted they probably netted 8 or 9 cents per pound. Profitability will be figured at both price levels. The amount of cotton produced per slave (y) is determined by multiplying the bales per slave (Table 6) by the poundage per bale. The census forms called for 400 pound bales, but there is much evidence that Harrison County planters pressed their lint into bales averaging at least 500 pounds each. Perhaps the distance to market was a factor, or maybe it is just one more example of everything being bigger in Texas. Annual maintenance costs per slave (C) have been set at $17.50 in the most careful studies of profitability, and there is no reason to alter this estimate where Harrison County is concerned.[27]

[25] This formula is presented and explained in Foust and Swan, "Productivity and Profitability of Antebellum Slave Labor," 49.

[26] Ibid.

[27] Gray, *History of Agriculture in the Southern United States to 1860*, II. 705, 1027; Harold D. Woodman, *King Cotton and His Retainers: Financing and Marketing*

The total capital investment per slave (K) was composed of four major items: average price per slave, cost of land per slave, and investments in farm implements and in livestock per slave. Estimates of slave prices depend on information from local records; those for the other three factors are derived from census data.

Virtually all studies of slavery's profitability have utilized the price estimates developed by Ulrich B. Phillips from bills of sale at major slave markets such as New Orleans. There are, however, more appropriate sources for slave values in antebellum Harrison County: estate inventories and appraisals preserved in the community's probate records. When a deceased person's estate went into probate, one necessary step in the process was to list and evaluate all his property, including slaves.

the Cotton Crop of the South, 1800-1925 (Lexington, Ky., 1968), 177; Foust and Swan, "Productivity and Profitability of Antebellum Slave Labor," 50.

TABLE 6

Cotton Productivity per Slave, 1850 and 1860

	Number of Cotton Producers	Number of Slaves	Number of Bales	Bales per Slave
		1850		
Large Planters	41	1,383	1,229	.89
Small Planters	49	675	615	.91
		1860		
Large Planters	68	2,544	6,589	2.59
Small Planters	54	739	2,197	2.97

The inventory was made by established members of the community who knew property values. In many cases, they listed every slave by sex, age, and condition before giving a dollar value; in almost every case they at least indicated the sex of the bondsman. It might be argued that the appraisals gave slave values rather than prices, but surely the two were closely related. And in the absence of numerous bills of sale for transactions in Harrison County, probate record data are the best available. On the basis of forty slaveholders' estates selected at random for the 1849-1860 period, slave values, regardless of the age, sex, or condition of the bondsman, averaged approximately $400 in 1850 and $780 in 1860.[28]

The cost of land to be worked by the slave is a second major component of investment per slave. Instead of attempting to estimate the amount of acreage necessary to employ the slave during his working life, it is assumed that all the land, both improved and unimproved, owned by slaveholding cotton planters was an investment for the present and future labor of their bondsmen. This assumption probably biases upward the costs of land since few slaveholders worked all their land at any given time. But it also allows us to assume that there was enough land of sufficient quality to employ each slave for thirty years, the same length period as the average slave's working lifetime. Thus we need not be concerned about the costs of additional investments in land to employ the slave at some future date. The method of determining the cost of land per slave is shown in Table 7. First, the dollar value of land per acre for slaveholding cotton farmers was determined by dividing the cash value of their farms by the amount of improved and unimproved acreage in those farms. The cost amounted to approximately $4.60 per acre in 1850 and $5.75 in 1860. Then, the number of acres per slave on these plantations was calculated by dividing the total acreage by the number of slaves. Finally, the value of land per

[28]Ulrich B. Phillips, *American Negro Slavery: A Survey of the Supply, Employment and Control of Negro Labor as Determined by the Plantation Regime* (New York, 1918), 368-370; Randolph B. Campbell, "Local Archives as a Source of Slave Prices: Harrison County, Texas as a Test Case," *The Historian*, XXXVI (Aug., 1974), 660-669.

acre was multiplied by the number of acres per slave to arrive at the total cost of land per slave. The results, which must be regarded as estimates only, rose notably for both large and small planters between 1850 and 1860 (from $157.30 to $226.98 for large planters and from $208.21 to $307.80 for their smaller counterparts).[29]

[29]Data discussed in this paragraph are drawn from Seventh Census, 1850, Schedules 2 and 4 and Eighth Census, 1860, Schedules 2 and 4.

TABLE 7

Calculation of the Value of Land per Slave among Cotton Planters, 1850 and 1860

Cash Value of Farms Divided by Total Acreage

	1850	1860
Large Planters	$217,596 ÷ 48,134 = $4.52	$577,496 ÷ 99,218 = $5.82
Small Planters	$140,789 ÷ 29,931 = $4.70	$227,649 ÷ 39,911 = $5.70

Total Acres Divided by Number of Slaves

	1850	1860
Large Planters	48,134 ÷ 1,383 = 34.8	99,218 ÷ 2,544 = 39.0
Small Planters	29,931 ÷ 675 = 44.3	39,911 ÷ 739 = 54.0

Acres Per Slave Multiplied by Cash Value Per Acre

	1850	1860
Large Planters	34.8 × $4.52 = $157.30	39.0 × $5.82 = $226.98
Small Planters	44.3 × $4.70 = $208.21	54.0 × $5.70 = $307.80

Estimates of the costs of farm implements and livestock were also derived from census data (Table 8). The reported dollar value of slaveholding cotton planters' equipment and tools was divided by the number of slaves to obtain a cost-per-slave estimate. These amounted to $12 and $17 per slave for large and small planters respectively in 1850 and $12 and $18 for the two classes in 1860. It could not be assumed, however, that one set of farm implements would last thirty years or the slave's entire working lifetime. Therefore the present value (cost) of the investments necessary at an 8% interest rate to replace these implements after fifteen years was calculated and added to the estimates. In the case of livestock, it was assumed that natural increase would replenish the supply so that cost was limited to the original investment. This part of the cost per slave was determined simply by dividing the value of livestock on slaveholding cotton farms by the number of slaves.[30]

At this point, we have the estimates necessary to calculate the rate of return per slave using the following formula (Table 9).

$$r \quad r = a + \frac{P(y) - C}{K}$$

The most striking feature of these results is the great increase in profitability during the decade. Where the rate of return was generally between 5% and 6% in 1850, it was consistently higher than 10% in 1860. To some extent, this was accounted for by the fact that 1859 was a better crop year than 1849 in Harrison County. But it also seems clear that rising productivity due to the commitment of more land to cotton offset higher costs and led to greater profitability. As a benchmark for comparison, it should be noted that Alfred H. Conrad and John R. Meyer in their 1958 path-breaking study of slavery's profitability indicate that in "contemporary chronicles southerners and northerners alike considered 6-8 percent a reasonable rate of return and a reasonable asking price for loans."[31] Thus, although this

[30] Ibid.

[31] Alfred H. Conrad and John R. Meyer, "The Economics of Slavery in the Antebel-

TABLE 8

Cost of Non-Slave Investment per Slave among Cotton Planters, 1850 and 1860

	Cost of Land Per Slave	Cost of Equipment Per Slave*	Cost of Livestock Per Slave
1850			
Large Planters	$157.30	$15.78	$46.00
Small Planters	$208.21	$22.36	$53.35
1860			
Large Planters	$226.98	$15.78	$63.06
Small Planters	$307.80	$23.67	$87.35

* Calculated on the basis of the original investment plus the present value of the investment necessary to pay for replacements in fifteen years at 8% interest.

TABLE 9

Rate of Return per Slave among Cotton Planters, 1850 and 1860

	Pounds Per Slave	8 Cents Per Pound	9 Cents Per Pound
1850			
Large Planters	445	5.07	5.79
Small Planters	455	4.91	5.58
1860			
Large Planters	1,295	10.08	11.27
Small Planters	1,485	10.60	11.84

analysis is based on a number of assumptions and estimates, the conclusion strongly suggests that the rate of return per slave on cotton plantations in Harrison County was not terribly low even in a poor crop year such as 1849 and that it was at least satisfactory at the close of the antebellum years.

Did the community's planters sacrifice self-sufficiency for profit; that is, did they concentrate on cotton to such an extent that they did not produce enough food for the human and animal populations on their farms? It has often been assumed that antebellum planters generally were not self-sufficient and had to import grain and meat from the Northwest, contributing to a capital outflow and general economic backwardness in the South.[32] Was antebellum Harrison County's economy weakened in this manner? The evidence from traditional sources is mixed. As early as 1852, one observer complained that all crops except cotton were neglected. "Most of the bacon and flour used here is brought from New Orleans," he wrote. Business papers of the William J. Blocker family support this observation in part, showing purchases of flour in both 1860 and 1861. On the other hand, the correspondence of planters such as William T. Scott and Levin Perry is filled with references to their corn crops, and some, John B. Webster, for example, engaged in extensive cultivation of small grains, including wheat and rye. Clearly too, many planters provided their own bacon. John B. Webster recorded the slaughter of ninety-eight hogs weighing 18,689 pounds in January, 1859, and Levin Perry killed 27,000 pounds of pork in January, 1860. Scattered traditional evidence suggests then, as might be expected, that some planters paid more attention than others to self-sufficiency.[33]

lum South," *Journal of Political Economy*, LXVI (Apr., 1958), 101-103 (quotation on p. 102). Conrad and Meyer also note that this rate of return was comparable to that from bond investments in New York.

[32] See, for example, Douglass C. North, *The Economic Growth of the United States, 1790-1860* (New York, 1966), 122-134.

[33] The quotation is from a letter reprinted in Edwards, "Texas Agriculture," 35-36. See also Estate of William J. Blocker, Harrison County Probate Papers. Virtually every letter written during the 1850s by William T. Scott, Rose Family Papers, and by Levin Perry, Person Family Papers, had some reference to cotton production. For the

Census data permit a more systematic investigation of self-sufficiency in general. The returns for 1850 and 1860 also reveal the increasing emphasis on cotton production in antebellum Harrison County. As Table 10 indicates, the ratio of corn to cotton grown in the community decreased dramatically from sixty-five bushels of corn for every bale of cotton in 1850 to twenty-four bushels per bale in 1860. So, cotton received more energy and attention as the decade passed. But the census also shows a consistently high level of food production (see Table 11). Even with the increased emphasis on cotton, Harrison County farmers and planters produced more corn for every person (free and slave) on their farms in 1860 (51.8 bushels) then they had in 1850 (46.5 bushels). According to the most thorough study of this subject, humans consumed an average of thirteen bushels of corn per year. Harrison County farmers in 1860 met this requirement with plenty to spare for their livestock. Moreover, as Table 11 indicates, the community's farmers did not rely solely on corn for food. Other grains such as wheat, oats, and rye, and food crops including peas, beans, and potatoes added ten to twenty bushels per person to the supply of edible crops in both 1850 and 1860. Finally, there was the matter of meat supply.

references to hog killing, see Webster Plantation Journal and Louisa Perry to Theophilus Perry, January 3, 1860, Person Family Papers.

TABLE 10

Ratio of Corn (Bushels) to Cotton (Bales), 1850 and 1860

	1850	1860
All Farmers	80.5/1	27.9/1
Large Planters	65.0/1	23.6/1
Small Planters	75.6/1	28.5/1
Yeomen Farmers	120.3/1	39.2/1

TABLE 11

Volume of Food Crops per Farm Resident, 1850 and 1860

1850

	All Farmers	Large Planters	Small Planters	Yeomen Farmers
Free Residents	1,532	266	327	939
Slave Residents	2,627	1,427	768	432
Total Residents	4,159	1,693	1,095	1,371
Bushels of Corn Produced	193,565	79,950	46,540	67,075
Bushels of Other Grains	3,971	2,231	1,648	92
Bushels of Peas & Potatoes	76,011	32,552	19,845	23,614
Value of Animals Slaughtered	$30,183	$11,194	$7,009	$11,980
Bushels of Corn Per Person	46.5	47.2	42.5	48.9
Bushels of Food Crops Per Person*	65.8	67.8	62.1	66.2
Value of Animals Slaughtered Per Person	$7.26	$6.61	$6.40	$8.74

1860

	All Farmers	Large Planters	Small Planters	Yeomen Farmers
Free Residents	1,833	406	312	1,115
Slave Residents	3,858	2,612	761	485
Total Residents	5,691	3,018	1,073	1,600
Bushels of Corn Produced	294,810	155,600	62,630	76,580
Bushels of Other Grains	24,433	16,632	3,423	4,378
Bushels of Peas & Potatoes	60,834	23,096	10,217	27,521
Value of Animals Slaughtered	$73,334	$23,375	$12,111	$33,848
Bushels of Corn Per Person	51.8	51.6	58.4	47.9
Bushels of Food Crops Per Person*	66.8	64.7	71.1	67.8
Value of Animals Slaughtered Per Person	$12.89	$9.07	$11.29	$21.16

*Includes corn, other grains, and peas and potatoes.

Harrison County farmers and planters slaughtered $7.26 worth of livestock per person for home consumption in 1850 and increased the amount to $12.89 in 1860. These figures may seem low until we remember that hogs were valued at $2 to $5 each and cattle at $5 to $7 during this period. It is interesting to note too that yeomen farmers apparently slaughtered more livestock per person than did the planters; perhaps they ate more meat than the slaveholders fed their bondsmen. But in any case, the average Harrison County farm probably slaughtered at least two hogs for every person living there during the 1850s.[34]

In summary, while there were planters who at times imported food products they could have grown for themselves, antebellum Harrison County agriculture appears to have been essentially self-sufficient. Cotton was king, but not to the neglect of everything else.

What was the future of the community's agricultural economy in 1860? Prospects must have appeared relatively good. There had been strong gains in the productivity and profitability of slave/cotton culture during the 1850s. Planters had made great strides, and yet yeomen farmers had improved their property-holding position vis-a-vis their larger counterparts. At the same time, self-sufficiency had not been sacrificed for cash-crop production. In short, the agricultural economy as such showed notable development during the decade. There were, however, some clouds on the horizon of this bright economic scene. Would the soil have held out? Some planters were careful to at least fertilize, but the tendency was to crop the land hard and clear new ground as needed. The soil could have been saved or replenished, but possibly the planters would have worked it out and then moved on. After all, many of them had come from the Old South primarily in search of richer lands than those left behind. More importantly, agricultural expansion by 1860 depended almost completely on the demand for cotton. Har-

[34]The data for Table 11 were drawn from Seventh Census, 1850, Schedules 1, 2, and 4 and Eighth Census, 1860, Schedules 1, 2, and 4. Sam Bowers Hilliard, *Hog Meat and Hoecake: Food Supply in the Old South, 1840-1860* (Carbondale, Ill., 1972), 157-158.

rison County planters were overwhelmingly committed to producing for an external market far removed from their influence. A fall in cotton demand, which some experts believe was inevitable within a few years, would have wreaked havoc with their economic fortunes.[35]

Harrison County's agricultural economy performed well during the last antebellum years, but it had the weaknesses inherent in any one-crop plantation system. Sound prosperity required the development of non-agricultural activity too. This, unfortunately, was no simple matter for most southern communities during the antebellum period.

[35]Gray, *History of Agriculture in the Southern United States to 1860*, I, 445-451, discusses soil depletion across the South. Armstrong, "History of Harrison County," 67-68, argues, although without documentation, that the community's soils were being cropped to death. Wright, *Political Economy of the Cotton South*, 89-97, argues that stagnation in world demand for cotton was coming shortly after 1860 regardless of what happened in the United States.

3

The Non-Agricultural Economy

SIGNIFICANT ECONOMIC diversification in antebellum Harrison County depended on the development of manufacturing, commerce, and transportation. These kinds of activities, especially manufacturing, could provide profitable investment opportunities to local businessmen and employment to workers in a way that would generate economic momentum for the community independent of outside demand for agricultural cash crops. Overwhelming dependence on agriculture did not change during the 1850s; nevertheless, it should be understood that the non-agricultural economy was not totally dormant. There were some interesting attempts at industrialization, commercial activity expanded, and one of the earliest railroads in Texas was built from Swanson's Landing on Caddo Lake to Marshall.

The censuses of 1850 and 1860 provide the only systematic assessments of manufacturing in antebellum Harrison County. As the decade opened, there were only eleven "industrial" establishments in the community with a total capital investment of $59,700. These businesses employed ninety workers and produced $61,200 worth of goods. When we remember that the county's farms were valued at more than a million dollars in 1850 and that the value of 150 slaves (the county had 6,213) would have equalled the total investment in industry, the relative position of manufacturing becomes very clear. Furthermore, an occupational breakdown of the population in 1850 shows only 1% of all household heads engaged as manufacturers. On the other hand, Harrison County led all others in Texas in total capital investment and stood fifth in the value of goods produced. Perhaps there was some small hope for diversification after all. The next census revealed, however, that the county had fallen to eighth place in both investment ($84,575) and value of annual product ($203,942). Only 100 hands were employed, and fewer than 1% of all household heads were manufacturers. Investment in manufacturing had increased 42% during the decade while the cash value of farms had grown 138% and ever-more-numerous slaves had nearly doubled in price. The community was hardly on the road to balancing agriculture with industry.[1]

A look at the manuscript census returns suggests that even these statistics on industry may be somewhat misleading in a discussion of economic diversification. The problem is one of definition. In 1860, for example, there were eight blacksmiths and three small-scale shoemakers reported in the Products of Industry schedule. These individuals could more properly have been termed skilled tradesmen; at least they were not really manufacturers who would contribute to genuine diversification of the economy. Only a few of the community's businessmen were.[2]

[1] DeBow (ed.), *Statistical View of the United States*, 313, 319; U.S. Bureau of the Census, Eighth Census, *Manufactures of the United States in 1860; Compiled from the Original Returns of the Eighth Census* (Washington, 1865), 580-593; Seventh Census, 1850, Schedules 1 and 5; Eighth Census, 1860, Schedules 1 and 5.

[2] Eighth Census, 1860, Schedule 5.

J. S. Alexander's cotton gin factory was probably Harrison County's outstanding industry throughout the 1850s. Located just outside Marshall, Alexander employed three workers and manufactured ten gin stands in 1850 with a total value of $2,600. He advertised regularly, often utilizing testimonials such as the following from a satisfied customer:

> This is to certify that I purchased of Mr. J. S. Alexander a 70 saw gin of his make, which is equal in all respects to any gin I have ever used. It will average six bales of 500 lbs each per day; the gin running by water power.
>
> J. F. Rosborough

Alexander, well-established early and manufacturing an item for which there was considerable local demand, increased production during the 1850s. The 1860 census reported the manufacture of twenty gins valued at $3,500, twenty "mills" worth $500, and twenty wheat "thrashers" valued at $600. All this was accomplished with the addition of only one more hand to his labor force. He had, however, acquired two slaves during the decade, and it is likely that they contributed too. Although hardly an industrial giant, J. S. Alexander's gin factory was the largest such establishment in the state throughout the 1850s, and he represented one of the few true manufacturers in antebellum Harrison County.[3]

Gins, mills, wheat threshers, and other types of farm machinery were essential to the community, and thus invited the attention of local manufacturers. But there was also a need for what might be called "consumer items," goods such as cloth and clothing that would not themselves be utilized in agricultural production. In 1850, Harrison County manufacturers were totally deficient in this area as a correspondent who signed himself "W" pointed out to the readers of the *Texas Republican*. Arguing that $675,000 worth of osnaburg, a coarse cotton cloth used for slave clothing, could be manufactured for an investment of $550,000

[3]Seventh Census, 1850, Schedule 5; Eighth Census, 1860, Schedules 2 and 5; Marshall *Texas Republican*, May 23, 1850 (quotation); White, "Cotton Ginning in Texas," 267.

in a plant, labor, and raw material, "W" insisted that the wealth of old and New England, based on the spindle and the loom, could be duplicated in Harrison County. Cotton, labor, and steam power, generated by burning wood, were readily available. Why, he asked, "defer to grasp what Nature and Art have clearly designated our lawful inheritance?"[4]

By the end of the decade, Henry Ware, a large planter situated a few miles southeast of Marshall, was attempting to meet the challenge. (Perhaps Ware was "W" in the first place?) He had invested $10,000 in a steam-powered textile mill that employed thirteen hands, six male and seven female, at a cost of approximately $4,080 per year. Raw materials, including cotton, wool, and wood to fire the boiler, cost him approximately $10,000 annually. The mill produced 45,000 yards of cotton and woolen cloths including linseys, kerseys, and tweeds with a total value of $20,500. It may be noted that at 1860 prices a $10,000 investment would have purchased only twelve to thirteen slaves. At the same time, it would have taken 450 bales of cotton weighing 500 pounds each and netting 9¢ per pound to earn $20,500, the value of Ware's textile output. No one in Harrison County produced that much cotton in 1860; William T. Scott's 326 bale crop was the largest. This is not to say that Ware's investment was spectacularly profitable because too many factors are unaccounted for here, but it does suggest that there were indeed opportunities in textile manufacturing.[5]

Henry Ware also ran a tanyard and a "shoeshop" that produced 1,700 pairs of russet shoes worth $2,550. The *Texas Republican* carried his advertisements for "Superior Negro Clothing, Blankets and Shoes" which he offered to deliver in Harrison, Rusk, Panola, and Cass counties as well as Caddo and DeSoto parishes in Louisiana. Ware also explained that he wanted to sell directly to his customers:

> I look to the Planters to sustain me in this enterprise, as merchants cannot do it; for goods as heavy as mine and of such

[4]Marshall *Texas Republican*, August 10, 1850.

[5]Eighth Census, 1860, Schedule 5.

> material with merchants' profits added, cost more than Planters are willing to pay for Negro clothing. Hence it is that manufacturers do not put good material into coarse heavy goods, . . . if the Planters prefer paying merchants larger profits on poor linseys, rather than buy mine at cost of material, and a reasonable price for manufacturing, I will quit the business.

Ware's position was not likely to win favor with local merchants, and we can only wonder if his goods really were of higher than usual quality or if his costs of production were simply greater than those for other textile mills. In any case, he was the largest manufacturer in the community in 1860, advertising his products that year as "A Good Chance to Encourage Home Manufactures."[6]

There was another seemingly more ambitious but unsuccessful attempt to establish textile manufacturing during these years. On August 15, 1856, the state legislature incorporated the "Harrison Manufacturing Company" and authorized it to issue $500,000 in capital stock to build and operate a "cotton and woolen manufactury." The incorporators were among the most capable and wealthy men in the community, and it seems that some effort was made to combine individuals of varying backgrounds and interests. William T. Scott, the county's largest slaveholder, was involved along with several other large planters including John B. Webster and Lodwick P. Alford. George G. Gregg, one of the largest merchants in Marshall (he was worth more than $100,000 in 1860) was an incorporator as was James M. Curtis, mayor of the town during the late 1850s. Technical expertise was brought to the enterprise by A. D. Burress, a Kentucky-born engineer who had for years operated a steam mill near Marshall, sawing lumber, grinding grain, and making wagons and carriages. Burress also operated, at least for a while, an iron foundry in Marshall. George B. Adkins, brickmaker turned hotelkeeper, and another very wealthy member of the community, also participated. Thus the Harrison Manufacturing Company appears to have had the support of men who

[6]Eighth Census, 1860, Schedule 5; Marshall *Texas Republican*, June 3, 1859 (first and second quotations), September 15, 1860 (third quotation).

were familiar with success. It came to nothing, however; perhaps because it was never a primary concern for any of those involved.[7]

By 1860 then, Harrison County had several reasonably large manufacturers, J. S. Alexander and Henry Ware being the best examples, who recognized the opportunities in economic diversification and were successful in developing local industries. The community also had numerous processing plants such as sawmills and gristmills. H. Sheppard, for example, ran a steam-powered saw- and gristmill combination that produced pine lumber valued at $3,000 and $4,500 worth of meal. F. Land, a German immigrant (and, incidentally, a slaveholder) operated a steam turning plant for the manufacture of furniture. Nevertheless, a good deal of what the census called industry amounted to skilled trades; few consumer items were manufactured in the community.[8] Even Ware's textiles were aimed at the market for Negro clothing where there was no choice on the part of the ultimate consumers. There was, of course, some home manufacturing on most farms and plantations, but most finished products and all "fancy" items were imported.

Why was Harrison County so backward in industrial development? No definitive answer is possible, but the best explanation seems to lie in a combination of economic and social considerations. In the first place, the community's planters, those who would have to provide the funds to develop manufacturing, were reasonably well satisfied with their slave/cotton economy. Most appear to have been making profits and living self-sufficiently. They had no pressing reason to seek other areas of investment. Secondly, the planters were largely natives of the South who had been reared as agriculturalists and slaveholders, and they preferred the social arrangements that accompanied farming and slavery. This is not to argue that men such as Wil-

[7]Gammel (comp.), *Laws of Texas*, IV, 610 (quotation), 611-614. For information on George G. Gregg, Lodwick P. Alford, James M. Curtis, and George B. Adkins, who have not been previously identified, see Eighth Census, 1860, Schedule 1. The "industrial" operations of A. D. Burress may be seen in the Marshall *Texas Republican*, June 22, 1849, June 7, 1851.

[8]Eighth Census, 1860, Schedules 1, 2, and 5.

liam T. Scott were opposed to making the money that might have come from manufacturing or that they were committed to agrarianism at all costs. The point is that the great majority of the community's leaders were basically satisfied with existing economic and social institutions and simply did not have good enough reasons to risk change. The letters and diaries of planters were filled with complaints about the uncertainties of agriculture, but none voiced a desire to trade those problems for the more unfamiliar ones of the business investor and factory manager.[9]

Commercial activity in Harrison County, like manufacturing, was carried on by a very small part of the population. Merchants constituted less than 4% of all heads of households in the community in both 1850 and 1860. As would be expected, commerce centered in Marshall. There were stores in Port Caddo, Elysian Fields, Swanson's Landing, and the smaller crossroads settlements, but the majority of merchants lived at the county seat. Most sold general merchandise, and some clearly prospered. George G. Gregg from Tennessee, for example, was a partner in Evans, Gregg, & Key in 1850. In his late twenties at the time, Gregg had $2,800 worth of real property and owned three slaves. William Evans, the senior partner, was considerably wealthier ($7,000 in real property and twenty-six slaves) while Hobart Key, a young man from the District of Columbia, had less property and no slaves. In 1852, the business became Gregg and Key as Evans apparently chose to concentrate on planting, and then in 1854, Key went into partnership with his brother leaving only G. G. Gregg & Co. in control of the store located on the west side of the Marshall town square. For the remainder of the decade, Gregg offered the community general merchandise: including, for example, dry goods, hosiery, gloves, bonnets, boots, cutlery, saddlery, nails, china, glassware, wood-

[9]Fred Bateman and Thomas Weiss, *A Deplorable Scarcity, The Failure of Industrialization in the Slave Economy* (Chapel Hill, N.C., 1981), is an outstandingly thorough study of the South's backwardness in manufacturing. The authors examine all hypotheses concerning industrial backwardness and reach the conclusion that the explanation is a combination of the South's comparative advantage in agriculture and the attitude of the planter class.

ware, jewelry, school books, stationery, and "Yankee notions." He also served as an agent in Marshall taking orders for out-of-town businessmen such as the Phoenix Foundry and Agricultural Works of St. Louis, Missouri, makers of various farm machines, and the Aetna Insurance Co. of Hartford, Connecticut. In the census of 1860, Gregg reported real and personal property valued at a total of $133,500. Certainly he had enjoyed success as a retail merchant during the 1850s. Other general merchandisers such as King Thetford and the partners, William Bradfield and C. E. Tally, offered an equally broad array of goods to the public.[10]

Marshall also had a number of more specialized retail commercial ventures. There were drugstores, groceries, E. Wolz's furniture store (with a stock imported directly from New York), J. B. Edwards's saddlery, and S. Jacobs's clothing store advertising "quick sales and small profits." The Marshall Music Store opened in 1859 to sell pianos and other instruments and sheet music.[11]

Skilled craftsmen who generally sold their handiwork and services directly to the public were in effect as much a part of the community's commercial life as were retail merchants. Some tradesmen, primarily blacksmiths, were, as we have seen, regarded by the census takers as manufacturers, but most were not; and they accounted for between 5% and 10% of the population. There were tailors, shoemakers, carpenters, cabinetmakers, house painters, watchmaker-jewelers, bakers, a photographer, barbers, a mattressmaker, and a nurseryman. In short, the basic skilled services of the era were available in Marshall. And there were some that might not be expected in such a rural community. As early as 1850, for example, "Mons. Ruffier" on the

[10] Seventh Census, 1850, Schedule 1; Eighth Census, 1860, Schedule 1. The business career of Gregg may be traced in the Marshall *Texas Republican*, June 8, 1849, June 6, 1852, December 9, 16, 1854, May 12 (quotation), 19, 1860. Advertisements for Thetford and for Bradfield and Talley appeared regularly during the late antebellum period. See, for example, Marshall *Texas Republican*, January 7, 1860.

[11] Marshall *Texas Republican*, January 7 (quotation), May 12, 1860, December 10, 1859.

square advertised "curls, wigs, and toupees" made to order with hair imported from New Orleans and the North. Business must have been reasonably good (Ruffier was a barber too) because he still offered his services in 1860.[12]

In the larger towns of antebellum Texas such as Galveston and Houston, the foreign-born dominated the skilled trades. This was the case in Marshall too, in spite of the fact that immigrants from abroad were only 5% or less of the community's population. Most were German — Charles Deckart and Joseph Bruckmuller, shoemakers; James Bechtold, mattressmaker; M. Dopplemayer, baker; and F. Ludolph, cabinetmaker; for example. But Ruffier was from France, and John Duncan, the nursery operator, was a native of England. Interestingly, too, the immigrants' supposed dislike for slavery is not readily apparent among these tradesmen. Duncan, Deckart, and Dopplemayer all held bondsmen as did a number of other foreign-born members of the community.[13]

Thus, although only a small fraction of Harrison County's people were directly involved, retail merchandising and skilled trades were reasonably diversified and thriving during the 1850s. Commercial activity in the community, however, was severely limited in two important ways. There were virtually no large wholesale merchants, and resident businessmen did not generally handle the marketing of the cotton crop. Harrison County storekeepers had to buy their wares from someone, and the community's planters exported thousands of bales of cotton annually to the northern United States and Europe. Wholesaling and cotton marketing and the profits made from them fell, therefore, to larger commercial concerns located primarily in New Orleans and to a lesser extent in Shreveport.

Factorage and commission merchant houses were especially

[12] Seventh Census, 1850, Schedule 1; Eighth Census, 1860, Schedule 1; Marshall *Texas Republican*, June 27, 1850 (quotation).

[13] Seventh Census, 1850, Schedules 1 and 2; Eighth Census, 1860, Schedules 1 and 2. Terry G. Jordan, *German Seed in Texas Soil: Immigrant Farmers in Nineteenth-Century Texas* (Austin, 1966), 110, points out that while Germans generally did not own slaves their reasons were economic rather than moral. Most Germans simply could not afford slave property.

important in taking local business out of the community. Factors marketed Harrison County cotton by arranging steamboat transportation to New Orleans, providing insurance, paying for handling and storage, and selling the crop for what they judged to be the best price attainable. For their services, they deducted a 2½% commission plus all other costs. It was also common for factors to hold much of the large planters' money and honor drafts drawn on their accounts. Factors often provided the services of commission merchants too by filling orders for plantation supplies and shipping them up river to Harrison County. This service also cost a 2½% commission. Some New Orleans businesses advertised strictly as commission merchants. At times, factors worked in cooperation with local merchants by using them as suppliers for plantation customers. Evans, Gregg, & Key, for example, announced in 1851 that they would supply rope, bagging, and other plantation necessities to those shipping cotton to Rawlins & Co. in New Orleans. Thomas F. Swanson announced in 1860 that he would make advances on cotton consigned to Winston, Harrison, & Co. Generally, however, most of the profits to be earned in marketing the county's cotton crop and supplying its largest consumers went to non-resident businessmen.[14]

A good example of the operation of this system is found in a series of letters written by Brander and Hubbard, New Orleans factors and commission merchants, to the family of William J. Blocker following his death in June, 1859. When Blocker died, he was in debt to Brander and Hubbard to the extent of $5,866.60. The New Orleans firm informed his family in January, 1860, that they felt the debt to be too heavy, but that in light of their long business relationship with Mr. Blocker they would handle the current cotton crop, arrange the debt, and send a note to be signed by Mrs. Blocker as administratrix of the

[14] The best discussion of the cotton factorage system is Woodman, *King Cotton and His Retainers*. Advertisements for New Orleans and Shreveport factors and commission merchants are found in the Marshall *Texas Republican* throughout the 1850s. For the Evans, Gregg, & Key advertisement, see Marshall *Texas Republican*, June 7, 1851; for Swanson, September 15, 1860.

estate. "We shall, of course, expect to furnish you with your supplies," they added. In February, 1860, Brander and Hubbard shipped $464.65 worth of plantation supplies such as a barrel of molasses ($19.80), four barrels of flour ($32), four barrels of sugar ($64.91), five rolls of bagging ($81.25), six coils of rope ($86.40), and a bale of oznaburg cloth ($63.94). After adding the cost of insurance and a 2½% commission, the total came to $486.46. The Blockers shipped ninety-one bales of cotton to New Orleans that same month. Brander and Hubbard sold it for $4,249.46 (39,995 pounds at 10 5/8¢), deducted $527.87 in charges and commission (12.4% of the gross), and credited the Blockers' account with $3,721.59. Of course, the family continued to have expenses. For example, one son, Eugene, attended the New Orleans School of Medicine (now Tulane University), in 1859-1860 and drew on the family's funds with the factors. By mid-1860 then, in spite of the income from cotton, the Blockers' debt with Brander and Hubbard stood at slightly more than $6,000 in the form of 10% notes due in 1861.[15]

The point of this discussion is not the Blocker family's finances, but rather the role of Brander and Hubbard as commercial agents. Although we cannot say how much money the New Orleans firm made, they had an opportunity to profit from mark ups on the plantation supplies sold, the 2½% commissions on all transactions, the costs of insurance, and the interest due on notes securing the debt. The Blockers, of course, spent money locally; their bill at Thomas F. Swanson's store in 1860 amounted to $137.69, and they bought $304.59 worth of goods from G. G. Gregg & Co. over a sixteen month period in 1860-1861. Local purchases, however, while numerous were generally small—a thimble for 50¢, a padlock for 40¢, a pair of kid gloves for $1.25, and so on. To repeat, the Blockers provide an excellent example of how major purchases and marketing arrangements were handled by merchants outside the community.[16]

[15] This entire discussion is based on materials in Estate of William J. Blocker, Harrison County Probate Papers.

[16] Ibid.

In short, antebellum Harrison County did not have a mercantile interest capable of handling the most lucrative local business, let alone of developing Marshall as a trade center for the area. Commercial activity was limited, of course, by geography. New Orleans merchants were simply in a perfect place to control supply and marketing. But commercial development in East Texas was hindered too by the state's constitutional prohibition on banking. Without banks to concentrate and loan capital, businessmen had great difficulty in advancing beyond simple retail ventures. Robert W. Loughery of the *Texas Republican* in effect recognized this in an 1852 editorial. Banks, he said, are fine for mercantile communities but not for farming communities.[17] It seems likely that an absence of banks helped keep Harrison County totally agricultural. Finally, the lack of adequate transportation also restricted the community's growth, especially in the area of commerce. The county had reasonably good outlets (excellent for East Texas) by water, but in this respect it was the "end of the line" during the 1850s. If there could be developed a means of transportation going through and beyond the community into the hinterlands of East Texas, then Marshall would have an opportunity to grow commercially as a link in the chain supplying the Texas cotton frontier and marketing its crop. What were the chances for such a development in the nonagricultural economy?

The first settlers in Harrison County generally provided their own transportation by horseback and wagon. During the 1840s, cotton was hauled to the Red River at Shreveport on ox-drawn carts. Public transportation began in 1850 with the installation of stagecoach service from Shreveport to Marshall, and stage lines through East Texas developed rapidly during the following decade. By 1854, a line ran southwesterly to Austin, and, in 1858, a connection was made with the famed Butterfield Overland Express which ran from St. Louis and Memphis to California by a route across the Southwest. On the eve of the

[17] Marshall *Texas Republican*, June 12, 1852. The restrictions on banking in antebellum Texas are explained in Avery Luvere Carlson, *A Monetary and Banking History of Texas, . . . 1821-1929* (Fort Worth, 1930), 6-10.

Civil War, Marshall was a transportation center with eight stage lines radiating from it. The bugle blast signalling the arrival of a coach with passengers and mail was an exciting but not uncommon occurrence in the community.[18]

Travel by horseback, wagon, and stagecoach had many drawbacks, even by mid-nineteenth-century standards. For passengers it was time-consuming and often uncomfortable, especially since the roads tended to become virtually impassable during inclement weather. Where freight was concerned, reliance on slow and inefficient ox- or horse-drawn carts and wagons to move cotton and other goods had a seriously negative impact on the economy. Fortunately for Harrison County, a readily accessible water route to New Orleans — via Caddo Lake, the Red River, and the Mississippi — was available.

Steamboat transportation between New Orleans and Jefferson on Big Cypress Creek at the head of Caddo Lake north of Harrison County began during the 1840s. Paddlewheel steamers carrying passengers and cargo stopped regularly at Part Caddo during all but the few dry months in late summer and early fall when low water often interfered with navigation. In January, 1850, for example, the *Texas Republican* carried advertisements for two steamers, the *Caddo* and the *Monterrey*, the former able to carry 1,550 bales of cotton and the latter making the run to New Orleans in fifteen days. Incidentally, in April of that same year, the *Monterrey* struck a snag twenty-five miles above Shreveport and sank with the loss of one life and an entire cargo. Steamboat transportation was in many ways superior to land travel, but there certainly were hazards. Regardless of fires, explosions, and snags, however, steamboating flourished along Harrison County's northeastern boundary throughout the antebellum years. Without it, large-scale cotton production would have been virtually impossible, and the community would have been very different.[19]

[18]Max S. Lale, "Stagecoach Roads to Marshall," *East Texas Historical Journal*, XVII (Fall, 1979), 18-32.

[19]Webb, Carroll, and Branda (eds.), *Handbook of Texas*, I, 266; Marshall *Texas Republican*, July 20, 1849, January 10, 17, 1850, May 2, 1850.

The water connection to Shreveport and New Orleans was vital; certainly it gave Harrison County an advantage over most of the East Texas uplands. And yet, by the mid-nineteenth century, the majority of the community's leaders believed that there had to be something more. They wanted a railroad, at least to provide transportation to Caddo Lake or Shreveport and at best to give them direct links with the Mississippi River and California. It was to benefit the agricultural economy, but surely it would mean greater diversification and thus promote nonagricultural activities as well. During the last antebellum decade, the community was swept by one railroad enthusiasm after another, and finally one of the projects proved successful. It was not much of a railroad, but it was the only one in that part of the state.

Interest in railroad building was evident as early as October, 1849, when a public meeting in Marshall chose Charles C. Mills, a prominent Whig planter, to represent the community at a southern railroad convention in Memphis. Early the next year, a group of Harrison County residents led by James McCown, a planter with fifty-five slaves, received a charter from the state legislature incorporating the Marshall Rail-way and Plank Road Company. It was to build a railway or plank road from Marshall to the Louisiana border and then hope, apparently, for an extension to Shreveport or the Red River. Nothing was accomplished by this company, and the charter eventually lapsed. In February, 1852, the legislature chartered a second railway corporation involving residents of Harrison County — the Texas and Louisiana Railroad Company. It was to build from the eastern boundary of Texas through Marshall and on to El Paso by way of Austin. This ambitious project, headed by a merchant named William R. D. Ward, was to lose its charter unless it had completed twenty miles of track within six years. The company organized, sold stock, and even picked a spot on the Texas border 18½ miles east of Marshall as the starting point. The *Texas Republican* argued that utilization of railway transportation from Harrison County to the Mississippi rather than the usual Port Caddo to New Orleans via Shreveport route would reduce marketing costs from $7.45 to $4.10 per bale. But then, in spite of all the talk of its advantages to the community, this railroad project died too. Within a year, on February 7, 1853, a group of Harrison County residents led by merchant-planter William Evans, received yet another charter from the state legislature; this one creating the Marshall Railroad Company. They were to build a line linking Marshall with a proposed transcontinental road called the New Orleans, Texas and Pacific Railway. Neither company, however, built any track.[20]

Obviously, then, the community wanted a railroad; the chartering of three companies headed by local citizens within a four-year period proves this point. But the actual construction of a road took more than local interest and plans on paper. And it seems that the necessary capital, the engineering and managerial ability, and the willingness to persevere in the face of financial and physical obstacles were generally lacking in Harrison County. The basic problem was that the men involved were farmers and planters, not railroad builders. Of the fifteen incorporator of the Marshall Rail-way and Plank Road Company, for example, all were slaveholders, and eight had twenty or more bondsmen.[21] These men needed railroads, but transportation was not their primary interest. Railroad building was a career in itself; it could rarely be handled by those who had to manage slave labor and cotton production as well.

In 1853, businessmen-promoters from outside the community became involved importantly in railroad building in Harrison County. This was probably necessary, but it amounted to a mixed blessing. The project began in July, 1853, when the New York state legislature chartered an Atlantic and Pacific Railroad Company empowered to build from the Mississippi River or the

[20] Marshall *Texas Republican*, October 4, 1849; June 6, 19, December 18, 25, 1852; Gammel (comp.), *Laws of Texas*, III, 587-589, 1184-1189, 1404-1410; Seventh Census, 1850, Schedules 1, 2, and 4; St. Clair Griffin Reed, *A History of the Texas Railroad and of Transportation Conditions under Spain and Mexico and The Republic and the State* (Houston, 1941), 123; Muir, "Thirty-Second Parallel Pacific Railroad," 23. Mills's Whig affiliation will be documented below.

[21] Gammel (comp.), *Laws of Texas*, III, 587; Seventh Census, 1850, Schedule 2.

Gulf of Mexico to California across any states that would allow it. When the Altantic and Pacific organized later that year it amounted to little more than a paper structure with many promises and virtually no capital. William R. D. Ward of Harrison County was one of the twenty-five directors, but the guiding spirits were Dr. Jeptha Fowlkes of Memphis, former-Congressman Thomas Butler King of Georgia, and ex-Secretary of War Robert J. Walker of Mississippi. One historian has remarked that "one would have to search assiduously to find three equally consummate knaves involved in any one scheme." They soon found just what they wanted in Texas when the state legislature on December 21, 1853, passed a law for the building of a Mississippi and Pacific Railroad without creating a corporation for that purpose. Instead, the law invited some existing company to sign a contract to build the road and receive a subsidy of twenty sections of land (12,800 acres) for every mile built. The contracting company would have to make a $300,000 deposit in gold as security that it would begin construction within sixty days and build fifty miles of track within eighteen months. These conditions would be very difficult to meet, but the Atlantic and Pacific promoters thought they saw an opportunity and soon had residents of Harrison County talking enthusiastically about "our railroad."[22]

Editor Loughery of the *Texas Republican* had always championed railroads, but to insure an even more favorable press, W. R. D. Ward and others set up their own paper, the Marshall *Meridian and Pacific Railroad Advocate*, in the late fall of 1853. The Atlantic and Pacific Company was so certain of success in signing a contract that in May, 1854, E. A. Blanch, former professor of mathematics at the University of Virginia, was sent to survey the first fifty miles of the railroad across Harrison County. An official groundbreaking was held at Marshall on July 4, 1854. Thomas Jefferson Green, one-time military leader during the Texas revolution and now associated with the Atlantic and

[22] Muir, "Thirty-Second Parallel Pacific Railroad," 25-27, 28 (first quotation), 37-38, 41-61; Gammel (comp.), *Laws of Texas*, IV, 7-13; Reed, *History of Texas Railroads*, 99-100, 123; Marshall *Texas Republican*, June 3, 1854 (second quotation).

Pacific Company, hailed the Mississippi and Pacific as the "great slavery road." Robert Loughery thought Green meant only to impress rather than to announce significant action. But work did begin that month at Swanson's Landing on Caddo Lake where the railroad was to make contact with water transportation to the Mississippi. Charles C. Mills of Harrison County helped hire the force of 230 men who went to work there.[23]

The Mississippi and Pacific scheme, then, having attracted the New York-based Atlantic and Pacific Company to East Texas, went further in 1853-1854 than had any previous railroad corporation toward actual construction. In the process it involved a number of local railroad enthusiasts led by Ward and M.J. Hall and Louis T. Wigfall who also became directors. But, after the ground-breaking and a little work at Swanson's Landing, the project came to nothing. In fact, it left a good many people in the community with a distaste for railroad promoters of any sort. The basic problem was that Fowlkes and his cohorts could not put up even the $300,000 in sound security as required by the Texas law, let alone actually finance construction. To cover this situation, they used Atlantic and Pacific stock to buy several Texas-chartered railroads and invited local investors to become involved with the expectation that every mile of track built would be rewarded with the land grants promised in each of these charters. Editor Loughery argued that no intelligent person could believe such a promise and soon pronounced the whole scheme a "Gigantic Humbug." The railroad promoters then sought in August, 1854, to use $300,000 in stock of the Sussex Iron Company of New Jersey as the deposit necessary to secure their contract. Paper from an out-of-state corporation was hardly gold, however, and Governor Elisha M. Pease rejected the offer. Loughery was pleased. "We want the road built," he wrote, "but we are opposed to humbug and dissimulation."[24]

[23]Only one copy of the Marshall *Meridian and Pacific Railroad Advocate*, January 28, 1854, is extant. It is at the Eugene C. Barker Texas History Center, University of Texas at Austin. For the progress of the railroad to July, 1854, see Muir, "Thirty-Second Parallel Pacific Railroad," 72-73 (quotation), 74; Marshall *Texas Republican*, July 8, 1854.

[24]Marshall *Texas Republican*, June 3, July 1, 15 (first quotation), November 11, 1854 (second quotation); Muir, "Thirty-Second Parallel Pacific Railroad," 41-61.

Loughery was inclined to blame the non-Texans for the railroad's questionable operations, but others in the community were suspicious of Ward's and Hall's involvement too. And at least one observer recognized very quickly that the promoters were in over their heads. Hobart Key commented in June, 1854: "Two of the Directors [Hall and Wigfall] have just returned from the North — all this windy railroad news in our village papers, is only a ruse to cover their retreat."[25]

The retreat was strategic, however; railroad enterpise in the community had by no means seen the end of the combination involving outside promoters such as Jeptha Fowlkes and local planter-businessmen such as M.J. Hall, William T. Scott, and others. As the Mississippi and Pacific project was falling through in 1854, the railroad men decided on a new approach. Meeting in Montgomery, Alabama, in December, 1854, they reorganized under the charter of the Texas Western Railroad Company, a corporation created by the Texas state legislature on February 16, 1852, and bought by the Atlantic and Pacific Company earlier in 1854. In the process, the promoters abandoned their hopes for the Mississippi and Pacific contract and dropped the Atlantic and Pacific corporation charter from New York. The Texas Western charter required no deposit and called only for the completion of twenty miles of track within six years of incorporation in order to remain operative. Upon the completion of twenty miles of track, the company would receive eight sections of land (5,120 acres) for every mile.[26]

The financial details of this reorganization are hazy; a circumstance typical of the finances of Harrison County railroad enterprise in this era. It appears that the Atlantic and Pacific's original purchase of the Texas Western charter was made with

[25] Hobart Key to "Mag," June 2, 1854, Key Family Papers.

[26] Muir, "Thirty-Second Parallel Pacific Railroad," 62, 75-78. The Act of incorporation for the Texas Western is found in Gammel (comp.), *Laws of Texas*, III, 1245-1250. Curiously, the railroad was called the "Vicksburg and El Paso Railroad Company" in the act's title and the "Texas Western Railroad Company" in section one of the same act.

$600,000 in Atlantic and Pacific stock. Then when the New York company reorganized under the Texas charter, all stock in the former was transferred to the latter. Thus, the men who had sold the Texas Western for Atlantic and Pacific stock wound up once again as stockholders in the Texas-chartered company. William T. Scott, one of the original incorporators, served on the executive committee, while William R. D. Ward, one of the original directors, sat on the new board of directors. Not so incidentally, Jeptha Fowlkes also served on the executive committee along with other non-resident businessmen. Loughery of the *Texas Republican* worried that the "controlling spirits" were the same in the reorganized Texas Western as in the Atlantic and Pacific and asked his readers to consider how Scott and others could wind up in control of a company they had just sold.[27]

The Texas Western promoters set out in 1854 to sell $25 million in stock (only 5% was to be actually paid in) and continue the construction already begun. Work moved at the proverbial snail's pace in 1855-1856, however. Any number of problems hampered progress. Iron rails, for example, were bought in the Northeast, shipped by water to Shreveport, and hauled by wagon to Texas. Then in August, 1856, new life came to the project when the Texas legislature, with considerable prompting from state Senator William T. Scott, passed a law amending the company's name to the Southern Pacific Railroad Company and offering sixteen rather than eight sections of land for every mile of track completed, providing that ten miles were graded and furnished with crossties within five years of the original charter (by February 16, 1857) and twenty miles were built by February 16, 1858. The renamed company held its first stockholders meeting on October 6, 1856, and although Harrison County was represented on the new board of directors by Scott, Ward, and Hall, ten of the nineteen were from the North. The president was Horatio Allen, a native of New York who had been involved in railroading since the late 1820s. Apparently he

[27] Marshall *Texas Republican*, January 13, 1855 (quotation); Muir, "Thirty-Second Parallel Pacific Railroad," 62.

was brought in primarily for the prestige his name could lend to the operation.[28]

The Southern Pacific Company raised enough money from stock sales and giving mortgages on its few assets, such as the Sussex Iron Works stock, to get down to serious work early in 1857. On January 30, one of William T. Scott's sons informed his uncle P. R. Rose that nearly 400 hands were ''making the dirt fly.'' E. A. Blanch, the Atlantic and Pacific's surveyor who had stayed on as chief engineer for the reorganized and now renamed company, told the *Texas Republican* that 800 hands were at work by mid-February. Many of the workers were Irish, but local planters reportedly responded with ''alacrity'' when asked to supply slaves. Under these circumstances, ten miles were graded and furnished with ties by February 16, and the company kept its charter. George S. Yerger of Mississippi became president in 1857, and a contract was signed with John T. Grant & Co. of Georgia to grade seventy miles and lay track over the twenty-eight miles from Swanson's Landing to Marshall, a portion of which was already prepared for rails. Increasingly, it seemed, the Southern Pacific was a southern enterprise.[29]

Construction continued through 1857 into 1858. Twenty miles of track were laid by February 12, 1858, four days before the deadline. The Company purchased a second-hand locomotive called the ''Ashuelot'' in 1857, and by the end of February, 1858, announced its readiness to haul cotton and other freight from Scott's depot seven miles east of Marshall to Swanson's Landing, a distance of approximately twenty miles. In the meantime, costs mounted and the company's finances deteriorated, Funds came from stock sales, mortgages, and from prom-

[28]Muir, ''Thirty-Second Parallel Pacific Railroad,'' 76-78, 82-84; Gammel (comp.), *Laws of Texas*, IV, 622-624. Governor Pease vetoed the Southern Pacific bill because he distrusted the out-of-state interests involved, but the legislature overrode the veto. Marshall *Texas Republican,* August 2, 1856. Information on the first stockholders' meeting of the Southern Pacific Railroad Company is in Muir, "Thirty-Second Parallel Pacific Railroad," 87-88.

[29]P. R. Scott to P. R. Rose, January 30, 1857 (first quotation), Rose Family Papers; Marshall *Texas Republican*, February 14, 21 (second quotation), 1857; Muir, ''Thirty-Second Parallel Pacific Railroad,'' 91-92.

ises based on the land to be received once the track was completed. The company even circulated its own paper currency, but by August 1, 1857, it was broke. To save the charter, President Yerger mortgaged the entire railroad to secure payment of the construction company engaged in building the track from Swanson's Landing.[30]

Within less than a year, on June 1, 1858, although the railroad was operative, it was sold to pay the debts for which it had been mortgaged. Dr. Jefferson M. Saunders of Marshall bought the property for $40,000 and immediately sold it for the same price to a group of investors composed primarily of Harrison County residents already involved in the project. William T. Scott became vice-president and W. R. D. Ward, secretary-treasurer. Wigfall, Saunders, and former county judge Trenton A. Patillo were among the stockholders. This so-called "New Company" was immediately challenged by an "Old Company" headed by Jeptha Fowlkes who claimed that the deed of trust executed by Yerger in 1857 was illegal. Harrison County residents including C. C. Mills, Josiah D. Perry, and Levin Perry, all large planters, were also involved in the "Old Company" so the issue was not drawn strictly between local and outside interests. An amazingly complex court battle followed, ending finally in October, 1859, with yet another reorganization of the company. Fowlkes wound up as president and Scott as vice-president.[31]

Somehow, in spite of this "snarl," as Scott called it, among the promoters, construction continued in 1858-1859. State Engineer Edwin F. Gray spent two weeks inspecting the road in late 1858. He found approximately twenty-five miles of track, two locomotives, four flat cars, and several construction cars. The service to the public, begun in 1858, continued irregularly into 1859. The company reported that it hauled 4,411 bales of cotton during the year ending September 1, 1859. Daily service

[30] Muir, "Thirty-Second Parallel Pacific Railroad," 93-94, 95-97; Marshall *Texas Republican*, June 5, 1858. Southern Pacific paper money is mentioned in Marshall *Texas Republican*, June 6, 1857.

[31] Muir, "Thirty-Second Parallel Pacific Railroad," 95-121.

as a common carrier began with the rise of the Red River in the fall of 1859. Cotton was hauled from the railhead a mile and a half east of Marshall to Swanson's Landing on the Lake at a charge of 75¢ a bale including all the costs of handling at the company's wharf and storage in the company's warehouses. Stops were made at Scottsville, Jefferson Crossing, and Perry's Crossing along the route. Freight from the Lake to Marshall cost 25¢ per hundred weight. The twenty-seven mile trip took two hours, leaving Marshall in the morning and then departing Swanson's Landing in the afternoon for the return trip. Business boomed as the county's huge 1859 cotton crop went to market. During the first months of 1860, steamboats could not take the cotton away from Swanson's Landing as fast as the railroad delivered it. Plans were made and grading began for extending the road west of Marshall.[32] For a while it seemed that the Southern Pacific would bring the commerce of East Texas through the Harrison County community. The Civil War, however, disrupted the cotton trade at New Orleans and for a while at least slowed transporation development.

Obviously the Southern Pacific Railroad had a chaotic financial history during the 1850s. Money was raised in nearly every imaginable way (except by lottery), and it was spent freely on materials and salaries. State Engineer Gray estimated the costs of construction at approximately $500,000 in late 1858, but the Company claimed to have spent $3 million by that time. And its finances did not stablize in 1859 or 1860, even after it began to earn money. Reorganizations and trustees' sales came almost annually. The whole story is best summarized by a careful student who wrote: "The financial standing of the company, at any time, is impossible to determine." It seems unlikely that any of the promoters, from Harrison County as well as outside the community, were greatly enriched. But then it is difficult to say just how much real money they had invested in

[32] W. T. Scott to P. R. Rose, July 30, 1858 (quotation), Rose Family Papers; Muir, "Thirty-Second Parallel Pacific Railroad," 123-129, 145-150; Marshall *Texas Republican*, December 3, 1859, February 25, March 10, November 17, 1860.

the project in the first place. Perhaps it is best simply to point to one established fact: Harrison County, thanks to a combination of outside entrepreneurs and local planter-businessmen, had one of the few operating railroads anywhere in antebellum Texas and the only one in that part of the state.[33] Although intended primarily to serve the needs of the agricultural economy, railroading was a non-agricultural activity in itself with the potential to promote manufacturing and commerce as well.

At the close of the antebellum period then, the people of Harrison County, especially the planters who were the community's economic leaders, generally remained committed to slave/cotton agriculture. Concurrently, there was considerable interest in non-agricultural activity, even among some of the largest slaveholders in the community. Henry Ware's involvement in producing textiles and shoes and William T. Scott's work in railroad promotion are good examples. The county had progressed beyond most in Texas at that time and was not nearly so devoid of non-agricultural development as the traditional view of the antebellum South might lead one to expect. Nevertheless, the community was not likely to change greatly in the direction of industrialization and commercialization so long as economic and social institutions continued to work, as they did during the 1850s, to the basic satisfaction of the planter class.

[33]Muir, "Thirty-Second Parallel Pacific Railroad," 88 (quotation), 123-127, 138-145.

4

Community Institutions and Social Life

LAW, MEDICINE, religion, and education constituted vital aspects of nineteenth-century Harrison County's biography. The legal and medical professions provided many community leaders as well as offering services that at one time or another affected virtually everyone living there. Churches and schools not only ministered to spiritual and intellectual needs but were focal points of social life as well. Cultural activities and events designed purely for entertainment also provided social interaction and eased the burdens of everyday life.

Antebellum Texans were famed as a violent and litigious people; characteristics that created business aplenty for those who chose law as a profession. The courts of Harrison County were kept busy with legal disputes over land, slaves, and railroads as well as with the trials of accused criminals. Court days were social events bringing men together for business and pleasure with the lawyers often providing the chief entertainment as they argued their cases. And the community had nearly as many attorneys as merchants or manufacturers. In mid-1850, the *Texas Republican* carried the professional cards of sixteen attorneys, most of whom were residents of Marshall.[1] Local spokesmen frequently boasted of the brilliant legal talent available in their community, and the boast had a basis in fact. Many of Harrison County's lawyers received recognition as leaders locally, and a number attained notoriety statewide.

William B. Ochiltree, a native of North Carolina and one of the best-known Whig politicians in Texas, practiced law in the district court at Marshall through the 1850s before moving there from Nacogdoches late in the decade. Ochiltree ran for congress in 1851 and for governor in 1853 when he finished second among five candidates. Although known as a Whig unionist during the early 1850s, Ochiltree represented Harrison County in the secession convention in 1861 and was elected to the Provisional Congress of the Confederacy that same year.[2]

Louis T. Wigfall, Ochiltree's law partner in Marshall, was perhaps the most spectacular member of the Harrison County bar. A native of South Carolina and graduate of South Carolina College, Wigfall possessed a high temper and a touchy sense of honor that led to a number of duels and shooting scrapes before he came to Texas. Once settled in Marshall (1848), he became widely known as an ultra-southern secessionist and bitter critic of Sam Houston. Wigfall was elected to the state senate in 1857 and to the United States Senate in 1859 where he supported

[1]Seventh Census, 1850, Schedule 1; Eighth Census, 1860, Schedule 1; Marshall *Texas Republican*, June 27, 1850.

[2]Webb, Carroll, and Branda (eds.), *Handbook of Texas*, II, 300; Marshall *Texas Republican*, June 27, 1850, July 26, 1856; Eighth Census, 1860, Schedule 1. On Ochiltree's career as a Whig, see Randolph B. Campbell, "The Whig Party of Texas in the Elections of 1848 and 1852," *Southwestern Historical Quarterly*, LXXIII (July, 1969), 22, 26.

secession and welcomed war. During the Civil War, he served in the Confederate Congress and led the opposition to President Jefferson Davis.[3]

Several other Harrison County lawyers, while perhaps not so outstanding as Ochiltree and Wigfall, had careers that extended beyond their community. Edward Clark, the descendant of a politically prominent Georgia family, was secretary of state from 1853 to 1857 under Governor Elisha M. Pease. Elected lieutenant governor in 1859, Clark completed Governor Sam Houston's term when the latter was forced from office by secession. Pendleton Murrah, a native of South Carolina, won the gubernatorial election of 1863 and the dubious honor of presiding over the defeat and break up of Confederate authority in Texas. Murrah left the state and died in Mexico during July, 1865. John T. Mills, who moved to Marshall from Clarksville in the mid-1850s, did not have an outstanding career after arriving there, but he had been a candidate for governor in 1849 and, although he did not attend, was chosen as a delegate to the Nashville Convention in 1850.[4]

Attorneys were almost always at the center of local public affairs. The chief justices of the commissioners court for much of this era, Trenton A. Patillo (1848-1856) and George Lane (1860-1865), were lawyers. Three of the county's four delegates to the secession convention in 1861, Ochiltree, Alexander Pope, and Gil McKay, were lawyers. Any political rally, July 4th celebration, or public meeting was certain to feature members of the bar as organizers and orators.[5]

In short, members of the legal profession exercised influ-

[3] Alvy L. King, *Louis T. Wigfall, Southern Fire-eater* (Baton Rouge, 1970), passim.

[4] Justin Whitlock Dart, Jr., "Edward Clark, Governor of Texas" (M.A. Thesis, University of Houston, 1964), passim; Webb, Carroll, and Branda (eds.), *Handbook of Texas*, II, 251, 200. For the relationship of Mills to the Nashville Convention, see Randolph B. Campbell, "Texas and the Nashville Convention of 1850," *Southwestern Historical Quarterly*, LXXVI (July, 1972), 7, 11.

[5] The officeholding records of Patillo and Lane are shown in Election Registers, 1846-1880, State Archives. Ochiltree, Pope, and McKay as delegates to the secession convention are shown in Marshall *Texas Republican*, December 22, 1860. All these men ran law cards in the *Texas Republican*, see the issues of June 27, 1850 and September 15, 1860, for example.

ence far beyond their numbers in Harrison County. Most lived in Marshall and were not distracted by the demands of operating a plantation or a business. They were perfectly situated to concern themselves with and to lead in public affairs. Moreover, lawyers were the county's best-known citizens statewide. They put the community "on the map."

The medical profession was also relatively well-developed in antebellum Harrison County. Doctors were more numerous than lawyers, heading approximately 3% of all households in 1850 and 1860. They had their own professional organization, the Marshall Medical Society, as early as 1850. A Marshall physician, Dr. Joseph Taylor, helped found the Texas State Medical Association in 1853 and served as its first president.[6]

Perhaps doctors were so numerous because many did not depend solely on the medical profession as a means of support. Some physicians such as E. P. M. Johnson, the brothers Benjamin F. and William H. Dial, B. F. Young, and N. W. Eames lived in Marshall or the smaller settlements and practiced medicine full-time. But a large proportion were planters to whom medicine may well have been a complementary or secondary pursuit. In 1860, for example, Dr. Harwood P. Perry owned seventy-two slaves; Dr. S. K. Haywood, twenty-two; Dr. William C. Swanson, seventy-two; Dr. Joseph Taylor, forty-seven; and Dr. William F. Baldwin, twenty. Although these men practiced medicine, they generally did not place cards in the newspapers and seek patronage. They were planters first and physicians second.[7]

Information on the educational backgrounds of Harrison County's doctors is limited, but it is clear that a good many held degrees from medical schools in the East. William H. Dial and E. P. M. Johnson earned diplomas at the University of New York; Benjamin F. Eads and W. G. Thomas at the University of

[6]Seventh Census, 1850, Schedule 1; Eighth Census, 1860, Schedule 1; Marshall *Texas Republican*, February 21, 1850; Pat Ireland Nixon, *A History of the Texas Medical Association, 1853-1953* (Austin, 1954), 8-9, 18, 25. The TMA did not function importantly until 1869.

[7]Eighth Census, 1860, Schedules 1 and 2; Marshall *Texas Republican*, June 7, 1851, June 6, 1852.

Pennsylvania; Addison Sears at the University of Louisville; and H. C. Gray and William W. Perry at the University of Louisiana. Eugene B. Blocker, the son of William J. Blocker, studied at the New Orleans School of Medicine (now Tulane University) during the late 1850s, graduated in 1861, and returned to practice in the community.[8] Harrison County residents had no difficulty in finding doctors who were reasonably well qualified by the standards of that day.

The inadequacies of medical knowledge during the mid-nineteenth century are well-known. Indeed, in some cases, prescribed treatments may well have been more dangerous than the original illness. Harrison County's doctors doubtless had the limitations common to their profession. They did the best they could under the circumstances, but their best was often not very good. They were largely powerless against such dreaded killers as yellow fever and cholera and were unable to combat the appallingly high mortality rate among infants and children. William J. Blocker and his wife Mary had fourteen children, only seven of whom survived beyond the age of six. Of the nine children born to John B. Webster and his wife Julia between 1847 and 1864, four died in infancy or childhood.[9] Examples of this sort could be piled upon each other indefinitely, but the point is clear.

Medical attention, regardless of its effectiveness, was not inexpensive in antebellum Harrison County. Doctors made house calls, but the charge was usually three dollars, a not inconsiderable amount in that day. When William J. Blocker suffered a fatal illness that lasted from April until June 13, 1859, his estate received bills of $166 from Dr. S. K. Haywood and nearly $200 from Dr. H. P. Perry for visits over a period of two months. Inci-

[8]Medical Register, District Clerk's Office, Harrison County Courthouse, Marshall; Estate of William J. Blocker, Harrison County Probate Papers; Randolph B. Campbell, "Family History from Local Records: A Case Study from Nineteenth Century Texas," *East Texas Historical Journal*, XIX (Fall, 1981), 13-26.

[9]William J. Blocker Family Bible, Property of Mrs. Robert M. Claypool, Bellaire, Texas; quotation from Woolsey Finnel, Sr., compiler, "The Reverend Daniel Brown of Culpepper County, Virginia, and Allied Families . . . Compiled . . . during the Period, 1948-1954" (Unpublished genealogical booklet in the possession of Douglass V. Blocker, Marshall, Texas.)

dentally, as the end neared, the Blocker family also called in Dr. William N. Head from Caddo Parish, Louisiana, and were presented with a bill for $307 for two visits, one of which involved three days and nights of attendance to the dying man.[10]

If a resident of the community chose to doctor himself, he found local druggists ready to assist with a host of "miracle" cures. Evans and Trawick in 1849 advertised Genuine Balm of Columbia for the restoration of hair, a Magical Pain Extractor, Dr. McNair's Acoustic Oil for curing deafness, Longley's Great Western Indian Panacea for the relief of all digestive ailments, and Dr. Larzetti's Juno Cordial or Procreative Elixir for the cure of impotence.[11] The fact that anyone would resort to such patent medicines is further suggestive concerning the state of medical science during this era.

Harrison County's physicians probably compared favorably to those elsewhere in East Texas. Their limitations were those of their profession rather than personal. Nevertheless, it must have been terrifying to members of the community when illness struck their families, especially if infants or young children were involved. They sought the help of their doctors, but at the same time many sought solace in their faith. The lives of the seriously ill were truly in the hands of God.

Organized religion was a strong institution in Harrison County, as would be expected in an area settled by people reared on the evangelical traditions of the Old South. Census-takers enumerated eleven churches in the community in 1850 and twenty-four in 1860. It is not possible to identify all these churches, let alone to say what proportion of the people actually belonged to or attended them.[12] Clearly, however, the influence of religion was strong. Ministers preached strict theologies and a stern morality; religious activities provided meeting places for

[10]Estate of William J. Blocker, Harrison County Probate Papers.

[11]Marshall *Texas Republican*, June 22, 1849.

[12]Seventh Census, 1850, Schedule 6; Eighth Census, 1860, Schedule 6. The reported seating capacity of all churches in 1850 was 3,500; in 1860, 13,100. If the 1860 figure was correct, there was room for more than 85 percent of the community's population, free and slave, in the churches.

the people; and church members supported the one important social reform of antebellum Harrison County — the temperance crusade.

"I would suppose a preacher could live in Texas," James C. Quillin observed somewhat cryptically in 1852. Whatever his meaning, more than a few Harrison County ministers found him correct. Louise Wigfall Wright remembered how, ". . . from their pulpits the theologians of the different schools pronounced a sufficient variety of dogmas to daunt the souls and bewilder the minds of ordinary mortals." Neither Quillin or Wright felt the need to point out that the preachers and dogmas were all protestant. That was taken for granted. Most churches were Methodist or Baptist, but Presbyterians, Episcopalians, Cumberland Presbyterians, and Christians (Disciples of Christ or Campbellites) were present too.[13]

There appear to have been only minor social distinctions involved in membership in one denomination or another. The Board of Trustees of one Methodist church in 1850 included William T. Scott, William J. Blocker, Billington Smalley, and Albert B. Stone, all of whom ranked among the wealthiest planters in the county. John B. Webster and James McCown, each the owner of more than fifty slaves, were Baptists. Trinity Episcopal Church, organized in 1850-1851 in Marshall, included lawyer-politicians Louis T. Wigfall and George Lane as well as the merchant Hobart Key among its members. Beverly L. Holcomb, a planter whose daughter Lucy married Francis W. Pickens of South Carolina, ambassador to Russia and wartime governor of his state, headed the most prominent Presbyterian family. Joseph Mason and Eli T. Craig, both large planters were Cumberland Presbyterians. Khleber M. Van Zandt, son of the famed soldier-politician of the Republic, Isaac Van Zandt, helped found the first Christian Church in Marshall.[14]

[13]James C. Quillin to Ezekiel Quillin, August 13, 1852, Quillin Family File; Wright, *Southern Girl in '61*, 14-15; Seventh Census, 1850, Schedule 6; Eighth Census, 1860, Schedule 6. There were only Methodist and Baptist churches reported in the census of 1850. The other denominations mentioned were present in 1860.

[14]Harrison County Deed Records, County Clerk's Office, Harrison County Court-

There is some evidence that members of the older denominations looked slightly askance at the Cumberland Presbyterian and Christian churches. The former ordained ministers without requiring the usual Presbyterian standards of training, and the latter emphasized New Testament concepts of God's love and mercy rather than harsher Old Testament religion. Khleber M. Van Zandt recalled that when he returned to Marshall in 1854 after attending Franklin College in Nashville and helped found the first Christian Church there, his was such an outcast among churches that only the Cumberland Presbyterians were friendly. Incidentally, Thomas B. Wilson, the Cumberland Presbyterian minister after 1850, was a doctor of divinity who also headed the Marshall Masonic Female Institute. He was anything but an uneducated minister.[15]

Denominational differences may have loomed large in the eyes of a few, but the desired impact of religious teachings was almost certainly the same for all churches in the community. They were to inspire men to salvation through faith and teach a basic protestant morality based on the Ten Commandments. For some at least, emphasis on morality extended well beyond obvious biblical injunctions. "We did a little dancing," young Louisa Perry wrote her brother Theophilus in describing a wedding party at Christmas time in 1859; "it was such a Methodist crowd [however] there were but few to dance."[16]

Protestant morality also figured heavily in the one reform

house, Marshall, Book M, 111; Mrs. M. P. McGee, "A Brief History of the First Baptist Church, Marshall, Texas" (Unpublished paper, Lentz Collection, East Texas Baptist College, Marshall); Max S. Lale, *As It Was in the Beginning* [History of Trinity Episcopal Church] (Marshall, Texas, 1950), 3; Mrs. Milton Lothrop, "The Organization and History of the Presbyterian Church" (Unpublished paper, Lentz Collection, East Texas Baptist College, Marshall); Thomas H. Campbell, *History of the Cumberland Presbyterian Church in Texas* (Nashville, 1936), 59-60; Khleber M. Van Zandt, *Force Without Fanfare, The Autobiography of K. M. Van Zandt*, ed. by Sandra L. Myres (Fort Worth, 1968), 65. Information on the economic status of the individuals named is from Seventh Census, 1850, Schedules 1, 2, and 4 and Eighth Census, 1860, Schedules 1, 2, and 4.

[15] Van Zandt, *Force Without Fanfare*, 64-66; Campbell, *History of the Cumberland Presbyterian Church*, 60.

[16] Louisa Perry to Theophilus Perry, January 3, 1860, Person Family Papers.

movement of the era that reached importantly into Harrison County, the temperance crusade. The consumption of alcoholic beverages may or may not have been regarded as a sin in itself, but a good many people were persuaded to support the temperance reform by the evils that accompanied drinking. Methodists seem to have led the way. For example, William J. Blocker announced a temperance celebration near his home northeast of Marshall on July 4, 1849, featuring an oration by the Methodist minister, Reverend F. H. Blades. At Christmas that year, a temperance meeting at the Rock Springs Methodist Church featured food prepared by Mrs. William T. Scott. This movement carried enough force statewide that in February, 1854, the legislature in Austin passed an act prohibiting the sale of intoxicating liquors in quantities of less than one quart in any county unless a majority of the voters approved licensing such sales. On August 7, 1854, Harrison County voted 615 to 316 in favor of this restriction. Demon rum was on the run, and the churches were primarily responsible. The victory for temperance was temporary, however, because during 1858 the commissioners court began licensing storekeepers to sell liquor in quantities of less than a quart. Saloons were in business by 1859. Pratt Hughes, for example, received a license in February to sell liquor at the Adkins House hotel in a room known as the "Hole in the Wall."[17]

Antebellum Harrison County's churches not only provided spiritual and moral guidance and impetus for the temperance reform; they also served as a focal point of social life. In a primarily rural community, families did not associate with their neighbors on a daily basis, and churches provided a welcome break from the relative isolation of farm life. Even among young people in town, religious services apparently amounted to a welcome social event. Fifteen-year-old Pleasant Vickers's record of Sunday activities in 1854-1855 almost invariably included at-

[17] Marshall *Texas Republican*, June 8, 1849, January 3, 1850; Gammel (comp.), *Laws of Texas*, III, 1560-1561; Marshall *Texas Republican*, August 5, 12, 19, 1854; Harrison County Commissioners Court Minutes, November, 1859, and March, 1859, County Clerk's Office, Harrison County Courthouse, Marshall. Blades is identified as a Methodist in the 1850 census. Seventh Census, 1850, Schedule 1.

tendance at one and often two churches. He was eclectic in taste, attending Methodist, Baptist, Presbyterian, and Cumberland Presbyterian services.[18]

Religious activities that aided community social life did not end with Sunday services. There were also church-sponsored events such as fund-raising dinners, and, most importantly, camp-meeting revivals that offered social contact as well as spiritual inspiration. In September, 1849, the *Texas Republican* carried notices for a "protracted meeting" by the Cumberland Presbyterians in Marshall and a three-day meeting by the Methodists at a church near Delia Harwell's, five miles south of Port Caddo. Hobart Key wrote his wife in June, 1852, that the Baptists, Methodists, and Christians were all holding protracted revivals. Later that year, Key found Marshall nearly deserted due to a camp meeting at E. M. Wilder's. "I thought," he wrote, "if some people would take as much trouble and pains to get to *heaven,* as they do to get to *preaching* — that they certainly would succeed."[19] Apparently Key recognized the social nature of such religious activities and did not fully approve. But he lived in town, ran a store, and more than likely did not lack for contacts with a variety of his fellow citizens. For many, preaching was quite properly a social as well as a spiritual event.

In many areas of antebellum Texas, it was common for churches to be heavily involved in education as well as in immediate religious activities. Interestingly, however, this was not the case to any important extent in Harrison County. Churches were vital to the community for spiritual leadership, moral guidance, and social interaction. But they did not establish schools, and few ministers served as teachers.[20] Instead, education was handled to a large extent by men and women who made it their profession.

[18] Vickers Diary, February 19, March 4, July 2, 1854, July 15, 22, 1855.

[19] Marshall *Texas Republican*, September 13 (quotation), 20, 1849; Hobart Key to Mary Key, June 13, 1852, October 17, 1852 (second quotation), Key Family Papers.

[20] For the role of churches in education, see Rupert N. Richardson, Ernest Wallace, and Adrian Anderson, *Texas, The Lone Star State* (Englewood Cliffs, N.J., 1970), 173-175. As mentioned above, Thomas B. Wilson of the Cumberland Presbyterian Church was a notable exception to this generalization.

Harrison County, like all others in Texas, had no public schools in 1850, and formal education throughout the last antebellum decade fell largely to a variety of private institutions including one-room country schools, academies, Marshall University, and the Marshall Masonic Female Institute. One room schools were apparently the most common, although they were highly informal and impermanent and, therefore, difficult to document. Khleber M. Van Zandt, for example, remembered that his first schooling took place in a single room establishment near Elysian Fields taught by E. C. Beazeley who soon became county clerk. Academies were more formally organized, and a number may be identified from their advertisements in the *Texas Republican*. The trustees of the Republican Academy in Marshall announced in 1849 that their teachers, Virgil M. DuBose and W. A. Tarlton, combined to render their institution ". . . unsurpassed, in point of usefulness by any institution in the South." J. B. Williamson, a young teacher from Pennsylvania, advertised his Golden Rule Academy a few miles south of Marshall in 1850. At the same time, Levin Perry, a wealthy planter living northeast of Marshall, sent his children to an institution called the Central Academy. Frank J. Patillo, younger brother of the county judge and originally a printer by trade, opened the Marshall Grove Academy in 1856-1857, and V. M. DuBose, formerly of the Republican Academy, began a school of his own in the late 1850s called the Glade Springs Academy. Several of these schools taught girls as well as boys, usually in a separate female department. But if a parent wanted a school exclusively for girls, that too was available in Marshall. Mrs. Emma Bonfoey opened her first school for young ladies in September, 1849, and continued in one capacity or another throughout the next decade as the leading female educator in the community.[21]

Academies came and went during the antebellum years, and many of the teachers shifted positions regularly too. But the

[21] Van Zandt, *Force Without Fanfare*, 12-13; Marshall *Texas Republican*, June 15, 1849 (quotation), January 24, 31, 1850, June 6, 1857, June 19, 1858; Levin Perry to Theophilus Perry, March 24, 1849, Person Family Papers. The Republican Academy, for example, had male and female departments. Marshall *Texas Republican*, June 15, 1849.

most ambitious of all educational endeavors in the county, Marshall University, functioned without interruption. Chartered by the Congress of the Republic of Texas in January, 1842, the University at the opening of the spring session in 1850 was headed by Professor Elisha Petit (A.M.), a native of New York. John H. McLean who attended the school during the early 1850s remembered that its three-man faculty "attracted boarding pupils from the surrounding country." Another student, William P. McLean, wrote his uncle P. R. Rose in January, 1851, that he was one of seventy-five male scholars at the university. The school was hardly a threat to major institutions in the older states, but in spite of numerous changes in leadership and frequent turnover in faculty, it continued to operate. The census of 1860 reported sixty-five students and a faculty of two so it had not grown during the decade. Nevertheless, as the antebellum period ended, Marshall University, now under the firm leadership of Frederick S. Bass, a graduate of Virginia Military Institute, still aspired to academic leadership in Texas.[22]

Until early 1850, Marshall University offered a course of instruction to female as well as male students. The spring session opened that year with the Reverend Thomas B. Wilson (A.M.) serving as principal of the female department. Newspaper notices in February, 1850, clearly distinguished the female from the male department so the school was probably not coeducational in the modern sense. In any case, within a month, the local lodge of the Masonic Order bought the brick building that housed the female department and created the Marshall Masonic Female Institute. The state legislature soon conferred the power to issue collegiate degrees on the Institute's board of directors thus raising it to a status comparable to the University. By the next year, the Institute had 100 students, and Reverend Wilson had been joined by Mrs. Emma Bonfoey and two other

[22] Webb, Carroll, and Branda (eds.), *Handbook of Texas*, II, 149-150; Marshall *Texas Republican*, November 29, 1849, February 7, 1850, December 15, 1860; John H. McLean, *Reminiscences of Reverend Jno. H. McLean* (Nashville, 1918), (quotation on p. 38); William P. McLean to P. R. Rose, January 28, 1851, Rose Family Papers; Eighth Census, 1860, Schedule 6.

female instructors. This school, like Marshall University, underwent numerous changes in leadership and faculty during the 1850s, but it too survived and grew; in fact, more rapidly than the male school. The census of 1860 reported a faculty of six and a student body of 130 for the community's female college.[23]

Courses of instruction in antebellum Harrison County schools are difficult to describe in that there was no established progression of study over a period of years culminating in a particular diploma or degree. Schools advertised for students and, therefore, apparently sought to be as encompassing as possible in their offerings. All had courses in the primary basics: reading, spelling, writing, arithmetic, and grammar. The academies provided more advanced instruction. The Republican Academy, for example, boasted in 1849 that it had "all the advantages of a primary as well as a high classical institution," and the Marshall Grove Academy in 1857 offered instruction in Latin, Greek, Hebrew, Higher Mathematics, Natural Philosophy, Metaphysics, Declamation, and Composition. Marshall University, regardless of its title, had a primary department and also taught essentially the same secondary courses. During the spring session in 1851, for example, William P. McLean studied Greek, Latin, Algebra, Composition, Criticism, and Declamation. Undoubtedly, there were variations in instruction according to the ages and attainments of particular students, but in general even the University was more of a secondary school than a true institution of higher learning; at least that was the opinion of K. M. Van Zandt who left Marshall in 1852 to attend Franklin College in Nashville, Tennessee.[24]

[23]Webb, Carroll, and Branda (eds.), *Handbook of Texas*, II, 155; Marshall *Texas Republican*, February 7, March 14, 1850, June 7, 1851; Gammel (comp.), *Laws of Texas*, III, 854; Eighth Census, 1860, Schedule 6. Mrs. Emma Bonfoey lost her position at the Masonic Female Institute in 1852 and opened another school for girls in 1853. Hobart Key to Mary Key, December 19, 1852, Key Family Papers; Marshall *Texas Republican*, December 3, 1853.

[24]Marshall *Texas Republican*, June 15, 1849 (quotation), June 6, 1857. Tuition in the University's primary department was less than in higher departments. See, for example, Marshall *Texas Republican*, December 15, 1860. William P. McLean to P. R. Rose, January 28, 1851, Rose Family Papers; Van Zandt, *Force Without Fanfare*, 47.

Several other aspects of the courses of instruction provided by Harrison County schools bear mentioning. First, the Female Institute and Mrs. Bonfoey's several schools for girls apparently offered the same basic courses of primary and secondary instruction as did the schools for boys. An advertisement for the Institute in 1852, for example, listed geometry, trigonometry, and ancient languages among the upper-level subjects. It was possible to take "ornamental" courses such as instrumental music, art, and modern languages, but these were generally not part of the regular curriculum and there was usually an additional charge involved. In short, female education did not necessarily take the "finishing school" approach. Second, by 1860, Marshall University under President Bass emphasized military training with courses in engineering and field fortifications. As early as 1858, all students over the age of fourteen wore uniforms and attended military exercises twice a day. Military schools were popular in the South, but in light of the approaching Civil War, Marshall University's trend in that direction is especially interesting.[25]

The level of academic achievement in these schools is even more difficult to measure than the courses of instruction. Most had two or three teachers offering a great variety of classes to pupils of all ages. This difficult teaching situation was probably made worse by matters of discipline. Edmund Key remembered that one of his teachers was hired on the basis of a reputation for "thrashing" boys large and small. In any case, the schools had a tradition of ending each session with a public examination that showed off the learning of their students. Parents and local newspaper editors apparently loved these events and overlooked the fact that the "examinations" were more on the order of recitations of prepared and rehearsed materials. Levin Perry proudly informed his son Theophilus in June, 1850, that Isaac and Hugh, two of the family's younger members, were facing examinations. "They both expect to mount the stand and speak forth for themselves," he wrote. Nearly ten years later when one of

[25] Marshall *Texas Republican*, June 7, 1851, June 6, 1852, June 12, 1858, December 15, 1860.

his daughters performed at the Masonic Female Institute's examinations, Perry stayed two days in Marshall and sent Theophilus a copy of the program. Almost invariably the newspapers commented on these public examinations with enthusiastic praise for teachers and students alike. Educational critics in some areas of Texas, however, felt that these affairs were carefully prepared performances rather than true indicators of learning. Harrison County educators, to their good fortune, did not have to face the wrath of an editor like E. H. Cushing of the Houston *Telegraph* who condemned calling secondary schools "universities" and considered public oral examinations "humbuggery."[26]

Tuition was relatively expensive at antebellum schools. A five-month session typically cost from $15 per student in the primary department up to $30 for senior-level instruction. Modern languages added $10 each, and instrumental music at the Female Institute was $30. Boarding students paid $10 to $15 per month. And then, of course, there were expenses for books, clothes (uniforms at Marshall University by 1860), and so on. A male student living at Marshall University for the fall, 1860, session and studying ancient languages, mathematics, "solid" sciences, civil and military engineering, and field fortifications would have paid at least eighty dollars in tuition and board. A senior student at the Female Institute taking French and piano in addition to regular courses would have paid more.[27] When it is remembered that the best land in the county sold for less than ten dollars an acre and that a bale of cotton grossed less than fifty dollars, the relatively high costs of schooling become apparent.

Formal education was probably beyond the means of a large proportion of the community's families during the 1850s. Table 12 drawn from the censuses of 1850 and 1860 bears out this sug-

[26]Edmund Key, "Memoranda for My Children" (first quotation), Key Family Papers. For examples of the general attitude toward public examinations, see Marshall *Texas Republican*, May 26, 1849; Vickers Diary, June 27-28, 1854; Levin Perry to Theophilus Perry, June 6, 1850 (second quotation), June 20, 1859, Person Family Papers. E. H. Cushing's criticism is quoted in Earl Wesley Fornell, *The Galveston Era: The Texas Crescent on the Eve of Secession* (Austin, 1961), 72-74.

[27]Marshall *Texas Republican*, June 6, 1852, December 10, 1853, June 6, 13, 1857,

gestion. Among large planters, more than three-quarters (78% in 1850 and 80% in 1860) of the families with school-aged children (ages five through seventeen) had at least one of those children attending school. At the other extreme, only one in every three poor white families with school-aged children had at least one child in school in 1860. Even among yeomen farmers, approximately half could not afford formal education for their children.[28] Clearly, the progress that could come with broader educational opportunities depended on the development of public schools.

There was considerable interest across Texas during the 1850s in the establishment of a free public-school system. Many Texans shared the traditional American faith in education as an essential to a democratic society. Moreover, they wanted to keep their boys at home, away from the influences of northern educators. And there was a desire to establish a fund that could be used to subsidize railroad building while the interest went to support public schools. These interests prompted the state legislature in January, 1854, to pass "An Act to Establish a System of Schools." This measure set aside two million dollars of the 5% United States bonds received from the boundary settlement in the Compromise of 1850 as a "Special School Fund." The interest from this fund was to be allocated annually to the counties for their public schools on a per student basis. (Two years later, another act provided for loans from the Special School Fund to Texas railroads, thus combining two major improvements of the era.)[29]

The school-system law of 1854 was to be carried out primarily by county commissioners courts. They had to divide their county into school districts and see to the election of school trustees in each. The tax assessor/collector in each county had the job of conducting a census of all children aged six to sixteen. Once trustees were elected for a district, a school house provided

June 12, 1858, June 3, 1859, December 15, 1860.

[28] Seventh Census, 1850, Schedule 1; Eighth Census, 1860, Schedule 1.

[29] Frederick Eby, *The Development of Education in Texas* (New York, 1925), 112-116; Gammel (comp.), *Laws of Texas*, III, 1461-1465; IV, 449-455.

by the school patrons in that district, and a teacher hired, funds would be made available from the Special School Fund to pay the teacher's salary. If more was due the teacher, it would come from assessments on the district's patrons. Indigent and orphaned children were to have their tuition paid from the one-tenth of annual state revenues set aside for "free public schools" by the Constitution of 1845. Finally, the law included a provision allowing the trustees and patrons of any district to employ a

TABLE 12

School Attendance by Social Class, 1850 and 1860

	Percentage with at Least One Child Aged Five to Seventeen	Percentage with at Least One Child Aged Five to Seventeen Who Had at Least One Child in School
	1850	
Large Planters	83.7	77.8
Small Planters	80.0	65.9
Yeomen Farmers	68.0	52.2
Poor Whites	52.0	15.4
Non-Farmers	58.0	51.1
	1860	
Large Planters	71.8	80.4
Small Planters	67.9	63.2
Yeomen Farmers	68.3	46.3
Poor Whites	48.6	38.5
Non-Farmers	61.8	60.0

teacher in the primary department of an existing academy or college and thus convert the private institution into a common school. This provision reflected the entrenched position of private-school interests statewide.[30]

The Harrison County Commissioners Court designated the community's nine voting precincts as school districts and set the election of trustees for the first Monday in August, 1854. Interest was minimal, it seems, but three trustees were elected for each district. In the meantime, the tax assessor/collector conducted a census and enumerated 1,268 children aged six to sixteen in Harrison County.[31]

The trustees of Harrison County school districts did not establish new public schools; instead, they used existing private schools. They probably had no choice in that the per capita allowance for 1854 from the Special School Fund was only $.62. Harrison County's share, asked for by the commissioners court in March, 1855, came to only $786.16. For 1855, the per capita allowance rose to $1.50 which, when multiplied by the 1,184 students reported in the census, came to $1,776. These amounts were hardly sufficient to support a free public-school system with approximately 1,200 students.[32] There are no records of the number of students who actually benefitted from state allotments in 1854 and 1855, but there must have been very few. Education still depended on the ability of parents to pay.

By 1856, there was a tendency to use state monies primarily to support the education of indigent and orphaned children. An act of August 29, 1856, recognized this by combining the General School Fund arising from the constitutional provision dedicating one-tenth of all state revenue to free schools and the Special School Fund created in 1854 into a Permanent School Fund.

[30] Eby, *Development of Education in Texas*, 116-118; Gammel (comp.) *Laws of Texas*, III, 1461-1465.

[31] Harrison County Commissioners Court Minutes, May, 1854; Marshall *Texas Republican*, August 19, 1854; Scholastic Census, 1854-1874, Texas Department of Education Records, Archives Division, Texas State Library, Austin.

[32] Eby, *Development of Education in Texas*, 120-121; Harrison County Commissioners Court Minutes, March, November, 1855; Scholastic Census, 1854-1874.

The interest from this combined fund would go to the counties on a per student basis and be used first for those unable to pay tuition. Any remainder would be distributed to the other patrons. This act also abandoned the school-district concept and left management of the schools entirely up to county commissioners courts.[33]

Harrison County's commissioners put the new law into effect for the 1857 school year. Their list of teachers due payments from state funds for instructing indigent and orphaned children reveals that the public school laws had been turned completely to the benefit of private educators. Major recipients of tuition payments included Mrs. Emma Bonfoey, Frank J. Patillo, Virgil M. DuBose, and other well-known private-school teachers in the community. The commissioners court announced that the school year would run from September 1 of one year to August 31 of the next and that the court would not pay for instruction in "music or any other of the ornamental branches of education." This system begun in 1856 continued through the remainder of the decade and into the 1860s. The public subsidized the education of more than one hundred poor children every year, undoubtedly to the benefit of those children and of the private-school teachers. At the same time, many families that could not be classified as indigent could not afford formal education for their children, and there was no true public school system.[34] Investment in the development of human resources remained essentially an individual rather than a social concern in antebellum Harrison County.

Social life in Harrison County was enhanced by a variety of cultural events and entertainments. The Marshall Lyceum organized by lawyers and teachers offered public debates on such topics as; "Is a Division of the State of Texas Desirable?"

[33] Eby, *Development of Education of Texas*, 121-122; Gammel (comp.), *Laws of Texas*, IV, 525-530.

[34] Harrison County Commissioners Court Minutes, December, 1857 (quotation), September, 1858, September, 1859, October, 1860, October, 1861, June, 1863. For the number of school children in the county each year, see Scholastic Census, 1854-1874.

Amateur acting groups staged plays for local audiences. The first offering of the Marshall Histrionic Society in 1850, for example, a show entitled "Idiot Witness or a Tale of Blood," was hailed by the *Texas Republican* as good entertainment. Concerts were provided by both local and touring musical groups. The Marshall Brass Band, composed of German members of the community, performed before overflow crowds at the Masonic Female Institute during the mid-1850s.[35]

Favorite southern sports such as horse racing and cock fighting were not common in antebellum Harrison County, although the newspaper carried occasional announcements of races in nearby Shreveport. It appears that the most common formal entertainment not associated with any cultural interest was the circus, a regular summer event in Marshall. Fifteen-year-old Pleasant Vickers recorded attending the Reynolds and Co. circus on four consecutive days during the summer of 1854. "Got acquainted with Davenport the circus actor," he wrote. In 1857, Washburn's Southern Circus performed the first four days in July. Interestingly, adult tickets cost 75¢ while admission for children was 50¢ and for "servants," 25¢. Apparently even slaves were expected to attend the circus, and some masters permitted their bondsmen to do so.[36]

Men associated in fraternal organizations such as the Masonic Order and the Independent Order of Odd Fellows. Although active in the community — the Masons, for example, owned the Female Institute — these groups were important simply as another way individuals met socially.[37]

A good many members of the community needed no cultural activity or formal entertainment as a reason for getting together; they simply organized affairs that were purely social. Parties and balls were common, especially during the Christmas season and on the Fourth of July, but at times any excuse would

[35] Marshall *Texas Republican*, February 14, May 16, 23, 1850, December 16, 1854, June 30, 1855.

[36] Ibid., March 28, 1850, December 16, 1853, June 27, 1857; Vickers Diary, July 11-14, 1854 (quotation from July 13).

[37] Marshall *Texas Republican*, January 17, May 25, 1850.

serve. In September, 1849, James McCown, owner of the Marshall Hotel, gave a ball in honor of the Battle of Monterrey. Throughout much of the decade, ''storm parties'' were popular. A group of celebrants gathered and ''stormed'' the house of a friend demanding a party. Once the Southern Pacific Railroad became operative, excursions to Caddo Lake became popular among young men and women. They rode to Swanson's Landing, spent the day boating and picnicking, had a dance, and then returned to Marshall.[38]

Finally, no description of antebellum Harrison County society would be complete without mentioning the violence that regularly marred life in the community. Violence may have been a product of the passing frontier, or it may have been, as some suggest, peculiarly southern. Perhaps too, antebellum Harrison County was no more violent than some areas in modern society. Nevertheless, men of all classes often went armed and resorted to force in settling any disagreement of personal slight.

''They have not forgot how to fight in Harrison County yet,'' R. R. Rose wrote in 1852, ''they have a fight in Marshall every week or two.'' This statement was prompted by a ''fuss'' between Wiley Ingram and D. Carwile over a piece of land. The two men, both farmers in their forties, married, with families, killed each other. Each fell, Rose reported, within five feet of the other. This was indeed a serious ''fuss.'' A few months later Hobart Key described in a letter to his wife how Mahone Fitzpatrick, son of the large planter Rene Fitzpatrick, argued with an unnamed man in Port Caddo, went home for a weapon, returned and killed his antagonist with a gunshot from behind. According to Key, no measures were being taken for Fitzpatrick's arrest. Pleasant Vickers's journal for Saturday, March 4, 1854, read: ''Dr. W. H. Dial killed Zed Casey in a Gambling room at 12 oclk at night.'' The *Texas Republican* reported that a ''difficulty'' between Dial and Casey had resulted in the death of the latter. Dial had given a $5,000 bond and faced

[38]Ibid., October 4, 1849, January 7 (quotation), May 5, 1860.

a trial at the next session of the district court. The results of this trial are unknown, but in 1860, Dial still lived in Harrison County as a doctor and a large planter.[39]

Institutionally and socially then, in spite of a continuing penchant for violence, antebellum Harrison County had advanced beyond most East Texas communities. Its lawyers commanded widespread respect; churches were numerous and strong; and private schools were among the best in the state. Plans for public schools had come to little — in large part because state support was truly inadequate — but at least some orphans and children from indigent families had their tuition paid. Cultural activities, entertainments, and parties were common in the community too. Social life centered in Marshall, but planters and farmers did not live in extreme isolation. In any case, a majority of those who lived in rural areas were constantly concerned with a social institution that overshadowed law, religion, education, and nearly everything else in their lives — the institution of Negro slavery.

[39]R. R. Rose to P. R. Rose, June 14, 1852, (first and second quotations), Rose Family Papers; Seventh Census, 1850, Schedules 1 and 4; Hobart Key to Mary Key, August 8, 1852, Key Family Papers; Vickers Diary March 4, 1854 (third quotation); Marshall *Texas Republican*, March 11, 1854 (fourth quotation); Eighth Census, 1860, Schedules 1, 2, and 4.

5

Slavery: "The Peculiar Institution"

NEGRO SLAVERY, said James S. Mayfield of Fayette County at the Texas constitutional convention of 1845, "is the most important institution of our land."[1] No one in antebellum Harrison County could have reasonably disagreed with this assessment. Their community was preeminently one of masters and slaves, and the "Peculiar Institution," as southerners called slavery, affected literally every aspect of life there.

Harrison had more Negro slaves than any other county in Texas during the 1850s. The census of 1850 reported 6,190

[1] Annie Middleton, "The Texas Convention of 1845," *Southwestern Historical Quarterly*, XXV (July, 1921), 44.

bondsmen; ten years later there were 8,726. Slaves constituted 52% of the community's total population in 1850 and 58% in 1860. In this respect Harrison was more typical of an Alabama "Black Belt" county than it was of Texas. Only a few plantation counties in the lower Brazos and Colorado river valleys matched Harrison in having a black majority during the 1850s. Statewide, slaves were only 27.3% of the total population in 1850 and 30.2% in 1860.[2]

Turning to the population samples for information on individual slaveholding, we find that 57.4% of all households in 1850 owned at least one bondsman. Ten years later 60.8% held slaves. In this respect too, Harrison County differed widely from the state as a whole where only 30.1% owned bondsmen in 1850 and 27.3% in 1860. Thus the proportion of slaveholders statewide was a decreasing minority during the 1850s while in Harrison County they were an increasing majority.[3]

The average slaveholding numbered 10.9 bondsmen in 1850 and increased to 13.7 by 1860. Averages, however, can be misleading concerning the distribution of slaves among masters, a matter of considerable importance to the community. Table 13 presents a clearer picture. It reveals that in both 1850 and 1860 more than half of all slaveholders owned fewer than ten slaves. On the other hand, fewer than one-quarter of the households owning bondsmen had twenty or more. Thus the "typical" slaveholding in the community was relatively small, whereas by 1860 the planter minority held a majority (61.5%) of all bondsmen. Put another way, slave property was concentrated in the hands of a minority of slaveholders, even when the nonslaveholders in the community are not considered.[4]

The relatively high degree of concentration notwithstanding, however, the institution was very strongly rooted in ante-

[2] DeBow (ed.), *Statistical View of the United States,* 310-319; U.S. Bureau of the Census, *Population of the United States in 1860*, 484-486.

[3] Seventh Census, 1850, Schedules 1 and 2; Eighth Census, 1860, Schedules 1 and 2; Campbell and Lowe, *Wealth and Power in Antebellum Texas*, 44.

[4] Table 13 is based on data drawn from Seventh Census, 1850, Schedules 1 and 2 and Eighth Census, 1860, Schedules 1 and 2.

bellum Harrison County. A majority of households owned slaves. And in spite of steeply rising prices, a subject to be discussed below, there was a rise in the percentage of those owning slaves and a trend toward larger holdings from 1850 to 1860. Simply stated, more members of the community owned slaves in 1860 than in 1850. The institution apparently was on the way up rather than on the way out.

The establishment of slavery in Harrison County and its strength there was first and foremost a matter of economics. Settlers came to the area with full knowledge that Texas was the cotton frontier of the 1840s and 1850s. Encouraged by a mild climate, rich and inexpensive land, relatively good transportation outlets, and strong if not always stable world markets, they saw every advantage in moving quickly into large-scale cotton culture. The only additional necessity was adequate labor, and slavery met that need.

TABLE 13

Distribution of Slaves among Slaveholders, 1850 and 1860

Number of Slaves	1–4	5–9	10–19	20–49	50–99	100+	Totals
1850							
Percentage of All Slaveholders	36.6	25.4	22.0	13.9	1.8	.3	100.0
Percentage of All Slaves	7.8	15.7	27.9	35.1	10.2	3.3	100.0
1860							
Percentage of All Slaveholders	34.2	21.1	21.0	19.4	4.0	.3	100.0
Percentage of All Slaves	5.9	10.4	20.6	42.1	18.5	2.5	100.0

Commercial agriculture was impossible in the antebellum South without slave labor. Certainly it was in Texas. Farm families were often large, but none had children enough to cultivate and pick cotton on a plantation scale. Free labor was unavailable and unreliable. Very few men would work for wages when it was so easy to acquire land and become a farmer on their own. Moreover, free laborers were just that; free to leave whenever they chose. And that might be at the height of picking season or at any other busy time. In comparison, slaves could be bought in any quantity that a planter could afford, and as property, their labor was totally at his disposal. Harrison County had slavery, then, because only bondsmen could provide the labor essential to commercial agriculture, the heart of the community's economy. It might be argued that the community would have benefitted in the long run had it concentrated on family farming or on developing manufacturing and commerce and never relied on slavery. These alternatives, however, even if feasible, would have required a deliberate decision to forego rapid economic expansion for no immediately compelling reason.[5]

Slavery worked well in its primary economic function in Harrison County. As demonstrated in Chapter 2, slave labor applied to cotton production returned a profit to farmers and planters. The institution thus met the first requirement for any capital investment as a factor of production: it paid. Moreover, the community's agricultural economy, although commercially oriented to a large extent, was self-sufficient in food supply. Slave labor successfully produced cotton for profit and food for subsistence.

Slaveowners who did not employ their bondsmen in agricultural production or need them to serve in some other capacity often profited nevertheless by hiring them out. Traditionally the first Monday and Tuesday in January were slave hire days when contracts were made for the new year, usually from that day un-

[5]There are many outstanding studies of the economics of slavery in the United States. Robert E. Gallman, "Slavery and Southern Economic Growth," *Southern Economic Journal*, XLV (April, 1979), 1007-1022, is an excellent historigraphic essay that summarizes the interpretations presented here.

til the following December 25. Owners received a cash payment or rent and the person doing the hiring was responsible for maintenance of the slave throughout the year. Records concerning the estate of Seaborn J. Arnett who died in 1853 provide a good example of the slave-hire system. Arnett's will directed that the administrator of his estate sell or hire the slave property as was thought best. Solomon R. Perry, who was named administrator, chose to hire them. In 1855, four males, three of whom were boys under the age of fifteen and the other a man over forty, and three females, two girls and one thirty-year-old with an infant, were hired to four different masters for a total of $431. The following year the same seven slaves were hired for $549. In effect then, with only minor expenses such as taxes, slave hires brought in a significant amount of cash for the Arnett estate. And only one of these bondsmen, the thirty-year-old female, was of prime age.[6]

There was always special demand for female house servants, although it appears that an owner could usually place men and boys too. By 1854, adult males hired for $200 to $300 a year and females brought from $100 to $200. Skilled craftsmen were so valuable that it was possible to hire them out on a day-by-day basis. John B. Webster, for example, owned a brickmason named Richmond whom he commonly hired out for three dollars a day. From Webster's plantation journal of 1858-1859, it seems that Richmond worked at that rate whenever he could be spared from the plantation.[7]

Slave property steadily appreciated in value throughout the 1850s. The average slave regardless of age, sex, or condition increased in value from approximately $400 in 1850 to nearly $800 by 1860. By 1860 field hands sold for $1,800 or more and skilled workers commanded $2,000 to $2,500. Rising prices were significant in two ways. First, the increase in slave prices bore out the productivity and profitability of the institution in Harrison

[6] Estate of Seaborn J. Arnett, Harrison County Probate Papers. For typical comments on hire days in January, see Marshall *Texas Republican*, January 7, 1854.

[7] Marshall *Texas Republican*, January 7, 1854; Webster Plantation Journal.

County. Robert W. Loughery of the *Texas Republican* made this point repeatedly through the decade. Commenting on high prices in January, 1854, he wrote: "The natural inference would be that a country must be very productive when people can afford to pay such prices for labor." Two years later Loughery noted that "a stranger would scarcely have supposed . . . that there was any reality in the cry of hard times" given the demand for slaves. In 1860, he told his readers:

> The South has never been pecuniarily in so prosperous a condition as at the present time. The newspapers from every portion of the southern country represent negroes as selling at enormous prices. On the general selling and hiring day in this county, (the first Tuesday in January), common field hands brought seventeen, eighteen, and even as high as nineteen hundred dollars. Last Tuesday, a number of negroes were sold for cash, at public auction. One man, a carpenter, brought $2755, and a boy 11 years old was knocked off at $900.

Second, rising prices were in themselves a source of profit. As one economist has observed: "The fact is that virtually every slaveholder who was careful enough to keep his slaves alive made at least a normal profit during the 1850s from capital gains alone." He might have added, of course, that the owner stood to gain also from the birth of slave children. Slaves were not only profitable as workers or as property for hire; they and their children were worth more every year too.[8]

Slavery returned profits from agricultural productivity, hiring out, and capital gains; it also was a very flexible institution. Critics sometimes argue that southern capital was "tied up" in slaves, but in fact investments in bondsmen were highly liquid. A slaveowner could generally sell his human property for cash more quickly that a manufacturer could sell his machinery. Too, slaves could be and were used as security in mortgage agree-

[8]Campbell, "Local Archives as a Source of Slave Prices," 669; Marshall *Texas Republican*, January 7, 1854 (first quotation), February 5, 1856 (second quotation), February 11, 1860 (third quotation); Wright, *Political Economy of the Cotton South*, 141 (fourth quotation).

ments to raise money or purchase property. The "Peculiar Institution" was not necessarily a hindrance to what is loosely called business. Slaves also functioned as a useful means of distributing property in estate settlements. John J. Webster's will, for example, probated in 1854, divided his estate into three equal shares for his son and the heirs of his two daughters. To achieve this distribution, the son, John B. Webster, received twenty-nine slaves and more than half of the land while the heirs of the daughters received thirty-seven and thirty-four slaves respectively and smaller amounts of land. The slaves were readily movable, and by giving more of them to his daughters' heirs, Webster was able to leave his plantation largely intact to his son.[9]

Slave property offered economic security to widows and their families. John P. Thompson, for example, at his death in 1849 left his wife Elizabeth Ann with eight children at home. Thompson's will bequeathed his farm and seven slaves to his wife; the remaining sixty bondsmen on his estate were to be divided among his children. The family paid taxes on 67 slaves in 1850 and reported a 840-acre farm producing twenty-nine bales of cotton during the census year. Ten years later at least one of Elizabeth Thompson's children had left home, but she and her husband's minor heirs still owned forty-two slaves and produced 140 bales of cotton on their plantation. Obviously the Thompson family was well-to-do and would not likely have been destitute under any circumstances, but slave labor permitted them to live largely as they had before the death of the family head.[10]

As an economic institution, slavery worked well in so many ways during the 1850s that there was always a brisk demand for

[9]The many economic and social functions of slavery are emphasized in George R. Woolfolk, "Cotton Capitalism and Slave Labor in Texas," *Southwestern Social Science Quarterly*, XXXVII (June, 1956), 43-52. Estate of John J. Webster, Harrison County Probate Papers. Harrison County Deed Records contain many examples of mortgages on slave property. Book O, for example, contains a deed of trust dated March 15, 1855 wherein W. C. and G. B. Woods used three slaves as security for a loan of $1,800 from J. M. Swanson.

[10]Estate of John P. Thompson, Harrison County Probate Papers; Harrison County Tax Rolls, 1850; Seventh Census, 1850, Schedules 1, 2, and 4; Eighth Census, 1860, Schedules 1, 2, and 4.

bondsmen. It is impossible to determine exactly what proportion of the community's bondsmen came with their owners from older slave states and how many were imported via the interstate slave trade. The appearance of many new large slaveholders on the tax rolls during the 1850s suggests that a majority probably arrived with their immigrant masters. Nevertheless, there is evidence of a steady influx of Negroes brought to the community as merchandise. Many Harrison County planters traded directly with New Orleans, one of the largest slave markets in the South, but they did not have to go that far to find Negro traders. As early as 1849-1850, Hugh M. Farrior & Co. of Shreveport advertised that slaves were kept constantly on hand at New Orleans prices. In 1860, George J. Pitts of Shreveport advertised that he had "a choice lot of Virginia, Carolina, and Georgia Negroes, consisting of field hands, cooks, house servants, washers, ironers, and seamstresses; and will be receiving fresh supplies during the season, which I offer for sale low for cash or approved paper."[11]

Slave importation continued through the 1850s, although the numbers of bondsmen involved cannot be determined. There was also a busy intra-community trade in Negroes. An ad placed in the *Texas Republican* on March 21, 1850, by G. J. Roberts provides one example of many that appeared through the decade.

> I will offer for sale, in the town of Marshall, to the highest bidder, on the last Monday in this month, a likely Negro Man about 28 years of age. Said boy is well-disposed, is a tolerably good hewer, and otherwise handy, and is accustomed to plantation service.

Public auctions were common also. Pleasant Vickers's journal contained the following entry for Tuesday, February 7, 1854: "Auction day for negroes, they sold from 12 to 15 hundred

[11] Marshall *Texas Republican,* June 15, 1849, May 16, 1850, January 21, 1860 (quotation). Examples of large slaveholders who arrived in the community during the 1850s are provided by Cary McClure who appeared on the tax rolls for the first time in 1855 with twenty-six slaves, Zachariah Abney who appeared first in 1856 with twenty-four slaves, and A. J. Sandige who appeared first in 1860 with thirty-seven slaves.

dols. specie." Hobart Key, the merchant, provided an example of a private transaction in a letter to his wife on October 24, 1852. He proposed to buy a woman named Sarah and her three children (an infant, a girl aged four, and a two year old boy) from a Mr. Simpson for $1,350. The price was $100 too high, Key told his wife, but it "is as low as negroes are selling." Sarah was not a first-rate servant, he thought, but she could cook, wash, and sew. Moreover, the four-year-old girl would be a good nurse for Key's own young son. Mary Key replied that $1,350 seemed a reasonable price. "If you could make the arrangement," she wrote, "I should prefer Sarah to any servant I now know."[12]

Slavery, in spite of its productivity, profitability, and utility during the 1850s, contributed to the development of several underlying weaknesses in the community's economy. Slave labor permitted the agricultural economy to rely overwhelmingly on cotton, the price of which depended, as we have seen, on external demand. In a sense, this problem is inherent in cash-crop farming anywhere in any age, but slavery allowed cotton planters to pursue staple production without concern for diversification. Rising slave prices meant capital gains too through the 1850s, but obviously, inflated values for factors of production could fall if there was a decline in demand for the product involved. In other words, much of slavery's profitability depended on circumstances far from Harrison County, and therefore much of the community's future was well beyond local control or influence. Perhaps planters could have adjusted successfully to a fall in cotton demand, but the process would not have been easy.

Even more importantly, slavery may have played a role in retarding the long-run economic development of the county. Slaveholders, with adequate and reliable labor forces, found their circumstances acceptable both economically and socially. As noted in discussing the non-agricultural economy, they felt

[12] Ibid., January 17, 1850 (first quotation); Vickers Diary, February 7, 1854 (second quotation); Hobart Key to Mary Key, October 24, 1852 (third quotation), Mary Key to Hobart Key, November 21, 1852 (fourth quotation), Key Family Papers.

no pressing need to invest in manufacturing and commerce, and the community was underdeveloped, at least relative to the northeastern United States, in those areas. Slavery may also have contributed directly to the lack of non-agricultural development in several others ways. For one thing, bondsmen, although they constituted the majority of the working population, could not act as free consumers creating business for local merchants and manufacturers. The fact that they were slaves limited the market. Secondly, the presence of bondsmen may have discouraged the immigration of free workers to build the non-agricultural economy. There is evidence that those already in the community felt that slavery limited their opportunities. A Mechanics' Association was formed in Marshall in 1853 for the primary purpose of preventing "mechanical labor by slaves from coming in competition with that of white men."[13]

In summary, the "Peculiar Institution" was a mixed blessing economically to Harrison County. Highly productive and profitable in several ways, it unquestionably contributed to rising agricultural prosperity during the last antebellum decade. The community's slaveholders were quite rational in upholding the institution. It was viable at that time, and who can foresee the future? On the other hand, if long-run agricultural stability depends on diversification, and if economic development is measured in terms of commercialization and industrialization, slavery appears to have contributed negatively to the future of the community.

Slavery, of course, once established as an economic institu-

[13] Marshall *Texas Republican*, June 18, 1853 (quotation). There are many discussions of slavery's impact on southern economic development. Eugene D. Genovese, *The Political Economy of Slavery: Studies in the Economy and Society of the Slave South* (New York, 1965), is one of the best-known expositions of the negative impact of slavery on economic development. Bateman and Weiss, *A Deplorable Scarcity*, discusses the impact of slavery on southern industrial development in detail and concludes that slavery *per se* did not impose unbreakable restraints. Their conclusion, as noted in chapter 3, emphasizes the attitudes of the planter class as the key factor in retarding industrialization. Obviously, however, this involves slavery since the planters were defined as such by the ownership of bondsmen. See also Wright, *Political Economy of the Cotton South*. As mentioned above, Gallman, "Slavery and Southern Economic Development," is an excellent historiographic summary.

tion, became an integral part of the community's social structure as well. It placed Negroes at the bottom of the social ladder and prevented any threat to the white minority or to the idea of white superiority. Most Harrison County whites assumed inherent Negro inferiority. Louise Wigfall Wright, for example, felt that all blacks were "lazy and idle" and also "simple, true, and faithful." Slavery was therefore their natural station in life.[14]

In keeping with these views on race and slavery, free Negroes had no place in the community's social structure and were decidedly unwelcome there. Harrison County had only one free black family in 1850 and none by 1860. This was best, the *Texas Republican* argued. "Free Negroes are certainly a most obnoxious and dangerous population . . ." Editor Loughery wrote in 1856.

> Negroes are usually set free, as a reward for meritorious services. But as a general thing such kindness acts very injuriously upon the public. The negroes, when free, sometimes get idle and dissipated; and their offspring generally are more objectionable than the original stock. Besides, they increase very rapidly. For these reasons, they ought not to be permitted to remain in slave states any longer than is dictated by just motives of humanity.

Of course, Harrison County had no monopoly on this attitude. State law in effect required special legislative action to permit free blacks to live in Texas. A manumitted slave had to remove from the state immediately upon obtaining his freedom.[15]

What was slavery like for the enslaved? Generalizations must be handled carefully. Conditions differed from one master to another; and the size of slaveholding involved and the type of labor regularly performed by a bondsman also had an effect. A single slave belonging to a merchant in Marshall, for example, undoubtedly had a somewhat different existence than a field

[14] Wright, *Southern Girl in '61*, 18.

[15] Marshall *Texas Republican*, December 6, 1856 (quotations); Seventh Census, 1850, Schedule 1; Eighth Census, 1860, Schedule 2. Restrictions on free blacks and emancipated ex-slaves dated to the Republic of Texas. See Gammel (comp.), *Laws of Texas*, II, 325-327 and the Texas Supreme Court ruling in *Purvis v. Sherrod*, 12 *Texas* 140.

hand on a large plantation. Nevertheless, some aspects of life were the same for *all* slaves, and reasonably dependable generalizations may be made concerning the life of the majority.

Every slave existed under the law as personal property; a movable chattel subject to being bought, sold, hired, and mortgaged. Lee Pierce, a slave belonging to Evans Spencer, discovered at age eleven what it meant to be property. ''Marse Spencer done got in debt so bad he had to sell me off from mammy,'' he remembered. After some time with a speculator named Buckley, Pierce was taken to the ''nigger trader yard'' in Marshall. ''I was put on the block and sold jes' like a cow or horse, to marse Henry Fowler, what taken me to Sulphur Springs.''[16] All slaves had to live daily with the knowledge that they could be sold for any reason to any buyer willing to pay.

Furthermore, as a piece of property, every slave was subject to the will of his owner. ''The right of the master to the obedience and submission of his slave, in all lawful things, is perfect,'' read the Texas Penal Code in 1859, ''and the power belongs to the master to inflict any punishment upon the slave . . . which he may consider necessary for the purpose of keeping him in such submission and enforcing such submission to his commands. . . .'' Bondsmen had no property rights themselves and no legal protections for marriages or family ties. They were slaves for life with no legal avenues of escape from the institution. Under the Constitution of 1845, not even the state legislature could emancipate slaves unless their owners consented.[17]

Regardless, however, of the many ways in which *every* Harrison County slave could be treated as a piece of property, the community also had to recognize that slaves were human. This fact affected the lives of all bondsmen too. The Constitution of 1845 gave the legislature

> full power to pass laws, which will oblige the owners of slaves to treat them with humanity, to provide for their necessary

[16] Rawick (ed.), *American Slave*, V, Part 3, 185.

[17] Williamson S. Oldham and George W. White, (comps.) *A Digest of the General Statute Laws of the State of Texas . . .* (Austin, 1859), 26, 560 (quotation).

> food and clothing, to abstain from all injuries to them extending to life or limb; and in case of their neglect or refusal to comply with the directions of such laws, to have such slave or slaves taken from such owners, and sold for the benefit of such owner or owners.

The murder of a slave, except in case of insurrection, was to be punished as if the offense had been committed against a free white. From time to time, the legislature enacted laws under these constitutional provisions. Chapter VIII of the Penal Code as summarized in 1859, entitled "Cruel Treatment of Slaves," outlawed punishment disproportionate to the nature of an offense or an unusual degree of punishment without due provocation. One article read: "If, by reason of abuse or cruel treatment to a slave, death shall result, the offence is murder." Slaves also had a few civil rights. They were not, for example, to be deprived of a jury trial if accused of a crime greater than petit larceny, and they could not be held accessory to a crime committed by their master.[18] Enforcement of these laws recognizing the humanity of slaves was always uncertain; nevertheless, the injunctions were there for all.

The law also recognized all slaves as human in another way, that is, they, not their owners, were held responsible for their crimes. Bondsmen were not fined or jailed. They were punished by death if found guilty of a variety of offenses including murder, insurrection, arson, and rape or attempted rape of a white woman. All offenses against society not specifically enumerated were punishable by whipping.[19]

Thus all bondsmen in Harrison County were treated as property and yet had to be recognized as human. Perhaps the ultimate legal recognition of their unique status as human property came in 1852 when the state legislature passed "An Act to Indemnify the Owners for the Loss of Slaves Executed for Capital Offenses."[20] The slave was human enough to be tried for his

[18] Ibid., 26 (first quotation), 482, 542 (second quotation), 543.

[19] Ibid., 561.

[20] Gammel (comp.), *Laws of Texas*, III, 911-912.

crimes and property enough to be paid for if destroyed. It was indeed a "Peculiar Institution."

The great majority of Harrison County's slaves, more than 90% in both 1850 and 1860, belonged to farmers and planters. By 1860, as we have seen, more than 50% lived on plantations having twenty or more bondsmen. Most slaves, therefore, performed agricultural labor—plowing, planting, cultivating, and harvesting the cotton and food crops and handling the myriad other chores to be done on a farm. Men did the heavier work such as plowing and ditching, but women planted and harvested, and even children once they were ten or so had tasks such as knocking down the stalks from old crops. According to the narratives of Harrison County slaves, long hours were common. Wes Brady who belonged to John James remembered the overseer rousing his workers at three in the morning and having them weigh in cotton by candlelight at night. Martin Ruffin reported similar hours on Joshua Perry's plantation near Port Caddo. Simpson Campbell said that W. L. Sloan's slaves worked from four in the morning to six in the evening and then had a "task" to complete before bedtime at nine o'clock. According to Katie Darling, bondsmen on William McCarty's farm worked all day Saturday and on Sunday too if the crops were "in the grass." Undoubtedly the narrators remembered busy times of the year best. As Tesban Young who belonged to Buckner Scott pointed out, slaves worked especially late during hoeing and cotton-picking seasons. At other times, the hours were not quite so long.[21] In any case, the average slave's work was hard, boring, and—although it varied from season to season—never-ending.

Slaves worked and worked well or they were punished, usually by whipping. Virtually every bondsmen who narrated his experiences mentioned this form of punishment. Rube Witt remembered his owner, Jess Witt, as more liberal than most. "The Witts had a good set of niggers," he said, "and didn't

[21] Seventh Census, 1850, Schedules 1, 2, and 4; Eighth Census, 1860, Schedules 1, 2, and 4; Rawick (ed.), *American Slave*, IV, Part 1, 133-136, 191, 192 (first quotation), 278, 279 (second quotation), 280; V, Part 3, 265-267; V, Part 4, 235-237. Webster Plantation Journal provides an excellent example of farm labor performed by slaves.

have to whip much. Sometimes he gives us a light breshin' for piddlin' round at work." Only Jerry Moore who belonged to Mrs. Isaac Van Zandt insisted that "I never seed a slave whipped on our place." He also claimed, probably with pride, that other slaveowners in the community "called us 'Van Zandt's free niggers' " and "wouldn't have none of Van Zandt's niggers." Undoubtedly many masters preferred to avoid severe whippings, if for no other reason than the damage done to valuable property. According to Bert Strong, for example, Dave Caven fired an overseer for "cuttin' and slashin' " his slaves and used a Negro driver instead. Wise slaveholders offered incentives and morale boosters in addition to punishment. Dr. William Baldwin, for example, kept a demijohn of whiskey on his front porch and allowed his hands a drink on their way to the fields. Every slave knew, however, that he could be whipped, and apparently it happened frequently enough on most farms and plantations to serve as a constant reminder.[22]

Most Harrison County slaves had enough to eat. Two kinds of evidence support this generalization. First, as we have seen, slaveholders grew large quantities of pork, corn, sweet potatoes, and blackeyed peas. Thus the food was being produced. Second, we have the testimony of the ex-slaves themselves. Virtually all who mentioned food remembered having plenty to eat including garden vegetables, molasses, wild game, and fish in addition to the crops that show up in the census. Tesban Young, for example, believed slaves were well fed and recognized it as simply good business. "Marster Scott feeds all us niggers good. We'uns have beans, peas, milk, vegetables, 'lasses, and plenty of meat. . . . De marster says, 'De nigger mus' have plenty of food and keep warm for to work good.' " Not every owner, however, took this point of view. Betty Powers, a slave on Dr. Harwood P. Perry's plantation, remembered,

> All de rations measure out Sunday mornin' and it have to do for de week. It am not 'nough for heavy eaters and we has to

[22] Ibid., V, Part 3, 121 (third and fourth quotations), 122 (second quotation), 123-124; V, Part 4, 70-72 (fifth quotation), 208-209 (first quotation), 210.

> be real careful or we goes hungry. We has meat and corn-meal and 'lasses and 'taters and peas and beans and milk. Dem short rations causes plenty trouble 'cause de niggers has to steal food and it am de whippin' if dey gits catched. Dey am if dey can't work for bein' hungry 'cause it am de whippin' den sho', so dey has to steal, and most of 'em did and taken de whippin' Dey has de full stomach anyway.[23]

There were exceptions to the general rule that slaves had enough food; how many, we cannot say. It should also be noted that no matter the quantity of food and its caloric content, bondsmen's diets may still have been lacking in nutrition. There could have been deficiencies in certain vitamins, niacin and thiamin, for example, due to the heavy reliance on pork and corn. In general, however, slaves appear to have had at least as much variety in their food as did their masters and any dietary deficiencies were due more to ignorance of nutrition than deliberate deprivation. This is not a defense of inadequate diets; it only supports the argument that slaves were reasonably well fed by the standards of that day.[24]

Harrison County slaves lived in log cabins, arranged on larger plantations into slave quarters situated at some distance from the master's home. The quarters on Joshua Perry's place, Martin Ruffin said, looked like a "little town." Typically, slave cabins had a fireplace for heating and cooking, beds nailed or pegged to the wall, and a few boxes or benches for seats. There were, of course, individual variations in housing and furniture. According to Campbell Davis, cabins on Henry Hood's plantation had dirt floors whereas Ellen Payne boasted that at Dr. William Evans's: "We had good wood beds and hay mattresses with lowell covers." Generally one family was assigned to each cabin so crowding depended on the size of the family. Betty Powers lived with her father, mother, and eleven other children in one cabin on Dr. Perry's plantation. Overall, slave housing seems to

[23] Ibid., V, Part 3, 190-191 (second quotation), 192; V, Part 4, 235-236 (first quotation), 237.

[24] For a good discussion of slave diet in terms of caloric content and and nutritional qualities, see David et al., *Reckoning with Slavery*, 233-281.

have given reasonable protection from the elements and may in that sense be termed "adequate." It was hardly comfortable.[25]

Harrison County slaves had little to say about clothing. Perhaps their feelings were summarized in two of the narratives. Slaves, according to Tesban Young, had all the clothes necessary to stay warm. And Martin Ruffin remembered how unattractive and uncomfortable the clothing was. Slaveowners generally bought heavy cloth, cut and sewed pants, shirts and dresses, and gave out one or two outfits a year. Children often wore only a long dresslike shirt. Shoes, usually described as "brogans," were for adults only. There is no mention of underwear or socks. Slave clothing, like housing, was adequate, and not much more.[26]

Health care for slaves is difficult to evaluate. Bondsmen were subject not only to common illnesses and all the diseases of that era, but to accidents and injuries from their work too. One of John B. Webster's hands, for example, was "laid up" for weeks in 1858 with a snake bite. Undoubtedly infant mortality was as high as it was among the white population, and that was appalling. Slaves themselves said nothing about health care. The records of slaveholders indicate that at least some called in doctors regularly and spent a great deal of money on medical care for their property. The Blocker family, for example, paid Dr. H. P. Perry $335 in 1864, nearly all as a result of visits to sick slaves.[27] Given the state of medical knowledge during these years, however, it is doubtful that the doctors were much help. Perhaps the best conclusion on health care is similar to that on food. Slaves did not enjoy the same degree of attention as whites but the limitations of their treatment were primarily those of knowledge and practice in that day rather than the result of deliberate neglect or mistreatment. Again, humanity aside, slaves were too valuable for owners to ignore their health.

Harrison County slaves thus constituted a mudsill class in

[25] Rawick (ed.), *American Slave*, IV, Part 1, 285-288; V, Part 3, 177 (second quotation), 178-179, 190-192, 265 (first quotation), 266-267.

[26] Ibid., V. Part 3, 265-267; Part 4, 235-237.

[27] Webster Plantation Journal; Estate of William J. Blocker, Harrison County Probate Papers.

their community. As property they were born to a lifetime of hard labor and total submission to their masters. If faithful and hard-working, they could expect only to escape most punishments and to have their material needs met adequately. Slavery was indeed, as Rube Witt put it, a "tight fight."[28] Yet there were relatively few efforts to escape from bondage and virtually no overt resistance to the institution.

Individual slaves, usually young men, occasionally ran away from their masters. The following notice from the *Texas Republican* is an example of one such case.

> Ran away from the subscriber, living in Harrison County, Texas, eight miles from Port Caddo, on Wednesday night the 3rd of October, instant, a large and likely negro man named Mack, about twenty-one years of age, copper complexion, quickly spoken, and very brisk in his deportment. Said boy rode off on a black mare, in good order, about four years old last spring, with saddle marks on each side of her back, and a white spot on her forehead. It is supposed that he will go west or to Arkansas.[29]

Mack apparently hoped to escape slavery forever. So also did Willis, a "boy" described as five foot, ten inches tall and "well built," who ran away from the estate of W. S. Richardson in 1850. He went armed with a doublebarrel gun and a brace of pistols. Not all who ran away, however, were seeking lasting freedom. When Anthony left in 1849, his owner, Chesley M. Adams, noted that he was probably heading for Nacogdoches where his slave wife lived. Editor Loughery advertised in early 1865: "My boy George ran off last night, and is lurking about town." It is not possible to say with certainty how many runaways there were during any given period. The newspapers generally contained fewer than ten notices per year. Certainly there were never enough to constitute a real threat to slavery in the community.[30]

[28] Rawick (ed.), *American Slave*, V, Part 4, 208 (quotation), 209-210.

[29] Marshall *Texas Republican*, October 11, 1849.

[30] Ibid., November 9, 1850 (first and second quotation), November 29, 1849, March 3, 1865 (third quotation).

There were random acts of violence and even premeditated murder by slaves. Ezeriah Crofford, for example, was poisoned by one of his slave women in 1849. But there were no plots or general insurrections against the slave system. The community became alarmed in November, 1856, and had a committee investigate "the reports and rumors afloat in Harrison County of a plan or project on foot among the slaves with a view to insurrection . . ." The investigators found that news of the Republican Party had upset the slaves with visions of freedom but that there was no plot. On other occasions, slaveholders became alarmed over "abolitionists" and "incendiaries" in the community. The fact remains, however, that there were no significant slave plots or insurrections in antebellum Harrison County.[31]

Slaves did not run away in large numbers or rebel against the institution because there were strong physical and psychological obstacles to such actions. A runaway seeking freedom had to reach Mexico or Canada to be beyond the authority of federal fugitive slave laws. And even Mexico was more than five hundred miles from Harrison County. Distance then was a major obstacle. Second, the runaway slave, if caught, could expect certain and probably severe punishment. Whipping was most likely, but Gill Ruffin recounted how Henry Hargrove brought home a runaway and tied him to a tree all one night. After that, no one tried to run off again, Ruffin said. Finally, it must be remembered that the commissioners court appointed a slave patrol for each precinct or "beat" in the county. The "patterrollers," as the slaves called them, stopped all Negroes found away from home, inquired as to their business, and inspected their passes or permits. A bondsman caught off the plantation without his master's permission, whether a runaway or not, was likely to be in for a whipping.[32]

[31]Ibid., October 11, 1849, November 22, 1856 (first quotation), August 11 (second quotation), September 1 (third quotation), 1860. The scare associated with the Republican Party campaign in 1856 spread across the South. See Eugene D. Genovese, *From Rebellion to Revolution: Afro-American Slave Revolts in the Making of the New World* (New York, 1981), 129. The summer of 1860 also was marked by much concern over abolitionists. This will be discussed below.

[32]Rawick (ed.), *American Slave*, V, Part 3, 262-264. Slave patrols consisted of a

Distance, the certainty of punishment, and slave patrols presented major obstacles to running away; the restraints on insurrection were even stronger. The bondsman who ran away could expect a whipping, but one who plotted rebellion faced certain death if caught. Keeping a secret was no easy matter. Betty Powers insisted that Dr. H. P. Perry's wife had "spies" among the slaves and knew everything that went on. Owners, overseers, and patrols were armed; slaves were not. A surprise uprising in mass might have solved the problem of arms in one locality, but the insurrection would have had little chance once the news spread.[33]

There were also strong psychological obstacles to running away or engaging in rebellion. Harrison County slaves had been born in bondage and knew nothing else. Masters generally kept their Negroes as ignorant as possible while impressing upon them the idea that inherent inferiority fitted them only to be slaves. Katie Darling's mistress told her, for example: "Niggers was made to work for white folks." Moreover, at least some owners presented themselves as benevolent fathers heading a plantation family, and some slaves apparently accepted this. Ellen Payne who belonged to Dr. William Evans remembered that "I loved all my white folks and they was sweet to us." Will Adams said, "We thunk lots of our white folks" on Dave Caven's place. In short, runaways or rebels had to overcome fears of the unknown, notions of inferiority, and the idea of "family" in addition to all the physical restraints on their situation. An almost superhuman act of will was required.[34]

In summary then, most slaves served without attempting to escape or destroy the system, but this cannot be taken to mean

captain and four or five other men appointed to three-month periods of service. This is seen in the Harrison County Commissioners Court Minutes throughout the 1850s.

[33]Rawick (ed.), *American Slave*, V, Part 3, 190-192.

[34]Ibid., IV, Part 1 (third quotation), 2-3, 278-279, 280 (first quotation); V, Part 3, 177 (second quotation), 178-179. The psychological impact of slavery is highly controversial. The argument began importantly with the publication of Stanley M. Elkins, *Slavery: A Problem in American Institutional and Intellectual Life* (Chicago, 1959). Planter paternalism and the concept of "family" is emphasized in Eugene D. Genovese, *Roll, Jordan, Roll: The World the Slaves Made* (New York, 1974), 1-149.

that they were happy or content in bondage. It would be a mistake also to assume that slaves, since they did not often run away or rebel, lived as mindless "Sambos," childishly subservient to their masters. And on the other hand, it would be equally mistaken to believe that the institution so brutalized the bondsmen that they were reduced to the level of chained animals constantly whipped into obedience.[35] Survival under the "Peculiar Institution" was a more subtle process.

Slaves in Harrison County did resist the demands of their masters, not to the point of getting into serious trouble, but enough to express their feelings about involuntary servitude. They worked at their own pace and required a great deal of supervision. Martin Ruffin recalled how "Sometimes they'd slack on that hoe and old massa [Joshua Perry] holler, 'I's watchin' yous.' The hands say 'yas, suh, us sees you, too.' Then they brightened up on that hoe." John B. Webster's journal regularly contained an apparently good-natured notation that Lev was "piddling" at his trade. Slaves also were too unwell for labor when they could get away with it. Webster, for example, frequently noted that one or the other of his slaves was "trying to be sick." Bondsmen were notoriously hard on livestock and equipment. Somewhat amusingly in retrospect, although slaveowners doubtless saw no humor in it at the time, Singer Sewing Machines in 1860 advertised a three-year warranty on their product, "even in the charge of negroes."[36] These forms of resistance did not threaten the existence of slavery, but they allowed the enslaved to make a necessary point about their condition.

The institution of the family also helped Harrison County slaves endure without being totally subservient or brutalized.

[35]Elkins, *Slavery*, advances the "Sambo" hypothesis. Stampp, *The Peculiar Institution*, presents slavery as an extremely brutal institution. The "Sambo" hypothesis is criticized effectively in John W. Blassingame, *The Slave Community: Plantation Life in the Ante-Bellum South* (New York, 1972), 184-216, and Kenneth M. Stampp, "Rebels and Sambos: The Search for the Negro Personality in Slavery," *Journal of Southern History*, XXXVII (Aug., 1971), 367-392.

[36]Rawick (ed.), *American Slave*, V, Part 3, 265 (first quotation), 267; Webster Plantation Journal (second and third quotations); Marshall *Texas Republican*, April 7, 1860 (fourth quotation).

Families, of course, could be and sometimes were broken up by sales, the hire system, and estate settlements. It is not possible to say how often this happened or what proportion of the community's bondsmen were affected. Many slaveholders, however, attempted to respect families, and most slaves probably lived in a family situation. For example, Tesban Young remembered that Buckner Scott never sold her parents or siblings, "so dere was no separation of de family long's we lived on de marster's place." John J. Webster's will provided "that my Negroes be so distributed as to allot the families by families in the partition that members of the same family may remain together." The slave family, although subject to disruption and possibly adding to a bondsman's burden when he could not protect his wife and children from a whipping or sale, brought support and comfort not obtainable from any other institution. Men and women shared each other and influenced their children in a family setting.[37] In small ways then, they did their own bidding rather than the master's.

Harrison County slaves had many aspects of a culture of their own. In the area of religious beliefs, for example, slaves tended to resist the message of white ministers—obey your master and work faithfully—and to listen instead for words promising salvation for all men. Some had the opportunity to hear Negro ministers whose christian teachings, unless they were carefully monitored by whites, may have mentioned deliverance more often than obedience. Indeed, some white church leaders recommended that services conducted by "colored men" for servants be "discountenanced" by all whites.[38]

[37] Rawick (ed.), *American Slave*, V, Part 4, 235 (first quotation), 236-237; Estate of John J. Webster (second quotation), Harrison County Probate Papers. Emphasis on the slave family across the South is found in Herbert G. Gutman, *The Black Family in Slavery and Freedom 1750-1925* (New York, 1976); Blassingame, *Slave Community*, 77-103; Genovese, *Roll, Jordan, Roll*, 443-523; and Leslie Howard Owens, *This Species of Property: Slave Life and Culture in the Old South* (New York, 1976), 182-213.

[38] Comments on the religious message desired by whites are found in Marshall *Texas Republican*, August 23, 1849, February 11, 1860. Slave resistance to this message is found in Rawick (ed.), *American Slave*, IV, Part 1, 133-136, 191-192; and V, Part 3, 265-267.

Formal education for slaves was unknown, although some liberal owners taught their bondsmen to read and write. Nevertheless, slave families and the slave quarter served as "schools" to teach children about their background and the basic lessons of survival as bondsmen. Slaves also had their own songs and stories expressing a variety of views concerning white masters and black bondsmen. Dancing was common on Saturday nights and special occasions. As Horace Overstreet remembered it: "Seems like my folks was happy when dey start dancin'." Martin Ruffin said, "we'd dance all night when the corn shuckin' was over." July 4 and the Christmas season brought extended parties and dances.[39] In short, slaves, especially on plantations where the quarter housed large numbers of bondsmen, had room enough to express their feelings and maintain their own beliefs and values.

Harrison County's slaves were able to endure their slavery with some degree of humanity left to them; nevertheless, individual attitudes toward their circumstances still varied considerably. Some cursed slavery and hated their masters. Wes Brady at age eighty-eight remembered that his overseer had gone unpunished for killing a bondsman who allowed livestock to get into a crop field. During the Civil War, Brady said, "Massa Jeems [John James] cussed and 'bused us niggers more'n ever, but he took sick and stepped off to Hell 'bout six months 'fore we got free." Betty Powers told her WPA interviewer:

> Did we'uns have weddin's? White man, you know better'n dat. Dem times, cullud folks am just put together. . . . Dey thinks nothin' on de plantation 'bout de feelin's of de woman and dere ain't no 'spect for dem. De overseer and white mens took 'vantage of de women like dey wants to.

On the other hand, Dave Caven's slaves, three of whom left narratives, could hardly say enough about the kindness of their

[39] Rawick (ed.), *American Slave*, V, Part 3, 160 (first quotation), 161, 265, 266 (second quotation), 267. There is no information on slave education from Harrison County sources. Thomas L. Webber, *Deep Like the Rivers: Education in the Slave Quarter Community, 1831-1865* (New York, 1978), is a good recent study of the subject.

master. He bought their "little crops" and let them go to Jefferson to spend their money. At Christmas every slave hung a stocking on the plantation house gallery and received a present. Caven taught his slaves to read and write and allowed them to have their own preacher to hold church and conduct funerals. Bert Strong stayed with the Cavens ten years after freedom "cause they so good it ain't no use to leave." Probably the majority of slaves fell somewhere between these two extremes. Their attitude may have been much like that of Josephine Howard who served Tim Walton. "Marse Tim," she said, was not any "worser dan other white folks."[40]

It seems certain too that a great majority of slaves, regardless of their feelings toward their masters and their individual lives, ultimately took a clear-eyed view of the institution. Even Van Zandt's "free niggers" all wanted freedom. And no matter how kind Dave Caven was, Will Adams remembered his grandmother's reply when told that "the Cavins [sic] allus thunk lots of their niggers."

"Why shouldn't they," she said, "it was their money."[41]

Obviously the weight of slavery in Harrison County fell heaviest on the Negro bondsmen, but the instituion was part of the daily life of every white member of the community too. State law, for example, required all to recognize the status of slaves and the special treatment given this form of property. County government expected white males to serve on slave patrols, whether they owned Negroes or not. Even city ordinances limited contacts between whites and blacks. Marshall had a rule requiring Negroes to have written authorization from their masters before trading or selling any item within the corporation limits. Not only the law, but politics and religion as well protected and promoted slavery. In short, there was no place or institution in the community unaffected. Any person who did not

[40] Rawick (ed.), *American Slave*, IV, Part 1, 2 (third quotation), 3, 133-134, 135 (first quotation), 136; IV, Part 2, 163-164 (fifth quotation), 165; 130-132; V, Part 3, 190, 191 (second quotation); 192; V, Part 4, 70-71, 72 (fourth quotation).

[41] Ibid., IV, Part 1, 1-3 (quotations); V, Part 3, 121-124.

approve of the "Peculiar Institution" could either keep quiet or leave.[42]

Slaves, for those who owned them, were clearly a troublesome property. Efficient plantation management required constant attention either by the master or an overseer. And tension was inherent in the situation as owners demanded discipline and hard work while slaves generally gave no more than they had to. As we have seen, virtually every master resorted to the lash at some time. Sometimes owners sold recalcitrant bondsmen. Cary McClure, administrator of the estate of Zach Abney in 1862, petitioned the court for permission to sell four Negroes because they "cannot be controlled by any person but their owner without rigid severity, and their example in other particulars as well as that, will have a very bad effect upon the other negroes as they are young and prone to follow evil examples even when those examples are not followed with impunity." Finally, violence was not uncommon. "Dr. Stewart shot his man John for insubordination," Levin Perry matter-of-factly informed his son in 1859, "but it is thought he will not die."[43]

Slave property was also troublesome in that masters never felt very secure about it. "Slave Owners, Look Out" read a headline in the *Texas Republican* of January 3, 1850. "Incendiaries" were reportedly at work luring slaves into running away. There was an even greater dread, of course, of insurrection. Commenting on a supposed plot for rebellion in Tennessee in 1856, Loughery wrote:

> In a community of slaves so extensive as our own, it is not surprising that such a scheme may be in existence, and its speedy supression of course is necessary to the preservation of our lives and property.[44]

[42] Marshall *Texas Republican*, July 20, 1850. Smith, *Journey Through Northeastern Texas*, 85, advised prospective settlers not to become involved with slavery but not to attack it either.

[43] Estate of Zachariah Abney, Harrison County Probate Papers (first quotation); Levin Perry to Theophilus Perry, June 20, 1859 (second quotation), Person Family Papers.

[44] Marshall *Texas Republican*, January 3, 1850 (first and second quotations), December 20, 1856 (third quotation).

Finally, slaveholders in Harrison County were troubled by their human property because slavery was under attack in the United States. Antislavery leaders and radical abolitionists disagreed over how to attack slavery, but they both argued that the institution was morally wrong. Told that the ownership of human property was evil, slaveholders reacted by calling it a positive good. After John Brown's raid on Harper's Ferry in 1859, the ultimate radical attack on slavery, a mass meeting in Marshall declared that the institution was of divine origin, "handed down from God to man to accomplish some great end on earth." "I have no more doubt," District Judge C. A. Frazier of Harrison County told an Upshur County grand jury in 1860, "of the right of a civilized and christian nation to capture the African . . . and subject him to labor, enlightenment, and religion, than I have of one of our people to capture a wild horse on the prairies of the West, and domesticate and reduce him to labor."[45]

For all their very real determination to defend slavery, however, many Harrison County slaveholders recognized the humanity of their property. John P. Thompson's will of August 11, 1849, for example, referred to an "old favorite Negro man . . . whom I desire to maintain on the place with his mistress and to perform easy labor, but I do not wish him to be regarded as the property of anyone." Occasionally, as in the 1856 will of David Funderburke, a slave was set free, ending his status as property. Possibly such recognitions of the slave's humanity were an indication that masters themselves knew slavery was wrong. Why else would they have made freedom a reward for faithful service? Perhaps some slaveholders were bothered by the holding of humans as property and gave themselves away from time to time. Other masters probably truly believed that the institution was a civilizing and christianizing influence and had no second thoughts. John H. McLean, for example, insisted in his *Reminiscences* that he felt no guilt for having owned slaves.[46] In

[45] Ibid., December 3, 1859 (first quotation), December 8, 1860 (second quotation).

[46] Estate of John P. Thompson (quotation), Harrison County Probate Papers; Estate of David Funderburke, Harrison County Probate Papers; McLean, *Reminiscences*, 131.

either case, they could not escape the fact that their institution was a moral anachronism in the western world and as such under attack.

For whites, then, slavery was in many ways a valuable but troublesome institution. The human capacities of bondsmen enhanced their contributions as servants while ironically at the same time making them difficult to manage and morally troubling to hold. For blacks, slavery was something to be endured. The system afforded them the "room," created to a large extent by their own efforts, to survive as humans with their own institutions rather than as a degraded, brutalized class who either copied whites or had no culture of their own. Individual variations aside, the majority had no illusions about the heart of the master-slave relationship and eagerly looked toward freedom from bondage. The community could not be at peace with itself so long as the "Peculiar Institution" existed. Would it be once slavery ended?

6

Antebellum Political Life: Conflict within Consensus

POLITICAL LIFE in Harrison County during the 1850s reflected the community's preeminently southern economic and social structure. Men interested in land, cotton, and slaves generally dominated politics, representing what may be called a "southern consensus" on those interests. Under the leadership of slaveholders during the decade, the community moved toward the political disaster of secession from the Union. The road to disunion was not taken eagerly by all, however, and significant disagreement existed within the community concerning methods of defending southern interests. The story is best told by examining how the community was governed, the men who provided leadership in politics, and the nature of political conflict within the southern consensus.

Authority emanating from the national government was virtually non-existent within antebellum Harrison County. There were no federal taxes, no social services, no grants or subsidies for any purpose, and no regulatory agencies. Since the community was well removed from the frontier, United States troops were not needed for protection. The Federal District Court for East Texas was not located in Marshall. During a typical year, most members of the community probably never saw a representative of the national government outside the post office and were virtually never affected directly by its laws.

In many ways then, national politics had little immediate impact on the people of antebellum Harrison County. On major sectional issues of the day, however, such as the extension of slavery, decisions made in Washington were considered vital to the community. Voters paid particular attention to the views and actions of presidents, United States senators, and representatives when southern interests were at stake. National politics thus constituted an important part of political life in Harrison County during the 1850s in spite of the very limited presence of the federal government there.

Citizens of the community felt state authority far more often than federal power in their daily lives. The government in Austin, in addition to passing a body of civil and criminal law, set state property taxes, established a slave code, planned public education, and provided support for internal improvements such as railroads. Moreover, state law determined the basic structure of county and municipal government. Voters, perhaps recognizing the importance of state government and feeling a closer identity with it, frequently turned out in larger numbers for the elections of governors and state legislators than for presidential contests. The elections of 1848 and 1852, for example, attracted fewer than 750 voters while more than 900 voted in the state legislative races in 1851. Even the presidential election of 1860 had fewer participants (1,069) than the governor's race between Sam Houston and Hardin R. Runnels in 1857 (1,157).[1]

[1] Returns for the presidential elections of 1848, 1852, and 1860 are found in W.

County government handled more of the community's immediate public concerns than did either national or state authority. The commissioners court chaired by the chief justice directed the upkeep of roads, appointed slave patrols, provided for the care of indigent citizens, chose officials to handle elections, maintained necessary buildings such as the courthouse and jail, set county property taxes (within guidelines provided by the state legislature), oversaw the collection of state and county taxes, and paid the salaries of public officials. The county clerk, among his many duties, kept all records of property transactions in the community. The sheriff enforced decisions of the commissioners court and attempted to uphold the law and maintain order (there were no state police). Tax assessors/collectors compiled annual property tax rolls and gathered revenue on the basis of those rolls. Voters recognized the importance of these offices. The race for county chief justice in 1860, for example, attracted a larger turnout (1,141) than either the presidential election that year (1,069) or the second Houston-Runnels gubernatorial contest in 1859 (1,055).[2]

For those who lived in Marshall, there was also a municipal government during the 1850s. Headed by a mayor and five aldermen, it could pass and enforce by-laws concerning the development, peace, and safety of the town. A small property tax could be levied by this government also.[3]

In summary, antebellum Harrison County was governed primarily by local authority with less presence of the state and

Dean Burnham, *Presidential Ballots, 1836-1892* (Baltimore, 1955), 784-785. For returns on the 1851 state legislative races, see Marshall *Texas Republican*, August 16, 1851. Totals from the 1857 Houston-Runnels race are in *Texas Republican*, August 15, 1857.

[2] An excellent survey of mid-nineteenth-century county government in the lower South is found in Ralph A. Wooster, *The People in Power: Courthouse and Statehouse in the Lower South, 1850-1860* (Knoxville, Tenn., 1969), 81-106. Wooster emphasizes the importance of county government and its essentially democratic nature. The presiding officer of the commissioners court in Texas is now called the county judge rather than the chief justice. The many functions of county offices may be found in Harrison County Commissioners Court Minutes. The election returns are given in Burnham, *Presidential Ballots*, 784-785; Marshall *Texas Republican*, August 20, 1859, August 18, 1860.

[3] Gammel (comp.) *Laws of Texas*, III, 770-772; Marshall *Texas Republican*, July 13, 1850.

much less presence of the federal government than is common in the twentieth century. Accordingly, the community gave more attention to county government than is common today. Contests for offices such as chief justice were often heated and close. At the same time, men recognized that the governments in Austin and Washington could make decisions of great magnitude in their lives, especially where sectional issues related to slavery were concerned. And they did not always agree on the stands to be taken in defense of southern interests. Governments may not have governed during the antebellum period to the extent that became common later, but political life was active and exciting. Indeed, the community, at least its free population, might have been better off with a little less excitement in politics.

What was the nature of political leadership in antebellum Harrison County? A characterization of the men who held public office provides one indication. Officeholders were not necessarily more important as leaders than influential private citizens such as large planters, wealthy merchants, and newspaper editors who were involved in politics regularly without becoming candidates themselves. Robert W. Loughery of the *Texas Republican,* for example, was highly influential in public affairs as was William R. D. Ward, a merchant, planter, and Democratic Party stalwart. The roles of such men will appear in the discussion of political conflict during the 1850s. Those who actually held legislative and executive positions, however, acted as well as spoke directly on public concerns and were, therefore, even more clearly identified as leaders in the community. What sort of men were they, and how did they compare to the average citizen of Harrison County?

Two of the community's political figures served at the national level during the 1850s, and they presented a striking contrast. Lemuel Dale Evans, a native of Tennessee, was a Unionist Democrat of the Sam Houston mold. He represented Fannin County in the constitutional convention of 1845, but by 1850 he was living in Marshall as a state district judge. A consistent opponent of southern extremism, Evans associated with the Know-Nothing Party in the mid-decade, possibly because many of those involved, including Senator Houston, who had a brief flirtation with the movement, preached unionism. Evans won a seat in the U.S. House of Representatives in 1855 as a Know-Nothing and served one term before being defeated by Democrat John H. Reagan in 1857. His term was undistinguished, but he had at least attained national office. Evans persisted in his support of Houston and the Union to the point of openly opposing secession. Fifty years old in 1860, he left the community during the Civil War, and then, as we will see, reappeared in public life there during Reconstruction.[4]

Louis Trezevant Wigfall was as far removed from L. D. Evans politically as a resident of antebellum Harrison County was likely to be. A native of South Carolina, Wigfall came to Marshall in 1848 with a reputation as a capable lawyer, a bitter partisan and duelist, and a disciple of the ultra-southern views of Senator John C. Calhoun. He made Sam Houston his prime political and personal enemy and spent a decade preaching defense of "Southern Rights" at any cost. Always spectacularly controversial, Wigfall engendered strong feelings wherever he went. In a letter of October 3, 1852, Hobart Key described for his wife one misadventure of the young fire-eater.

> Col. W____ got a nice thrashing at Linden (the county seat of Cass County) the other day—he was as usual [attacking] Sam Houston, when one of the *Sovereigns* present remarked, that he had served in *Wars* with Sam Houston, and would not have him abused—and suiting the action to his words knocks W____ down at a single blow, and jumping on him, gave him a drubbing before the bystanders could interfere—I am rather a Quaker in feeling and don't like violence—but really I cannot think it misapplied in this case.

Wigfall had a checkered career through the 1850s but reached national stature when he was elected to the United States Senate

[4]Webb, Carroll, and Branda (eds.), *Handbook of Texas*, I, 576; Seventh Census, 1850, Schedule 1; Ben H. Procter, *Not Without Honor: The Life of John H. Reagan* (Austin, 1962), 91-98; Thomas Schoonover (ed.), "Documents Concerning Lemuel Dale Evans' Plan to Keep Texas in the Union in 1861," *East Texas Historical Journal*, XII (Sp.,1974), 35-38.

by the Texas state legislature in 1859. He took Abraham Lincoln's victory in 1860 as a sign for secession and dared the North to save the Union with blood if it could. Fittingly, he was present at Fort Sumter for the bombardment that began the war and served in the Confederate Congress throughout the conflict. He was forty-four years old in 1860.[5]

Edward Clark held several positions in state government including those of lieutenant governor and governor. Arriving in Harrison County from Alabama during the Republic period, he had a distinguished political and military career before 1850. He then served as secretary of state for Governor Elisha M. Pease from 1853 to 1857 before being elected as Sam Houston's lieutenant governor on the Independent Democratic ticket in 1859. Unlike Evans and Wigfall, Clark, who turned forty-five in 1860, was not an outspoken politician, but his willingness to run with Houston suggests that he was not ultra-southern in his views. However, when Houston was forced from office at the time of secession, Clark served out his term and thus became the first governor of Confederate Texas. He attempted to remain in that office in 1861 but was defeated by Francis R. Lubbock.[6]

Interestingly, Evans, Wigfall, and Clark were not wealthy men, at least not by the standards of that era as reported in census returns and on tax rolls. Harrison County tax rolls for 1850 show Clark as the wealthiest of the three with property assessed at $3,725 including five slaves. Wigfall had no taxable property and paid only the poll tax. Evans did not appear on the 1850 rolls, but in 1859 he paid taxes on two horses, a buggy, and a watch, valued in total at $235. By 1860, Clark lived in Austin, and Evans apparently was not an official resident of Marshall

[5]King, *Louis T. Wigfall*, passim; Seventh Census, 1850, Schedule 1; Eighth Census, 1860, Schedule 1; Hobart Key to Mary Key, October 3, 1852 (quotation), Key Family Papers.

[6]Dart, "Edward Clark," 5-7, 23-26, 122-123. Webb, Carroll, and Branda (eds.), *Handbook of Texas*, I, 354, states incorrectly that Clark was born in Georgia, the son of Governor John Clark. Actually John Clark was his uncle, and he was born in Louisiana. See ibid., III, 173.

either. Wigfall, according to the census that year, owned ten slaves and $200 worth of real property.[7]

The political activities of Evans, Wigfall, and Clark cannot be explained in terms of personal economic interests. Instead, they worked with men interested in politics, generally men who had much larger material stakes in society. Leaders such as these three men helped to shape and at the same time reflected the views of the politically active. They were lawyers by training, but each should perhaps have listed his occupation as "professional politician."

State legislators from Harrison County were generally farmers or planters first and politicians second. Seventeen men represented the community in Austin at some time during the 1850s, five as senators and twelve as representatives. Fourteen could be identified in the census of 1860. Table 14 indicates that eleven (78.6%) were farmers, and only three were full-time lawyers. These legislators were a little older on the average (44.6 years) than the typical household head in the community (40.5 years). But they differed most strikingly in slaveholding and total wealth. Every one of the legislators held slaves, and the average was 31.6 bondsmen each. They averaged nearly $14,000 in real property and $50,000 in personal property making them as a group approximately five times wealthier than the typical household head.[8] The inclusion of William T. Scott, the county's largest slaveholder and wealthiest individual, introduces an upward bias in these averages. But it is fitting that Scott, who served three terms in the senate from 1851-1857, be included. Representation in Austin during the 1850s was very much the province of slaveholding planters.[9]

At the local level, chief justices and county commissioners were the leading public officials. Together they comprised the

[7] Harrison County Tax Rolls, 1849, 1850, 1860.

[8] Table 14 is based on 1860 census data for fourteen state legislators, fourteen members of the commissioners court, and the general population sample of 500 households. Eighth Census, 1860, Schedules 1, 2, and 4.

[9] Ibid. State senators and representatives are listed in *Members of the Texas Legislature, 1846-1962* (Austin, 1962).

commissioners court, the main executive and legislative body in county government. Twenty-one men served on the commissioners court during the 1850s, fourteen of whom could be identified in the census of 1860. Table 14 reveals that, like the state

TABLE 14

Economic and Demographic Characteristics of Harrison County's State Legislators and Commissioners Court Members (1849–1861) Compared to the General Population in 1860

Characteristic	Legislators	Commissioners Court Members	General Population
Mean Age	44.6	50.9	40.5
Birthplace			
Upper South	42.9%	57.1%	43.4%
Lower South	50.0	35.7	47.0
Free States	7.1	0.0	3.6
Foreign Born	0.0	7.2	5.4
Unknown	0.0	0.0	.6
Occupation			
Farmer	78.6%*	78.6%	72.8%
Merchant	0.0	0.0	3.8
Professional	21.4	21.4	6.6
Other	0.0	0.0	16.8
Average Value of Real Property	$13,764	$4,406	$3,189
Average Value of Personal Property	$49,265	$22,332	$9,585
Percentage of Slaveholders	100.0	100.0	60.8
Mean Number of Slaves per Slaveholder	31.6	21.0	13.7

* Five of the state legislators were professionals as well as farmers.

legislators, they too were farmers and planters. This group was on the average older (50.9 years) than the legislators or the typical head of household. Where slaveholding-economic status was concerned, county-level leaders stood between state legislators and the general public. They all owned slaves, but their average holding was 21 bondsmen rather than 32 as was the case with state legislators. County leaders averaged more than $26,000 in real and personal property combined, making them more than twice as wealthy as the typical household head.[10]

In general, then, leadership in state and local politics, measured in terms of officeholding, came from men who had a substantial material stake in the community. This is not unusual in American politics from the colonial period until today. Voters generally defer to those who have succeeded economically and have the time and interest to be politically active. And it does not follow that men who have the same interests always agree on the means of protecting and promoting those interests. No one should expect to find an antislavery leader or a noted critic of slave/cotton agriculture in antebellum Harrison County politics. Support for slavery and cotton was the key to the southern consensus. But there still remained room within this consensus for significant political conflict concerning the value of the Union and the wisest course for defenders of slavery.

A strong majority in antebellum Harrison County gave allegiance to the Democratic Party. Most of these were southern Democrats who adhered to John C. Calhoun's doctrines employing the concept of state sovereignty as a means of protecting sectional interests, primarily slavery. Southern Democrats generally believed that slavery was inviolable where it stood and should be free of criticism by northern abolitionists, that slaveholders had a right to take their human property with them into any territory belonging to the United States, and that the election of a national administration dedicated to restricting the

[10]The list of men who served on the commissioners court is drawn from Election Registers, 1850-1860, and the Marshall *Texas Republican*, August 27, 1850, August 21, 1852.

spread of slavery would be a justification for secession from the Union. Pressure to conform to these views existed in that anyone who disagreed publicly opened himself to being labeled an opponent of slavery and, therefore, a traitor to his section and his race.[11]

Nevertheless, there always existed a minority who took a more conservative stand on the extension of slavery and on secession. They did not oppose the "Peculiar Institution," but above all, they cautioned against disunion. The role of this group, often referred to simply as the Opposition, was summarized very well by an editorial in the *Harrison Flag* on September 15, 1860. Southern Democrats, the editor insisted, were arguing that the choice in the current presidential contest was between their candidate, John C. Breckinridge, and disunion. He believed that this was a serious mistake in that it ignored the existence of a large minority in the community who felt that their rights and interests lay not with Breckinridge or disunion but with the Union instead. In political matters, the editorial said,

> the democratic party has an old, and hereditary and powerful adversary in the south.
>
> Call this party what you will—federalist, whig, American Union or Know-Nothing—it is still . . . a *power* within the state . . . Separate the two—the democratic party and the southern opposition—and you will find as much patriotism, as much intelligence, as much true statesmanship, as much virtue and moral courage, as much wealth, energy and enterprise in the opposition ranks as in the democratic party.
>
> If they [the disunion party] have not the self-denial, not the forebearance, not the patriotism to submit — not to Abraham Lincoln, but to the laws of their country—we may well doubt their *capacity* for self government, and dread to risk them as *our rulers* in a southern confederacy. The southern opposition have been accustomed to submit and submit for years. They submitted to Polk, they submitted to Pierce,

[11]Gerald M. Capers, *John C. Calhoun: Opportunist, a Reappraisal* (Chicago, 1960), 235-248. The development of southern Democratic views from the late 1840s into 1861 is explained in many places. See David M. Potter, *The Impending Crisis, 1848-1861* (New York, 1976). Pressures for conformity are explained in Clement Eaton, *The Freedom-Of-Thought Struggle in the Old South* (New York, 1964).

> and they submitted even to Buchanan. They never dreamed of disunion or threatened it. No man who has not learned to submit himself has yet acquired the first rudiments for governing others.[12]

The editor was correct; antebellum Harrison County did, as we will see, have an Opposition. They were Whigs in the early 1850s, Know-Nothings during the mid-decade, and Constitutional Unionists in the election of 1860. But, was the Opposition strong enough numerically and different enough in its views to constitute a significant threat to the Democratic majority? Second, what accounts for the existence of the Opposition? Were there demographic, socioeconomic, or ethnocultural characteristics common to Opposition leaders that help explain their political views? In short, was there an Opposition culture? Finally, did the Opposition represent meaningful political conflict within the southern consensus, or were their differences with the Democrats too slight to be of real importance?[13]

It is a testimonial to the fortitude of the Opposition that the Whig Party, their first organizational vehicle, even appeared in Harrison County. Nationally, the Whigs had failed to champion Texas annexation in 1844-1845 and been unenthusiastic about the Mexican War in 1846. Moreover, Sam Houston, the giant of Texas politics, was a strong Jacksonian Democrat. In spite of these and other difficulties, however, Harrison County was a center of Whig activity in 1848 as the party organized statewide, held a convention at Huntsville, and presented an electoral ticket to the voters in that year's presidential election. A convention to ratify the work of the Huntsville meeting, complete with a parade and banners honoring Zachary Taylor, the Whig nominee, was held in Marshall on July 22. William B.

[12] *Harrison Flag*, September 15, 1860.

[13] The term "Southern consensus" is from Eaton, *Freedom-Of-Thought Stuggle*, 382. Eaton emphasizes conformity while recognizing that there were dissenters. By contrast, Carl N. Degler, *The Other South; Southern Dissenters in the Nineteenth Century* (New York, 1974), 1-2, argues that "The South is not and never has been a monolith." The significance of the Opposition thus remains open to question. ("Culture," as used here, covers a broad range of characteristics including ethnicity, religion, occupation, slaveholding, etc.)

Ochiltree, a Whig elector from Nacogdoches who would eventually move to Harrison County, spoke. The Whigs then campaigned actively in the community, even establishing a partisan newspaper called the *Star State Patriot.* Their efforts were rewarded with 364 (48.9%) of the 745 votes cast in the county.[14]

Discussion of issues probably constituted an even smaller part of this campaign in 1848 than is usual in presidential elections. The Democrats attempted to portray Taylor as the candidate of a northern-oriented, antislavery party, but they could not deny that "Old Rough and Ready" was himself a southern slaveholder. That plus Taylor's military reputation undoubtedly helped the Whig cause in Harrison County. The issue of secession versus unionism was a year away from becoming heated. Whig leaders emphasized traditional policies of their party such as federal internal improvements; issues that were national rather than southern. Thus, the election of 1848 revealed a large Opposition vote in Harrison County, but, on the other hand, the issues in the campaign were not generally vital to the South.[15]

Within two years of Taylor's election, the Opposition was tested in a clearly sectional contest. North-South tension continued to build in the late 1840s as antislavery leaders sought acceptance of the Wilmot Proviso prohibiting slavery in the Mexican Cession while John C. Calhoun formulated an "Address of the Southern Delegates in Congress to their Constituents" urging unity in the South against northern "aggression" respecting the rights of slavery, especially the rights of expansion into new territories. Southern Whigs generally refused to sign Calhoun's "Southern Address" and even some Democrats including Senators Houston and Thomas Jefferson Rusk of Texas did not give approval. Democrats in Harrison County, however, held a meet-

[14] Whig Party organizational efforts in 1848 are discussed in Campbell, "Whig Party of Texas," 17-21. The vote is from Burnham, *Presidential Ballots*, 784-785. The Marshall convention of July 22 is described in Clarksville *Northern Standard*, August 5, 1848.

[15] Campbell, "Whig Party of Texas." 20-21. These comments are based on the Whig's Texas campaign in general. There are no details available on the campaign in Harrison County.

ing in May, 1849, and endorsed Calhoun's views wholeheartedly. Another meeting in October pronounced Houston and Rusk guilty of a "dereliction of duty to Texas" in not supporting the "Southern Address." Throughout the year, the strongly Democratic *Texas Republican* (under the joint editorship of Trenton A. Patillo and Robert W. Loughery from July to November and under Loughery's sole editorship thereafter) preached ultra-southern views. "The South has been slow to anger"; read an editorial on June 8, for example, "she has used patience till it ceased to be a virtue — not that she loves the union less, but her honor more, she is beginning to speak in words that cannot be misunderstood."[16]

Harrison County Democrats also became much interested in late 1849 in a convention of all slaveholding states called by a meeting in Mississippi to assemble at Nashville on the first Monday in June, 1850. The purpose was to "devise and adopt some means of resistance" by the South against northern aggression. Editor Loughery insisted that only by being represented at Nashville could Texas correct the impression given by her senators and much of the press that she was a "submissionist" state on slavery and southern rights. The Texas legislature acted in February, 1850, to provide representation in Nashville by eight delegates, four to be elected in each congressional district.[17]

Against this background, sectional tensions reached crisis proportions in 1850 over a number of disputes including the admission of California to the Union and the fugitive slave law. For citizens of Harrison County, the most emotional issue was the boundary between Texas and New Mexico. Since Texas, which claimed territory extending westward beyond Santa Fe, was a slave state while New Mexico would undoubtedly be a free

[16]Potter, *Impending Crisis*, 85; Margaret L. Coit, *John C. Calhoun: American Portrait* (Boston, 1950), 474-476; Marshall *Texas Republican*, May 26, June 8 (second quotation), November 1 (first quotation), 1849.

[17]For general background on the Lone Star State's role in this convention, see Campbell, "Texas and the Nashville Convention," 1-6 (first quotation on p.4). For Loughery's attitude, see Marshall *Texas Republican*, December 20, 1849 (second quotation), January 3, 1850.

territory, this question took on a strongly sectional cast. The Nashville Convention in June, for example, although it adopted relatively moderate resolutions, endorsed Texas's claims to the Santa Fe area and urged rejection of any monetary settlement. Later that summer, Congress passed a compromise measure proposed by Senator James A. Pearce of Maryland which would limit Texas to her modern boundaries and pay the state $10 million for use primarily in handling existing debts. Texans were to vote acceptance or rejection of the Pearce Bill in November, 1850. In September, a public meeting in Marshall, chaired by William T. Scott, voted to support Governor Peter H. Bell in his call for the use of force if necessary to control the Santa Fe area. By October, the *Texas Republican* was urging defeat of the "Infamous Texas Bribery Bill" as Loughery dubbed Pearce's proposal. Slavery extension and the Union itself seemed to be at stake.[18]

The issues in 1850 were not defined strictly in terms of Whig or Opposition versus Democrat in Harrison County. The *Texas Republican* insisted in August, 1849 that ". . . the question, is he a Whig?, or, is he a democrat? has nothing to do with the question of slavery in the South." In June, Loughery had editorialized, "The Southern people, without regard to party, will certainly unite in defense of their institutions." And indeed the Whigs did not attack slavery. The editor of the *Star State Patriot* was offended when the *Republican* accused him of supporting free-soil principles. The Whigs did, however, tend to oppose the Democratic majority by disputing the need for the Nashville Convention, supporting the Pearce bill, and calling for preservation of the Union. Loughery complained that the *Star State Patriot* believed that the Union was "paramount to everything else; to right, justice, and the constitution . . ." When Democratic leaders held a public meeting and called for rejection of the Pearce bill, Opposition spokesmen led by James

[18]Campbell, "Texas and the Nashville Convention," 11; Marshall *Texas Republican*, October 5, 19, 1850. Holman Hamilton, *Prologue to Conflict, The Crisis and Compromise of 1850* (Lexington, Ky., 1964) is the best account of the entire sectional controversy in 1850. Pearce's bill is discussed on pages 136-138.

A. Simpson supported the compromise. Democrats did not, of course, call directly for secession, and some leaders including L. D. Evans supported the Pearce Bill. Most, however, apparently agreed with the *Texas Republican* when it encouraged "united resistance" to the North and discussed the feasibility of disunion.[19]

The controversy of 1850 carried Democratic-Whig conflict into areas of the community's politics that were usually non-partisan. Harrison's state senator, James F. Taylor, decided to support the Pearce bill on the grounds that it was better to "sell" Santa Fe for $10 million than try to hold it against the national government. But State Representative J. M. Clough disagreed and in a surprise move resigned his seat in September, 1850. Senator Taylor apparently then felt compelled to follow suit, and these vacated seats had to be filled at the same time the Pearce bill vote was taken in November. The *Texas Republican* endorsed Taylor's opponent, John J. Kennedy, and condemned the *Patriot* which had "wheeled entirely over to the opposition" and was supporting the Pearce bill and Taylor's re-election. Loughery also endorsed L. T. Wigfall, the ultra-southern lawyer, who was running against M. J. Hall, a pro-compromise Democrat, for Clough's seat in the Texas House. All friends of "Southern Rights" were urged to "stand at their posts, and to do their duty." The southern Democratic majority did just that. When the votes were counted in November, 1850, the Opposition polled 275 for the Pearce bill (34.0% of the 809 votes cast), 296 for ex-State Senator Taylor (37.6% of the 788 votes cast in that race), and 276 for M. J. Hall (37.1% of the 743 votes cast in the contest for state representative). The Pearce bill carried statewide, so in one sense the Opposition's performance in Harrison County during the crisis of 1850 may be considered weak.[20] On

[19] Marshall *Texas Republican*, June 8, 1949 (second quotation), August 30, 1849 (first quotation), October 26, 1850. No copies of the *Star State Patriot* from 1850 are extant. For Whig views, see the attacks on them in Marshall *Texas Republican*, January 3, 1850 (third quotation), October 5, 12, 1850. L. D. Evans's position is also described in *Texas Republican* of October 12, 1850. For the ultra-southern views of the Democrats, see *Texas Republican*, December 20, 1849, May 30 to October 26, 1850.

[20] Marshall *Texas Republican*, October 5, 12 (quotations), 19, November 2, 1850.

the other hand, when it is remembered that their unionism and support for compromise was interpreted to the community as a lack of southern patriotism and possibly even a sign of antislavery sentiment, their vote appears more respectable.

The crisis atmosphere of 1850 continued into 1851 and remained important until the regular state legislative elections in August. Although Democrats insisted that they meant to preserve the Union "as it was designed by its framers," they consistently emphasized southern rights and the constitutionality of secession. Clearly, when Democrats spoke of the Union, they meant the Union on their terms only. By contrast, the *Star State Patriot* carried the following motto: "Without Union our independence and liberty would never have been achieved — without Union, they never can be maintained." Opposition spokesmen such as Silas D. Wood, an avowed Whig, and Nathan Smith, a unionist-Democrat, both candidates for seats in the Texas house of representatives, insisted that there was no constitutional right to secede. "I am scarcely able to distinguish between the right of secession and that of revolution," said Smith. Secession, like revolution, was a "natural right," he argued, not a constitutional procedure. In July, when a meeting in Marshall agreed to support Wood and Smith for the lower house and Dr. B. F. Dial, another avowed Whig, for the state senate, the *Texas Republican* referred to it disgustedly as a "regular union submission" assembly. The Democrats in turn supported planter William T. Scott for the senate and Dr. Joseph Taylor against Smith and L. D. Camp of Upshur County against Wood.[21]

The campaign closed in early August with the *Texas Republican* reminding the community that every vote for the Opposition was a vote for "Federal Consolidation." B. F. Dial polled 317 votes (34.3%) against Scott's 606 while Wood with 400 votes and Smith with 406 received 42.7% and 42.8% respectively of the votes cast in their races. It may be unfair to

Technically Senator Taylor represented Harrison, Upshur, and Smith counties.

[21] Ibid., June 21, 1851 (first quotation); July 5, 1851 (third and fourth quotations), July 12 (fifth quotation), August 2, 1851; Marshall *Star State Patriot*, August 23, 1851 (second quotation).

term the Democrats "disunionists" as the Opposition did at times in 1851, but there does appear to have been a genuine difference in views concerning the value of the Union and the right of secession. And a sizable minority in Harrison County voted for a position that was labelled unpatriotic and "submissionist."[22]

As the election of 1852 approached, the Whigs of Harrison County were prepared and apparently eager to oppose the Democrats on the issues of unionism and sectional compromise as well as traditional policies. Twenty-five Whigs from Harrison served as delegates to their party's convention for the eastern congressional district at Tyler in April, 1852, and Charles C. Mills, a planter from the community, served as chairman. The Whigs chose delegates to the national convention and adopted resolutions emphasizing their faith in "the permanency of our government" and "the Compromise Measures" of 1850. This platform also expressed faith that the party would not nominate an "abolitionist" and directed Texas's delegates to support no candidate who would repeal or modify the Fugitive Slave Act. East Texas Whigs may have been conservative about the Union, and they did not wish to agitate the slavery issue. On the other hand, they certainly did not mean to appear unsound on the "Peculiar Institution."[23]

The Whig national convention proceeded to make the Opposition's position especially difficult by nominating General Winfield Scott who, although Virginia-born, was known to be friendly with antislavery Whigs such as William Seward of New York. Harrison County Whigs met the challenge well. In August, they held a dinner to ratify Scott's nomination and begin the campaign. Even the *Texas Republican* admitted that the meeting was a respectable affair and warned local Democrats that Whigs were stronger in their county than any other in Texas. The Whigs campaigned on their traditional policies such

[22]Marshall *Texas Republican*, August 2 (first quotation), 16, September 23 (second quotation), 1851.

[23]Ernest W. Winkler (ed.), *Platforms of Political Parties in Texas* (Austin, 1916), 51-52, 53-54 (quotations).

as federal internal improvements, denying all the while that Scott was a threat to the South. The Democrats again made the election a test of southern patriotism by reminding the voters constantly that Scott was "the candidate of Seward" while Franklin Pierce was a true Jeffersonian states righter. Scott received 283 votes (41.3% of the total) as once more the Opposition demonstrated considerable strength at the polls under adverse conditions.[24]

By 1852, the issues debated so heatedly in 1850-1851 had cooled down in Harrison County and state elections passed off with relatively good feelings. William B. Ochiltree, a well-known Whig who denied secession as a constitutional right, received 416 votes for governor compared to 234 for Elisha M. Pease, the Democratic candidate. L. D. Evans, the unionist Democrat, polled 206 votes in the same race, leading the *Texas Republican* to conclude that many Whigs had voted for him. All three of the community's successful candidates for the state house of representatives had previous affiliations with the Opposition. M. J. Hall, a unionist Democrat in 1850-1851, and George W. Whitmore, a Whig sub-elector in 1852, led the ticket of seven candidates. Nathan Smith, unsuccessful unionist Democrat candidate in 1851, and Dr. Joseph Taylor, the southern Democrat who had defeated him then, tied with 437 votes each. A new election to fill this third position was held in September and the victor was Josiah Marshall, one-time editor of the *Star State Patriot*. "The state of Texas does not contain a more ultra, anti-state rights Whig," complained the *Republican* in 1854.[25] These victories should not necessarily be taken as proof that Harrison's voters approved diversity on issues vital to the South, but they do reveal that individuals who had previously taken stands counter to the southern consensus were far from dead politically in the community.

[24]Campbell, "Whig Party of Texas," 22-26; Marshall *Texas Republican*, August 14, September 10, 25, October 2, 9, 30 (quotation), November 13, 1852; Marshall *Star State Patriot*, October 30, 1852; Burnham, *Presidential Ballots*, 784-785.

[25]Results of these elections are in Marshall *Texas Republican*, August 13, 1853. See also ibid., October 26, 1850, June 21, 1851, September 30, 1854 (quotation). William

Thus, during the troubled years from 1848 to 1853, the Opposition in Harrison County received the support of one-third to one-half of the community's voters. Is there a demographic, socioeconomic, or ethnocultural explanation for the existence of this Opposition? How did this group differ from the southern Democrats? Because there is no way to identify the hundreds of voters who simply supported each side, investigation of this question is of necessity limited to leaders of the Opposition and of the Democratic majority. Lists of twenty outstanding leaders of each group were compiled from newspaper accounts of political activity during this period. These individuals were identified in the census of 1850; and a profile of each group was prepared. Table 15 presents these profiles in conjunction with a profile of the community as a whole.[26]

This table reveals that the leaders of the Opposition and the Democratic consensus were generally similar to each other. Indeed, in some ways, they were more comparable to each other than to the rank and file of the community. Leaders of the two groups differed most notably in place of birth with a higher proportion of the Opposition having originated in the upper South. The importance of this difference is difficult to assess, however. Eventually the upper South would be more conservative than the lower South where questions of the Union were concerned, but lower southern states such as Georgia certainly had their share of strong Whigs. Perhaps the overriding fact is that more than 90% of Harrison County's people and its politi-

T. Scott ran unopposed for the state senate.

[26] The lists of Opposition and Democratic leaders were compiled from the *Texas Republican* and the *Star State Patriot* during the years from 1849 to 1853. The definition of "outstanding" is subjective, of course, but every individual chosen appeared in at least several leadership positions during that period. Many appeared consistently on one side throughout the antebellum years. Statistical data in Table 15 is drawn from Seventh Census, 1850, Schedules 1, 2, and 4. Six of the Opposition leaders and one of the Democrats were not present in the census of 1850. They were located in the returns for 1860 and data on age and birthplace that could be determined regardless of census date were used. Other data in Table 15 such as average value of real property were drawn only from information in the census of 1850. It should also be noted that the averages on slaveholding and property holding for the Democrats are biased upward to some extent by the inclusion of William T. Scott, the county's richest citizen, in this group.

TABLE 15

Economic and Demographic Characteristics of Opposition Leaders, Democratic Leaders, and the General Population, 1850

Characteristic	Opposition	Democrats	General Population
Number in Sample	20	20	500
Mean Age	37.6	36.5	37.9
Birthplace			
Upper South	60.0%	50.0%	52.0%
Lower South	35.0	45.0	42.0
Free States	5.0	5.0	4.2
Foreign Born	0.0	7.2	1.2
Unknown	0.0	0.0	.6
Occupation			
Farmer	30.0%	30.0%	72.2%
Merchant	20.0	5.0	2.4
Professional	45.0	50.0	6.0
Other	5.0	15.0	19.4
Average Value of Real Property	$3,030	$4,249	$1,452
Percentage of Slaveholders	73.3	73.7	57.4
Mean Number of Slaves per Slaveholder	12.1	21.3	10.9
Number of Farmers with Land	6	9	267
Mean Number of Improved Acres per Farmer	195.8	247.0	111.5
Mean Number Bales of Cotton per Farmer	19.7	24.1	9.0

cal leaders were southerners. This made them alike in many aspects of culture that are not revealed in Table 15. The overwhelming majority of the community were protestants of Anglo-American heritage who had been reared and educated in the South.

In matters of occupation and property holding, these leaders were definitely more similar to each other than to the community as a whole. Farming, which was the primary occupation of nearly three-quarters of all families, was the chief support of only about 30% of the leaders. It should be noted, however, that in such an overwhelmingly agricultural society the professionals such as lawyers had to be concerned with the economic interests of the farmers. It is very unlikely that occupational differences provided a basis for conflict. Those leaders who were farmers, whether of the Opposition or of the majority, were generally wealthier than average in the community. Furthermore, nearly three-fourths of both groups of leaders were slaveholders.

In short, Harrison County in the late 1840s and early 1850s was a remarkably homogeneous society. A sizable Opposition existed in the community, but there is no obvious socioeconomic or ethnocultural explanation for it. Further attempts to analyze the Opposition may be reserved until the more critical period of the late 1850s and early 1860s has been examined.[27]

In 1854, the Kansas-Nebraska Act proved fatal to the Whig Party as a national organization, and the Opposition in Harrison County lost a valuable link with the traditional two-party system. They were unwilling to join the southern Democrats, but

[27] Wooster, *People in Power*, offers an extensive analysis of the personal characteristics of state legislators chosen by Whigs and Democrats in the lower South in 1850. He finds that while there were some notable differences in property holding, these differences were not "so great as to present a real barrier to those wishing to cross party lines" (p. 44). In his study of the upper South, Wooster found a "lack of any major social or economic differences between the individuals" who composed the Democratic and Opposition parties during the 1850s. Ralph A. Wooster, *Politicians, Planters, and Plain Folk: Courthouse and Statehouse in the Upper South, 1850-1860* (Knoxville, Tenn., 1975), 54. Apparently then, the situation in Harrison County where Democratic and Oppostion leaders were highly similar demographically and economically during the late 1840s and early 1850s was not unusual.

they could hardly support the Republican Party which emerged to replace the Whigs in the North; its very existence was regarded as a menace to the South. Under these circumstances in the mid-1850s, an unusual organization called the American or Know-Nothing Party became the new focal point of partisan Opposition activity in Harrison County. It does not seem that the appeal of the Know-Nothings in this East Texas community depended primarily on the antiforeign and anti-Catholic attitudes on which the party attempted to build a national following. Nativism may have helped in areas of Texas with heavy Mexican or German populations, but Harrison County's people were almost entirely Anglo and protestant. There is no evidence that they were very upset over foreign or Catholic influence in the United States. Although the *Harrison Flag,* the Know-Nothing newspaper, carried the slogan "Americans Must Rule America," the Opposition apparently supported their party not as a nativist movement but largely as the only partisan organization through which they could speak.[28]

The numerical strength of the Opposition during the Know-Nothing period was as great as or greater than it had been before the destruction of the Whig Party. In 1855, the Know-Nothing candidate for governor, David Dickson, carried Harrison County with 59.7% of the 1,674 votes cast. The party's three contenders for the Texas House of Representatives, Nathan Smith, A. D. Burress, and William A. Tarleton, were all victorious by wide margins over their Democratic opponents. Lemuel D. Evans received 63.1% of Harrison's votes in his successful quest for a seat in congress. Evans disavowed Know-Nothing support, and he had never been a Whig, but his unionism had placed him with the Opposition before and would do so again. In the presidential election of 1856, former Whig, Millard Fillmore, the Know-Nothing candidate, barely lost to James Buchanan, polling 47.2% of the 1,070 votes cast in the community. The Democrats were forced to organize and

[28] For brief surveys of the Know-Nothing movement in Texas, see Richardson, Wallace, and Anderson, *Texas*, 144-145 and Ralph A. Wooster, "An Analysis of the Texas Know-Nothings," *Southwestern Historical Quarterly*, LXX (Jan., 1967), 414-423.

work as never before, and the *Texas Republican* hailed their narrow margin as a "Glorious Victory!"[29]

Following the election of 1856, the Know-Nothing movement generally died out in Texas, but it remained active in Harrison County for several more years. Sam Houston, under attack for his vote against the Kansas-Nebraska Act in 1854, had tended to support the new party in 1855-1856 so when "Old Sam" ran for the governorship in 1857, the Opposition attempted to return the favor. They also supported Evans for re-election to Congress and endorsed candidates for seats in the state legislature. Democrats in the community, remembering their losses in 1855, fought hard. The *Texas Republican* endorsed Hardin R. Runnels against Houston and John H. Reagan to unseat Evans. A local meeting chose the fiery L. T. Wigfall as their candidate for state senator and two popular planters, Eli T. Craig and William F. Baldwin, along with a rising young lawyer, Pendleton Murrah, as nominees for the lower house. And they were plainly worried. William R. D. Ward, a Democratic party leader in Marshall, informed John H. Reagan of their efforts in June, 1857. "But to tell you the truth," he wrote,

> old Sam and Lem have a stronger hold upon the people of this county than did Fillmore in the last election, and if we succeed in beating them we yet have to manufacture the strength to do it with for you know this is a Lem county and old Sam is the strongest man in the state in the opposition.

The results were close in August, 1857, but the Democrats managed to defeat the Opposition in every contest. Runnels defeated Houston 601 to 556; Reagan bested Evans 598 to 558; and the state legislative races were decided in favor of the Democrats by similar margins.[30]

[29] Marshall *Texas Republican*, August 4, 11, 18, 1855, November 8, 1856 (quotation); Richardson, Wallace, and Anderson, *Texas,* 145; Burnham, *Presidential Ballots,* 784-785.

[30] Llerena Friend, *Sam Houston, The Great Designer* (Austin, 1954), 226-230, 238-245, 248-250; Marshall *Texas Republican*, June 6, 20, August 15, 1857; Procter, *Not Without Honor*, 95-97; William R. D. Ward to John H. Reagan, June 3, 1857 (quotation), John H. Reagan Papers, Archives, Barker Texas History Collection, University of Texas at Austin.

Houston returned to the political arena in 1859, campaigning once more for the governorship against Runnels. Know-Nothingism was largely dead so the Opposition group now identified themselves as Houston independents. The *Harrison Flag,* the Know-Nothing paper, endorsed Houston, and L. D. Evans defended him by charging the regular Democrats with disunionism. The *Texas Republican* furiously denounced Houston and said that Edward Clark, his running mate from Harrison County, was "politically demoralized and disgraced." In the meantime, Congressman John H. Reagan who had defeated Evans in 1857 confused the issue by speaking against southern extremist proposals such as reopening the African slave trade, thereby infuriating many southern Democrats. William B. Ochiltree, the old Whig unionist, perhaps seeing an opening for political gain, became the candidate of the ultra-southerners against Reagan. The community's Democratic Party divided badly over the congressional race. Levin Perry described the situation to his son in June: "The split in the ranks you will at once perceive is of no ordinary character when I tell you Col. Ward, Genl. Greer, Maj. Blanche, Col. Long, Dr. Swanson, Dr. Haywood, etc. etc. are open mouthed against Reagan."[31]

Houston, who won statewide, carried Harrison County over Runnels by a margin of 560 to 495 while Clark, who also won across the state, narrowly lost to Francis Lubbock, 499 to 487, in the county. Ochiltree defeated Reagan by a huge margin, 604 to 267; apparently Opposition voters remained loyal to him while southern Democrats rejected Reagan. Of the nine candidates for the state house of representatives, two of the three winners, George W. Whitmore and Eli H. Baxter, were identified with the Opposition. The other victorious candidate, Eli T. Craig, was a Democrat. Mixed results were not enough for Editor Loughery of the *Texas Republican.* The vote for Houston and others, he wrote, proved that all "love of country" and "patri-

[31] Marshall *Texas Republican*, July 16, 30 (first quotation), 1859; *Harrison Flag*, June 27, 1859; Procter, *Not Without Honor*, 107-112; Levin Perry to Theophilus Perry, June 20, 1859 (second quotation), Person Family Papers.

otism'' was dead in the ''States Rights, Southern Rights county of Harrison.''[32]

Opposition voters had one more opportunity to demonstrate their strength in the community before the critical election of 1860. A special election had to be held on December 31, 1859, to fill the state senate seat left vacant when the legislature elected Louis T. Wigfall to the United States Senate. E. A. Blanch won the contest with 292 votes; defeating Josiah Marshall, 261 votes; J. M. Morphis, 57; Charles C. Mills, 24; and A. D. Burress, 3. The *Texas Republican* and the *Flag* both pointed out that all of the candidates except Blanche had voted with the Opposition at times. Loughery believed that the Democrats owed their victory primarily to the splitting of the vote between Marshall and Morphis.[33]

The voting strength of the Opposition as Know-Nothings and as Houston Independents may be clearly established then, but the question remains—did this vote represent genuine ideological diversity within the community? The evidence is very mixed. Harrison's Democrats taunted the Know-Nothings for belonging to a party without principles and insisted that the whole movement was an attempt to gain office by ''artifice.'' On the other hand, they charged the Opposition with being inimical to the interests of the South. Fillmore was called an abolitionist in 1856, and the *Republican* regularly decried the ''federal'' and ''interventionist'' doctrines of the Know-Nothings. Houston was constantly under attack as a traitor to his state and section. The Democrats are poor witnesses against the Opposition, however, since they had a natural tendency to distort for partisan purposes. Moreover, the Know-Nothings themselves were capable of winning elections in the community; a fact that probably led them to handle the issues as matters of political expediency at times. For example, in 1856, the *Flag* attempted to

[32]*Harrison Flag*, August 5, 1859; Marshall *Texas Republican*, August 6 (quotation), 20, 1859; Friend, *Sam Houston*, 325.

[33]King, *Louis T. Wigfall*, 70-76; Marshall *Texas Republican*, December 24, 1859, January 7, 1860; *Harrison Flag*, January 6, 1860.

raise doubts concerning James Buchanan's views on slavery. Overall, however, when compared to the Democrats, the Know-Nothings did offer a discernibly different approach on the important issues. They were not opponents of slavery; instead they insisted that the institution must have all its rights including the opportunity to expand into new territories. But they generally opposed agitation of the issue in the South or the North and rarely attempted to use it for partisan purposes. Where the permanency of the Union was concerned, the Know-Nothings were more conservative than the Democrats. They were not as adamant about their unionism as the Whigs had been, they attempted to use the issue politically at times by painting the Democrats as disunionists, and there was no proof that under pressure some might not change to a more ultra-southern stance. Nevertheless, the Opposition's unionism appears genuine. They voted for Sam Houston after he had made himself unacceptable to many Democrats by opposing the Kansas-Nebraska Act and become famed as a unionist. And they voted for L. D. Evans whose anti-secession sentiments were well-known. In effect, then, through the mid-1850s, the Opposition backed up their unionist rhetoric by voting for conservative candidates.[34]

Political prospects were frightening in Harrison County as the election of 1860 approached. The rapidly growing Republican Party had a chance to win control of the national government without the aid of a single southern vote. In that event the

[34]For examples of Democratic attacks on the Know-Nothings, see Marshall *Texas Republican*, August 4 (first quotation), 11 (second and third quotations), 1855; June 7, July 19, October 18, 1856, August 6, 1857. For attacks on Houston, see Friend, *Sam Houston*, 221-269. For the *Flag's* attack on Buchanan, see Marshall *Texas Republican*, July 19, September 13, 1856. For the Know-Nothings' official stance on issues, see Winkler (ed.), *Platforms of Political Parties*, 68-71. Josiah Marshall, a Know-Nothing spokesman, was reported in 1856 to have said that the Union was more important than slavery and that non-slaveholders would not fight for slavery anyhow. Marshall *Texas Republican*, November 8, 1856. Wooster, "Analysis of Texas Know-Nothings," 417-419, and Frank Smyrl, "Unionism in Texas, 1856-1861," *Southwestern Historical Quarterly*, LXVIII (Oct., 1964), 172-175, 192-195, agree that Know-Nothingism was an expression of unionism in the mid-1850s. They also conclude that there was little or no correlation between Know-Nothing unionism and opposition to secession in 1861. This matter is dealt with below.

pressures for disunion might be irresistible. Democrats insisted that the South would be safe only if the government remained in the hands of their party. The Opposition, on the other hand, began to talk as early as March, 1860, of the need for a "conservative Union party" to support a moderate unionist such as John J. Crittenden of Kentucky, John Bell of Tennessee, or Sam Houston. There was an organizational meeting of the newly forming Constitutional Union Party in Marshall on April 14, and six delegates including the old-line Opposition leaders, James F. Taylor, George W. Whitmore, and N. V. Board, were sent to a regional meeting in Tyler. In May, the national Constitutional Union Party convention nominated John Bell and Edward Everett. Harrison County's Opposition held a ratification meeting on July 7 chaired by Nathan Smith. William Woodson, a real "union shrieker," sneered the *Republican,* and state representative Eli H. Baxter spoke. The *Flag* made a masthead endorsement of Bell and Everett, and the Opposition prepared for an uphill fight.[35]

In the meantime, the Democratic Party had split. The northern wing supported Stephen A. Douglas of Illinois; his nomination, the *Texas Republican* warned, would be regarded in the South as "the first step to a final surrender to the demands of Black Republicanism." Texas Democratic delegates to their convention in Charleston, South Carolina, including General Elkanah Greer of Harrison County, walked out rather than accept a platform expressing Douglas's views. The community's Democrats approved this walk out and resolved "that the time for compromising and temporising on the question of slavery has passed." A second Democratic convention in Baltimore resulted in the nomination of Douglas by the northern wing of the party. Southern bolters named John C. Breckinridge of Kentucky as their candidate on a largely sectional platform. Harrison County's Democrats enthusiastically endorsed Breckinridge and in effect made him the only "right" choice for southerners. Lincoln

[35] *Harrison Flag*, March 23 (first quotation), April 20, July 6, 13, 1860; Marshall *Texas Republican*, April 21, July 14 (second quotation), 1860.

was out of the question, they said, Douglas was hopelessly northern, and Bell could not protect the South. Democrats did not want disunion, according to Robert W. Loughery, but they certainly could not tolerate the "submissionist" stance of the Opposition. "The South will fight," said the *Texas Republican,* "and ought to fight, rather than purchase peace at the price of honor."[36]

In attempting to counter this Democratic challenge, the Opposition did not attack slavery, and they gave no indication that violations of "southern rights" were to be accepted. Most of their campaign consisted simply of appeals to save the Union and to consider the costs of the alternative. The Constitutional Union Party's declaration of principles read simply: "The Constitution of our Country, the Union of the States, and the Enforcement of the Laws." As the campaign developed, George W. Whitmore of Harrison County served as an alternate elector for the first congressional district, and Gil McKay acted as a subelector for the community. In September, Josiah Marshall, an old Opposition spokesman serving as interim editor of the *Flag,* blamed the approaching crisis on "vandal hordes" in the North and "Fiery dragons" in the South and warned that the burdens of conflict would fall on "the great conservative *mass*" who constituted a majority in both sections. "These are the parties," he said, "to fight all, pay all, and be ruined." The *Texas Republican* scorned this Opposition campaign as "Union shrieking."[37]

In September, 1860, under the leadership of L. D. Evans, the Opposition in East Texas tried a new tactic. They sought to form a fusionist ticket composed of Bell and Douglas forces.

[36] Marshall *Texas Republican*, April 21 (first quotation), June 2 (second quotation), July 7, 28, September 8, 15 (third quotation), 1860. Douglas was unacceptable to southern Democrats in 1860 because he had opposed admitting Kansas to the Union as a slave state under the Lecompton Constitution and because he has announced the Freeport Doctrine explaining how a territorial legislature could refuse to protect slavery and thus circumvent the Supreme Court's Dred Scott decision (1857) that the institution had to be permitted in all territories of the United States. See Gerald M. Capers, *Stephen A. Douglas: Defender of the Union* (Boston, 1959), 160-169, 186-187.

[37] *Harrison Flag*, September 1 (first quotation), 8 (second-fifth quotations), 1860. Josiah Marshall replaced John W. Barrett as editor on September 8 due to the latter's ill health. Marshall *Texas Republican*, September 15, 1860 (sixth quotation).

This move created confusion because it involved altering the Constitutional Union electoral ticket, thus creating charges of inconsistency for Opposition spokesmen who had previously condemned Douglas. It also alienated some who could not accept the northern Democratic nominee. Gil McKay, for example, reigned as sub-elector for the county when he could no longer support a straight Bell-Everett ticket. Nevertheless, fusion was accomplished, and the *Flag* explained it to the community's voters as follows: "This is a union for the sake of the Union, and for it, and for it alone, we shall battle 'till November." If the ticket won, they meant to cast their votes for Bell, Douglas, or even Breckinridge if necessary to defeat Lincoln.[38]

For most of the campaign of 1860, then, the Opposition in Harrison County focused on the future of the Union. They attacked Breckinridge as a disunionist, but apparently they could have accepted Bell, Douglas, or even Breckinridge as the winner. Little was said about what they would do if Lincoln won. The *Texas Republican* called them "submissionists," but only a few — including Josiah Marshall, John W. Barrett (publisher of the *Flag*), and state representative George W. Whitmore — said publicly that the simple fact of Lincoln's election would be no cause for resistance by the South, Perhaps many agreed with Gil McKay, the resigning Bell-Everett sun-elector: "But whatever the result may be, I am with the South. Whatever the South will say, I will do; and wherever the South will go I will follow, but to submission."[39] Soon, as the Opposition feared, going with the South meant leaving the Union.

As expected, Breckinridge carrried Harrison County with 681 votes as opposed to 388 (36.3%) for the Bell-Douglas fusion ticket.[40] This was a respectable Opposition vote under the circumstances. But they had run out of time. By mid-November, 1860, the community knew that Abraham Lincoln, candidate of

[38] Marshall *Texas Republican*, September 15, 29, 1860; *Harrison Flag*, September 22 (quotation), October 13, 20, 1860.

[39] *Harrison Flag*, September 15, October 13 (quotation), 20, November 10, 1860; Marshall *Texas Republican*, September 29, November 3, 1860.

[40] Burnham, *Presidential Ballots*, 784-785.

the hated "Black Republicans," would be the next president. The majority's reaction was swift and extreme. They moved to leave the Union.

Before considering secession in Harrison County, we may conclude this examination of politics during the 1850s by once more looking for an explanation of the differences between the Democratic majority and the Opposition on major sectional issues. Table 16 reveals that, as in 1850, leaders of both groups were somewhat more similar to each other than to the average head of household in the community. Compared to the population in general they were slightly older, more likely to be natives of the upper South, less likely to have farming as a primary occupation, and far wealthier. Virtually every leader was a slaveholder. As in 1850, the most notable difference involved place of birth. Nearly three-fourths of the Opposition leaders were natives of the upper South. Given the many similarities in socioeconomic status and the general homogeneity of the community, it seems unlikely that differences associated with birthplace could account for an Opposition culture. On the other hand, in light of the vote by Virginia, Tennessee, and Kentucky for the Constitutional Union Party ticket in 1860, it seems reasonable that Texans native to these and the other border states would also be less willing than deep southerners to agitate the slavery question and break up the Union.[41]

In summary, there was significant political conflict in antebellum Harrison County. Throughout the 1850s one-third to one-half of the voting population consistently supported candidates who emphasized calming down the slavery question and preserving the Union. There were, however, limits to dissent. Opposition spokesmen never seriously attacked slavery, and, as we will see, with a few notable exceptions they did not oppose

[41] The names of leaders in the late 1850s and early 1860s were taken from the Marshall *Texas Republican* and the *Harrison Flag*. Table 16 is based on data derived from the Eighth Census, 1860, Schedules 1, 2, and 4. Wooster, *Politicians, Planters, and Plain Folk*, 52-54, found comparable similarities among legislators elected by the Opposition and by the Democrats in the upper South during the late 1850s.

TABLE 16

Economic and Demographic Characteristics of Opposition Leaders, Democratic Leaders, and the General Population, 1860

Characteristic	Opposition	Democrats	General Population
Number in Sample	19	24	500
Mean Age	45.7	42.9	40.5
Birthplace			
Upper South	70.6%	50.0%	43.4%
Lower South	23.5	41.6	47.0
Free States	5.9	4.2	3.6
Foreign Born	0.0	4.2	5.4
Unknown	0.0	0.0	.6
Occupation			
Farmer	58.8%	41.7%	72.8%
Merchant	5.9	4.2	3.8
Professional	23.5	50.0	6.6
Other	11.8	4.2	16.8
Average Value of Real Property	$9,352	$10,301	$3,189
Average Value of Personal Property	$24,827	$37,918	$9,585
Percentage of Slaveholders	100.0	95.8	60.8
Mean Number of Slaves per Slaveholder	22.9	24.7	13.7
Number of Farmers with Land	12	12	326
Mean Number of Improved Acres per Farmer	399.1	648.0	184.2
Mean Number Bales of Cotton per Farmer	61.8	138.9	32.4

secession once it was virtually an accomplished fact after the election of 1860.

The contention that the antebellum Opposition represented a genuine and significant division of opinion in the community would be strengthened by the existence of an identifiable Opposition culture. It does not appear, however, that leaders of the Democratic majority and the Opposition during the 1850s divided according to any demographic, socioeconomic, or ethnocultural characteristics. Antebellum Harrison County was an extremely homogeneous society, and leaders of both groups were probably more similar to each other than to the population as a whole. They were virtually all wealthier than average and slaveholders. There was a tendency for Opposition leaders to be natives of the upper South, but this was not marked enough or a vital enough factor that it could be considered a crucial difference. It would appear that the explanation of political differences in so homogeneous a society was a highly individual matter. A man may have been conservative on slavery agitation and on preservation of the Union due to the influence of his family, because Henry Clay was his hero, or because of the preaching of a particular minister. Real differences of opinion were present in the community, but it would be difficult to predict the views of any individual on the basis of his age, birthplace, occupation, wealthholding, or slaveholding.[42]

Ultimately then, there was a southern consensus in the political life of antebellum Harrison County. Leadership came from men with essentially the same backgrounds and economic interests. Slavery and "southern rights" were to be defended at

[42] There is a relatively large body of historical literature on the subject of socioeconomic differences among leaders of antebellum political parties. Many of these works are cited in Wooster, *Politicians, Planters, and Plain Folk*, 45-54. There is argument over detail, of course, but most, including Wooster, tend to agree that party affiliation cannot be predicted on the basis of economic, social, or demographic characteristics. In an important recent study, for example, Burton W. Folsom II found that "no clear socioeconomic differences" separated Whigs and Democrats in antebellum Davidson County, Tennessee. Folsom, "The Politics of Elites: Prominence and Party in Davidson County, Tennessee, 1835-1861," *Journal of Southern History*, XXXIX (Aug., 1973), 359-378 (quotation on p. 376).

all costs. The Opposition's conservatism was meaningful, however. It represented conflict within consensus; a type of partisan contest not unlike that which many historians believe to be characteristic of the United States as a whole.[43]

[43] For a summary of how American historians have handled the questions of conflict within consensus, see Bernard Sternsher, *Consensus, Conflict, and American Historians* (Bloomington, Ind., 1975). Party politics is discussed in chapter 4 and summarized on pages 206-207.

PART TWO

Secession and Civil War

7

The Secession Crisis: 1860–1861

ABRAHAM LINCOLN'S victory in November, 1860, created an immediate crisis in Harrison County. A majority of county voters vowed not to acquiesce in the election of a ''Black Republican'' and began a secession movement that quickly gained momentum and overwhelmed the community by the end of February, 1861. The secession winter is best understood by first examining the events of disunion and then attempting to analyze and explain the decision to secede.

Secession in Harrison County was truly a grass-roots movement in that local leaders took the initiative with no prompting from individuals or groups outside the community. The first step was a public meeting held in Marshall on Friday, November

16. Chairman James M. Curtis, the town's mayor, appointed a resolutions committee that included three current or former Democratic state legislators, Pendleton Murrah, M. J. Hall, and J. M. Clough; County Judge George Lane; the former Whig leader turned ultra-southerner, William B. Ochiltree; and two men, Gil McKay and Eli H. Baxter, who had announced as Constitutional Union Party electors during the recent election. The meeting adopted a resolution vowing no submission to Lincoln. The Republican leader threatens slavery, it said, and his election means a loss of the South's equality in the Union. Other resolutions called for a state convention to consider disunion and a second Harrison County meeting to be held on Saturday, November 24. Ochiltree spoke of resisting federal tyranny as the Lone Star flag was raised. In the meantime, John W. Barrett of the *Harrison Flag* asked the community to remember that Lincoln was a conservative man who did not propose to attack slavery where it existed. Let us wait for an overt act by the Republican administration, he argued, before we commit an overt act ourselves.[1]

The majority, however, were not in a waiting mood. "Harrison County Speaks," read the *Texas Republican's* front page headline on December 1. According to Editor Loughery, the gathering on November 24 was "The Largest and Most Imposing Meeting Ever Convened in the County." John B. Webster, a large planter from northeast of Marshall, presided and delivered the "keynote" speech. Webster, said the *Republican,* is "a gentleman who has never occupied a prominent position as a politician, and who, on this occasion, was selected on account of his moral worth, his prudence, and known conservatism." He proved to be an excellent choice from Loughery's point of view.[2]

Webster's speech was anything but conservative. He insisted that the South was being denied equal rights under the Constitution, that northern fanaticism threatened the South and

[1] Marshall *Texas Republican*, November 24, 1860; *Harrison Flag*, November 10, 24, 1860.

[2] Marshall *Texas Republican*, December 1, 1860.

the Union, and that to accept Lincoln's professions of conservatism would be "fatal and suicidal." Our government has failed, Webster said. Speaking of the South's situation, he continued:

> I have given it my solemn and most serious thought. I am not ashamed to say it — I profess to be a christian — I have made it a subject of prayerful consideration; and before God, and with a full sense of the responsibility encountered, I say the South should withdraw from the Union!

The *Texas Republican* reported that this statement drew applause from those listening.[3]

Webster was realistic enough to expect war as a result of secession; a war he did not welcome.

> I have a wife and five children. My principles, my feelings and inclinations are all for peace; the pride, pomp and circumstance of war have no attraction for me. I deprecate war; but bad as war is, with its long train of evils, there is something worse; and the people who will not rise in defense of their rights and their honor, will soon be fit for servitude and for chains.

Some may smile at the irony of a slaveholder referring to the horrors of servitude, but Webster was in good company. Less than one hundred years before, many American revolutionaries had protested that Great Britain was seeking to reduce them to slavery. Editor Loughery, no doubt accidentally, touched on the same note when he said of Webster's speech: "It takes us back to the days of the revolution, when men forgot everything in their patriotic devotion to their country."[4]

Seven other speakers, including William T. Scott, Gil McKay, and Eli H. Baxter, followed Webster. Those assembled then adopted resolutions endorsing the concept of state sovereignty, condemning Lincoln as a dangerous radical, and calling

[3]Ibid.

[4]Ibid. The tendency of slaveholders to equate political oppression with slavery (and the contradictions this created within their own society) at the time of the American Revolution is discussed in many places. See, for example, Bernard Bailyn, *The Ideological Origins of the American Revolution* (Cambridge, Mass., 1967), 232, 246, and Donald L. Robinson, *Slavery in the Structure of American Politics, 1765-1820* (New York, 1971), 54-97.

for yet another local meeting on December 1 to elect delegates to a state convention. Loughery, who had previously voiced the hope that "every reference to past party divisions will be laid aside and that we will assemble as a band of brothers," was delighted with the community's unity against "Black Republican" rule.[5]

By late November, 1860, Harrison County was not alone in calling for a state convention to consider disunion; mass meetings were making similar demands in one community after another across Texas. The "anti-submissionists," however, collided head on with the formidable figure of Governor Sam Houston who adopted a wait-and-see position, refusing to convene a special session of the state legislature or call a convention until Lincoln took some unconstitutional action against Texas. "Old Sam" hoped for public support to calm the crisis atmosphere and avoid precipitant action.[6] He would find little in Harrison County, in spite of the strong record of Opposition groups there during the 1850s.

The *Texas Republican,* as noted above, constantly emphasized unity in the community and denounced the submissionists who "contend that Lincoln's election furnishes no cause for secession." "It is gratifying to *know,*" Loughery wrote on December 1, "that they form but a small minority of this county, and, as we believe, but a meager squad in the state of Texas." In the same issue, a correspondent who signed himself "Inquirer" rejoiced that the adherents of John C. Calhoun and Henry Clay had finally joined hands to defend the South. Loughery and "Inquirer" were essentially correct; the community was unified as never before. Nevertheless, there were those who dissented. Lemuel D. Evans eventually left Texas rather than accept disunion. John W. Barrett of the *Flag* opposed secession in editorial after editorial through November and December. Breaking up the United States, he said, is "the most momentous political decision that has ever demanded the attention of mankind."

[5]Marshall *Texas Republican*, November 24 (quotation), December 1, 1860.
[6]Friend, *Sam Houston*, 330-332.

And he invoked the old Opposition warning that secession was revolutionary rather than constitutional in nature. "Haste, haste has always been the watchword of revolution," he told his readers. His position was like Governor Houston's — wait-and-see. State Representative George W. Whitmore dissented most spectacularly. Whitmore, a long-time Opposition leader, was accused first of saying that he would fight against the South in the event of secession. He denied that charge in a letter to the *Texas Republican* on November 24, but argued in the same communication that Lincoln's election in itself was no reason for secession. Loughery, of course, disagreed, and as we will see, a bitter dispute followed.[7]

The December 1 meeting in Marshall was chaired by Rene Fitzpatrick, another large planter who was not usually active politically. John B. Webster was ill. This gathering nominated William T. Scott, William P. Hill, Gil McKay, and Alexander Pope as delegates to the hoped-for state convention; the election to take place on December 24. Scott was the wealthiest planter-businessman-politician in the community; the other three were lawyers. Hill soon declined to serve due to professional commitments and was replaced by William B. Ochiltree. This meeting also authorized formation of a "batallion" of "Minute Men" in Harrison County and called on George W. Whitmore to resign if Governor Houston called the legislature into session. Whitmore's views, the resolution said, are better suited to a northern than to a southern constituency.[8]

Whitmore's reply on December 4, published in the *Republican* on December 8, should have earned respect for the courage of his convictions, even among those who disagreed. The tone, however, was angrily sarcastic. "I was not aware," he wrote, "that my opinions were of so much importance as to occupy the attention of such an august body of men, assembled for so momentous a work as that of the destruction of one of the best, freest, and happiest governments that was ever framed, by the

[7] Marshall *Texas Republican*, November 24, December 1 (first and second quotations), *Harrison Flag*, December 15, 1860 (third and fourth quotations).

[8] Marshall *Texas Republican*, December 8, 1860.

combined wisdom of men." I have lived this long, Whitmore wrote, without being "dictated to by any self constituted caucus, or *would-be* political leaders," and I do not intend to change. The voters who put him in the legislature, he said, were the only ones who would convince him to leave.[9]

The secession movement steadily gained strength during the last month of 1860. When it became apparent that Governor Houston would not call the legislature into special session, secessionist leaders in Austin issued a call on December 3 for a state convention to meet on January 28, 1861. "Old Sam," his hand forced and still hoping to forestall drastic action, countered on December 17 by calling the legislature into session for January 21. Harrison County leaders had no difficulty in complying with the request from the Austin secessionists; their delegates to the convention were already nominated. When the vote was taken on Christmas Eve, the four unopposed nominees received 534 votes. Loughery declared that Opposition candidates favoring the Union would not have received 75 votes.[10]

Word of South Carolina's secession reached Marshall on Saturday, December 29, touching off an enthusiastic celebration. A public meeting passed resolutions of concurrence. Marshall was illuminated that night, and the firing of anvils could be heard in Jefferson sixteen miles to the north. Numerous speakers endorsed secession including the Reverend E. A. Wagner, a recent arrival from South Carolina, who pointed out that his state had been right about sectional issues for thirty years. The South must, Wagner said, put aside all except questions of right, and slavery is right. "God sanctions it . . ." Clearly, the Opposition's position was untenable in Harrison County. John W. Barrett, ill and confined to his room, suspended publication of the *Flag* on January 12.[11] George W. Whitmore, however, headed for Austin and the special legislative session on January 21.

[9] Ibid.

[10] Ernest Wallace and David M. Vigness (eds.), *Documents of Texas History* (Austin, 1963), 194; Friend, *Sam Houston*, 333; Marshall *Texas Republican*, December 29, 1860.

[11] Marshall *Texas Republican*, January 5, 1861 (quotaton); *Harrison Flag*, January 5, 12, 1861.

Governor Houston asked the legislature to avoid precipitant action and to look instead to a general southern convention aimed at a redress of grievances. The secessionists, now firmly in control, gave no heed and voted to validate the convention scheduled to meet on the 28th. The only restriction was that actions of the convention were to be submitted to the voters for ratification. Once the convention assembled, dissolution of the Union took only a few days. An ordinance of secession was adopted on February 1 by a vote of 166 to 8 with the ratification election scheduled for the 23rd of the month. Disunion, once approved, would become effective on March 2, 1861.[12]

Meanwhile, the excitement generated by crisis continued in Harrison County. On January 24, citizens of Marshall awoke to find an effigy of Abraham Lincoln hanged at the courthouse square. Loughery contended that he did not like such things hanging about. "If we had the original we would not hang him longer than half an hour," he wrote. The community's legislators and delegates to the state convention kept Loughery and his readers informed of developments in Austin. All were satisfactory except for the conduct of Representative Whitmore who opposed secession and the convention. Adding insult to injury from the disunionists' point of view, Whitmore remained in Austin after the special legislative session and signed the "Address to the People of the State" which argued that slaveholders would rule the confederate States of America, then in the process of formation, in ways that were oppressive to nonslaveholders. Only a "Black Republican" would sign such a document, the *Texas Republican* fumed. A mass meeting in Marshall, calling Whitmore's conduct "repugnant," "incendiary," and "treacherous," demanded his resignation. It was decided to have voters express their opinions on the removal of Whitmore on the 23rd when they ratified disunion.[13]

On February 23, 1861, Harrison County voted approval of

[12]Seymour V. Connor, *Texas: A History* (New York, 1971), 192-194; Friend, *Sam Houston*, 336-337.

[13]Marshall *Texas Republican*, January 26 (first quotation), February 9, 23 (third, fourth, and fifth quotations), March 2 (second quotation), 1861.

secession by a margin of 866 to 44. George Whitmore was nearly as unpopular as disunion was popular. The vote was 706 to 46 in favor of his resignation. He ignored this expression of opinion, however, and returned to Austin when the legislature met in mid-March. "In the history of individual political profligancy and moral obtuseness," said the *Texas Republican,* "we have never known a case equal to it." Meanwhile, the secession convention reassembled and took the steps necessary to have Texas formally join the Confederate States of America. Governor Houston refused to swear allegiance to the Confederacy and was forced from office. Back in Marshall, Robert W. Loughery grudgingly praised Houston for the way he met his political death.

> How strikingly does this contrast with our misrepresentative, George Washington Whitmore! He in the agony of a suicidal death, clings to a dishonored life only that he may seize with the spasmodic energy of the miser's grasp his per diem. Judas Iscariot, we believe, repenting the betrayal of our savior, cast from him the thirty pieces of silver; so will not G. W. Whitmore, but we predict will invest it in a farm in Collin or Grayson.

Whitmore apparently dealt with the oath of allegiance to the Confederacy by going through the forms but not repeating the oath as it was read to him. Incidentally, N. V. Board, another old-line Opposition leader in the community, resigned his position on the commissioners court rather than take the oath.[14]

Harrison County's overwhelming approval of secession surprised no one and, at first glance, appears so one-sided as to offer nothing to analyze. The Opposition vote that had supported the Whigs, Know-Nothings, and Constitutional Unionists largely disappeared in 1861. Most strikingly, the Marshall precinct that had cast 189 votes for the Fusionist ticket (against 312 for Breckinridge) in 1860, voted 444 to 0 for secession. Only 4.8% of the participating voters rejected disunion, and Loughery of the *Texas Republican* insisted that most of the 44 individ-

[14]Ibid., March 2, 16 (first quotation), April 13 (second quotation), May 18, 1861; Friend, *Sam Houston*, 338-339.

uals who had opposed secession were simply "uninformed."[15] Thus, with a few notable exceptions such as Whitmore and Board, the community appears to have closed ranks in favor of secession.

A closer look at the vote, however, suggests that at least a few reservations are in order concerning the county's enthusiasm for disunion. In the first place, there were 159 fewer votes cast in the secession contest (910) than in the election of 1860 (1,069). Voter turnout may have been lighter because the result was certain in 1861. But on the other hand, there may have been a good many individuals who were unwilling to vote against secession and yet could not actively support it either. Secondly, 39 of the 44 negative votes were cast in two of the county's eleven voting precincts, a situation indicating that for some reason neighbors in these areas encouraged each other to stand against the tide of disunionism.[16]

A precinct-by-precinct comparison of the vote on secession with returns in the 1860 presidential election also raises doubts concerning the total disappearance of the old Opposition. Official returns printed in the *Texas Republican* in November, 1860, showed two precincts, Craig's and Craver's Mill, returning majorities of 24 to 16 and 23 to 15 respectively for the Fusionist ticket. Two other precincts, Marshall and Coppedge's Store, gave Breckinridge a majority, 312 and 189 and 58 to 35 respectively, but at the same time gave the Fusionist ticket a larger proportion of the vote than it received countywide. In February, 1861, Marshall, as noted above, changed dramatically and gave unanimous support to secession, and no official returns were ever reported for the Craver's Mill precinct. However, Craig's box favored disunion by a margin of only 14 to 11, and Coppedge's Store approved by a 37 to 28 vote. These two precincts appear to have been consistently conservative. Perhaps Craver's Mill would have been also had its returns been reported in 1861.[17]

[15] Marshall *Texas Republican*, November 10, 1860, March 2, 1861.

[16] Ibid., March 2, 1861; Burnham, *Presidential Ballots*, 784-785.

[17] Precinct-by-precinct returns for 1860 are in Marshall *Texas Republican*, November 10, 1860. Those for 1861 are in Ibid., March 2, 1861. Identification of the

Interestingly too, just as there were no major economic-social differences between Democratic and Opposition leaders during the 1850s, there was no consistent pattern of contrast between these two precincts and the rest of the community. Coppedge's Store was in the far northwestern part of the county in an area settled primarily by nonslaveholding farmers. Only about 25% of the households there owned slaves, and bondsmen constituted approximately one-quarter of the population. Perhaps in this precinct Harrison County had a minor example of the classic division between slaveholders and nonslaveholders over secession. Loughery no doubt had this area in mind when he wrote: "There is a portion of the county cut off from mail facilities, and where the people are uninformed of the real condition of the country, which will account for there being as many as 44 against secession." But the situation in Craig's precinct located south of Marshall was entirely different. A majority of the households there held slaves, and bondsmen constituted nearly 66% of the population. The precinct's election judge and namesake, Eli T. Craig, was a large planter. The consistent conservatism of this area cannot be explained by nonslaveholding. Perhaps it was a matter of the personal influence of unionists such as N. V. Board who lived in Craig's precinct.[18]

In summary, Harrison County strongly endorsed secession, but the community was somewhat less united than the official returns indicated or than the *Texas Republican* wanted to believe. Most individuals who disagreed with disunion in February, 1861, probably did so not because they opposed slavery or had other economic-social differences with the majority. Instead they apparently felt that the action was too extreme for the situation. This is suggested by the fact that the few negative votes

various precincts was done with the aid of lists of election judges published in the *Texas Republican* on October 6, 1860, and December 1, 1860. The judges were identified in the United States census of 1860 where election precincts coincided with census "beats." They were then located geographically in the county by determining the original grantees of their land from the tax rolls and finding those original grantees on the General Land Office map of Harrison County. Thus, it was possible to identify each precinct and characterize it in terms of total population, slaveholding, etc.

[18] Ibid. The quotation is from the *Texas Republican*, March 2, 1861.

cast were in areas that had also been inclined to support a conservative approach in 1860.

Harrison County thus committed itself in 1861 to disunion and probable war. In the broadest sense, the community's purpose was essentially conservative, to preserve existing institutions and the "southern way of life." Certainly there was no desire to win new freedoms or to change the existing economic, social, and political structure. At the same time, however, secession was a revolutionary step aimed at escaping the authority of the United States. Harrison County, like other communities in the Confederacy, was fighting for independence and the creation of a new nation. In short, the events of 1860-1865 constituted a conservative revolution in the community; one that would perhaps bring more change in failure than it would in success.

As befits a conservative revolution, leadership in the movement for secession in Harrison County came from those who had a great deal to preserve. It was entirely proper that a large planter, John B. Webster, presided over the most important local secession meeting and that William T. Scott served in the state convention. These leaders were bolstered by the constitutional theories of John C. Calhoun emphasizing state sovereignty and secession as a legitimate remedy for the South's problems as a minority section of the nation. Also, they were alarmed at the steadily rising economic and political power of the North. But constitutional theories and jealousy of northern strength did not create secession. Instead, large planters led, and slavery stood at the heart of the matter.[19]

[19]The interpretation of secession presented here is based primarily on the idea that planters dominated the society and politics of Harrison County and sought disunion to protect their interests from external threats. This view of the antebellum South is associated in recent historiography with the work of Eugene D. Genovese. See his *The World the Slaveholders Made: Two Essays in Interpretation* (New York, 1971). Wright, *Political Economy of the Cotton South*, 40-41, has questioned the nature of this "domination." And several other recent studies, including Michael P. Johnson, *Toward a Patriarchal Republic: The Secession of Georgia* (Baton Rouge, 1977), and J. Mills Thornton III, *Politics and Power in a Slave Society: Alabama, 1800-1860* (Baton Rouge, 1978), have found the fears of the planter class concerning the loyalty of nonslaveholders and the fears of yeomen concerning a loss of freedom to be at the heart of secession. In a

Virtually every issue between the South and the North stemmed from or related importantly to the "Peculiar Institution." Eventually many southerners would argue, as did Khleber M. Van Zandt of Harrison County in his autobiography:

> I was never an advocate of slavery, and slavery was not the direct cause of the War. War came because the North was getting too strong. The northern states imposed on the South in different matters. . . . It was the invasion by the North that fired the South.

Secession, however, was the step that led to war, and prior to secession there were few attempts in Harrison County to disguise the key issue. The community regarded slavery as an essential economic and social institution. It provided the labor necessary to the agricultural economy and, as slaveholders saw it, the means to control an inferior race incapable of existing on the basis of equality with whites. Any attack had to be resisted, even to the point of revolution.[20]

Most of Harrison County's slaveholders had grown up concurrently with the development of radical abolitionism in the North. Beginning with the appearance of William Lloyd Garrison's *Liberator* in 1831, radical abolitionists demanded that slavery be destroyed everywhere in the United States by any means possible. The abolitionists, their attack based almost entirely on moral grounds, gave slaveholders no opportunity to defend their institution on the basis of economic necessity or the requirements of social control. When radicals said that slavery was a monstrous evil, defenders in areas such as Harrison County could only reply that it was a positive good, a moral and social blessing. The more they were attacked, the more bitterly defensive they became. By 1859, when John Brown's raid on Harper's

single community as homogeneous in population as Harrison County and where slaveholding was so widespread, however, there appears to have been little or no conflict of class or economic interest. Although it is true that an area of the county with relatively few slaves cast most of the votes against secession, planters dominated without compulsion and gave no evidence that fears of who would rule locally had anything to do with secession.

[20] Van Zandt, *Force Without Fanfare*, 79 (quotation); Marshall *Texas Republican*, August 3, 1849, December 3, 1858.

Ferry received the public blessing of northern radicals such as Wendell Phillips, emotions in the community were overflowing. A mass meeting on November 26 expressed shock "at the madness and blind fanaticism of the Abolitionists of the North" and declared slavery to be an institution "handed down from God to man to accomplish some great end on earth." There is, the resolutions continued, "no crime, sin, or moral turpitude known to our laws human or divine, more culpable or injurious, than that which is expressed in the term, 'Abolitionist.' " Since all were in danger of being "murdered or destroyed by these northern fanatics," it was necessary to "use every effort to capture and punish any and all persons who may be found in this State, advocating, speaking, or publishing any of the diabolical sentiments of the abolitionists."[21]

Radical abolitionists were never more than a tiny minority, however, and their effect was more to ignite emotions in the South than to convince the North to support immediate emancipation. Undoubtedly, Harrison County's slaveholders could see, in spite of their anger, that there was no practical or effective abolitionist party in the North. When they sought emissaries of radicalism stirring up their bondsmen, they found none. So the abolitionists infuriated the community and in that way prepared the emotional complex for secession, but they were not the immediate cause of action in 1860-1861. Instead, disunion came when Abraham Lincoln was elected to the presidency, and Lincoln was no abolitionist.

The Republican Party did not at any time before the Civil War propose the immediate destruction of slavery. Its position, rather than abolitionist, was antislavery. Abraham Lincoln and the majority of Republicans thought slavery wrong, but they were too conservative and constitution-conscious to propose abolition. Moreover, they meant to win elections, and radicalism attracted few northern voters. They took a stand only against the spread of slavery into any new territory. Some, perhaps convinced by the radical abolitionists that slavery was wrong, took

[21] Marshall, *Texas Republican*, December 3, 1859.

this stand as a matter of right and looked to the institution's ultimate extinction; others probably cared little about slavery and less about Negroes but did not want to compete with slave labor in the West. In any case, the Republicans did not mean to pose the danger of immediate abolition in communities such as Harrison County.[22]

Lincoln, however, his conservatism notwithstanding, was perceived as an intolerable threat to slavery. Slaveholders recognized the moral condemnation implicit in restricting the spread of their institution, and they also understood the assumption that slavery, once limited, would eventually die. Other dangers were more immediate and concrete, as the *Texas Republican* pointed out as early as 1849. First, if Texas were to have free states on her northern and western boundaries, the problem of runaways would be compounded. Second, restriction would not end slavery in Texas, but what would it do to slave prices? "Anything that would impair slave labor, or render that species of property precarious in value, would be detrimental in proportion to the extent of its influence—not only to the slaveholder, but to those who do not own that species of property." More than eleven years later, after Lincoln's election, the *Republican* approvingly reprinted an editorial from the Charleston *Mercury* that made exactly the same points. The Republicans, ran the argument, will repeal the Fugitive Slave Act, thus encouraging runaways to free soil. Also, loss of confidence in the future will cause slave property to be "greatly depreciated." The *Mercury* calculated that slave values would drop $100 each upon the inauguration of a Republican president.[23]

In the eyes of slaveholders, then, Abraham Lincoln, abolitionist or not, did indeed constitute a dangerous threat. And the *Texas Republican* encouraged this view by confusing the distinc-

[22]The views of Republicans and Lincoln on slavery and abolitionism are developed in many places. See, for example, Stephen B. Oates, *With Malice Toward None: The Life of Abraham Lincoln* (New York, 1977), 197-199, and Richard N. Current, *The Lincoln Nobody Knows* (New York, 1958), 214-236.

[23]Marshall *Texas Republican*, August 3, 1849 (first quotation), November 17 (second quotation), December 8, 1860.

tion between antislavery and abolitionism in 1860. Lincoln, said Loughery on December 1, is as opposed to slavery as any abolitionist. The "House Divided" speech proves that he is a dangerous radical. Is not his election "an overt act justifying the secession of the Southern States?" At the very least, the South could expect a Republican administration to bring increasing strength for the abolitionists. If Lincoln and the northerners want to save the Union, said Loughery, they must put a stop to abolitionist agitation, uphold the Fugitive Slave Act, and give slavery equal rights in the territories.[24]

A majority of Harrison County's people entered the secession crisis of 1860-1861 determined to preserve slavery. Enraged by radical attacks and distrustful of the North in general, they blurred distinctions between abolitionism and antislavery and saw Abraham Lincoln as a serious threat to their key economic and social institution. As District Judge Charles A. Frazier put it, Lincoln's election was "equivalent to summing up all the injuries and indignities inflicted upon the Southern states and Southern people for the last twenty years, and spitting them in their faces." Furthermore, emotional reactions aside, they were correct about Lincoln in one sense. He did mean to put slavery on the road to ultimate extinction. They could have "submitted" and kept their slaves, but there probably would have been a loss of confidence, an increase in the incidence of runaways and rebellions, and a decline in slave prices. "Ultimately" — the Republican death date for slavery — could well have been a long time, but the community apparently agreed with a *Texas Republican* correspondent calling himself "Texas" who contended on December 8, 1860, that submission meant suicide.[25] Unwilling to accept the end of slavery, even if the death was slow, Harrison County enthusiastically joined other Deep South communities in risking all on a conservative revolution.

[24] Ibid., December 1, 1860 (quotation). Calhoun had demanded the same concessions as the price of union in 1850. Hamilton, *Prologue to Conflict*, 71-74.

[25] Marshall *Texas Republican*, December 8, 1860, January 5, 1861 (quotation).

8

The Community at War: 1861–1865

SECESSION, AS MOST leaders in Harrison County expected, soon led to war. President Lincoln insisted on upholding the Union and refused to recognize the Confederate States of America as an independent nation. He was, therefore, determined to hold the few federal positions—including Fort Sumter at Charleston, South Carolina—that remained in the hands of United States troops when he took office. The Confederate government in turn believed that any United States presence in its territory was a denial of independence. When Lincoln attempted to send supplies to Sumter in early April, 1861, Jefferson Davis and his advisors decided to attack rather than allow the federal fort to stand. Eventually there would be considerable dispute over who started the war, but placing blame for the outbreak of fighting was not a matter of much concern in Harrison County. When, on April 17, Robert W. Loughery brought news of the surrender of Sumter, the community reacted enthusiastically, Marshall resounded with cannon fire and patriotic speeches.[1] Secession and the outbreak of war seem to have been akin to an emotional release for many; at last the sectional conflict was in the open and would be settled.

Harrison County was already preparing to contribute to the military effort of the Confederacy when news of Fort Sumter arrived. In response to a call from the state secession convention for ten companies of mounted rangers, Sheriff A. W. Crawford began to enroll volunteers from his community in early April. The company, consisting originally of 103 men and officers, was organized and sworn into the service of Texas on April 19. Of the volunteers 41 came from Harrison County; young men from eight other counties filled out the ranks. They designated themselves the "W. P. Lane Rangers" in honor of Walter P. Lane, a noted veteran of the War for Texas Independence and the Mexican War and brother of County Judge George Lane, and elected Samuel J. Richardson as their commanding officer. After a rousing farewell ceremony during which many partook liberally of "old bustskull," Captain Richardson marched his company west out of Marshall on April 20. They proceeded to Camp Wood, 140 miles north of San Antonio, and took up the job of patrolling and protecting the Texas frontier from hostile Indians. On May 23, the W. P. Lane Rangers were sworn into Confederate service and became Company F of the 2nd Texas Cavalry commanded by Colonel John S. "Rip" Ford.[2]

Other early volunteers from the community headed directly

[1] Marshall *Texas Republican*, April 20, 1861. There are numerous in-depth studies of the outbreak of conflict. See, for example, Richard N. Current, *Lincoln and the First Shot* (Philadelphia, 1963).

[2] Marshall *Texas Republican*, April 6, 27, 1861; William W. Heartsill, *One Thousand Four Hundred and Ninety-One Days in the Confederate Army: A Journal Kept by W. W. Heartsill* . . . ., edited by Bell I. Wiley (Jackson, Tenn., 1953), xv, 2-14. Heartsill was an original member of the W. P. Lane Rangers.

for theaters of expected conflict with United States troops. Frederick S. Bass, graduate of Virginia Military Institute and president of Marshall University, organized and drilled a company that designated itself the "Marshall Guards." On May 28, 1861, they left for Richmond, Virginia, by way of New Orleans. Alexander Pope gave the farewell address and presented a battle flag made by the young women of Marshall. At Richmond, the Marshall Guards became Company E of the 1st Texas Infantry. In October, the 1st Texas was joined by the 4th and 5th Texas and the 18th Georgia infantry regiments to form the unit that became famous as Hood's Texas Brigade. Far from home as part of General Robert E. Lee's Army of Northern Virginia, they fought in 38 battles and skirmishes including Antietam, Gettysburg, and the Wilderness. More than half of those who served in the company were killed, wounded, or captured. If there was glory to be won in the military defense of the "Lost Cause," the Marshall Guards earned their share. Frederick S. Bass, having risen to the rank of colonel in command of the 1st Texas, surrendered the company at Appomattox in April, 1865, only a few miles from a spot they had passed on their way toward Richmond nearly four years earlier.[3]

The Marshall Guards came primarily from town; at the same time, another company was being formed by young men from the eastern portion of the county. Adopting the name "Texas Hunters," they received their battle flag in a ceremony at Jonesville on May 1, 1861. The flag, made of silk by the neighborhood ladies, had a hunting scene on one side and the first flag of the Confederacy on the other. Trained as a cavalry unit by Captain Thomas W. Winston, a 32-year-old planter, the Texas Hunters left Marshall on June 1 and marched westward to Dallas where they were sworn into the service of the Confederate States of America and became Company A of the 3rd Texas Cavalry. Their commanding officer was Colonel Elkanah Greer, a

[3]Marshall *Texas Republican*, June 8, 22, 1861; Harold B. Simpson, *The Marshall Guards: Harrison County's Contribution to Hood's Texas Brigade* (Marshall, Texas, 1967), 1-6; Marcus J. Wright (comp.), *Texas in the War, 1861-1865*, edited by Harold B. Simpson (Hillsboro, Texas, 1965), 98, 208.

resident of Harrison County who had served with Jefferson Davis's famed "Mississippi Rifles" during the Mexican War. Walter P. Lane, namesake of the "W. P. Lane Rangers," who had enlisted as a private in the "Texas Hunters" was elected the regimental lieutenant colonel. Once organized, the 3rd Texas moved northeastward toward the Arkansas-Missouri border to support General Sterling Price's forces in that area. Missouri, although a slave state, had not seceded, and Confederate success in that area was considered vital to their cause.[4]

Thus during the spring of 1861 Harrison County furnished all or most of the men and officers of three volunteer companies. And two of these units, the Marshall Guards and the Texas Hunters, had moved into areas that would soon see the first real battles of the Civil War. In the meantime, those at home took other steps to support the Confederacy. On May 7, the commissioners court ordered the appropriation of $16,000 to buy arms and ammunition and provide support for the families of volunteers. There was no money in the county treasury so bonds were issued to raise the money. Later that month, a committee of public safety for the county was organized with James F. Taylor, a large planter who had once been an Opposition leader, as chairman of its executive board. The vigilante like nature of this organization is revealed in one of the resolutions adopted at the formative meeting.

> The powers of the Committee shall be to take up or cause to be taken up and brought before them for trial any and all persons black or white charged with committing any act touching in these treacherous times the safety of the South, and to determine whether they or any of them are guilty and inflict such punishment as the articles of the organization of this society authorizes or as the Committee in the exercise of a sound discretion may deem proper for the safety of the County.

[4]Marshall *Texas Republican*, May 4, June 8, 22, 1861; Wright (comp.), *Texas in the War*, 79, 85-86, 112; Albert B. Blocker, "The Boy-Bugler of the Third Texas Cavalry: The A. B. Blocker Narrative," edited by Max S. Lale, *Military History of Texas and the Southwest*, XIV ([1978] #2), 73-76; Clement Eaton, *A History of the Southern Confederacy* (New York, 1961), 154.

> They shall also have power to bring before them, or have brought before them all persons suspected of disaffection to the South and deal with them as the safety of the country requires.

Later the Committee was authorized to "inspect" all letters going to the North and arriving for individuals of questionable loyalty in the community.[5] Fortunately for all concerned, Harrison County had no active opponents of the South; had they existed, the Committee of Public Safety might have taken highly repressive action.

The first war news to reach the community during the summer of 1861 undoubtedly convinced many that the "God of Battles" was with the South. Confederate troops routed a Union army advancing into Virginia at the first Battle of Bull Run (or Manassas) on July 21. The Marshall Guards were rushed north from Richmond on the day of the battle but arrived too late to do more than help pursue the retreating Federals. A few weeks later in southeastern Missouri the Texas Hunters became the first Harrison County unit to engage in actual combat when they fought in the Battle of Wilson's Creek (or Oak Hills) on August 10. This battle, far bloodier than the more famous fight at Bull Run, was also a complete victory for the Confederacy. These victories proved the superiority of southern troops, Robert Loughery thought, and the news brought "unbounded confidence" to the Marshall area. But there was sobering news as well. A number of young volunteers including Lieutenant A. B. Stone, Jr., the 19-year-old son of a large planter, were wounded at Wilson's Creek, and one, F. J. Willey, the son of a nonslaveholding farmer from England, was killed. He was probably the first Harrison County soldier to die in action against the enemy during the Civil War.[6]

[5]Harrison County Commissioners Court Minutes, May, (quotation), June, 1861. The bonds bore 10% interest. They were to be retired over the next four years.

[6]Eaton, *History of Southern Confederacy*, 152-154; Simpson, *Marshall Guards*, 5; Blocker, "Boy-Bugler of Third Texas Cavalry," 77-83; Marshall *Texas Republican*, August 31, 1861 (quotation), February 1, September 6, 1862; Key, "Memoranda for My Children," Key Family Papers; Eighth Census, 1860, Schedules 1 and 2. Lieutenant

The community remained enthusiastically in support of the war through the first summer and stood ready to furnish supplies and additional troops. A Central Relief Committee was formed to aid the families of soldiers, and a Women's Volunteer Aid Association organized to help the sick and wounded. Mrs. F. C. Van Zandt, widow of the Republic of Texas leader, headed this group. Two more volunteer companies, the "Bass Grays" commanded by Captain Khleber M. Van Zandt and the "Texas Invincibles" with Captain William B. Hill, a 44-year-old minister, in command, left Harrison County in the early fall. They became respectively Companies D and H of the 7th Texas Infantry Regiment under Colonel John Gregg. J. M. Clough of Marshall, Van Zandt's law partner and brother-in-law who volunteered as a private, was elevated to the position of lieutenant colonel of this regiment.[7]

The 7th Texas Infantry was sent to western Kentucky as part of General Albert Sidney Johnston's army that stretched in a defensive posture from the Allegheny Mountains to the Mississippi. When General Ulysses S. Grant saw that the Tennessee and Cumberland rivers provided the gateways to breaking Johnston's line and invading Tennessee in early 1862, both companies from Harrison County, already greatly weakened by disease, wound up trapped in Fort Donelson on the Cumberland in northwestern Tennessee. As Joseph Bruckmuller, a private in the Bass Grays remembered it, the Confederates attacked the beseiging Federals and appeared on the verge of victory until a return to the fort was ordered. Two of their generals disappeared that night leaving the entire force at Donelson to surrender the next day.[8]

Stone was later accused of cowardice at Oak Hills, but Captain Winston defended him by explaining that he was wounded. *Texas Republican*, February 1, 1862

[7]Marshall *Texas Republican*, July 8, July 27, October 12, 1861, February 1, 1862; Wright (comp.), *Texas in the War*, 20, 80, 163; Van Zandt, *Force Without Fanfare*, 80-81.

[8]Eaton, *History of Southern Confederacy*, 155-158; Marshall *Texas Republican*, February 12, 1862; Joseph Bruckmuller, "Description of the Family and Life of Joseph Bruckmuller," Peter Joseph Bruckmuller Papers, University of Texas Archives, Barker Texas History Center, Austin.

Bruckmuller's memory was essentially correct. Generals John B. Floyd and Gideon J. Pillow, both described as "incompetents" by Clement Eaton, after allowing themselves to be trapped in Fort Donelson by Grant's army, succeeded in opening the road to Nashville on February 15 but then almost inexplicably ordered their troops back to the fort. Again beseiged by superior forces, the Confederate generals decided that night to surrender. Floyd and Pillow escaped by the river leaving the capitulation to General Simon Bolivar Buckner. The surrender was the first great military disaster for the South costing more than 12,000 prisoners and 20,000 stand of arms and forcing retreat from Kentucky.[9]

The fighting and surrender at Fort Donelson was a terrible blow directly to Harrison County. It showed the community a side of war not experienced in 1861. Lieutenant Colonel J. M. Clough was killed in the fighting on the 15th, falling in the presence of his brother-in-law, Captain K. M. Van Zandt. Six others from the county died including Captain William B. Hill, commander of the Texas Invincibles. Twelve were wounded, and the rest made prisoners of war at Camp Douglas in Illinois. Apparently the captives were generally treated well. Joseph Bruckmuller, for example, escaped in April, 1862, probably with the knowledge of his guards, and made his way home. Within a year, all the officers and men in these companies, including Captain Van Zandt, were exchanged.[10]

Less than a month after Donelson, Confederate forces on the Arkansas-Missouri border, including the Texas Hunters as Company A of the 3rd Texas Cavalry, also suffered a major defeat. General Earl Van Dorn, hoping to build on earlier southern successes such as the Battle of Wilson's Creek, planned to capture St. Louis and threaten an invasion of Illinois. He was turned back at the Battle of Pea Ridge (or Elkhorn Tavern) in northwestern Arkansas on March 7-8, 1862, and Missouri was

[9]Eaton, *History of Southern Confederacy*, 157-160 (quotation on p. 158).

[10]Marshall *Texas Republican*, March 1, 8, 1862; Van Zandt, *Force Without Fanfare*, 86-96; Bruckmuller, "Family and Life of Joseph Bruckmuller," Bruckmuller Papers; Wright (comp.), *Texas in the War*, 163.

lost to the confederacy. Company A played no important part in the fighting; it was part of the force covering Van Dorn's retreat. The Texas Hunters thus fared better than their compatriots at Donelson, but the war seemed to be going against the soldiers from Harrison County. Only the Marshall Guards with Lee's army in Virginia fought in successful campaigns during early 1862, and they faced bloody Antietam later that year.[11]

The fall of Fort Donelson and the defeat at Pea Ridge alarmed but did not discourage those at home in Harrison County. A citizens meeting in early March, 1862 called for even stronger support for the war effort, and the *Texas Republican* screamed "To Arms, To Arms." The community's remaining men responded. Some joined existing companies, and many formed their own units. By mid-summer, eight new companies raised primarily or to a large extent in Harrison County joined the five already in Confederate service. The "Clough Rangers" under Captain J. J. Kennedy and "Hendricks' Company" under Captain Sterling B. Hendricks became Companies K and E respectively of the 17th Texas Cavalry commanded by Colonel George F. Moore. They were sent to Arkansas. Although technically cavalry outfits, these companies were dismounted after July, 1862. The "Harrison County Lancers," Captain Phil Brown commanding, were actually armed with lances as well as breech-loading rifles and pistols. Every man supplied his own horse in this unit which became Company F of the 28th Texas Cavalry under Colonel Horace Randal. They left for Little Rock, Arkansas, on July 9, 1862. The "Marshall Mechanics" under Captain N. S. Allen, the "Clough and Hill Avengers" under Captain H. L. Berry, and the "Cypress Tigers" under Captain John F. Buchan, became respectively Companies A, B, and H of the 14th Texas Infantry commanded by Colonel Edward Clark of Marshall. They would serve as part of General John Walker's Division in Louisiana during 1863 and 1864. The last two companies, known simply as "Hec McKay's Company" and "S. W.

[11]Eaton, *History of Southern Confederacy*, 155; Blocker, "Boy-Bugler of Third Texas Cavalry," Part II, 157-163; Simpson, *Marshall Guards*, 6, 17. Hood's Brigade fought with Lee's army during the Peninsula Campaign in 1862.

Webb's Company'' for their captains, went to Arkansas in 1862 as Companies E and L respectively of Crump's Regiment of Texas Cavalry.[12]

By the end of 1862, then, Harrison County had contributed heavily to 13 companies fighting for the Confederacy. It is virtually impossible to determine exactly how many of these men volunteered and what proportion of those eligible for military duty served. Clearly those who joined the army before the spring of 1862 did so voluntarily. But on April 16, the Confederate Congress passed a conscription act drafting all able-bodied white males between the ages of 18 and 35 for three years. Volunteers already in the army had their service extended to a total of three years. The age limits were broadened to 45 years in September, 1862, and from 17 to 50 in February, 1864. To be drafted was considered a disgrace, thus some who volunteered after April, 1862, may have done so under the threat of forced service. Robert W. Loughery, as a southern patriot, implied that most went willingly. ''There will be no conscripts in Texas,'' he wrote, ''for everyone between the ages of 18 and 35 is volunteering.'' So far as the number who served is concerned, only a rough approximation is possible. The first five companies raised in 1861 averaged 88 men and officers. Assuming that this average held true through 1862, the total number of men in the 13 companies would have been approximately 1,144. Not all were from Harrison County, however. If we assume that only one-half were, probably a low estimate, the number would be 572. There were 1,664 white males aged 15 through 49 living in the community at the census of 1860. A conservative estimate, therefore, supports the conclusion that during the first two years of war one-third to one-half of all Harrison County males capable of military service entered the army.[13]

[12]Marshall *Texas Republican*, February 15, March 1 (quotation), 8, 15, 22, 29, May 10, 24, June 3, July 5, 12, August 9, 1862; Wright (comp.), *Texas in the War*, 106-107, 117, 125, 164; Theophilus Perry to Thomas Person, May 6, 1862, Person Family Papers. Perry was a lieutenant in the ''Harrison County Lancers.'' Walker's command became known as the ''Greyhound Division'' due to their ability to march rapidly.

[13]Albert Burton Moore, *Conscription and Conflict in the Confederacy* (New York, 1924), 13-15, 140-141, 308; Eaton, *History of Southern Confederacy*, 90-92; Marshall

Support for the Confederacy remained strong through 1862 in Harrison County. In March, the commissioners court appointed a person in each precinct to look after the families of volunteer soldiers. Money was to come from donations and from the county government. A resolution expressed the commissioners' sentiments: "The faith of our county is pledged to these men who are now in (and more about to enter) the field in defense of the country that their families should not suffer." Gradually, however, the war began to exert pressure on the home front; pressure that would erode support in some cases. Food supplies were abundant, but shortages soon developed in certain imported and manufactured items. Coffee, for example, was in short supply, and paper was so difficult to find that Loughery reduced the size of the *Texas Republican* in March. Most upsetting, however, was the depreciation of Confederate money. Gold and silver virtually disappeared from circulation once the war began, and the currency issued by the Confederate government did not inspire confidence for long, especially since it did not bear interest, was not backed by precious metal, and poured from the printing presses. An item costing one dollar in Confederate currency on September 1, 1861, cost two dollars by April 8, 1862, three dollars by September 14 of that year, and four dollars on January 1, 1863. Put another way, the Confederate dollar lost three-quarters of its purchasing power in just a little more than one year. Some members of the Harrison County community reacted by refusing to accept the depreciated currency; an action that brought a strong reaction from southern patriots. A mass meeting in December, 1862, chaired by William T. Scott, condemned anyone who refused Confederate notes or demanded specie as a traitor and recommended blacklisting of the guilty parties and driving them from the country.[14]

Texas Republican, May 3, 1862 (quotation); U.S. Bureau of the Census, *Population of the United States in 1860*, 474-475.

[14]Harrison County Commissioners Court Minutes, March, 1862 (quotation); Theophilus Perry to Thomas Person, May 6, 1862, Person Family Papers; Marshall *Texas Republican*, March 15, December 20, 1862, January 3, 1863; Eaton, *History of Southern Confederacy*, 228-229; Emory M. Thomas, *The Confederate Nation, 1861-1865* (New York, 1979), 197, 257; Henry Fox, "Fluctuations of Confederate Cur-

Regardless of all efforts to sustain the currency, however, depreciation would continue and grow worse.

The county government also decided to issue scrip or emergency paper money, adding to the public's tendency to lose confidence in the monetary system. The first large issue of scrip began in September, 1862 when the commissioners court authorized $13,700 worth of "Treasurer Drafts" in denominations ranging from 10 cents to $5. G. G. Gregg, a Marshall merchant, was appointed as the agent to put these drafts into circulation by using them to pay off the county's bond obligations. He was also directed to exchange the county's paper for Confederate notes and hold the notes to use in eventually redeeming the scrip! A second issue of $12,229.55 worth of treasurer drafts began in November, 1862, and then $52,000 worth of "Treasury Warrants," all in denominations of $2 or less, was authorized in February, 1863. Due to the shortage of paper, Harrison County scrip was printed on small pieces of whatever was available. One local historian wrote that the blank side of forms used to register stock in the Southern Pacific Railroad Company served for the printing of a great deal of the scrip issued.[15]

Paper money depreciated and upset the exchange of goods and services in the community. The Confederacy's conscription or draft system embodied in the act passed on April 16, 1862, created even more social tension. The law drafted white males aged 18 to 35, but five days later the Confederate Congress added a long list of exemptions. Moreover, a conscript could avoid fighting by sending a substitute. In October, 1862, an addition to the original act exempted all planters or overseers charged with the supervision of 20 or more slaves. This law made sense in terms of economic need and police control at home, but it appeared as flagrant evidence that the conflict was a "rich man's war and a poor man's fight." George W. Whit-

rency in the State of Texas from . . . 1861 to . . . 1865," in *The Texas Almanac for 1867* (Galveston, 1866), 213-214.

[15]Harrison County Commissioners Court Minutes, August, November, 1862, February, 1863; Sallie Lentz, "The Use of Scrip to Pay for County Government," Lentz Collection, East Texas Baptist College Library, Marshall.

more could not resist saying "I told you so" in a letter published in the Shreveport *South Western* and reprinted by Loughery in Marshall. I warned about "invidious distinctions" between slaveholders and nonslaveholders at the time of secession, Whitmore said. At least, he argued, if those with fewer than 20 slaves are going to do the fighting, those with 20 or more should pay for it. Loughery devoted two columns of editorial prose to a reply. Whitmore, he wrote, is a demagogue or traitor—and probably both—who is seeking to array class against class and aid the enemy.[16]

Wartime pressures and tensions at home were not alleviated by military successes for Harrison County soldiers or the confederacy in general during late 1862 or 1863. Lee's invasion of the North was turned back at Antietam, or Sharpsburg as southerners called it, on September 17, 1862. The Marshall Guards were heavily involved in this battle, the bloodiest single day's fight during the war, and suffered 16 wounded and three killed. Among the dead were Lieutenant Clinton E. Perry, son of Josiah D. Perry, and his cousin Corporal Harwood Earl Perry, son of Dr. Harwood P. Perry. Each of these planter families also had a son wounded in the same battle. The wounded boys got home in mid-October; no doubt creating joy at their survival and renewed sadness over the deaths of their brothers. "I am so sorry for them all," wrote the wife of a family member. "They are in great distress."[17]

The Texas Hunters of the 3rd Texas Cavalry, following General Van Dorn's defeat at Pea Ridge, were ordered to join General Pierre G. T. Beauregard's army at Corinth, a strategic railroad center in northern Mississippi, where it had retreated to after the bloody battle of Shiloh in April 1862. They crossed the

[16]Moore, *Conscription and Conflict*, 27, 53, 67-68; Eaton, *History of Southern Confederacy*, 89-91; Marshall *Texas Republican*, December 20, 1862 (quotations).

[17]Eaton, *History of Southern Confederacy*, 186-188; Simpson, *Marshall Guards*, 7, identifies all four Perrys as brothers, but this is incorrect. The quotation is from Harriet Person Perry to "My Dear Sister" [Mary Person?], October 22, 1862, Person Family Papers. Both Clinton and Harwood Earl Perry had attended military school in Kentucky before the war.

Mississippi at Memphis and arrived in time to help cover the retreat southward from Corinth at the end of May, 1862. Lieutenant Colonel Walter P. Lane and the 3rd Texas fought so aggressively in this action that they earned praise from General Beauregard in general orders read to the entire army. Nevertheless, the Federals gained control of northern Mississippi. In the early fall, the 3rd Texas, still under the command of Van Dorn, participated in a thrust aimed at regaining control of the area, but they were defeated at Iuka in northeastern Mississippi on September 19 and again at Corinth on October 4. Thus the Texas Hunters met with little success; certainly not enough to merit the cost. By mid-September, 1862, before the battles of Iuka and Corinth, the company had suffered 15 deaths from battle and disease.[18] The fall of 1862 brought only news of defeat and death to Harrison County.

The next year, 1863, began disastrously with the fall of Fort Hindman, or Arkansas Post as it was commonly called, at the mouth of the Arkansas River. Although the surrender of Arkansas Post was a relatively unimportant part of Grant's campaign against Vicksburg, it was very damaging to Harrison County because three of the community's volunteer companies were trapped there. Companies E (Hendricks' Company) and K (the Clough Rangers) of the 17th Texas Cavalry were already stationed at Arkansas Post in late November, 1862, when they were joined by the W. P. Lane Rangers. The Lane Rangers had served a year on the Texas frontier near San Antonio, re-enlisted, and during late 1862 returned to Marshall and been ordered to Arkansas. Immediately upon their arrival, Gil McKay, now captain of the Clough Rangers, greeted them with the opinion that Arkansas Post was "Ft. Donaldson *[sic]* No 2." McKay's fears proved correct in a matter of weeks as a strong United States force supported by a fleet of gunboats forced the surrender of the fort. W. W. Heartsill of the Lane Rangers noted that Federal casual-

[18]Blocker, "Boy-Bugler of Third Texas Cavalry," Part III, 217-225, 227 n. 80; Walter P. Lane, *The Adventures and Recollections of General Walter P. Lane, A San Jacinto Veteran* . . . (Marshall, 1928), 95-102; Eaton, *History of Southern Confederacy*, 189; Marshall *Texas Republican*, September 16, 1862.

ties were heavier than Confederate and that few weapons were captured. Nevertheless, the people at home had to absorb the news of another surrender sending hundreds of the community's young men into Yankee prison camps. Most were interned at Camp Butler near Springfield, Illinois.[19]

The beginning of the end for the Confederacy came during the first week of July, 1863. In the East, Lee's invading army was turned back at Gettysburg, while in the West, Vicksburg surrendered to the forces of General Grant. Harrison County soldiers fought in both theaters. The Marshall Guards were at Gettysburg with Hood's Brigade, and the 7th Texas Infantry including remnants of the Bass Grays and Texas Invincibles fought at Vicksburg. Members of these two companies fared only slightly better than they had at Fort Donelson in 1862; they were paroled immediately rather than being held as prisoners of war.[20]

A few days after the fall of Vicksburg, Port Hudson at the mouth of the Red River, the last Confederate stronghold on the Mississippi also surrendered. The United States thus cut the Confederacy in two and greatly reduced the flow of men and supplies from West to East. These defeats hit hard at morale in Texas and thoughout the South. In Harrison County, however, the surrender of Vicksburg and Port Hudson meant worse than a loss of confidence or spirit; there was also the recognition that these Union successes had opened northeast Texas to invasion along the Red River. Apparently everyone in the community saw the threat. "I fear the federals will be here soon," Louisa Perry, a teenaged daughter of Levin Perry, wrote her brother in August, 1863.[21]

Harrison County was indeed an inviting target for Federal invasion once Vicksburg and Port Hudson fell. The community

[19]Marshall *Texas Republican*, February 12, 1863; Heartsill, *One Thousand Four Hundred and Ninety-One Days in the Confederate Army*, xvi-xvii, 85-106.

[20]Eaton, *History of Southern Confederacy*, 193-200; Simpson, *Marshall Guards*, 17; Wright (comp.), *Texas in the War*, 163.

[21]Eaton, *History of Southern Confederacy*, 201; Louisa Perry to Theophilus Perry, August 10, 1863 (quotation), Person Family Papers.

had one of the few railroads in Texas, the Southern Pacific, which, in spite of all its financial difficulties, had been extended during the war to Greenwood, Louisiana, only 14 miles from Shreveport. Marshall was the site of a powder mill and ordnance works moved there during 1863 as the Confederacy's hold on Arkansas became increasingly untenable. More importantly, General Edmund Kirby Smith, commander of the Trans-Mississippi Department after February 9, 1863, gradually located his whole base of operations near and in Harrison County. The Quartermaster Bureau, for example, was based in Shreveport after March, 1863, but the main nerve center for paperwork was at Marshall. The bureau to enforce the Tax-in-Kind Act of April, 1863, was also located in Marshall. Once Federal control of the Mississippi in July impeded communications with Richmond, General Kirby Smith virtually ruled the Confederacy west of the river; "Kirby-Smithdom," some southerners called it.[22] Clearly, a successful Federal military operation up the Red River into northwestern Louisiana and northeastern Texas could be expected to destroy military resources and disrupt the entire Trans-Mississippi Department. Harrison County had good reason to fear the Federals after July, 1863.

The dreaded invasion came early in the spring of 1864. General Nathaniel P. Banks moved up the Red River with more than 25,000 troops supported by Admiral David D. Porter's flotilla of gunboats. Confederate forces under the command of General Richard Taylor surrendered Alexandria and Natchitoches without a fight, leaving Banks's army only eighty miles from Shreveport. If the retreat continued, as Banks thought it would, Marshall would soon be occupied. On April 8, however, near Mansfield, Louisiana, some 40 miles south of Shreveport, Taylor took a stand and fought. The resulting Battle of Mansfield (or Sabine Crossroads) was a complete success for

[22] Muir, "Thirty-Second Parallel Pacific Railroad," 169; Clive J. Luke, *The Marshall Powder Mill Site: The 1973-1974 Excavation* (Austin, 1978), 5-10; James Lynn Nichols, *The Confederate Quartermaster in the Trans-Mississippi Department* (Austin, 1964), 5; Eaton, *History of Southern Confederacy*, 202; Robert L. Kerby, *Kirby Smith's Confederacy; The Trans-Mississippi South, 1863-1865* (New York, 1972).

the Confederates who took 2,500 prisoners and drove the Federals five miles southward. During the night Banks retreated to Pleasant Hill, 15 miles southeastward, where he was attacked on April 9 by Taylor's pursuing forces. Union troops held their positions and dealt heavy losses to the Confederates, but they again retreated during the night. Banks considered another move against Shreveport but then gave up his Red River campaign in failure.[23]

Harrison County contributed heavily to its own defense in 1864. Six of the volunteer companies raised largely in the community fought at Mansfield and Pleasant Hill. The Harrison County Lancers of the 28th Texas Cavalry and the Marshall Mechanics, Clough and Hill Avengers, and Cypress Tigers of the 14th Texas Infantry all entered the battles as part of General John G. Walker's Texas Division. The Lancers saw especially heavy action in both battles and suffered numerous casualties including Captain Theophilus Perry who died a few days after Pleasant Hill. Hec McKay's Company and S. W. Webb's Company fought as part of the 1st Regiment of Texas Partisan Rangers, General Thomas Green's Division. Walter P. Lane, commander of a brigade in this division (although he was not promoted to brigadier general until 1865), received a serious wound at Mansfield as did Captain S. W. Webb. In general, successful defense of the Shreveport-Marshall area was dearly bought as General Taylor's army suffered more than 2,500 casualties on April 8 and 9.[24]

Harrison County thus escaped invasion and occupation in 1864, and the community's people continued to avoid serious material privation. There were shortages, of course. Items such as coffee, flour, good quality cloth, leather, and paper were very scarce. Cards, the wire-toothed brushes used to prepare cotton and wool fibers for spinning, were in effect rationed. By the fall of 1863, each county received an allotment from the Texas

[23] Ludwell H. Johnson, *Red River Campaign: Politics and Cotton in the Civil War* (Baltimore, 1958), 94, 112, 129-169.

[24] Ibid., 129-169; Kerby, *Kirby Smith's Confederacy*, 290-308; Wright (comp.), *Texas in the War*, 107, 119, 125, 164; Lane, *Adventures and Recollections*, 108-112.

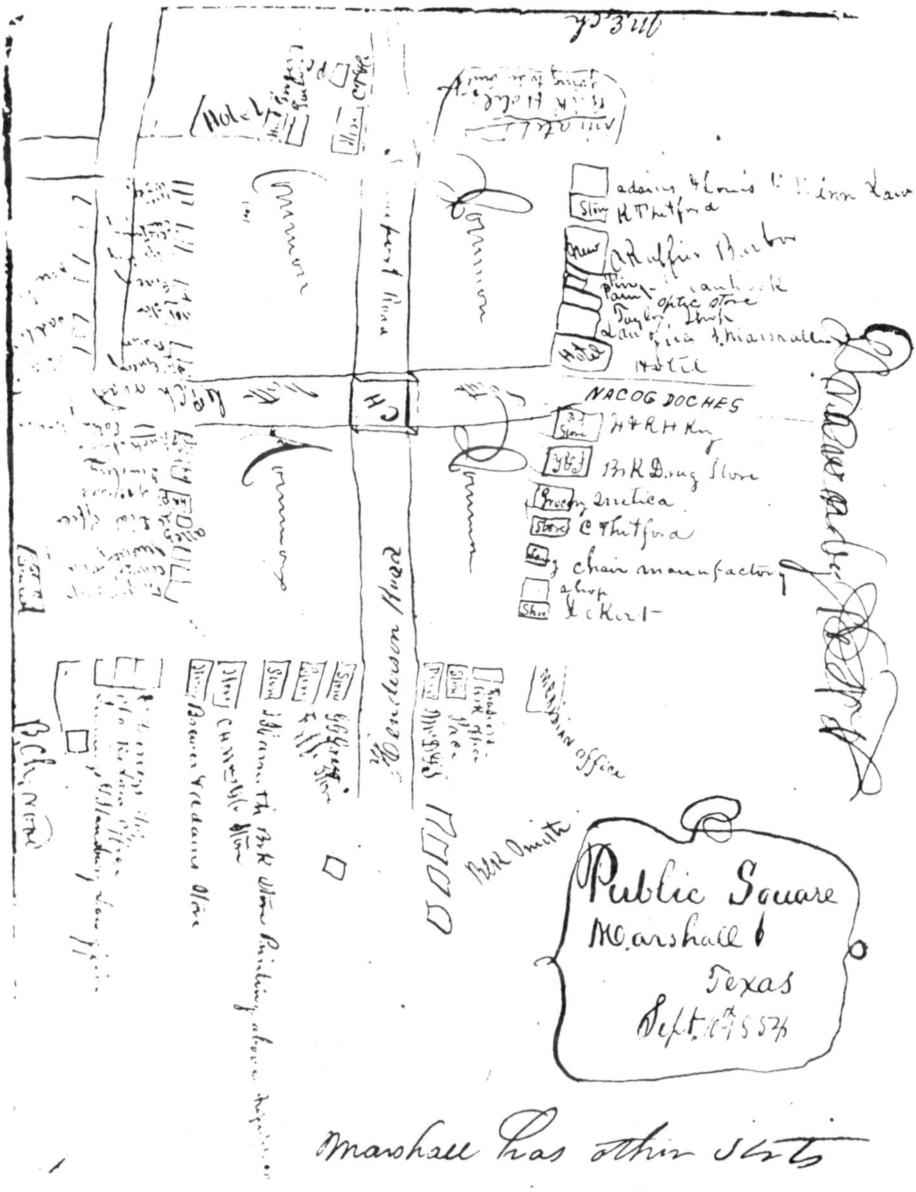

Diagram of the Marshall courthouse square, drawn by Pleasant Vickers. Unless otherwise indicated, pictures in this section are used courtesy of the Harrison County Historical Museum, Marshall.

Harrison County's 1852 courthouse.

George Lane: county judge.

William T. Scott: planter and political leader.

William B. Ochiltree: lawyer and politician.

John B. Webster: planter. A daguerretype made when he was a student at William and Mary. Courtesy of Mrs. Claire Claypool, Houston.

Robert W. Loughery: editor of the *Texas Republican*. Courtesy of the Collection of the Texas/Dallas History and Archives, Dallas Public Library.

N. V. Board: unionist political leader.

David Abner: Member of the Constitutional Convention of 1875. Courtesy of the Texas State Archives, Austin.

George W. Whitmore: unionist politician and Republican congressman. Courtesy of the Library of Congress, Washington, D.C.

''Mimosa Hall'': built on the Webster plantation by the family slaves.

''Edgemont'': The plantation home of Montreville J. Hall.

Military Board, and the commissioners court then distributed them to individuals. Generally, however, people in the community had the necessities of life, food from their farms, gardens, and livestock, fuel from the forests, and clothing from homespun. The correspondence of Harriet Perry, wife of Captain Theophilus Perry of the Harrison County Lancers, as we will see, reflects loneliness and fear throughout the war but does not mention material want. When K. M. Van Zandt arrived home from the army in 1864, he found his family in need only of shoes. His saddlebags provided the leather to supply that want.[25] There is no evidence to suggest that the Perrys and Van Zandts were especially well supplied.

Continuing currency depreciation proved more upsetting to the community than material want. The Confederacy continued to print money, and county government scrip remained in circulation. This flood of money coupled with declining fortunes in the war led to wild depreciation and hence inflation in prices. By September, 1864, for example, fifty Confederate dollars were necessary to match the purchasing power of one dollar three years earlier. The commissioners court considered a new issue of scrip in October, but concluded that "the necessity for such issue does not now exist." Paper money probably was literally not worth the material on which it was printed. Harriet Perry's letters to her husband reflect the dismaying rise in prices. In January, 1864, she wrote him that the price of cotton cards had risen from forty to eighty dollars during the past month. By February, a single town lot in Marshall sold for as much as $15,000. Such wild inflation created general demoralization and disrupted commerce. Theophilus Perry reflected the prevailing view when he wrote his wife in March, 1863: "I do not want any Confederate money except to pay debts with."[26]

[25] Harrison County Commissioners Court Minutes, September, 1863; Van Zandt, *Force Without Fanfare*, 107-108.

[26] Fox, "Fluctuations of Confederate Currency," 213-214; Harrison County Commissioners Court Minutes, October, 1864 (first quotation); Harriet Perry to Theophilus Perry, January 18, February 14, 1864; Theophilus Perry to Harriet Perry, March 8, 1863 (second quotation), Person Family Papers.

Harrison County thus suffered from some material shortages and from currency depreciation during 1863-1864 but escaped the worst privations and horrors of war. The community had little else to celebrate, however. There was no escaping the fate of the Confederacy. The loss of Chattanooga in November, 1863, after several months of bitter fighting in northwestern Georgia and south-central Tennessee, opened the southern heartland to invasion. Almost unbelievably, the Marshall Guards fought in this campaign too. They were part of General James Longstreet's corps detached from Lee's army after Gettysburg to aid General Braxton Bragg in defending Chattanooga. Other Harrison County companies joined them there. Some of the W. P. Lane Rangers who had been exchanged at City Point, Virginia, in April served in General Thomas J. Churchill's Brigade while the 7th Texas Infantry including the Bass Grays and the Texas Invincibles fought in a Tennessee brigade commanded by General John Gregg. The 17th Texas Cavalry including the Clough Rangers and Hendricks' Company, also exchanged in the spring after surrendering at Arkansas Post, served as part of General James Deshler's Brigade. "Nearly all of the Texans east of the river are concentrated here," commented W. W. Heartsill of the Lane Rangers, "and they will give a good account of the 'Lone Star State.' " Under the command of General Bragg, the Confederates won a great victory at Chickamauga Creek on September 19-20, 1863, but then failed to follow up their advantage. Union forces held Chattanooga and on November 23-25 badly defeated Bragg's army attempting to trap them there.[27]

In the spring of 1864, General Grant, now supreme commander of all the Union armies, mounted a campaign of inexorable pressure on Richmond. General William T. Sherman, using Chattanooga as his base, invaded Georgia and headed toward Atlanta. The Marshall Guards, back with Lee's army following their service at Chattanooga, fought in virtually every major engagement occasioned by Grant's move on Richmond.

[27]Eaton, *History of Southern Confederacy*, 268-272; Simpson, *Marshall Guards*, 17; Heartsill, *One Thousand Four Hundred and Ninety-One Days in the Confederate Army*, 152 (quotation); Wright (comp.), *Texas in the War*, 80, 117.

At the Battle of the Wilderness in May, 1864, for example, the company lost seven wounded and three killed including Eugene O. Perry whose brother had died at Antietam. The 7th Texas Infantry and 17th Texas Cavalry, both of whom included Harrison County companies, fought in the defense of Atlanta, and after Atlanta fell in September, 1864, they were part of General John B. Hood's thrust into Tennessee that was turned back at Nashville in December. The Texas Hunters of the 3rd Texas Cavalry, part of Ross's Texas Brigade since December, 1863, also served in both the Atlanta and Tennessee campaigns.[28]

As the Confederate armies suffered defeat after defeat in 1864, some leaders began to advocate accepting the inevitable and seeking an armistice to be followed by peace negotiations. It was believed that northern Democrats would be especially interested in ending the war through a "peace convocation." In late September, 1864, William W. Boyce, a Confederate congressman from South Carolina, published an open letter to President Jefferson Davis advocating this course. Robert W. Loughery of the *Texas Republican* furiously denounced this suggestion as ill-timed and ill-advised. And then to his great disgust found that at least one prominent member of his own community agreed with Boyce. Henry Ware, a large planter and manufacturer who had lived in the county since the mid-1840s, argued that since the South was already failing in its effort to protect states rights and slavery, any proposal for an honorable peace would do credit to those suggesting it. Loughery replied that Ware represented "a class of grumblers, whose sole purpose seems to be to sow the seeds of discontent in the country. . . ." He deserved credit only for coming into the open with his "pernicious counsels" where they could be opposed. Loughery also insisted that not twelve sensible men in the county would agree with Ware, but he then closed his paper to Ware's views, saying that a man of the latter's wealth and influence should support his country.[29]

[28] Simpson, *Marshall Guards*, 17, 19-24; Wright (comp.), *Texas in the War*, 82-83, 91, 117, 163; Eaton, *History of Southern Confederacy*, 280-282.

[29] Eaton, *History of Southern Confederacy*, 257; Marshall *Texas Republican*,

Those who wanted peace did not give up easily. In early 1865, they circulated a petition favoring negotiations to end the war and claimed majority support in the community. "Incipient treason has dared to raise its serpent head in our midst," said the *Texas Republican*. A public meeting to rally support for the war and to counter the opposition was held on February 4. Henry Ware attended and introduced resolutions favoring peace. He spoke against the resolutions committee's proposals calling for continuing resistance to the North. According to Loughery, only two or three men present agreed with Ware. Nothing came of this brief reappearance of the Opposition.[30]

By springtime, Confederate armies were so depleted that Congress approved arming 300,000 slaves for military duty. Loughery was worried. "Can the Negroes be relied upon to fight on our side?" he asked. It was too late, however, for even such desperate measures. The *Texas Republican* of April 14 carried news of the fall of Richmond. By the 28th, the community knew that Lee's army had surrendered at Appomattox. Loughery's first reaction was to demand no surrender, but by May 12, he was counseling only against surrendering with too much haste. In the meantime on May 9-12, General Kirby Smith held a meeting at Marshall with the governors of Louisiana, Arkansas, and Missouri. Governor Pendleton Murrah of Texas, a Marshall resident, was unable to participate due to illness, but he was represented by Guy M. Bryan. Kirby Smith and the governors worked out a set of proposals for ending the war without a formal surrender, but the situation was out of control. The Trans-Mississippi Department did not so much surrender as it simply disintegrated.[31]

Conditions around Marshall in April and May, 1865, were apparently typical of East Texas. As early as April 18, Confederate troops in the area lost discipline. General Thomas J. Church-

November 18, 25, December 2, 9 (quotations), 23, 1864.

[30] Marshall *Texas Republican*, January 27 (quotation), February 10, 1865.

[31] Ibid., April 14 (quotation), 28, May 12, 1865; Kerby, *Kirby Smith's Confederacy*, 417-423.

ill, commander of the forces fortifying Marshall for possible defense, issued the following order:

> It having been reported to these headquarters that the soldiers of this division have been committing depredations upon and otherwise annoying the citizens in the vicinity of Marshall, brigade commanders are directed to place strict guards around their respective commands when not engaged in the fortifications and adopt such other measures as they think most effectual in keeping their men in camp and preventing further molestation of the citizens living in the vicinity of their respective encampments.

Within a month as defeat became obvious, the men of Churchill's Division simply threw away their arms and went home. The arsenal and powder mill were left open for pillage. As Edmund Key remembered it, "Boys and men helped themselves — no guards, no precautions — bags were torn, kegs shattered and powder covered the floor. Fortunately, no explosion occurred." K. M. Van Zandt, who was then serving as tax-in-kind collector for the Confederacy, allowed the word to go out that his bureau's storehouse was unlocked. The supplies were soon well-distributed.[32]

The South's revolutionary war for independence ended as an unsuccessful civil rebellion. Harrison County, although paying a price in lives, goods, and prosperity, escaped invasion and occupation. Political institutions, social arrangements, and ways of making a living continued throughout with no fundamental alterations. As the community lay defeated at the end of May, 1865, however, it was possible that peace would bring more change than had the war. What would be the price of defeat?

[32]Robert N. Scott (comp.), *The War of the Rebellion: A Compilation of the Official Records of the Union and Confederate Armies* (Washington, 1880-1901), Series I, Vol. 48, Part 2, 1282 (first quotation); Vol. 53, 975; Edmund Key, "Memoranda for My Children" (second quotation), Key Family Papers; Van Zandt, *Force Without Fanfare*, 108; Luke, *Marshall Powder Mill Site*, 9-10.

9

Theophilus and Harriet Perry: "War Makes Its Widows by the Thousand"

THE CIVIL WAR meant tragedy to countless Americans, North as well as South. Historians recognize this, of course, but the story often has to be told in terms of depersonalized statistics and faceless generalizations about the sufferings of soldiers in the field and their families at home. Only in this way can we appreciate the magnitude of the struggle and its consequences. At the same time, however, we must not forget the war's impact on individual men and women. Their stories, taken singly, constitute a minute part of the conflict, but for millions of Americans, including many people in Harrison County, the real tragedy of the Civil War came at a personal level. Such was the case of Theophilus and Harriet Perry of Marshall, Texas.

The Perry family was prominent among the planter elite of antebellum Harrison County. Levin Perry, a native of North Carolina, arrived in the community during the late 1840s and took up the life of a large planter at "Spring Hill" in the area northeast of Marshall. His brother, Joshua, and two cousins, Dr. Harwood P. Perry and Josiah D. Perry, all of North Carolina, also established large plantations in the same neighborhood before 1850. Theophilus Perry was Levin Perry's eldest son, born in North Carolina on February 5, 1833.[1]

The Perrys could well afford educational opportunities for their children. During the late 1840s and early 1850s, Theophilus lived with relatives back "home" in Louisburg, North Carolina, and prepared to begin studies at the University of North Carolina in Chapel Hill. Levin Perry reminded his son of the need for "constant and untiring effort in the prosecution of your studies. . . ." "Think not," he wrote, "that anything truly desirable or praiseworthy can be attained in indolence, nor suffer yourself discouraged nor energies relaxed in the accomplishment of any purpose."[2]

Theophilus Perry heeded his father's advice, at least to the extent of completing a course of study and graduating from the University in 1854. He then moved to Marshall and began reading law preparatory to applying for admission to the Bar in Texas. At first, the aspiring lawyer felt that he had neglected his opportunities at Chapel Hill. "I have," he confessed, "an indirect need for all the prescribed college studies, and an urgent and direct one for the power of application and vigor of mind and strength of memory, a course of constant close study would have insured me. . . . How then can I help looking towards Chapel Hill without solemn regrets?" Difficulties and doubts

[1]The Perry families appear in the censuses of 1850 and 1860. Seventh Census, 1850, Schedules 1, 2, and 4; Eighth Census, 1860, Schedules 1, 2, and 4. References to "Spring Hill" appear regularly in the correspondence of Levin Perry. See Levin to Theophilus Perry, June 5, 1849, Person Family Papers. Theophilus specified his birthday in a letter to his wife Harriet Person Perry on February 21, 1864, also in the Person Family Papers.

[2]Levin Perry to Theophilus Perry, June 5, 1849 (quotations), June 6, 1850, April 21, 1852, Person Family Papers.

notwithstanding, however, Theophilus Perry applied to District Judge W. W. Morris to be examined for admission to the Bar during the fall of 1855. Having passed the examination, he bought part of a lot in Marshall in March, 1856, and opened a law office. The next spring Levin Perry gave his son ten slaves and 130 acres of land one mile east of town.[3] Thus Theophilus Perry at age twenty-four was an attorney, landholder, and slave-holder. Soon he would complete the process of settling in the community by marrying and beginning a family.

In 1859, Theophilus Perry returned to North Carolina and urgently courted his cousin Harriet Eliza Person. The Perry and Person families lived in Louisburg and were allied in many ways, so Theophilus probably knew Harriet from his days as a student. He pressed her—"the supreme object of my love"—for an early marriage. "Write to me immediately and write as you feel," he urged in September, 1859. "I demand a candid expression of your thoughts and feelings now. I dislike luke warmness, Cousin Harriet." Her reply must have been to his satisfaction for they were married on February 9, 1860. The couple arrived in Marshall that spring, bought an eight acre lot situated in town, and with the aid of eight Negro slaves established housekeeping.[4]

Harriet Person Perry was twenty-four years old in 1860, three years younger than her husband. Apparently she was not physically strong; Theophilus confessed a fear that friends would oppose his courtship because of her "feeble health." It is doubtful that she had extensive formal education, but she was highly literate, sensitive, and deeply religious. Her first months

[3]Kemp B. Battle, *History of the University of North Carolina* (Raleigh, N.C., 1912), I, 805; Theophilus Perry to an "Old Friend" (otherwise unidentified), March, 1855 (quotation); Theophilus Perry to Judge W. W. Morris, Fall, 1855, Person Family Papers. Copies of the deeds for the lot in Marshall (bought from George B. Adkins) and the land and slaves given to Perry by his father are in the Person Family Papers and the Harrison County Deed Records, County Clerk's Office, Marshall.

[4]Theophilus Perry to Harriet Person, September 28, 1859 (quotation), Person Family Papers. The marriage date is specified in a letter from Harriet P. Perry to Theophilus Perry, February 9, 1863, Person Family Papers. On July 19, 1860, Perry signed a note for $1,100 due May 1, 1862, to pay John A. Harris for the lot, Person Family Papers. Eighth Census, 1860, Schedule 2, shows Perry as the owner of seven bondsmen, but in 1861 he paid taxes on eight slaves. Harrison County Tax Rolls, 1861.

in Marshall left her homesick for Louisburg, but the transition from unmarried daughter in North Carolina to housewife in Texas was eased by the attentions of her husband. Theophilus came home at noon from his office for "dinner" and often sent Harriet affectionate notes during the afternoon. One read:

> Dear Wife: the desert you sent me was excellent. The tart was very good, but as for the apple pie allow me to say that I think the French cooks might learn a profitable lesson in your kitchen. Your devoted and loving husband, Theophilus Perry.

Harriet planned a flower garden with the assistance of a neighbor, Mrs. Catherine Marshall, recognizing that her husband would do the necessary work. "I can do what I please," she wrote her sister, "and leave the rest for him. I consider myself *very fortunate* in most respects . . . He is in better health than he ever was he says and looks very well *which you know is nothing unusual for him to do.*"[5]

Harriet Perry's adjustment to the community was also eased by the presence of so many North Carolinians. She visited often with "Mother Perry," as she called Levin Perry's second wife, Nancy Green Perry, and she liked Henry Hargrove who, she said, "goes like a steam engine as his red head would indicate." She could not resist gossiping a little about Henry's wife: ". . . *between you and me,*" she wrote her sister, "she [Lizzie Hargrove] is *one poor and dirty* housekeeper."[6] One is tempted to conclude that Harriet Person Perry was a thoroughly normal young wife.

While Theophilus and Harriet Perry were making themselves a home in Marshall, sectional tensions reached a climax in the election of 1860 and secession. The Perrys had not been notable political activists during the 1850s, and the family did not

[5]Theophilus Perry to Harriet Person, September 28, 1859, (first quotation), undated note (second quotation); Harriet Perry to her sister [Mary Person?], November 16, 1860 (third quotation), Person Family Papers.

[6]Harriet Perry to Sallie Person, December 17, 1860 (first quotation), Harriet Perry to her sister [Mary Person?], November 16, 1860 (second quotation), Person Family Papers. Levin Perry's first wife, Theophilus's mother, had died at the age of thirty-three.

play a leading role in the crisis of 1860–1861. Theophilus Perry, it seems, was a conservative whose political sympathies lay with the Opposition. Among his papers are several undated essays on filibustering during the early 1850s which he defined as the attempt to revolutionize Cuba and annex it to the United States. Filibustering activity of this sort was popular with ultra-southerners who sought additional slave territory, but Perry castigated it as lawlessness and the filibusterers as "adventurous prodigals." Also, during the crisis of 1860-1861, Perry committed to paper his reaction to a public letter from Royal T. Wheeler, chief justice of the Texas Supreme Court, approving secession. The young attorney decried the extremism of South Carolina's reaction to Lincoln's election and questioned Wheeler's assurances that there would be no conflict with federal authority. He pointed to the "grand army of voters that were marshalled at the last election" who did not vote Republican and who were not just southerners either.

> Here is the noble army of northern patriots that have stood up like a rock in the sea amidst the surging billows of abolitionism, grounded and rooted upon the firm foundation of justice the constitution and brotherly love. There they stand in unswerving and intrepid defense of southern rights and animate the patriot's heart with the proud declaration, my country with all your faults I love you still.

There is no evidence that Perry expressed his views publicly; perhaps he did not wish to risk the unpopularity that came with unionism at the time. Nevertheless, he must have been distressed at the course of events from November, 1860, through February, 1861.[7]

Theophilus Perry did not rush to volunteer for military duty

Theophilus to Harriet Perry, February 21, 1864, Ibid.

[7]Undated essays entitled "Filibusterism" by Theophilus Perry, (first quotation); undated and untitled paper by Theophilus Perry (second and third quotations), Person Family Papers. Judge Wheeler's letter appeared in the Austin *State Gazette* on December 15, 1860, and was reprinted by the Marshall *Texas Republican* on January 26, 1861. Levin and Joshua Perry did serve on the resolutions committee at the key secession meeting in Marshall on November 24, 1860. Marshall *Texas Republican*, December 1, 1860.

when the war began in April, 1861. This is not surprising in light of his views on secession in the first place. Moreover, Harriet bore their first child that summer, a girl named Martha or "Mattie." The proud parents were unable to write more than a few lines without reference to their "Sugar Lumpy," as Theophilus called her.[8]

Perry did, however, keep up with the war news, and undoubtedly as a relatively young man, felt pressure to do his part for the Confederacy. His younger brother, Hugh, volunteered with relatives in North Carolina and fought in the East throughout the war. At least four of his cousins from the community, Harwood Earl and Eugene O. Perry, sons of Dr. Harwood P. Perry, and Clinton and Bose Perry, Josiah D. Perry's sons, joined the Marshall Guards and went to fight in Virginia. The *Texas Republican* constantly demanded more volunteers. "Shall we stand idly by," Loughery asked on February 15, 1862, "with our arms folded, while our brothers are fighting the enemy on the border, and making breastworks of their bodies to repel the invaders?" Finally then, in the spring of 1862, Theophilus Perry decided to fight in a war brought on by secession, a step he had never favored. Duty and honor demanded that he serve.[9]

Perry volunteered for service with the Harrison County Lancers, a company raised by Captain Phil Brown to become part of Colonel Horace Randal's 28th Texas Cavalry. As a testimonial perhaps to his age, status, and leadership qualities, Perry was elected first lieutenant of the company when it organized in May, 1862. On Tuesday evening, July 8, 1862, the ladies of

[8]Harriet to Theophilus Perry, August 3, 1862, Louisa Perry to Theophilus Perry, November 15, 1862, Mrs. Catherine Marshall to Theophilus Perry, December 24, 1862 (quotation), Person Family Papers.

[9]Simpson, *Marshall Guards*, 20, 22. Marshall *Texas Republican*, February 15, 1862 (quotation). Perry may have been pressured into volunteering by the Confederacy's draft law in mid-April, 1862. However, the company that he joined was being formed before the Conscription Act passed, and it is clear that he had joined by early May, too soon most likely for the act to have had much effect. Theophilus Perry to Thomas Person, May 6, 1862, Person Family Papers. Hugh Perry was in the army as early as February, 1862. Theophilus Perry to Levin Perry, February, 1862 (date inferred from reference to surrender of Fort Donelson), Ibid. The role of Perry's cousins is also documented in Harriet to Theophilus Perry, October 26, 1862, Ibid.

Marshall presented the Lancers with a battle flag. Lieutenant Perry received the banner with "an appropriate speech," according to the *Texas Republican*. His remarks were not recorded, but more than likely he emphasized defense of the South against northern aggression. The next morning, July 9, Lieutenant Perry left with his company for Little Rock. He was accompanied by a slave named Norflet who was provided by Levin Perry as a body servant.[10]

Randal's regiment moved east to Shreveport, and Theophilus Perry soon found that an officer's duty could often be "disagreeable." The Louisiana town apparently offered special attractions to young soldiers from Texas, and Lieutenant Perry had the job of bringing them back to camp. "I had to go to some places a gentleman ought never to be caught at," he wrote Harriet, "and take them out of the presence of their amours." He also quickly discovered the pain of being separated from his family. "I never knew how much my life is wrapped up in you and daughter, as I know now," he wrote on July 17. "With you I could be happy on bread and water. Without you, wealth, fame, and glory would be worthless and indeed, misery. I am doing the best I can to preserve my health in order to return again. God grant to us all to meet again." As his regiment prepared to move on toward Little Rock, Perry told his wife that he expected "a great deal of hard fighting on this side of the Mississippi if the war continues throughout the year." "But," he added, "God grant it may be stopped." Theophilus Perry wanted the war over; he was hardly a glory seeker eager for battle and victory.[11]

Left at home in Marshall, Harriet Perry faced loneliness, sickness, fear, and depression. She was in the fifth month of her second pregnancy when Theophilus left. "I have had palpitations of the heart nearly every morning since you left, . . ." she wrote on August 3. "I attribute it to my situation. . . ." Their

[10] Marshall *Texas Republican*, February 15, May 4, July 5, 12 (quotation), 1862; Theophilus to Harriet Perry, July 14, 17, 1862, Person Family Papers.

[11] Theophilus to Harriet Perry, July 14 (first and second quotations), July 17 (third quotation), July 18 (fourth and fifth quotations), 1862, Person Family Papers.

first child, still an infant, was frequently ill. Harriet described a typical bout with a fever in early September. "I had all the care of her myself; no one to help or sympathize as you *always do*, and as no one else *could* do but your sweet self. . . . I was *very* fearful she would have spasms, her fever was so high—but I applied cold cloths to her head and that seemed to relieve the symptoms of spasms she exhibited." Harriet had some friends in Marshall, and Theophilus's family was nearby. Her own immediate family, however, was far away in North Carolina. At times she could hardly bear the absence of her husband. "I frequently wake up at night and feel as though my heart would break, tears are my greatest relief," she wrote. "I do not sleep at all. I often get up and sit by the window for some time and would give worlds, if I had them, if you could be with me." But at the same time, she was determined not to despond in the first months after Theophilus left.

> You must be cheerful and not get low-spirited, for I shall do the very best I can under *all* circumstances. I have a great many things to divert my mind, for I have much to employ me to keep everything going strait *[sic]* about the place. We have got on every well so far. The Negroes seem to do as well as when you were here so far. I can't tell how long they will hold out.

Thus she had at least an adequate labor force for her small household and as much help in caring for her daughter as she needed.[12]

In mid-August, Harriet and "Sugar Lumpy" visited Theophilus at Lewisville in southwestern Arkansas where his company stopped on the way from Shreveport to Little Rock. The visit raised her spirits. "I feel better satisfied since I saw you than I did before," she wrote upon her return home. But improved spirits did not last long in the face of renewed loneliness. "Oh husband I feel as if I shall die here all alone," Harriet's letter of September 24 read. "I can't take any interest in anything in the

[12]Harriet to Theophilus Perry, August 3 (first, third, and fourth quotations); September 15 (second quotation), 1862, Person Family Papers.

world . . . and I don't think anything could arouse me but your presence." Their daughter continued in poor health. "I have humored and spoiled her until I scarcely know what to do with her. She sits in my lap *all* the time and loves me better than ever, it's mamma all the time with her. I don't know what I shall do with two babies." And as the birth of a second child neared Harriet was more anxious than ever. "I cannot sleep at night," she wrote Theophilus. "I experience daily and nightly all the horrors of giving birth to an infant in mind, and the recollection of it is as vivid as the hour of my baby's birth. I dread it much more, for I know how bad it is. My being alone is worse still." She begged her husband to come home, but in the same line recognized that he could not and hoped that she would not make him sad.[13]

Developments in the war during 1862 compounded Harriet's fears. In mid-October, she learned of the deaths of Theophilus's cousins, Harwood Earl and Clinton Perry, at the Battle of Antietam. "I don't know what is to become of us," she wrote her sister. "We are sorely scourged if any people ever were." She longed to be with her family in North Carolina but could not bear to be so far from her husband. "I want to stay as near him as I can while he lives for I have no idea he will ever return to stay. War makes its widows by the thousand." Fear for Theophilus's life went largely unmentioned in Harriet's letters to him, but it gave a morbid cast to her thought as the war progressed. Finally, in addition to everything else, she began in 1862 to worry over the attitude of slaves. "I am very much alarmed about Lincoln's Proclamation," she wrote Theophilus on October 26. "I had not been afraid to stay here till now."[14]

Theophilus Perry remained in the vicinity of Little Rock through the fall of 1862 well removed from any engagement with the enemy. Serving as acting brigade quartermaster he had

[13]Theophilus to Levin Perry, August 17, 1862; Harriet to Theophilus Perry, September 5 (first quotation), 22 (second quotation), October 26 (third quotation), 30 (fourth quotation), 1862, Person Family Papers.

[14]Harriet Perry to Sallie Person, October 22, 1862 (first and second quotations); Harriet to Theophilus Perry, October 26, 1862 (third quotation), Person Family Papers.

a great deal of time to observe his fellow officers and army politics. He still had no desire for military glory; his only hope was that the "clouds and storm of war which like a blast have swept over the land, may soon be swept away, and leave the skies clear again." He urged Harriet to be cheerful in that expectation and told her how he fixed his eyes on the future. "I make many plans about fixing my place, and practicing law, educating Sugar Lumpy and providing you with a thousand little conveniences and comforts about home. The humblest home in the Confederacy is preferable to the life of a soldier in camp."[15]

Harriet expected her baby in late November, 1862, but three weeks into December it had not yet been born. Waiting without Theophilus was almost more than she could bear. "I nearly die with low-spirits and depression, . . ." she wrote. "You don't know how I feel and never can. I know you are the most sympathetic and best of husbands and I feel grateful for such an one, but you can never feel enough for your wife. I don't think any *man* can." She feared a Federal invasion up the Red River and expected to have to leave home. "I don't feel confident of our success by any means. I think the South is nearly exhausted." At least their daughter was well, and Harriet obviously enjoyed describing her good health and disposition. "She is sweet tempered and amiable as she can be, *not at all like* her mother."[16]

Harriet Perry's second baby was born at noon on Christmas Eve. She was attended only by an aunt and her friend, Mrs. Catherine Marshall. The latter wrote Theophilus Perry informing him that he was the father of a "fine boy weighing 8½ pounds, which *we* have named Theophilus." Harriet was relieved and proud but not even the birth of her son and her own physical recovery cheered her for long. On January 6, 1863, she wrote her sister, "It is the worst thing in the world to live as I do, it nearly kills me, but I don't know what to do. I sometimes

[15] Theophilus to Harriet Perry, November 22 (first quotation), September 23 (second quotations), 1862, Person Family Papers.

[16] Harriet to Theophilus Perry, December 3 (first quotation), December 23 (second and third quotation), 1862, Person Family Papers.

think of breaking up and maybe I will this year.'' And she did have reason for her gloomy outlook. There were slaves to keep the place, plant a garden, kill hogs, and so on, but they required supervision. Once her aunt left in January, she had to care for an infant and a young child. A slave named Louisiana helped with the children, but the pressures of motherhood fell heavily on Harriet Perry. To make matters worse, Mattie developed a serious intestinal disorder during the Christmas season. ''I do not think I shall ever raise her,'' Harriet wrote Theophilus in January. She ''is more trouble than the baby.''[17]

The war dragged on for Theophilus Perry during the early months of 1863 in the area of Little Rock and Pine Bluff, Arkansas. He was distressed at the surrender of Arkansas Post with the capture of so many Harrison County men and believed that his division should be sent to Vicksburg where they might do some good. He continued to handle quartermaster duties but hoped for a promotion to regimental commissary officer, a position with the rank of captain. Above all, however, he wanted the conflict ended. ''Oh God!,'' he wrote on January 30, 1863, ''that this war would close, and we all could return to our homes and families.''[18]

In February, 1863, seven months after Theophilus left for the war, Harriet reluctantly decided to break up housekeeping and move in with Levin Perry's family at Spring Hill. Her father-in-law advised it. She rented the house in Marshall to a refugee from Arkansas and hired out most of the slaves, being satisfied that they would earn more in that manner than any other. She was able to pay their bills and promised to be especially frugal in the future. The move immediately seemed to bolster her spirits. ''Husband,'' she wrote, ''I shall endeavor to manage the best I can, so that when you return our circumstances will be more easy

[17] Catherine Marshall to Theophilus Perry, December 24, 1862 (first quotation); Harriet Perry to Sallie Person, January 6, 1863 (second quotation); Harriet to Theophilus Perry, January 13, 1863 (third quotation), Person Family Papers. The reference to ''breaking up'' meant that she was thinking of abandoning her own household and moving in with her in-laws.

[18] Theophilus to Harriet Perry, January 30, 1863, Person Family Papers.

than now." The morbid tone of earlier letters was gone, at least temporarily. Both children were healthy and had a housefull of playmates with Theophilus's young half-brothers and sisters. In fact, Levin Perry's second wife gave birth to another baby in March, 1863. Late that month Harriet wrote: "I am well and as happy as I could be separated from your sweet self. I am better satisfied than I was before I broke up."[19]

Doubtless Theophilus Perry was relieved at the news from his wife; especially since his life in the army became much more active during the spring of 1863. When General Grant menaced Vicksburg by crossing the Mississippi north of the town and moving southward along the river in Louisiana before crossing again on April 30 to attack from the south, Lieutenant Perry's company as part of Randal's 28th Texas Cavalry regiment in General John G. Walker's Division was ordered from Pine Bluff in Arkansas southward into Louisiana. A few weeks before the army marched, Perry was made acting inspector general of the second brigade, a position he held for most of the campaign. Walker's Division reached Monroe in early May and marched on to Alexandria in central Louisiana later that month. By early June, they had moved northeastward to Delhi only nineteen miles west of Vicksburg. They could hear the sounds of battle there, and they covered what Theophilus sarcastically called the "withdrawal" of General Henry E. McCullough's forces following the Battle of Milliken's Bend on June 7. The Harrison County Lancers, like the rest of the second brigade, were not actively engaged, however, and suffered no losses.[20]

Theophilus discounted most of the talk of Confederate successes around Vicksburg and was not surprised when the town surrendered on July 4, 1863. Walker's Division moved to the west of Monroe as the southern commanders sought to deter-

[19]Harriet Perry to Sallie Person, February 18, 1863; Harriet to Theophilus Perry, February 8 (first quotation), March 24 (second quotation), 1863, Person Family Papers.

[20]Eaton, *History of Southern Confederacy*, 199-200. The movements of Perry's company may be traced in a series of letters to his wife. Theophilus to Harriet Perry, April 14, 23, 25, May 7, 18, 23, 27, 29, June 1, 11 (quotation), 1863, Person Family Papers.

mine Grant's next move. Perry did not expect an invasion immediately, and again he was correct. His company awaited orders in late July, expecting to be sent back to Alexandria in the event of a Federal attack along the Red River. In the meantime, Captain Phil Brown of the Lancers died. Theophilus Perry ended his service as inspector general and rejoined his company. Soon he became its commander.[21]

Perry was troubled throughout the busy months from March to July, 1863, by the fact that his servant, Norflet, was missing. Norflet had been of "inestimable value" to his master after they left home together in July, 1862. But in January, 1863, Perry loaned him to Colonel and Mrs. Randal because their servant had run away. Norflet, Theophilus had written Harriet at the time, "thinks Mrs. Randal hard to please but that is neither here or there; he has got to cook for them yet awhile." Apparently he had no thought that Norflet might take a lesson from the Randal's own "boy." Norflet disappeared from camp near Pine Bluff, Arkansas, in early March, 1863. Perry was hopeful at first that he had headed for home, but soon became convinced that he had gone to the Federals instead. The loss of a valuable slave was upsetting, and Perry commented on it in letter after letter to his wife. Yet he seemed to accept running away as part of slavery and did not express anger over what Norflet had done. Within several months, he was thinking in terms of having another servant sent from Harrison County to join him.[22]

As he reached the end of his first year in the army, Theophilus Perry became increasingly convinced that the war would not end soon. Perhaps, he wrote Harriet, a great man could bring it to a speedy conclusion.

> If the North was blessed with a great military genius like Alexander or Caesar, our armies and secession would melt away faster than snow in the plain of the Tropics. But if Heaven

[21] Theophilus to Harriet Perry, June 11, 20, July 4, 12, 29, 1863, Person Family Papers.

[22] Ibid., August 17, 1862 (first quotation), January 30, 1863 (second quotation). Norflet's disappearance is mentioned in each of the following: Theophilus to Harriet Perry, March 8, 24, April 11, May 7, 27, June 11, 1863, Person Family Papers.

> chooses to bless our nation with that man, we will soon dictate peace. If however as is generally the case no wonderful man arises to fix the eyes of the nation and this war has to be fought out by "great men in the more common acceptance of the word" in all likelihood it is yet a war of months and years. Accustom yourself to think of it as a long war.[23]

Once more Perry's primary concern appears to have been not victory, but an end to the fighting.

When Theophilus Perry had time to think about things other than his immediate military duties in early 1863, personal finances worried him as much as the loss of Norflet and the lengthening war. He sent $500 to Harriet in March. "I think it will be enough to pay all of my little debts," he wrote. He began to list his creditors but concluded: "I am afraid since I have begun to enumerate that the $500.00 will not pay the half of them." Taking advantage of the fact that Harriet had moved to live with his father, he directed her in letter after letter to sell their land and anything else necessary to pay existing debts. Depreciation of Confederate money also encouraged him to seek "freedom from our creditors." "At the conclusion of this war," he wrote on April 23, "the smallest indebtedness will break a man. Now is the golden opportunity to pay out. Sell everything that can be spared for that purpose." He was so anxious to be freed of debt that in July, 1863, he returned the eight acre lot in Marshall to John A. Harris for the $1,100 note he had signed in 1860. Apparently too he disposed of the 130 acres given to him by his father back in 1857. The tax rolls for 1864 show Theophilus Perry as the owner of only eight slaves. In 1862, he had paid taxes on two parcels of land, eight slaves, a horse, four head of cattle, and $72 worth of miscellaneous property. Service in the army was costing him what small fortune he had.[24]

By the summer of 1863, Theophilus Perry had become disgusted with many of the men at home, a not uncommon or un-

[23] Theophilus to Harriet Perry, April 11, 1863, Person Family Papers.

[24] Ibid., March 8 (first and second quotations), April 23 (third and fourth quotations), 1863; Harriet to Theophilus Perry, July 28, 1863, Person Family Papers; Harrison County Tax Rolls, 1862, 1864.

reasonable reaction among soldiers in the field. He was angered at the lack of necessary equipment for the army and the apparently weak morale back in Texas. Those he regarded as war profiteers were condemned too. "I have a great contempt for noisy men like G. G. Gregg and his stripe, who . . . talked of whipping the reluctant youth of the land off to the war, and who themselves have ignobly speculated upon the necessities of the soldier and his family, accumulated fortunes out of the sacrifices of those that have bared their bosoms to the bayonets, and yet sculk away from danger themselves." Perry's most bitter denunciations were saved for the radicals who had whipped up sentiment for secession and left others to do the fighting. "Every little editor and stump speaker ought to be put under a musket and a rucksack," he wrote Harriet on July 9. "But they think the world would cease to turn unless their weekly issues [appear]. What will Loughery do? What will Pope? I have no faith in their sort." Harriet cautioned against bitterness, but his feelings remained strong. "You admonish me against indulging in bitter feelings against those people that stay at home and shun the service," he wrote on July 17.

> I yield to sentiments of kindness for all that class that were tolerant and respectful towards the opinions of others; but the rabid violent secessionist who denounced all persons that differed from him, ought to have shouldered his gun at the beginning of the war; and I feel a contempt for him that I in vain strive to suppress. He that denounced others, is himself denounced.[25]

Theophilus Perry finally received a long-awaited furlough and came home in mid-August, 1863. Sadness and heartbreak awaited him, however. The baby born to his stepmother in March had died in July, and his half-sister Geneva died of dyptheria in August. Then, his own daughter Mattie, who had often

[25] Theophilus to Harriet Perry, June 20, July 12 (first quotation), July 9 (second and third quotations), July 17 (fourth and fifth quotations), 1863, Person Family Papers. G. G. Gregg, as already noted, was a wealthy Marshall merchant; Loughery, of course, was editor of the *Texas Republican*; Alexander Pope was the ultra-southern lawyer who represented Harrison County in the secession convention.

been in poor health, died in late August or early September. At least he was home to comfort his wife. "It was my first great sorrow," Harriet wrote her sister, "but I know it is all for the best." Theophilus left to return to the army in mid-September but became ill on the way and was taken back home for a couple more months. It was late November before he went back to the army in Louisiana.[26]

Shortly after Theophilus left, Harriet Perry received the news that two of her brothers had died in the war in the East. Jessee Person was killed while leading a charge at Gettysburg on July 3, and Tom Person died from wounds received at Bristol Station near Culpepper Courthouse in Virginia on October 14. "Now sorrow is added to sorrow," Harriet wrote her mother. "Truly misfortunes come not singly. . . . God doeth all things well, however hard it may seem to us."[27]

Theophilus Perry rejoined the Harrison County Lancers in east-central Louisiana near the mouth of the Red River, the expected route of invasion if the Federals sought to attack the Trans-Mississippi Department command center in the Shreveport-Marshall area. He took with him a slave called Doctor to serve in the place of the runaway Norflet. Shortly after he and his new servant departed, however, Harriet wrote that Norflet had been located at Bonham in North Texas. Levin Perry immediately rode to the Fannin County town to claim his property. He returned twelve days later, and Harriet recounted Norflet's odyssey to Theophilus. According to the slave, he had not run away. Instead, he had been picked up by "Jay Hawkers," while on an errand to purchase eggs and butter for Mrs. Randal, and been taken to the Federals. He was present at a battle near Helena, Arkansas, in which Negroes were placed in the front ranks where they were killed by the Confederates. Norflet himself was

[26]These events are documented in Theophilus to Harriet Perry, July 17, 1863; Louisa Perry to Theophilus Perry, August 10, 1863; Harriet Perry to Sallie Person, October 18, 1863 (quotation); Theophilus Perry to Thomas Person, December 23, 1863; Harriet Perry to her Mother, December 23, 1863, Person Family Papers.

[27]One of Harriet Perry's sisters wrote to her of their brothers' deaths on November 14, 1863. Harriet Perry to her Mother, December 23, 1863 (quotation), Person Family Papers.

being drilled at the time and was promised action in the next fight. With that in mind, he did run away—from the Federals. A man from Arkansas then brought him to Texas with the promise of taking him home, but Norflet decided that he was being led in the wrong direction and ran away again. He was then "taken up" at Bonham in Fannin County by Confederate troops and worked for the quartermaster department there until Levin Perry arrived. "This is his story," Harriet wrote, "we know not what to believe — I knew he would have a good tale made up. . . . He says," she added, "he is glad to get home for no one ever tried harder than he did." It would be interesting to have seen the expression on Norflet's face when he made that statement. Perhaps he was sincere. He had a wife at Spring Hill who wrote to him and sent him little presents while he was with Theophilus Perry in Arkansas.[28]

Theophilus Perry's company spent January and February, 1864, in camp near Marksville, Louisiana. They were not immediately menaced by the Federals, and Perry again allowed himself to think about the future. Having extricated himself from most of his debts during 1863 by sacrificing his small landholdings, he decided that whatever the outcome of the war, landed property would be a useful and secure investment. The situation now seemed ripe for a man to exchange depreciated Confederate currency or even slaves for debt-free property of lasting value. In letter after letter, he urged his father and Harriet to use currency or his few Negroes to buy a "little, improved place" of four or five hundred acres. On January 18 he wrote:

> Land is the best property a man can have. I want a place if one can be had. I care not what it costs. I wish to spend five thousand dollars for land. I can raise about this amount, or near it. . . . Our Confederate money is rapidly coming to nothing. Before it does this I wish to secure a little Home,

[28]Theophilus to Harriet Perry, December 8, 1863; Harriet to Theophilus Perry, December 6, 13 (quotation), 1863; Fannie to "My Dear Husband," December 28, 1862, Person Family Papers. For the full context of Fannie's letter, see Randolph B. Campbell and Donald K. Pickens (eds.), " 'My Dear Husband': A Texas Slave's Love Letter, 1862," *Journal of Negro History*, LXV (Fall, 1980), 361-364.

> where I can finally resort and make a subsistence by the sweat of my brow, if I should be reduced to the necessity of field labor. I know that Papa thinks landed property as insecure and worthless as any other kind in the event of our subjugation. I do not think so and cannot. I do not wish to be considered as believing that we will be subjugated, but whatever our fortune may be I think that our money will be worthless in all likelihood, and that our Negro property will be rendered very insecure and precarious. . . .
>
> In revolutions like this, landed property is far safer than any other. It behooves every man to procure a little home for his family.

Harriet replied in February that she and Levin Perry could not comply with Theophilus's wish. Land costs a "small fortune," she wrote, and there was no place to buy even if they had the money. Perry's accurate analysis of the economic situation thus came to nothing.[29]

Theophilus Perry had his thirty-first birthday in early February, 1864. Remembering that his mother had died at thirty-three, he wrote Harriet, "I shudder at the thought of being so old." He expected a Federal attack in the spring but took what was for him an unusually warlike attitude. "Our army is stronger and in better condition than even. We will show our strength this summer."[30]

General Nathaniel P. Banks began his Red River campaign in early March, 1864. Troops under his command supported by Admiral David D. Porter's gunboats moved upriver from the Mississippi and took Fort DeRussy near Marksville on March 14. General Walker fell back to Alexandria and beyond, leaving the city to the pursuing Federals without a fight on March 16. Confederate forces, now under the overall command of General Richard Taylor, retreated to Natchitoches which fell without resistance on March 31. General Banks expected to cover the last eighty miles to Shreveport by April 10. His primary fear was that

[29] Theophilus to Harriet Perry, January 8, 18 (first and second quotations), 1864; Harriet to Theophilus Perry, February 14, 1864 (third quotation), Person Family Papers.

[30] Theophilus to Harriet Perry, February 21 (first quotation), March 1 (second quotation), 1864, Person Family Papers.

the rebel army would continue to withdraw necessitating pursuit into the interior of Texas.

The 28th Texas Cavalry including Captain Perry's company retreated with Walker's Division from the lower Red River to a point about forty miles below Shreveport near the town of Mansfield. There General Taylor did what General Banks apparently did not expect. He turned and fought. Walker's Division including Randal's Brigade stood astride the stage road three miles from Mansfield occupying the center of Taylor's lines. On the afternoon of April 8, Federal troops attempted an unprepared attack on the Confederate position and were driven back in a defeat that turned into blind panic. Banks lost nearly 700 men killed or wounded and 1,500 military and 1,000 non-military prisoners. Rather than attempt to press on toward Shreveport, he retired during the night to Pleasant Hill about twenty miles south of Mansfield. General Taylor decided to follow up his advantage and crush the Federals. The next afternoon, April 9, with Walker's Division once more occupying the center, Taylor's outnumbered and exhausted forces battered themselves to pieces attacking Union troops in a defensive posture. Confederate forces took 1,600 casualties; Banks suffered just as many. The Federal army retreated again and abandoned the Red River campaign.[31]

Theophilus Perry had premonitions of death from the outset of this campaign. "I feel very solemn," he wrote Harriet on March 13.

> I cannot help it. It is a trying thing to join in Battle. The most horrible and blasphemous thing perhaps on earth. I shall try to be true to our cause. . . . I love you more than my life. My love to all my family. I send this to them all. I may never see them again. I love my people and I die in their defense. God look in mercy upon us all and forgive our sins, and collect us at death into his glory. Farewell, my Dear Wife

[31] The Red River campaign has been discussed above in Chapter 8. The most detailed study is Johnson, *Red River Campaign*. Kerby, *Kirby Smith's Confederacy*, 294-311, also deals with this campaign in some depth from the Confederate point of view.

> and child, Farewell my Father, Mother, sisters, Brothers, Aunt Betsy, and All, Farewell again.

He wrote several more letters during the retreat up Red River and finally on April 6 sent Harriet a note from a point near Mansfield telling her to look for his baggage to arrive in Marshall. Theophilus Perry survived the Battle of Mansfield on the 8th, but he was wounded at Pleasant Hill the next day and died on April 17, 1864.[32]

Harriet Perry eulogized her husband as a martyr to the cause of southern independence; a cause that would yet triumph. But more importantly, she wrote, he died a Christian warrior, enabling her to take consolation in the thought that "the toil, the privations and hardships of a soldier's life are now exchanged for the glories of a brighter world—the roar of cannon and clash of arms for the songs and shouts of a New Jerusalem — and the smiles and endearments of the beloved on earth, for the smiles and approval of a crucified Redeemer." She concluded by quoting William Cullen Bryant's *Thanatopsis.*[33]

Theophilus Perry's will was probated in Marshall during June, 1864. It left all his property to Harriet, but except for his slaves, he had virtually none. Harriet Perry had often longed for her home in North Carolina while Theophilus was in the army and remained in Harrison County only to be close to him. Soon after his death, probably within a year, she left the community with Theophilus Jr., and went home.[34]

Harriet Perry was hardly the idealized heroine of the beleaguered Confederacy standing steadfastly through hardship at home while uncomplainingly supporting her husband in the field. From one point of view, she was a morbidly fearful young woman who constantly bemoaned her plight while surrounded

[32] Theophilus to Harriet Perry, March 13 (quotation), 17, 19, 23, 24, April 6, 1864, Person Family Papers. The date of Perry's death is fixed in the "Eulogy" written by his wife and retained among the family papers.

[33] Harriet Perry, "Eulogy" of Theophilus Perry, Person Family Papers.

[34] Louisa Perry (from Spring Hill) to Harriet Perry (in North Carolina), November 8, 1865, Person Family Papers. Copies of Perry's will, dated November 13, 1863, and of the probate action on the will are preserved in the Person Family Papers.

by servants, relatives, and friends. On the other hand, she may be seen as an intelligent and sensitive wife almost borne under by the pressures of bearing and rearing children and managing a household while worrying about the fate of her husband in the army.

From any point of view, the Civil War brought tragedy to the lives of Theophilus and Harriet Perry. He had not favored secession or war and clearly wanted no part of the conflict. He fought as a matter of duty and hoped only for peace. She hated her husband's absence and felt that she could not live without him. Amidst the tensions of war, they suffered the deaths of brothers, of sisters, and of their own first child. The Harrison County community lost an entire family.

PART THREE

Reconstruction

10

Presidential Reconstruction: May, 1865–March, 1867

HARRISON COUNTY emerged from the Civil War relatively unscathed. Many families mourned the loss of sons or husbands, but there had been no invasion and occupation, no seizure of property or emancipation of slaves, and no destruction of towns and plantations. From the secession winter of 1860–1861 until the Confederacy disintegrated in May, 1865, the community's basic economic, social, and political structure stood unchanged. It was possible, however, that peace and Reconstruction after the war would bring fundamental change where the conflict had not.

What would the victorious North demand of the defeated South? Robert W. Loughery summarized the possibilities for

Harrison County readers in a *Texas Republican* editorial on May 25, 1865. The North, he wrote, may attempt to establish military rule, confiscate property, disfranchise whites, and "elevate" the Negro. Or, the policy could be one of reconciliation aimed at binding up the wounds of war and reviving the southern economy. Loughery warned against adoption of a harsh policy designed to bring drastic change to southern communities such as his own. "Our armies, it is true, are destroyed, but the spirits of the people are unbroken. . . . They are not yet fit for slaves. . . ."[1]

Loughery urged the community to accept the restoration of Federal authority gracefully and to maintain law and public order. He was not pleased at the manner in which the powder mill and arsenal at Marshall were pillaged during the Confederacy's last days, and the apathy of the public on this and other local matters troubled him. Nevertheless, by mid-June, he felt that civil government was functioning smoothly in Harrison County and across Texas. In his opinion, it would be "useless to send a single company of soldiers to garrison any portion of the territory."[2]

Loughery also expressed a hope that Negro slavery would continue in spite of the Confederacy's defeat, the Emancipation Proclamation, and the proposed Thirteenth Amendment. Some planters are freeing their bondsmen, he noted, but the great majority, actuated by attachment to the race and gratitude for the past, "continue to support and control their Negroes as formerly." In Loughery's opinion, this was necessary. "The Negro race is naturally idle and migratory," he wrote, and at least 2,500 of the 10,000 slaves in the community cannot take care of themselves. He did not expect the constitutional amendment to win approval within ten years; so emancipation, if it had to come, could be partial and gradual.[3]

Loughery's hopes concerning military occupation and the

[1] Marshall *Texas Republican*, May 26, 1865.

[2] Ibid., May 26, June 2, 16 (quotation), 1865; Luke, *Marshall Powder Mill*, 9-10.

[3] Marshall *Texas Republican*, June 16, 1865.

preservation of slavery, which undoubtedly reflected the views of many in the community, soon proved false. On June 19, 1865, General Gordon Granger arrived at Galveston to take formal possession of Texas for the United States. Granger immediately issued the famous "Juneteenth" order ending slavery everywhere in the state. Events in Galveston were not news in Marshall, however. Federal troops — the 8th Illinois Infantry regiment and a company of cavalry under the command of Lieutenant Colonel Loyd Wheaton—had arrived there from Shreveport on Saturday, June 17. Military government replaced local civilian authority, and the community was informed that slavery had been destroyed by Lincoln's Emancipation Proclamation.[4]

Steps toward reconstructing loyal state and local governments in Texas began the same day federal authority arrived in Harrison County. President Andrew Johnson appointed Andrew Jackson Hamilton, a noted Texas unionist, as provisional governor on June 17 and directed him to call a convention for the purpose of restoring Texas to its proper constitutional relationship with the United States. Hamilton would have to oversee the registration of qualified voters (those who had taken an amnesty oath prescribed by President Johnson on May 29 and could meet the qualifications to vote effective in Texas prior to secession); supervise the election of delegates to the convention; and approve their work in revising the constitution and laws of Texas. In the meantime, he had to create provisional local governments to cooperate with federal authority and aid in the process of Reconstruction.[5]

Through July and early August, 1865, Hamilton received numerous requests for appointments in Harrison County. Isaac W. Johnston, for example, sought the position of sheriff. "I am and have been of the conservative class of citizens of the state,"

[4]Ibid., June 23, 1865; Charles William Ramsdell, *Reconstruction in Texas* (Austin, 1970), 40. Federal troops were rushed to Marshall because of the Confederate quartermaster operations based there. Scott (comp.), *War of the Rebellion: Official Records*, Series I, volume 48, part 2, 903.

[5]Ramsdell, *Reconstruction in Texas*, 55-59; Marshall *Texas Republican*, August 4, 1865.

he wrote, "who preferred a settlement of all national questions between the State and United States government by compromising of mutual concessions on the part of both in preference to open conflict." N. H. Wilson, an Ohio-born lawyer, wanted the appointment as district judge. "Slavery is at and [*sic*] end here," he informed Hamilton, "and should be so regarded by our people. Having been born and educated in a free state, I know something of the free labor system, and believe it can be . . . inaugurated in the South." Hamilton also received at least four letters from Asa H. Willie, a Marshall attorney whose brother, James Willie, had been attorney general of Texas during the mid-1850s. Willie apparently wrote as a personal acquaintance and perhaps a friend of Hamilton, but as a Georgia-born, former slaveholder, and ex-Confederate army officer, he generally recommended long-time residents of Harrison County who had the confidence of the community. His recommendation for sheriff, for example, was Solomon R. Perry, the incumbent who had won that office four times since 1850.[6]

Hamilton appointed a provisional government for Harrison County on August 7, 1865. The men chosen for the most important positions, J. B. Williamson for district judge of the Sixth Judicial District and Davis B. Bonfoey for county judge, were both northerners by birth, and neither had been a secessionist or an officeholder prior to secession. Williamson and Bonfoey, however, could hardly be called "carpetbaggers," as northern settlers in the post-war South came to be known, since both were resident in the community as early as 1850. Williamson had participated in Democratic Party politics during the antebellum years, and Bonfoey had been a slaveholder. The latter's wife, Emma Bonfoey, was one of Marshall's leading antebellum educators. Among the other county officials appointed, three of the four county commissioners (N. V. Board, E. B. Blalock, and J. S.

[6]Isaac W. Johnston to Andrew J. Hamilton, July 20, 1865 (first quotation); N. H. Wilson to Andrew J. Hamilton, August 3, 1865 (second quotation); Asa H. Willie to Andrew J. Hamilton, July 20, 21, August 1, 4, 1865, Executive Department, Governors' Letters, Archives Division, Texas State Library, Austin; Webb, Carroll and Branda, (eds.), *Handbook of Texas*, II, 918; Eighth Census, 1860, Schedules 1 and 2; Election Registers, 1850-1865.

Powell), the sheriff (S. R. Perry), and the tax assessor/collector (G. W. Young) had held those offices previously — during the 1850s and early 1860s. Only a few men such as County Commissioner Silas D. Wood, a merchant who had lived in the community since 1850, and District Clerk Alexander R. Woodall joined Williamson and Bonfoey as new local officeholders. Thus, although federal troops remained present, the first Reconstruction government in Harrison County was run by men very familiar to the local citizenry. Even Loughery of the *Texas Republican* felt reassured about the federal government's approach to political restoration.[7]

In the meantime, Harrison County's residents, both white and black, began to adjust to the end of slavery. Most owners freed their bondsmen in June, 1865, once federal authority arrived. The financial loss, while not unexpected, had to be staggering. There is no way to ascertain exactly how many slaves were freed in the community that summer, but it is possible to calculate the slaveholders' losses in terms of 1860 numbers and values. The 8,784 bondsmen enumerated in the census of 1860 were valued at approximately $780 each regardless of age, sex, or condition. Emancipation at that time would have cost $6,851,250. When it came in 1865, there were even more slaves in the county, perhaps 10,000. Slave values were, of course, upset by wartime conditions, but under normal circumstances they probably would have continued upward during the early 1860s. It seems reasonable to conclude, then, that emancipation cost Harrison County slaveholders at least $7,000,000.[8]

[7] Marshall *Texas Republican*, August 18, September 29, 1865; Election Registers, 1850-1865; Seventh Census, 1850, Schedule 1; Eighth Census, 1860, Schedule 1. J. B. Williamson appears in the census of 1850 as a twenty-five-year-old schoolteacher from Pennsylvania. Seventh Census, 1850, Schedule 1. For his participation in Democratic Party politics, see Marshall *Texas Republican*, November 22, 1856. Davis B. Bonfoey appears in the census of 1860 as a forty-eight-year-old "trader" from Connecticut and the owner of five slaves. Eighth Census, 1860, Schedules 1 and 2.

[8] The number of slaves in 1860 and the value of those bondsmen is discussed above in Chapters 1 and 2. The Marshall *Texas Republican* of June 16, 1865 estimated 10,000 slaves in the community. Interestingly, Harrison County Tax Rolls for 1864 listed 8,680 Negroes. However, on the basis of a comparison of tax and census records in 1850 and 1860, it seems that owners had a tendency to "overlook" one or two slaves for tax pur-

Planters at least had the consolation of extremely high post-war prices for cotton grown in 1865. The crop was well on the way toward maturity when emancipation came, and it appears that most farmers succeeded in persuading enough of their slaves to remain with them to handle the harvest that year. Josephine Howard, who belonged to Tim Walton recalled: "Dey wants us to git in de pickin', so my folks and some more stays. Dey didn't know no place to go to." At least there were virtually no complaints about cotton going unpicked, and records available on a few plantations indicate that the owners did reasonably well in 1865. William J. Blocker's family, for example, sold twenty-seven bales (12,344 pounds) in February, 1866 at 42 cents per pound and another fifteen bales (6,671 pounds) in May at 31 7/8 cents. The crop grossed $7,339.54; approximately $3,000 more than the ninety-one bales sold in early 1860.[9] Wise planters undoubtedly enjoyed this situation but at the same time recognized that it was temporary. Cotton prices would fall, and black labor was not secure in the future.

For their part, most of the Negroes had been slaves since birth, and freedom, no matter how much it had been desired, came as a shock. Will Adams, for example, remembered "lots of cryin' and weepin'." Many slaves, he said, "didn't want to be free, 'cause they knowed nothin' and had nowhere to go." Bondsmen on Joshua Perry's plantation reacted differently, however. Martin Ruffin recalled that the announcement of freedom was puzzling at first, but then someone said, " 'we is free — no more whippings and beatings,' " and all began to celebrate. Jess Witt's slaves responded to the news of emancipation by pulling off their "croaker sack clothes."[10]

poses. Slaves were not counted for taxes in 1865.

[9] Rawick (ed.), *American Slave*, IV, Part 2, 164 (quotation); Estate of William J. Blocker, Harrison County Probate Papers. C. R. Hargrove, in a memoir on Reconstruction preserved in the Lentz Collection at East Texas Baptist College, recalled that all his family's slaves stayed except for those recently purchased. By October, 1865, the *Texas Republican* carried numerous advertisements by cotton factors, suggesting a boom at that time.

[10] Rawick (ed.), *American Slave*, IV, Part 1, 1-3 (first quotation); V, Part 3, 265-267 (second quotation); V, Part 4, 208-210 (third quotation).

Almost without exception, slaveowners asked their bondsmen to remain on the farm or plantation and work for wages. Jess Witt, for example, told his Negroes that if they stayed they would have plenty to eat and wear but if they left "it'd be root hawg or die." A good many freedmen, having nowhere to go and nothing to do, accepted this kind of advice, at least long enough to cultivate and harvest the 1865 crops. Some remained with their former masters for many years, but most left relatively soon. Freedom of movement was one of the most tangible benefits of emancipation. "It was harder'n being a slave at first," Horace Overstreet remembered, "but I likes it better, 'cause I kin go whar I wants and git what I wants." Many tested their freedom to move at will. By late June, the *Texas Republican* was complaining of idle Negroes roaming the countryside by the hundreds. Planters were concerned, Loughery wrote, and some ladies had been "reduced to the necessity of doing their own housework without assistance. . . ."[11]

Harrison County's slaves thus gained control of their own bodies during the summer of 1865, but they received virtually nothing more. Federal authorities soon made it clear that they did not intend to offer much material assistance in the transition from slavery to freedom and that they would have little patience with Freedmen who did not work hard and behave responsibly. The first general order issued by Lieutenant Colonel Wheaton after the arrival of his troops in Marshall directed that "Negroes will not be allowed to collect about the city or camps and all Freedmen must have passes from their employers or they will be arrested and punished as vagrants." Similarly, General Granger in Galveston told Freedmen to remain with their employers and avoid vagrancy or idleness. The Freedmen's Bureau, he said, would oversee the creation of permanent labor arrangements.[12]

The Freedmen's Bureau, created by Congress in 1865 to

[11] Ibid., V, Part 4, 208-210 (first quotation); V, Part 3, 160-161 (second quotation). Judgments of what "many" or "most" bondsmen did are based on all twenty-two narratives left by ex-slaves from Harrison County. Marshall *Texas Republican*, June 30, 1865 (third quotation).

[12] Marshall *Texas Republican*, June 23 (quotation), July 28, 1865.

help emancipated slaves find homes, work, and educational opportunities, and, in general, adjust to a new life, arrived in Harrison County during the fall of 1865. Ordered to the area in October, Colonel H. Seymour Hall used Marshall as a base for his work as sub-assistant commissioner for East Texas. One of his first steps was to publish a circular urging Negroes to uphold their labor contracts, be responsible, and earn for themselves. You have the same freedom and rights as other men, he said, and no more. Governor Hamilton told Freedmen the same thing a little later. "You are free — free to work for yourselves and to do right. No man is free to do wrong and to live upon the labor of others."[13]

Regardless of the words of federal officers, Freedmen's Bureau agents, and Governor Hamilton, a rumor circulated persistently among the community's blacks that the government would divide among them the property of their former owners. This redistribution of land was to take place at Christmastime 1865. In mid-November, Colonel Hall made a speech to approximately 1,500 Negroes in Marshall denying this rumor and urging responsibility. A new rumor circulated to the effect that Hall did not really speak for the government; a huge crowd of Freedmen assembled again; and Hall told them to go home. In December, Governor Hamilton's address recommending work and sobriety was read to a large assemblage of Negroes in Marshall. The former slaves apparently felt that they deserved something more than control of their own bodies, but they were largely inarticulate and without leadership. All designated authorities denied their claim to anything more than simple freedom.[14]

[13]Claude Elliot, "The Freedmen's Bureau of Texas," *Southwestern Historical Quarterly*, LVI (July, 1952), 1-24, is a general introduction to this agency's work in the Lone Star State. United States Bureau of Refugees, Freedmen, and Abandoned Lands, 1865-1869, Records of the Assistant Commissioner for the State of Texas, General E. M. Gregory to Lieutenant Colonel H. Seymour Hall, October 6, 1865. These records, available on microfilm from the National Archives, will hereinafter be cited as Freedmen's Bureau, Records of the Assistant Commissioner for Texas, with appropriate correspondents and dates. Hall's circular dated November 1, 1865, and Governor Hamilton's address are reprinted in the Marshall *Texas Republican* of December 8, 1865 (quotation).

[14]Marshall *Texas Republican*, November 17, December 1, 15, 1865; Ramsdell, *Recon-*

Freedmen found too that they were still somewhat less than equal before the law. District Judge J. B. Williamson instructed a grand jury in September, 1865, to apply the law to former slaves exactly as it was applied to men of any color. Slave codes had died with slavery, he ruled. But Judge Williamson also said that legal restrictions on the testimony of blacks would have to stand until the legislature altered them. These laws, he said, derived from the mental and moral inferiority of blacks as well as their condition of servitude. Once the Freedmen's Bureau arrived, it created courts to adjudicate issues involving ex-slaves and to seek impartial justice. Even then, Negroes were frequently involved in state civil court cases where they were less than equal. Whites also believed that in spite of emancipation it was acceptable to continue to pass special laws concerning blacks. The town of Marshall, for example, adopted an ordinance in December, 1865 prohibiting the sale of liquor to blacks in any quantity except on a drink-by-drink basis at a bar.[15] Such laws, as will be noted below, eventually became known as "Black Codes." Finally, virtually no one expected the Freedmen to participate politically in Reconstruction. Presidents Lincoln and Johnson did not propose giving the vote to Negroes; most whites in Harrison County could not imagine such a thing.

On August 19, 1865, Governor Hamilton announced the beginning of registration for voters pursuant to electing the convention that would bring Texas back into its proper constitutional relationship with the Union. The people of Harrison County, like those across Texas, responded apathetically. Loughery complained on November 3 that only 600 to 700 voters had qualified. He and editor Silas D. Wood of the now-revived *Harrison Flag* urged prompt registration and acceptance of President Johnson's plans for Reconstruction.[16]

The election of delegates to the convention was finally held

struction in Texas, 71-72.

[15]Marshall *Texas Republican*, September 29, December 8, 1865; Elliot, "Freedmen's Bureau in Texas," 2, 12.

[16]Marshall *Texas Republican*, November 3, 1865; *Harrison Flag*, November 15, 1865; Ramsdell, *Reconstruction in Texas*, 61.

on January 8, 1866. In the meantime, a division of opinion similar to that existing between the Opposition and the southern Democrats before the secession crisis reappeared in the community. Differences between conservative unionists and ultra-southern secessionists had never entirely disappeared, and now they cropped up again. The *Flag* argued editorially that secession as the cause of war should be declared null and void and that conservative men rather than disunionists should direct the process of Reconstruction. County Judge Bonfoey, a former Whig, urged voters to choose "one who had been conservative in the past." Henry Ware who had drawn the wrath of southern patriots by advocating peace in 1864 came forward as the candidate of this revived Opposition. He declared publicly that secession had been wrong and argued that Freedmen deserved fair treatment and education. Perhaps in a generation, he said, blacks will be ready to vote. Old-line southern Democratic support soon focused on Colonel John Burke, a war hero who had served with the Marshall Guards in Hood's Texas Brigade. Burke admitted that slavery was dead, but he opposed the Thirteenth Amendment and wanted the state constitution to disfranchise Freedmen and bar them from office. His campaign statement to the community said "it is impossible for me to vote for any measure which makes the negro the equal of the white man." Loughery backed Burke and condemned Ware for not saying

> what every sensible, well informed Southern man, acquainted with negro character knows, that the negro can never become the political equal of the white man, and whether it is this year, or twenty, or a hundred years from now, the negro will still be a negro, and remain in the subordinate position in which nature has placed him.

Ware replied that Loughery had been a "political trickster" at the time of secession and had not changed his ways since.[17]

Burke defeated Ware 162 to 146 with five votes going to

[17] *Harrison Flag*, November 22, December 7, 21 (first quotation), 28, 1865, January 4, 1866 (fourth quotation); Marshall *Texas Republican*, December 29, 1865 (second and third quotations). For Burke's war career see Simpson, *Marshall Guards*, 8-10.

two other candidates.[18] The total vote of 313 was very light for such an important contest, but Ware's strength (46.6 percent) was impressive. Apparently Harrison County still had a strong Opposition group who believed that the South would be better served by conservative cooperation with the national government rather than all-out resistance. Antebellum moderation in the defense of slavery was now replaced with moderation in the treatment of Freedmen.

The community also shared one delegate to the convention with neighboring Panola County. That contest involved the old unionist leader Lemuel D. Evans against Charles A. Frazier, an ardent advocate of slavery. Evans, however, had left Marshall during the war and could be accused of siding with the North. Frazier defeated him in Harrison County by a margin of 263 to 11. The *Flag* expressed displeasure over the victories of Burke and Frazier, fearing that such leaders would obstruct Presidential Reconstruction and bring down far greater retribution on the state.[19]

The Texas convention assembled in Austin on February 7, 1866, and decided to handle the necessary Reconstruction measures as amendments to the state constitution of 1845. Delegates soon divided into conservatives including Burke and Frazier from Harrison County and radicals who were primarily old unionists. After bitter wrangling, they declared the act of secession null and void and repudiated all state debts incurred during the years of disunion. They did not ratify the Thirteenth Amendment, which was already part of the United States Constitution, but proposed a change in the state constitution guaranteeing the end of slavery and guaranteeing to Negroes their basic rights of person and property. Blacks could testify in cases involving their own race, and the legislature was empowered to broaden this to testimony in all cases if it wished. Freedmen were not given the right to vote or hold office. In general, then,

[18]Records of the Secretary of State, Election Returns, Harrison County, 1866, Archives Division, Texas State Library, Austin.

[19]Ibid.; Marshall *Texas Republican*, January 12, 1866; *Harrison Flag*, January 11, 1866.

when the convention adjourned on April 2, 1866, the conservative viewpoint had largely triumphed.[20]

The convention provided for the election of state, district, and local officials on June 25, 1866, and ordered a vote on the proposed constitutional amendments at the same time. It was hoped that Texas would be readmitted to the Union before the summer ended.[21] If this proved to be the case, Harrison County's white population would find Reconstruction relatively painless. And the black majority would receive freedom and some basic rights but nothing more.

In the meantime, however, during late 1865 and the first months of 1866, developments in Washington threatened the prospects for a quick and painless restoration of Texas to the Union. Most ex-Confederate states had completed Reconstruction during 1865, well ahead of Texas, but as they did so, there was increasingly strong opposition from Radical Republicans in Congress. Led by Senator Charles Sumner of Massachusetts and Representative Thaddeus Stevens of Pennsylvania, the Radicals objected to President Johnson's leniency with former Confederates who headed many of these Reconstruction governments across the South; they feared the political and economic policies of southern Democrats who were being returned to power in Washington; and they opposed the treatment of Freedmen as second-class citizens at best. None of the reconstructed governments allowed Negroes to vote; most passed special Black Codes regulating the conduct of former slaves. Radicals wanted to give the Negro equal civil and political rights, and some wished even to guarantee an economic foothold to former slaves. These Congressional leaders first blocked President Johnson's approach to Reconstruction by refusing to seat senators and representatives from those states that had completed the process under his direction. Then, in January, 1866, they created a Joint Committee on Reconstruction to investigate conditions in the South. Their

[20] Ramsdell, *Reconstruction in Texas*, 85-107; Connor, *Texas*, 216.

[21] Ramsdell, *Reconstruction in Texas*, 106-107.

intent was at least to modify the most objectionable aspects of Johnson's approach.[22]

The Joint Committee built an indictment of Presidential Reconstruction by hearing one witness after another testify to the unrepentant attitude of former Confederates and the unfair treatment being accorded Freedmen. Harrison County was directly involved. On February 20, 1866, Lieutenant H. S. Hall, the first sub-assistant commissioner of the Freedmen's Bureau in Marshall, testified in Washington. Leaders of the community, he said, "denounce most bitterly . . . the radical party" in Congress and consider the Freedmen's Bureau an "unmitigated nuisance." Their only regret "for any action during the past five years was, that they did not succeed." Hall also described the case of a Negro woman named Lucy Grimes beaten to death by two "discharged rebel soldiers" named Anderson and Simpson who went free because there were no witnesses except Negroes to testify to the murder. If military force were removed from the area, Hall said, the Freedman "would be, in many instances, forced to labor without any compensation, under some system of compulsion, nearly the same as formerly. He would be liable to worse treatment than ever before—to assaults in many cases, and even to murder."[23]

Congress and the President remained deadlocked into the spring of 1866, but gradually Johnson's uncompromising attitude and the testimony concerning conditions in the South added to the Radicals' strength. In April, Congress passed a Civil Rights Act guaranteeing citizenship and equality before the law to Freedmen. Johnson vetoed this act, but Congress overrode his veto. The president was in danger of completely losing control of Reconstruction; Radicals looked to the midterm congressional elections in November, 1866, as an oppor-

[22]There are many accounts of the development of Reconstruction issues during 1865 and early 1866. See, for example, John Hope Franklin, *Reconstruction After the Civil War* (Chicago, 1961), 32-57; Kenneth M. Stampp, *The Era of Reconstruction, 1865-1877* (New York, 1965), 50-111.

[23]United States House of Representatives, *House Reports*, 39th Congress, 1st Session, 1866, Report No. 30, 46 (first, second, and fifth quotations), 47 (fourth quotation), 48, 49 (third quotation), 50.

tunity to guarantee their take over. Harrison County watched developments in Washington with rising concern. Not surprisingly, Loughery's *Texas Republican* pictured Johnson as a constitutionally minded hero and the Radical Republicans as unconstitutional extremists. The more conservative *Flag* attempted to be more optimistic, emphasizing the need for responsible leadership in Texas and reporting that free labor was working well. But by March, 1866, the *Flag* too found the Radicals unacceptably extreme and came out in support of the president. As the election of state, district, and county officials approached on June 25, 1866, Harrison County was probably more unified in support of Presidential Reconstruction than it had ever been on any political issue, even secession in 1861.[24]

The candidates for governor in 1866 did not really represent the extremes of southern Democrat versus Radical, but they came to be seen in that way. James W. Throckmorton, an old-line Whig who had opposed secession before serving the Confederacy, became the Democratic nominee, although the *Harrison Flag* preferred to call his the "Conservative Union ticket." Elisha M. Pease, a former Democratic governor and unionist, represented the developing Republican Party. Perhaps unfairly, he was generally called a Radical. In Harrison County, both newspapers strongly endorsed Throckmorton. There were no acknowledged Radical or Republican candidates for local office or seeking to represent the community at the state level. Both candidates for the county's state senate seat, for example, E. A. Blanch and C. C. Coppedge, made a point of informing the voters of their total support for President Johnson.[25]

Throckmorton defeated Pease in Harrison County by a vote of 796 to 6. Robert C. Garrett and Samuel J. Richardson who won seats in the Texas House of Representatives were both ex-

[24]Franklin, *Reconstruction*, 57-67; Marshall *Texas Republican*, January 19, March 2, 1866; *Harrison Flag*, January 11, 25, March 1, 8, 15, 1866. The change of attitude at the *Flag* may be explained to a large extent by a change in editorship. In early March, Silas D. Wood became county judge and was replaced by William G. Barrett. The paper immediately swung to strong support of President Johnson.

[25]Ramsdell, *Reconstruction in Texas*, 108-112; Marshall *Texas Republican*, April 28, 1866; *Harrison Flag*, May 17, June 7, 14, 1866.

Confederate soldiers. District Judge Matthew D. Ector of Marshall had held the rank of brigadier general, and Hec McKay, the district attorney, had been a captain in the Confederate army. County Judge Obadiah Hendrick had twice held that position before 1860, and Sheriff Solomon R. Perry had held his office intermittently since 1850. All four county commissioners, Lodwick P. Alford, John Munden, George B. Conway, and R. W. Blalock, had been slaveholding residents of the community in 1860. The new county clerk, J. P. Alford, was L. P. Alford's son and a Confederate veteran, while the tax assessor/collector, George W. Young, had been elected twice to that position during the Civil War.[26]

Harrison County thus reconstructed its local government in 1865–1866 with as little change as possible. The same kind of men, and in many cases the same men, who had governed during the antebellum years were returned to political leadership. There was no major disfranchisement of whites and no significant confiscation of property. Negroes were free, but they had absolutely no part in the political process of Presidential Reconstruction.

In areas other than politics, the community also sought to maintain antebellum standards or continue with developments begun before the war. Taxes fell back nearly to their pre-war levels. The state tax rate in 1860 had stood at 12.5¢ per $100 evaluation in ad valorem property taxes and a 50¢ poll tax on males aged twenty-one to fifty. County taxes were exactly one-half the state level. By 1864, state taxes had increased to 50¢ on every $100 in property and a $1 poll tax on males twenty-one or older, and county taxes were 62.5¢ on the $100. In 1865, Provisional Governor Hamilton set state taxes back to the pre-war level of 12.5¢ per $100 of property and a $1 poll tax on adult

[26] Marshall *Texas Republican*, July 7, 1866. Previous officeholding is documented in Election Registers, 1850-1865. Ector's record is in Wright (comp.), *Texas in the War*, 77. Slaveholding is documented in Eighth Census, 1860, Schedule 2. Richardson and Garrett served with the W. P. Lane Rangers, Alford with the Bass Grays, and McKay with McKay's Company; see Marshall *Texas Republican*, June 22, July 27, 1861, June 28, 1862.

males. County taxes were 12.5¢ on the $100 too. The Reconstruction convention in 1866 set the state tax rate at 20¢ on the $100 and kept the $1 poll tax. County taxes were limited to one-half of state taxes.[27] Apparently inexpensive government had returned to the county.

The Southern Pacific Railroad, always in chaotic financial condition, had managed barely to survive during the Civil War. Where, for example, it had carried 4,274 bales of cotton in 1861, it transported 12 bales in 1864. And it continued to go through managerial reorganizations. Nevertheless, the railroad had received and sold land grants totalling 384,000 acres for the track built before the war, had gotten a $150,000 loan from the permanent school fund, and had managed to stay in business. The track from Swanson's Landing on Caddo Lake to Jonesville east of Marshall had been taken up and rebuilt eastward to Greenwood, Louisiana, fourteen miles from Shreveport. Thus when the war ended, only a little construction was necessary to complete a rail link from Marshall to the Red River at Shreveport. By the summer of 1866, the work was complete and the first train ran on this route. There was much celebration in the community as the *Texas Republican* hailed a "new era" for Marshall. The Southern Pacific was essentially a local enterprise too. Of the twelve directors elected in September, 1866, six — J. M. Waskom, William T. Scott, M. J. Hall, Joseph Mason, William Bradfield, and George G. Gregg — were from Harrison County. One director lived in Tyler, one in Shreveport, one in New Orleans, and three in Louisville, Kentucky.[28]

The community also remained interested, although still ineffectively, in public schools. The Constitution of 1866 authorized the state legislature to set up a public school system for "white scholastic inhabitants," using all moneys and sources of revenue such as land previously set aside for education. If the legislature levied an education tax, all money collected from

[27] Harrison County Tax Rolls, 1860, 1864, 1865, 1866; Ramsdell, *Reconstruction in Texas*, 59; Gammel (comp.) *Laws of Texas*, V, 890-891.

[28] Muir, "Thirty-Second Parallel Pacific Railroad," 162, 165-166, 169-171, 182; Marshall *Texas Republican*, August 4, September 8, 1866; *Harrison Flag*, August 2, 1866.

blacks would go to support black schools. The Eleventh Legislature, which assembled in Austin on August 6, 1866, passed "An Act Regulating Public Schools" on November 12 directing the creation of school systems that would draw financial support from the public school fund. There was no special school tax, hence no provisions for black schools. Establishment and operation of the schools was to be almost totally local in nature. Each county would be divided into school districts with their own popularly elected three-man board of trustees to choose teachers and direct their school. The Harrison County Commissioners' Court created eleven school districts in April, 1867, and called for the election of trustees in each. A school census was taken that year showing 1,228 white children aged six to sixteen. As we will see, however, other developments soon overshadowed public schools, and nothing came of this act. Education for whites remained primarily a private enterprise in the hands of institutions such as Marshall University and the Marshall Masonic Female Institute, both of which continued to operate in the postbellum years. Frederick S. Bass, back from his exploits with the Marshall Guards, continued as head of the University, and the Reverend Thomas B. Wilson remained as principal of the Female Institute.[29]

The Freedmen's Bureau rather than state or local authorities provided the first educational opportunities for Negro children in Harrison County. In May, 1866, Owen F. Baker, a federal appointee, opened a day school for Freedmen in Marshall. It was not necessarily free; students who could afford to paid tuition of $1.50 per month. Baker's monthly reports to the Bureau's superintendent of education for Texas, E. M. Wheelock, showed an increase in attendance from 47 pupils in May to 149 by July 31. Attendance at Sunday School reached more than 500, and Baker was assisted then by seventeen Freedmen who could read. The number of students declined during the late summer and fall, possibly due to the need for labor in

[29]Gammel (comp.), *Laws of Texas*, V, 882-885, 1088-1092; Eby, *Development of Education in Texas*, 265; Harrison County Commissioners Court Minutes, April, 1867; Scholastic Census, 1867; Marshall *Texas Republican*, September 29, 1866.

cotton picking, and the school suspended operations completely in November and December.[30]

At the beginning of January, 1867, two new Bureau teachers, Mr. and Mrs. C. E. Coleman from Illinois, began teaching in Marshall. They had some difficulty supplanting Baker who continued to teach for a while in spite of a financial dispute with the Bureau, but with the aid of a new sub-assistant commissioner, Captain Charles F. Rand, the Colemans soon established a thriving school. "The people here use us very well for Texas," C. E. Coleman wrote on January 13, 1867. "And the Freeds are anxious to learn and to have Bibles. . . ." Beginning with eighteen students the first week, the Colemans reached a total of 85 by March, 1867. Captain Rand reported that two divisions of the school were being created and praised the pupils for "rapidly advancing up the hill of education." The Colemans' "system and discipline cannot be excelled," he wrote, "and all who send their children are well pleased." C. E. Coleman himself reported that "we have very exalted hopes that soon the Freedman's school at Marshall will equal or outstrip the schools for white children."[31]

Enthusiastic optimism from Freedmen's Bureau teachers like the Colemans is understandable. They were doing "missionary" work under extremely challenging circumstances. Any success probably seemed a great victory. And their school was important. Still, with a total enrollment of less than 100 pupils through the first half of 1867, they were reaching only a tiny part of the community's black children.[32]

[30] United States Bureau of Refugees, Freedmen, and Abandoned Lands, 1865-1869, Records of the Superintendent of Education for the State of Texas, Monthly Reports by Owen F. Baker, May 31, June 30, July 31, August 31, 1866; ibid., Monthly Reports by State Superintendent E. M. Wheelock, August, October, November, 1866. These records, available on microfilm from the National Archives, will hereinafter be cited as Freedmen's Bureau, Records of Texas Superintendent of Education. See also Marshall *Texas Republican*, July 21, 1866.

[31] Freedmen's Bureau, Records of Texas Superintendent of Education, C. E. Coleman to E. M. Wheelock, December 30, 1866, January 13 (first quotation), January 28, March 3 (fourth quotation), 1867; Charles F. Rand to E. M. Wheelock, March 4, 1867 (second and third quotations); Monthly Reports by C. E. and E. E. Coleman, January 31, February 28, March 31, 1867.

[32] Ibid., Monthly Reports by C. E. and E. E. Coleman, June 30, 1867.

During 1865-1866 then, Presidential Reconstruction allowed Harrison County's whites to ignore Freedmen politically and to resume antebellum ways in areas such as taxes, railroad building, and public schools. Negro schools were an innovation, but they were sponsored solely by the Freedmen's Bureau. White Texans also sought to minimize the adjustments necessitated by emancipation in the treatment of the Negro as a laborer. Slaveholders and federal authorities alike had, with considerable success at the time of emancipation, urged the Freedmen to remain on the land and work for wages, but the new relationships between employers and laborers had to be formalized.

White leaders, especially landowners, were concerned in late 1865 and early 1866 with developing guarantees that ex-slaves became dependable free laborers. Local planters believed that annual "moneyed contracts" were the best means of bringing together land and labor. The Freedmen's Bureau agreed, and Lieutenant Colonel Hall, the first sub-assistant commissioner in Marshall, drew up a standard form to be used in 1866. An example of the terms prescribed is found in one of these contracts signed by Adam Hope and nineteen Freedmen for the period from January 24 to December 31, 1866. Hope promised to provide food, a weekly allowance of three and one-half pounds of bacon, one-quarter bushel of corn meal, and fresh vegetables (children received half rations), and to pay monthly wages. The Austin Powell family, which included four of the nineteen Freedmen involved, was to receive $9 per month for the father, $7 for his wife, $5 for fifteen-year-old Thomas, and $4 for twelve-year-old Samuel. Not more than one-third of the wages could be demanded or paid at the end of each month, the remainder came at the end of the year. Hope pledged his crop as security to pay the wages promised. The Freedmen promised to "perform all labor which is necessary or customary in carrying on a plantation, cheerfully rendering prompt and respectful obedience to all just and lawful orders . . . ." They were to work six days a week unless the weather was inclement; hours per day were not specified. Undoubtedly Hope could not expect the Freedmen to work as they had when enslaved, but on the other hand, farm laborers probably could not imagine a forty hour week.[33]

Hope's 1866 contract, approved by Colonel Thomas Bayley who replaced Hall as sub-assistant commissioner in Marshall early that year, probably amounted to reasonably fair treatment of the Freedmen by the standards of that day. Farm labor always meant long hours and hard work. The Powell family's wages totalling $25 per month may seem low, but beef and pork cost less than 5¢ a pound, land was less than $10 an acre, and other prices were correspondingly low. Also, Hope promised a weekly food allowance.[34]

It is likely, however, that many Freedmen signed contracts with more restrictions and found themselves unable to make any gains. M. J. Hall, whom we have already met as a planter-lawyer-businessman, kept ledger books for 1866 containing the accounts of several Freedmen who worked his land for monthly wages. Bill Haney worked twelve months at fifteen dollars a month and earned $180. However, he spent $55.77 at a store Hall operated in Marshall and lost sixty days from work for which Hall deducted fifty cents a day wages and twenty cents board. (Apparently Hall regarded a month as having thirty working days or the deduction would have been greater.) Total deductions came to $97.77, leaving Haney a balance of $82.23. And that was by far the best record of any of the Freedmen dealing with Hall. Cary Hall worked eleven months for $110 in wages but missed ninety-one days from work at a cost of $49.14 in wages and board and spent $65.92 at Hall's store. At the end of the year, his employer owed him $5.06. Henry Butts wound up $7.63 in debt to Hall, and Frances Lipscomb, who was paid only $8 a month, found herself with a $25.16 deficit at the end of the year.[35] It is possible that these Freedmen were spending

[33] *Harrison Flag*, January 11, 1866, announced that Hall had blank contract forms and urged local planters to use them. The Adam Hope contract is preserved in the Hope Family File, Harrison County Historical Museum, Marshall.

[34] Freedmen's Bureau, Records of the Assistant Commissioner for Texas, Special Orders, January 4, 1866, shows Bayley ordered to replace Hall. Prices are from S. J. Richardson, "Harrison County," in *The Texas Almanac for 1867* (Galveston, 1866), 114-116.

[35] Hall Ledger Books.

their money unwisely, but it seems unlikely that many would "get ahead" under such terms.

Harrison County planters accepted Negro wage labor reluctantly. Hugh Perry, Levin Perry's surviving younger son, wrote his widowed sister-in-law Harriet Person Perry in North Carolina of a cousin who "speaks of going to Cuba. He wants to work slave Africans again—has no confidence at all in 'freedmen.' " Nevertheless, labor contracts were accepted as the best arrangement consistent with freedom. The *Flag* claimed on March 1, 1866, that some farmers were ahead of schedule in planting their crops. Even the *Texas Republican* conceded that blacks, although not as industrious as before, were doing better than anticipated.[36] The new system of bringing together land and labor won support elsewhere in Texas too, and when the Eleventh Legislature assembled, steps were taken to formalize it in a manner especially reassuring to white farmers and planters. The leaders of Presidential Reconstruction in Harrison County undoubtedly approved.

On November 1, 1866, the Texas Legislature passed a measure entitled "An Act Regulating Contracts for Labor." Heads of families were to make contracts for themselves and their dependents. Once signed, a contract could not be broken by a laborer without forfeiting all wages, unless the employer gave his approval or broke the contract himself. Any employer who willfully violated his promises was to be fined with the fine going to the laborer. The laborer, however, would have sick days deducted from his wages, and he was bound by a stringent code of conduct. He could be fined one dollar for every time he was guilty of neglect of duty, leaving home without a permit, "swearing," or "impudence." In short, the Negro worker was placed in a position as near to slavery as a free man might be. This law was in the class with the infamous Black Codes created earlier in other southern states which added to the determination of Radical Republicans in Congress to block Presidential Re-

[36]Hugh H. Perry to Harriet P. Perry, June 5, 1866 (quotation), Person Family Papers; *Harrison Flag*, March 1, 1866; Marshall *Texas Republican*, February 9, 1866.

construction. It was never really operative because federal authorities ordered in January, 1867, that it be disregarded.[37] Nevertheless, this labor contract reveals the intention of most white Texans during Presidential Reconstruction to keep Negro workers as close to slaves as possible.

There were, of course, whites who encouraged ex-slaves to become more than wage laborers and Freedmen who successfully began the transition from being property themselves to holding their own land. The case of David Abner, Sr., provides an example of cooperation between a sympathetic white and an exceptional Freedman. Abner was born in Alabama and came to Upshur County, Texas, in 1843 at the age of twenty-three. When freedom came, he went to Marshall to see Mrs. Fannie Richardson, the sister of his first owner in Alabama. Mrs. Richardson "stood" Abner a mule and some farm equipment and rented forty acres of land to him on credit. By 1870, he owned 300 acres and reported a fifty-bale cotton crop. As we will see, Abner became active in local politics and represented Harrison County in the state legislature and the constitutional convention of 1875. David Abner, Jr., attended Fisk University in Nashville and became a noted educator in Texas; another son, E. W.D. Abner, became a doctor.[38] Thus economic success was not impossible for blacks, but there were very few like David Abner in the community during the first years after emancipation. Most signed labor contracts that promised little real gain.

Harrison County also had serious difficulty adjusting to the social implications of emancipation. Most whites were accustomed to thinking of Negroes as inferior and subservient. But many Freedmen expected at least to go and come as they pleased, to seek an education for their children, and to negotiate the best terms possible for their labor. They expected to be as secure in

[37] Gammel (comp.), *Laws of Texas*, V, 994-997; Ramsdell, *Reconstruction in Texas*, 123-125.

[38] *The Black Citizen and American Democracy: Black Culture in Harrison County, Past, Present, and Future*, (Marshall, 1976), 4-6; Letter by M. D. Moore, a descendant of David Abner, Sr., March, 1970, Abner Family File, Harrison County Historical Museum, Marshall; John Mason Brewer, *Negro Legislators of Texas and Their Descendants* (Dallas, 1935), 42-43; Ninth Census, 1870, Schedules 1 and 3.

their persons and property as any man. White attitudes clashed with black expectations, and racially based violence became a serious problem in the community during 1866, at least in the eyes of federal agents.

As mentioned above, Lieutenant Colonel H. S. Hall testified before Congress in February, 1866, that the murder of a Negro woman in the Marshall area had gone unpunished. Her offense, he said, had been to refuse to whip her child who was accused of stealing. In July, 1866, Colonel Thomas F. Bayley reported that "Many planters irritated by the loss of crops vent their displeasure upon the helpless Freedmen." Negroes could not get their grievances before grand juries, he said, because of "wicked men resorting to all means, even to force, to prevent any ill treatment becoming known." A majority of planters would do right, Bayley believed, but there were many bad men too. Captain Charles F. Rand, the third Bureau agent to serve in Marshall reported on December 31, 1866:

> There are bands of organized robbers in the southern portion of this county who prey alike upon white and black and several other counties are equally pestered by these marauders. With a company or a detachment I could rid the district and insure protection. The effect would be soon felt. Fifteen counties or all surrounding Harrison County would be quieted and freedmen would be protected. Yesterday a freedman presented himself with two bullet holes through him for no other cause than by being one of a Christmas jubilee dancing party. He was shot through a window. They dare not carry anything to protect themselves with for they would be surrounded and all arms and whatever else they had valuable would be taken away from them. Outrages are committed daily with impunity and all pass unnoticed for lack of assistance. They have been so long unchecked that they have no respect or fear of us and we are compelled to submit with silence.[39]

The situation worsened during the first months of 1867.

[39]Freedmen's Bureau, Records of the Assistant Commissioner for Texas, Colonel Thomas F. Bayley to General J. Kiddoo, July 31, 1866 (first and second quotations); Captain Charles F. Rand to General Kiddoo, December 31, 1866 (third quotation).

Owen F. Baker, the first Freedmen's Bureau teacher, reported on January 1, 1867, that "My house on last Monday evening was the target of an enraged rebel mob, the windows were smashed and fired into to such an extent that bullets were found on the floor the next morning." C. E. Coleman, the teacher from Illinois, reported on January 13: "This is the worst place for killing and shooting Negroes I ever saw, but not so much so right here as in adjoining counties. I do pity the poor Freeds. Nearly every day some one comes in robbed or shot for their money." Coleman felt that Colonel Bayley, who had recently been replaced, was partly responsible for the situation. Local Freedmen complained that he did not protect their rights, said Coleman, "and I see the citizens think too much of him for an agent of the B_____ . . ." Coleman believed that Captain Rand would do a better job. But Rand reported on February 1, 1867: "The state of the country in point of civil law is at its lowest ebb. . . . Numerous cases of murder, etc. are presented, but without mounted men, I can take no action." Rand's complaints reached Governor James W. Throckmorton who responded in early March by asking County Judge Obadiah Hendrick to investigate the charges and make a full report. The governor urged Hendrick to cooperate with Captain Rand and punish all crimes. But, he added, "As a matter of course, I do not believe one word of this . . . ."[40]

Federal agents such as Hall, Bayley, Rand, Baker, and Coleman expected the worst and may have exaggerated the frequency of violence directed at Freedmen in Harrison County. Governor Throckmorton seemed to think so. Nevertheless, by the spring of 1867, the community was notorious enough to be mentioned in Horace Greeley's New York *Tribune.* "In Harrison County, bands of organized robbers plunder whites and

[40] Freedmen's Bureau, Records of the Texas Superintendent of Education, Owen F. Baker to General E. M. Wheelock, January 1, 1867 (first quotation); C. E. Coleman to General Wheelock, January 13, 1867 (second and third quotations); ibid., Records of the Assistant Commissioner for Texas, Captain Charles F. Rand to General Charles Griffin, February 1, 1867 (fourth quotation); Governor James W. Throckmorton to Obadiah Hendrick, March 4, 1867 (fifth quotation), Executive Record Book, Archives Division, Texas State Library, Austin.

blacks alike, and in twenty-seven other counties in that district there is no safety for Negroes or loyal men." Local white leaders and spokesmen such as Loughery of the *Texas Republican* indignantly denied such reports of violence against persons and property. How, asked Loughery, could Negroes be considered unsafe in the county when 15,000 lived there and nearly 1,000 visited Marshall every weekend? Perhaps the majority were indeed left alone to pursue peaceful lives. But the testimony concerning mistreatment is strong, and it is very likely that, given their racial attitudes and the frustrations of defeat and federal occupation, many whites did react violently when ex-slaves got "out of their place" during the first years after emancipation.[41]

In the meantime, Radical Republicans in Congress continued through 1866 to block President Johnson's Reconstruction program. Senators and representatives from the restored government of Texas met the same fate in Washington as did those from other Presidential Reconstruction governments across the South; they were not seated. The Radicals' success was based on Johnson's own political ineptitude and on the general unrepentance of the South, the election of former Confederates to office, and the refusal of white southerners to accord more than the barest essentials of freedom to the Negro.[42] In other words, a good part of the Radicals' determination to block Presidential Reconstruction arose from conditions highly similar to those in Harrison County.

Both the president's supporters and the Radical Republicans looked to the mid-term congressional elections in November, 1866, as an opportunity for the voters to speak. Conservative observers such as Editor Loughery in Marshall dreaded a Radical victory. Once in complete control, he told his readers,

[41] For the charges made by the New York *Tribune* and Loughery's reply, see Marshall *Texas Republican*, March 16, 1867. For a survey of racial attitudes in Reconstruction Texas, see Barry A. Crouch and L. J. Schultz, "Crisis in Color: Racial Separation in Texas During Reconstruction," *Civil War History*, XVI (Mar., 1970), 37-49.

[42] This interpretation of the Radical Republicans' success is now common in the historiography of Reconstruction. It is found, for example, in Stampp, *Era of Reconstruction*, 83-118.

they will adopt the policies feared most — disfranchisement, confiscation, and Negro equality.[43]

Harrison County sent six delegates to a state convention at Navasota in July, 1866, that in turn chose representatives to the National Conservative or National Union Convention at Philadelphia in August. This meeting assembled for the purpose of supporting President Johnson in the up-coming elections. Lemuel D. Evans, the well-known unionist leader, served as a delegate, indicating once more the extent to which former unionists and secessionists were unified in support of Presidential Reconstruction. When the elections were held, Harrison County voted heavily for George W. Chilton of Smith County for the House of Representatives in the 39th Congress (2nd session, December, 1866) and William B. Ochiltree of Marshall for a seat in the 40th Congress (1867-1869). Chilton had been a Confederate colonel, and Ochiltree had been elected to the Congress of the Confederacy. The community's voters apparently felt that all was lost if the Radical Republicans won, so they made no effort to elect unobjectionable candidates.[44]

By mid-November, Harrison County knew that the Radicals had won overwhelmingly in the North and would enjoy a two-thirds majority in both houses of the next congress. Reconstruction, after nearly two years, remained very much up in the air. And local conservatives believed conditions were already beginning to change for the worse. In January, 1867, the Freedmen's Bureau ruled that the highly restrictive state contract labor law of November, 1866, would not be enforced. Loughery complained the same month that thousands of Negroes were refusing to sign labor contracts because they expected congress to give them property or handouts. He cheered the arrival of house servants from England, saying, "It is evident that white labor is destined to supplant, in a great measure, the present negro labor, which is every day becoming more and more worthless."

[43] Marshall *Texas Republican*, October 6, 1866.

[44] Ibid., July 21, 1866; *Harrison Flag*, August 4, September 27, October 25, 1866; Webb, Carroll, and Branda (eds.), *Handbook of Texas*, I, 340; II, 300.

Freedmen's Bureau courts continued to adjudicate minor disputes involving former slaves, much to the disgust of conservative whites in the community. In February, 1867, Loughery referred to the Bureau as an "engine of oppression."[45] Had he been able to foresee the exercise of federal authority that would begin with Congressional Reconstruction the next month, developments in 1865 and 1866 would have appeared far less negative and oppressive.

From one perspective, perhaps, the nearly two years of Presidential Reconstruction had brought drastic changes to Harrison County. Emancipation more than doubled the free population and cost the community's slaveholders approximately seven million dollars in capital investments. White men no longer owned black men as human property. United States troops occupied Marshall, and a federal appointee in Austin chose the officials for a provisional county government. The Freedmen's Bureau arrived to aid the former slaves in a variety of ways. Plantation agriculture began to disintegrate as it became clear that wage labor could not be controlled closely enough to maintain the old system. Summary statistics are not available, but almost certainly cotton production did not recover to pre-war levels in 1865 or 1866.

All these changes, however, were limited. Federal military presence created relatively few problems for the community. There was a minor incident involving townspeople and some of the Negro troops who arrived in the spring of 1866, but generally local citizens followed Loughery's advice and left the soldiers alone. Political control returned quickly to the same class that had governed before and during the war. Freedmen did not vote or hold office. Schools continued largely as before the war; at least there was no effort to educate all children, black as well as white, at public expense. Only slave property was disturbed; other forms including land were not confiscated or redistributed.

[45]*Harrison Flag*, November 15, 1866; Ramsdell, *Reconstruction in Texas*, 124-125; Marshall *Texas Republican*, January 12, February 2 (first quotation), 9, 23 (second quotation), 1867; Elliot, "Freemen's Bureau in Texas," 2, 12.

Negroes generally became wage laborers for whites under conditions that seemed likely to keep them one step above slavery. Cotton production remained below pre-war levels, but prices were high. Farmers bemoaned the unreliability of free labor, and yet there were relatively few pronouncements of "doom and gloom" for the future. Samuel J. Richardson's description of Harrison County for the *Texas Almanac for 1867* said that "the general behavior of the negro has been better than could reasonably be expected." Evidently, Richardson wrote, free labor will prove successful. In the meantime, as a further indication that agriculture in the community was not ruined, Marshall prospered. Loughery of the *Texas Republican* bragged regularly about the town's commercial bustle. Prosperity is everywhere, he wrote in February, 1867, in our "embryo city."[46]

Harrison County had been changed but not revolutionized by Presidential Reconstruction. Congress would take over in March, 1867, however, and most of the community's white population feared the worst.

[46]Marshall *Texas Republican*, April 28, May 5, September 29, October 27, 1866, February 9, 1867 (second quotation); Richardson, "Harrison County," 114-116 (first quotation). The troops from the 80th United States Colored Regiment remained in Marshall until February, 1867.

11

Congressional Reconstruction: March, 1867–April, 1870

CONGRESS UNDER the leadership of Radical Republicans took Reconstruction away from President Johnson in March, 1867. A Reconstruction Act of March 2 supplemented by a measure passed on the 23rd divided the South into five military districts and ordered the president to place an army general in command of each. Texas and Louisiana constituted the Fifth Military District; General Philip Sheridan commanding. Existing state and local governments (those created under Presidential Reconstruction) were considered strictly provisional and subject to military authority. Governor Throckmorton and Harrison County's officials elected in 1866 could be removed from office at any time. The entire process of political reconstruction was to be repeated; this time, however, under military supervision and according to rules established by Congress.[1]

The most important change brought by Congressional Reconstruction came in the area of suffrage requirements. Adult white and black males, except those disfranchised for their role in the Confederacy or for felony convictions, or disqualified from holding office by the Fourteenth Amendment, could vote. The latter limitation was especially important because it barred from office (and thus from voting) any person who had ever taken an oath to uphold the Constitution of the United States and then engaged in rebellion. This disqualification could be removed only by a two-thirds vote of both houses of congress. If enforced, it would disfranchise most of the traditional leaders of Harrison County since anyone who had ever held local office had taken an oath to uphold the constitution. Congressional Reconstruction would not be run by those who had always governed the community.

The Reconstruction Acts of March, 1867, also specified the procedures to be followed. Registration of qualified voters was to be followed by an election in which these registered voters decided whether or not to hold a constitutional convention and at the same time chose delegates to that convention. There would be no convention unless a majority of those registered participated in the election and a majority of those voting favored it. The new constitution also had to receive majority approval. Once a state government was operative under this new frame of government and the Fourteenth Amendment had been ratified, senators and representatives would be seated in congress. Political reconstruction would be complete when a state was readmitted to the Union. But of course there would still be the question of who would control the former Confederate states. Obviously a majority in congress hoped that black enfranchisement and the whole process of Reconstruction would create Republican governments in the South.

[1] The principles of Congressional Reconstruction outlined in this and the following paragraphs are drawn from Franklin, *Reconstruction*, 69-73; Ramsdell, *Reconstruc-*

Harrison County's initial reaction to Congressional Reconstruction followed two lines of thought, at least as it was expressed in the newspapers. First, there was indignation over "subversion of the constitution" and "persecution of the South." Enfranchisement of black men created even more outrage. The *Flag* was disgusted at the prospect of a Negro county judge, high taxes, corruption, expensive schools, and "all the horrors of social equality." "To exalt the common African," the editor wrote, "with his thick skin, wooly head, his superstition and silly notions, to a level or perfect state of equality with the proud race of Anglo-Saxon blood, is an attempt to place a libel upon the great and original purposes of God himself." On the other hand, Harrison County whites recognized that they had no choice but to submit to congress and make the best of a bad situation. Robert W. Loughery of the *Republican* urged whites to register if they could and plan to make a fight at the polls. Both local newspapers urged their readers to stay on good terms with Negroes and see that the Freedmen were not influenced by renegade whites. Negro schools were approved by the *Republican* and the *Flag* as offering essential improvements to would-be voters. Both papers also appealed to the community's blacks to trust their former masters and not be deceived by outsiders. "Listen to the pratings of no imported political teachers," the *Republican* urged, "for their only object is to ride to power on your backs." In short, Harrison County's white minority was shocked and outraged over Congressional Reconstruction, but they reacted within a democratic framework, hoping somehow to register enough whites and appeal to enough blacks to win at the ballot box.[2]

Registration of eligible voters in Harrison County began on June 24, 1867. The process was handled by a three-man board of registrars appointed by General Charles Griffin, General

tion in Texas, 145-149; Carl H. Moneyhon, *Republicanism in Reconstruction Texas* (Austin, 1980), 58-60.

[2] *Harrison Flag*, March 7 (first and second quotations), May 2, 9, 14 (third quotation), 30 (fourth quotation), 1867; Marshall *Texas Republican*, April 20, June 8, 15 (fifth quotation), 1867.

Sheridan's commander for Texas. These registrars had to swear the "Iron Clad Oath" of July 2, 1862 that they had never voluntarily aided the Confederacy; a requirement that disqualified a large proportion of the community's white population. Nevertheless, one of the registrars, N. V. Board, was a long-time resident who had served on the commissioners court during the antebellum years. Of the other two, Jacob Foster was a native of Pennsylvania who had apparently arrived in the community only recently, and Mitchell Kendall was a Freedman. Registration continued until August 28, by which time 2,480 blacks and 805 whites had enrolled. The voter lists were opened for one more week in September and again for a week in January, 1868. Total registration at this point came to 3,404, 2,521 blacks and 883 whites.[3]

Registration in Harrison County was relatively free of controversy. At first many whites refused to register because blacks were being allowed to; an attitude the *Flag* scorned as "puerile and womanish." There were also a few complaints that the local board of registrars was applying the rules concerning disfranchisement too strictly. It appears, however, that only those clearly prohibited from holding office by the Fourteenth Amendment were denied registration, Antebellum officeholders such as William T. Scott, George Lane, and Solomon R. Perry do not appear on the lists of qualified voters. Former Confederates who had not previously held office did register. The names of Captain Thomas W. Winston, W. W. Heartsill, Albert B. Blocker, Hugh H. Perry, and many other ex-soldiers are found among those permitted to register.[4]

The extent of white disfranchisement is difficult to assess. There were 1,069 votes cast in the last antebellum presidential

[3] *Harrison Flag*, June 27, 1867; Marshall *Texas Republican*, September 14, 1867; Ninth Census, 1870, Schedule 1; Ramsdell, *Reconstruction in Texas*, 161-162. The names of all registered voters with race and literacy indicated are found in List of Registered Voters in Texas, 1867 (Book three of nine), Archives Division, Texas State Library, Austin. The "Iron Clad Oath" is explained in James G. Randall and David Donald, *The Civil War and Reconstruction* (Boston, 1961), 553 n. 6.

[4] *Harrison Flag*, June 27 (quotation), August 1, 1867; List of Registered Voters, 1867.

election in 1860. In the first local elections held under Presidential Reconstruction during 1866, however, only 825 voters participated. Robert W. Loughery, in what was by his own admission a generous estimate, guessed that the community had 1,300 white voting-age males in September, 1867. In the light of these numbers, and the fact that a sizable minority of those eligible never cared to register or vote, the registration of 883 whites in 1867-1868 suggests that white disfranchisement in Harrison County was not drastic. Moreover, most whites probably recognized the basic fact that they were simply outnumbered. As Loughery pointed out to his readers, if all whites were allowed to register, their 1,300 votes would scarcely be enough to defeat the nearly 2,500 registered blacks.[5]

During the summer and into the fall of 1867, the community continued under a combination of military rule and local government run by those chosen during Presidential Reconstruction. There were few problems during this period with United States troops stationed at Marshall. A company of Negro soldiers from the 80th U.S. Colored Infantry had served as an occupying force since replacing the original two companies of the 8th Illinois in April, 1866. These black troops were in turn replaced in February, 1867, by Company C of the U.S. 20th Infantry under the command of Lieutenant William Hawley. The *Texas Republican* conceded that the black troops had generally behaved well but argued that white soldiers were preferable. It seems likely that armed blacks in uniform may well, from Loughery's point of view, have been a bad influence in the community. In September, he went out of his way to praise Lieutenant Hawley and Lieutenant Adam G. Malloy of the Freedmen's Bureau. There may be problems elsewhere in the South, Loughery said, but,

> Here the most complete accord and good feeling exists. A man might remain in Marshall a month without being aware there was a United States command here, unless he met a

[5]Marshall *Texas Republican*, September 14, 1867; Burnham, *Presidential Ballots*, 784-785; Election Returns, 1866.

> soldier on the street. The reason for this is, the officers are men of sense and good feeling.

Basically the military allowed civil authorities to govern.[6]

There were indications, however, from the onset of Congressional Reconstruction that the existing government of Harrison County faced a bleak future. General Griffin announced on April 15, 1867, that henceforth he would appoint all civil officers in Texas and that all persons serving on grand and petit juries must swear the "Iron Clad Oath." Then, as already explained, the board of registrars had to take this oath, and blacks constituted an overwhelming majority of those enrolled. And finally, in a development that was most upsetting of all to the white conservatives, radicals began to campaign among the community's Negroes. Loughery was complaining bitterly by late June and early July, 1867.

> Hireling emissaries are now, or recently have been, in Harrison County, . . . instilling into the minds of the black population poisonous and dangerous sentiments against the southern whites, and meeting with more success than we are willing to acknowledge, or ready to concede.

Loughery was not specific, but it seems clear that his references were to Republican activists establishing in Marshall a chapter of the Union League, their partisan organization of Negro voters. To make matters worse, George W. Whitmore, the former unionist state representative who had refused to resign at the time of secession, showed up to speak at a Negro celebration on July 4. Addressing the Freedmen as "My Fellow citizens," Whitmore told them to give their political support to white Republicans, men who would soon be termed and term themselves "radicals." Loughery raged that Whitmore was a fifth-rate lawyer and a "low demagogue" who was mean in his social relations and "cruel" to his slaves.[7]

[6]Marshall *Texas Republican*, April 28, 1866, February 9, September 14 (quotation), 1867.

[7]Ibid., May 11, June 29 (first quotation), July 13 (second and third quotations), 1867. Whitmore had moved to Tyler in Smith County by this time. The Union League

Conservative whites attempted to counter radical influence among Freedmen by arguing that the true interests of Negroes lay with their former masters. Mayor James Turner of Marshall, for example, at the same July 4 gathering addressed by Whitmore, urged blacks to remember that prosperity depended on co-operation between the races. Whites did not threaten Freedmen at this point, although Loughery suggested economic pressure, and some Negroes recognized that their former masters would not accept political equality with impunity. Will Adams, once a slave belonging to Dave Caven, recalled that his father told the radicals, "Listen, white folks, you is gwine start a graveyard if you come round here teachin' niggers to sass white folks."[8]

On July 30, 1867, General Griffin removed Governor Throckmorton from office as an "impediment" to Reconstruction and replaced him with former governor Elisha M. Pease. The new governor had to recommend appointees to fill vacant state and local offices and to replace disloyal or politically unacceptable men put into office during Presidential Reconstruction. He was immediately bombarded with letters from around the state requesting removals and appointments. J. B. Williamson of Harrison County who had been appointed district judge by Andrew J. Hamilton in 1865 and then lost that position to General Matthew D. Ector in the first election under Presidential Reconstruction wrote to Pease on August 22, 1867. Ector, he said, is disqualified from officeholding by the Fourteenth Amendment, and County Judge Obadiah Hendrick and County Clerk J. P. Alford should be replaced too. Williamson wanted Ector's position, and he recommended N. V. Board for county judge. Board, according to Williamson, "is one of the unterrified union men of the county. . . . He has been much persecuted and desires a kind act from the Government he has never failed to support." Elijah Blackwell, a farmer from Tennessee who had

appeared officially in Texas during the spring of 1867. Moneyhon, *Republicanism in Reconstruction Texas*, 63-64.

[8] Marshall *Texas Republican*, June 29, July 13, 1867; Rawick (ed.), *American Slave*, IV, Part 1, 3 (quotation).

not held office before, was suggested for county clerk. Williamson recommended A. Hotchkiss for the district clerk's office which was vacant due to the death of J. M. Henderson. He also noted that S. R. Perry, although he could not take the "Iron Clad Oath," was doing a good job as sheriff, especially in seeing to it that prospective jurors could swear the oath, and should be retained in that office. The county commissioners could be left alone unless "good union men" wanted their positions.[9]

General Griffin died of yellow fever on September 15, 1867, and was replaced by General J. J. Reynolds who acted on Pease's many requests for removals and appointments. Military Order #195 dated November 1 replaced Hendrick with Board as county judge and Alford with Blackwell as county clerk. John Munden and L. P. Alford were removed from the commissioners court in favor of John Polk and Frank M. Lynch. The *Republican* and the *Flag* were both bitterly critical of the removals. Loughery called the action "official tyranny" and described the appointees as men "devoid of merit or capacity" and "obnoxious personally and politically" to the white population. The *Flag* expressed surprise that long-time residents of the community such as Board and Blackwell would take military appointments. Desire to feed at the "public crib" was the explanation. Ector lost his position as district judge too, and J. B. Williamson took his place in early December.[10]

On December 18, 1867, General Winfield Scott Hancock, who had replaced General Sheridan in August as commander of the Fifth Military District, called an election for February 10-14, 1868, in each Texas county, to decide whether a constitutional convention should be called and to select delegates to that meeting if it was approved. Harrison County conservatives knew that they had little chance, but they planned to vote against the con-

[9] Ramsdell, *Reconstruction in Texas*, 169 (first quotation), 170-173; Marshall *Texas Republican*, August 3, 1867; J. B. Williamson to General Charles Griffin, August 22, 1867 (second and third quotations), Governors' Letters.

[10] Ramsdell, *Reconstruction in Texas*, 174-175; Marshall *Texas Republican*, November 16, 23 (first, second, and third quotations), 1867; *Harrison Flag*, November 23, 1867 (fourth quotation). Williamson's replacement of Ector is seen in Election Register, 1867.

vention and for their candidates at the same time. The mood of many whites was worsened by economic hard times at the end of 1867. Planters felt that cotton prices were too low in comparison to the costs of labor. Moreover, 1867 had not been a good crop year due to a cold spring and wet summer. As the planters struggled with financial ruin, so did the community's merchants. It is likely that lower farm prices, especially for cotton, resulted from recovering productivity across the South, but Harrison County's planters tended to blame the free labor system. They also felt that the continued presence of Federal authority kept alive the hope of something for nothing among Freedmen.[11]

Through 1867, in spite of tensions created by Federal "interference" with local government, the fear of Negro domination, and worsening economic conditions, the community remained relatively calm. "Things are moving along with much sameness in the neighborhood," Lizzie Hargrove informed Harriet Perry in late April. And this attitude seems to have prevailed generally. There was no violence in reaction to the first months of Congressional Reconstruction. The community was upset by several murders involving important people, however; one of which was so bizarre that it deserves some detail.[12]

Davis B. Bonfoey and his wife Emma had been well-known members of the Harrison County community since the early 1850s. He was a Connecticut-born merchant, and she, a native of Massachusetts, was a respected schoolteacher. The Bonfoeys were unionists who refused to support the Confederacy, and, as we have seen, he was appointed provisional county judge by Governor A. J. Hamilton when Presidential Reconstruction began during the summer of 1865. Then, in February, 1866, Bonfoey became a collector of internal revenue for the United States

[11] Ramsdell, *Reconstruction in Texas*, 175; *Harrison Flag*, November 2, 1867; Marshall *Texas Republican*, May 11, September 7, November 2, December 21, 1867, January 4, 11, 1868.

[12] Lizzie Hargrove to Harriet Person Perry, April 27, 1867 (quotation), Person Family Papers. John Burke, the ex-Confederate soldier elected to the Presidential Reconstruction convention in 1866, killed John C. Sloan in Marshall on June 3, 1867. Eventually he was acquitted of murder. Marshall *Texas Republican*, June 26, 1868.

Government. He had several deputies in his district, including W. H. Fowler in Jefferson. Early in August, 1867, Bonfoey visited Fowler, the two quarrelled over the latter's work, and Bonfoey shot and killed his deputy. He was arrested and held for trial in Jefferson. Emma Bonfoey was left at home in Marshall with her four sons and a safe believed to contain $13,000 belonging to the family and more than $30,000 in government revenues. She asked Lieutenant William Hawley, commander of Federal troops in Marshall, for protection, and two soldiers were placed on guard duty at her home. One night shortly thereafter, one of Mrs. Bonfoey's sons awoke to find someone running from his mother's room and discovered that she had been bludgeoned with an axe or a hammer. She died several days later without regaining consciousness. Robbery was the apparent motive, but the money in the safe was not stolen. The guards claimed to have heard nothing; some local citizens believed that they were the criminals. Civil authorities arrested the two soldiers, but Lieutenant Hawley secured their release. No one was ever tried for the murder, and the disposal of the money is unclear. One account contends that Federal authorities eventually took all the money in the safe, although a United States Senate investigation in 1892 was inconclusive. Davis B. Bonfoey, released on bail to visit his wife's grave in early October, 1867, collapsed at the site and died within a few hours.[13]

The significance of the Bonfoey murder is difficult to assess. It was claimed many years later that this incident contributed heavily to the end of Reconstruction and the overthrow of Republican government in Harrison County. This is unlikely, however, since Republican government had not yet begun in 1867 and would not end until 1878. Most likely, while Mrs.

[13] Identifying information on Davis B. and Emma Bonfoey is from Eighth Census, 1860, Schedule 1. Their careers in the community prior to 1867 have been described at various points throughout this study. Details of the murder story are from Harold T. Dimick, "The Bonfoey Case at Marshall," *Southwestern Historical Quarterly*, XLVIII (Apr., 1945), 471-483, and "Bonfoey," an unpublished note compiled by Sallie M. Lentz on the basis of conversations with Miss Annie Young on March 16, 1936, Lentz Collection, East Texas Baptist College Library, Marshall. Miss Young lived in Marshall at the time of the murder.

Bonfoey's position made her death especially upsetting to the community, the whole affair had no really important political implications. Undoubtedly some sought to blame it on the Federal military's presence, but it did not even produce an outburst of emotion against existing conditions.[14]

The relative calm of Congressional Reconstruction in Harrison County finally broke down to some extent on December 30, 1867 in the so-called "Marshall Riot." Several radical leaders including Judge Colbert C. Caldwell of the Texas Supreme Court arrived to campaign for candidates to the constitutional convention, and according to the judge, "the pent up wrath of all rebeldolm culminated and exploded."[15]

A severe norther and snow storm was blowing in Marshall on December 30. Caldwell and his fellow campaigners sought to use the county's main courtroom for a meeting, but finding that they needed written approval from County Judge Board, they agreed to use the basement hallways of the courthouse for their gathering. Caldwell spoke to the crowd of nearly 300 for a few minutes, urging them to vote in February, and then Scipio McKee, a Negro accompanying the judge, began singing "Rally Round the Flag, Boys." At that point, Marshall Chief of Police S. J. Richardson (formerly captain of the W. P. Lane Rangers) broke into the hallway, fired a shot into the ceiling, and drove the Freedmen out. Deputy Sheriff A. G. Adams came to preserve order, but Caldwell believed that he was supporting Richardson and claimed later that the two had ordered him out of town at pistol point. Caldwell took refuge with Lieutenant Hawley, the post commander at Marshall. The affair went further. Sheriff S. R. Perry, who had not been present at the courthouse, and Deputy Sheriff Adams came to the army post apparently seeking to explain the incident. But they wound up arguing

[14]The extreme claim about the murder's significance is made in the Marshall *News Messenger*, January 23, 1951. Dimick, "Bonfoey Case," 483, did not go so far, but he argued that the murder was especially upsetting since Mrs. Bonfoey was the wife of a United States government employee. If she was not safe, then who was?

[15]C. C. Caldwell to Major Longley (intended for Governor Pease), January 2, 1868, Governors' Letters.

with Judge Caldwell in the Freedmen's Bureau office and leaving in a rage when he accused Adams of sympathizing with assassins. Adams vowed that he would have "satisfaction" from Caldwell, and Sheriff Perry told Lieutenant Hawley to keep out of the way. Judge Caldwell feared for his life and later reported that only an attache of the Freedmen's Bureau armed with a double barrel shotgun saved him from grave danger. Lieutenant Hawley then arrested Perry, Adams, Richardson, and five others. Much to Caldwell's disgust, District Judge Williamson released them several days later on a writ of Habeas Corpus. "This man Williamson is a cheat," he wrote. "No union man has any confidence in him. Either from fear or sympathy he runs with the rebel element."[16]

Robert W. Loughery held the radicals responsible for the incident. Marshall is a peaceful community, he said, and radicals should not come to town at the end of a bad crop year when idle Negroes are numerous and stir everyone up. Personally, he regretted the whole affair and suggested that radicals were better ignored.[17]

On January 11, Sheriff Perry and several of the others released on Habeas Corpus were rearrested, apparently on the orders of General Reynolds. An angry letter from Judge Caldwell to Governor Pease may have been responsible. Colonel W. H. Wood was ordered to Marshall by General Hancock to investigate the incident. He reported in early February that Captain Richardson had begun the excitement and the others had only tried to keep peace. The report indicated that civil authorities in the county were fully competent to handle the situation and that there had been no need for the rearrests. He recommended that the prisoners be turned over to civil authorities.[18]

No one was injured then, and the "Marshall Riot" probably created more excitement that was justified. Nevertheless,

[16]This account (together with the second quotation) is taken from Caldwell's letter cited above, the Marshall *Texas Republican* of January 4, 1868 (first quotation), and a report by Colonel W. H. Wood printed in the *Texas Republican*, February 22, 1868.

[17]Marshall *Texas Republican*, January 4, 1868.

[18]Ibid., February 22, 1868. There is no evidence that those arrested were ever tried.

federal presence and the prospects of "Negro rule" did heighten emotions in the community to a level where violence was just beneath the surface. Judge Caldwell, although not exactly an unbiased witness, included some observations on the political atmosphere in Marshall at the beginning of 1868 that were probably not great exaggerations. He claimed to have been "expelled from the hotel because of my politics." Richardson and Adams told him that no radical speeches would be made in their town. "No man but a Johnson man will be tolerated here," Caldwell wrote. "Such an one would be lionized. He must *cuss Congress* and damn the *nigger.*" Negroes in Harrison County, he believed, were so "cruelly wronged and outraged" that they might attempt to take matters into their own hands and thus give conservatives an excuse for violence. At least, the judge wrote, "the last one of them will vote *if he can.*" Caldwell was thus convinced that radicals would control Harrison County's delegation to the constitutional convention if federal authorities made it clear that election "disturbances" would not be tolerated.[19]

The Loyal League of Harrison County met on January 20 and 21, 1868, to select a slate of candidates for the convention. The community's best-known unionist, Lemuel D. Evans, rejected their nomination, and N. V. Board, the county judge, was put in his place. The other nominees were C. E. Coleman, the white Freedmen's Bureau teacher from Illinois, Mitchell Kendall, a Freedman who had served on the board of registrars, and Wiley Johnson, also a Freedman. The radicals thus supported one "scalawag" (Board), one "carpetbagger" (Coleman), and two Negroes. And they campaigned for their candidates. Judge Caldwell, George W. Whitmore, and several other prominent Republicans spoke to a gathering of 1,000 Freedmen on January 27 endorsing Congressional Reconstruction and Negro suffrage. The *Texas Republican* protested that these speakers not only campaigned for radical candidates but told blacks that conservative whites were their enemies.[20]

[19] Caldwell to Longley, January 2, 1868, Governors' Letters.

[20] Marshall *Texas Republican*, January 25, February 1, 1868.

The Democrats nominated L. D. Evans, Thomas F. Purnell, J. M. Waskom, and J. M. Fain of Panola County. Waskom had been a slaveholding planter, but the other two candidates from Harrison County were not typical of the community's traditional leadership. Evans had opposed secession, and Purnell was a former Union soldier who had settled there since the war. Conservatives apparently recognized, although too late, that some concessions had to be made in recognition of military defeat. The four-day election went off quietly with 2,417 of the county's 3,404 registered voters participating. Many whites ignored the contest. According to the *Texas Republican*, 497 whites (56% of those registered) and 1,920 blacks (76% of those registered) voted; totals that correspond exactly with the numbers voting for and against the proposed constitutional convention. All four radical candidates won overwhelmingly too, although only Judge Board received more than 1,920 votes (1,928). C. E. Coleman received 1,886, indicating that not every one of the Freedmen voted for the lone "carpetbagger" in the contest.[21]

The constitutional convention authorized by congress, generally called the "Black and Tan" or "mongrel" convention by the Marshall *Texas Republican*, assembled in Austin on June 1, 1868. There were ninety delegates, primarily "scalawags" such as N. V. Board. Of the nine Negroes who served, Harrison County sent two, Mitchell Kendall and Wiley Johnson. The convention debated issues such as the legality of legislation passed while Texas was out of the Union, the establishment of a public school system, and the division of Texas to create two states. And in the meantime, the delegates did not accomplish their primary purpose. After two months in session, they exhausted their funds and had to adjourn until additional tax money could be raised. The first session thus ended on August 31, 1868, and a second one began on December 7. The convention finally concluded its work on February 6, 1869. Forty-five delegates including Johnson who had served on the Public Debt Committee and

[21] Ibid., February 8, 15, 1868, May 14, 1869.

Kendall who had been a member of the Public Lands Committee signed the proposed new frame of government. Board and Coleman were not present at the final sessions.[22]

The Constitution of 1869 included several provisions of importance to Harrison County. First, it guaranteed Negro suffrage. Thus, although white disfranchisement extended only to those barred from office by the Fourteenth Amendment, the community's black majority could control local government. Second, the constitution abolished the county court and vested its powers in five justices of the peace elected in separate precincts. There would be no county judge. Instead, the justice of the peace from Marshall, the county seat, was to preside. Third, the constitution mandated free public schools for all children in Texas aged six to eighteen. The school system was to be highly centralized with all power in the hands of a superintendent of public instruction in Austin. And it was to be funded by proceeds from all lands previously set aside for schools plus one-quarter of the revenue from general taxation and a one dollar poll tax on all males from twenty-one to sixty years of age. In general, the constitution of 1869 was not nearly so punitive as conservatives feared, and many observers have considered it a remarkably sound frame of government. Nevertheless, the great majority of Harrison County's whites opposed it as they would have rejected any constitution created by "scalawags," "carpetbaggers," and Negroes.[23]

Through 1868 and into 1869 white conservatives planned to contest democratically for control of the community. They held a meeting on May 9, 1868, but attendance was so small that nothing could be accomplished. Loughery found this apathy "extraordinary" and "inexplicable." A second effort on June 2 was more successful. Plans were made for the creation of a con-

[22] Ibid., March 7, May 29, 1868; Brewer, *Negro Legislators of Texas*, 20, 24; Ramsdell, *Reconstruction in Texas*, 200-260; Moneyhon, *Republicanism in Reconstruction Texas*, 82-103; Gammel (comp.), *Laws of Texas*, VII, 430.

[23] Ramsdell, *Reconstruction in Texas*, 252-255; Connor, *Texas*, 220; William A. Russ, Jr., "Radical Disfranchisement in Texas, 1867-1870," *Southwestern Historical Quarterly*, XXXVIII (July, 1934), 47. The entire Constitution of 1869 is in Gammel (comp.), *Laws of Texas*, VII, 395-430.

servative club in each election precinct in the county. Direction would come from a central committee in Marshall composed of Alexander Pope, Samuel J. Richardson, Solomon R. Perry, E. B. Gregg, and J. H. Van Hook. Precinct committees were appointed in July, and the organizational process went ahead in August. Thus Harrison County's conservatives were prepared to contest for control of local government well before the constitutional convention completed its work.[24]

White conservatives in Harrison County, however, no matter how thoroughly they organized, faced one fundamental problem: they were a minority. How could they win a democratic election when blacks with radical leaders constituted an overwhelming majority of eligible voters? The meeting on June 2 made it clear that there would be no concessions in the area of political and social equality for Negroes. And yet at the same time, Freedmen were invited to join the conservatives' precinct clubs. Negroes were told that radical leaders cared only for their votes whereas conservatives had their economic welfare at heart. It soon became apparent that while the whites' economic argument would be partly positive, emphasizing that prosperity would come through cooperation, it would also be heavily negative, threatening Freedmen with a loss of work if they supported the radicals. The conservative club in the fifth precinct, for example, adopted a resolution calling on all members to refuse employment to anyone, white or black, who did not belong to the club. The *Texas Republican* advised against hiring or having any business relations with "radical loyal league negroes." Tell them to go to their radical friends for help, Loughery said. It is difficult to say how widespread economic coercion actually became in the community, but the idea apparently won widespread acceptance in theory. Joseph Bruckmuller, for example, a German-born shoemaker turned shopkeeper in Marshall, informed a friend in New Orleans that he would never give work to a white or black radical. The Negro's position should be im-

[24] Marshall *Texas Republican*, May 15, June 5, July 17, August 7, 14, 21, 1868.

proved, Bruckmuller said, but demagogues and promises would not do it.[25]

Conservatives appeared at first to have some success with this appeal to blacks. The constitution of the conservative club in precinct nine was signed by forty-three whites and thirty blacks. A "Colored Conservative Club" of precinct five was created in Marshall, and more than 150 blacks attended a meeting in early December, 1868, to hear speeches by white (William Stedman and G. P. Lipscomb) and black (Willis McNair and George Tucker) leaders. Loughery exulted that Freedmen were beginning to open their eyes to the "enormities of radicalism." He was further encouraged at the end of the year when the Freedmen's Bureau ended its work except for educational activities.[26] Still, more than a year of military-directed government remained, affording the radicals more than enough time to remind black voters who had ended slavery and brought them the right to vote and the promise of social advance.

There was, of course, another method Harrison County whites could employ in dealing with the black majority: physical intimidation. Across the South during Congressional Reconstruction the Ku Klux Klan emerged as the best-known organization practicing threats and violence against Freedmen who were politically active or otherwise got "out of their place." The Klan as such probably did not operate in Texas, but Klan-type activities, carried on by local, imitative groups were common by 1868. Harrison County blacks were at times the objects of intimidation by armed men. In their narratives, several ex-slaves spoke of the Klan being active in the community during Reconstruction, and two identified "Colonel Alford" (Lodwick P. Alford?) as the leader. It appears, however, that due to the presence of federal troops, there was much less Klan-type activity in Harrison County than in neighboring areas such as Upshur and Panola counties. Captain T. M. K. Smith wrote from Marshall

[25]Ibid., June 5, July 24, September 11 (quotation), 1868; George Dinkel to Joseph Bruckmuller, August 30, 1868, Bruckmuller to Dinkel, September 7, 1868, Bruckmuller Papers.

[26]Marshall *Texas Republican*, August 14, December 4 (quotation), 25, 1868.

when he went to take charge of the Freedmen's Bureau there in June, 1868: "Freedmen fleeing for their lives are continually coming to this place, . . . In almost every instance the offence charged against these freedmen was their attachment to and their earnest support of the U.S. Govt. . . ." Smith complained that he did not have enough force at his disposal to do anything effective in outlying areas. "I will say though," he added,

> that any outrage or injustice done to the freedmen in this county (Harrison) is promptly punished. Aggravated assaults though are of rare occurrence, owing no doubt to the presence of the troops in the immediate vicinity. If they were removed the same reign of terror would be instituted.

Local whites undoubtedly would have disputed Smith's judgment. He was never one of their favorites. Nevertheless, he had a point; the presence of United States troops meant that Harrison County whites had no choice except to deal with the black majority in a largely nonviolent manner.[27]

Federal authority made itself felt locally again in the spring of 1869 when General Edward R. S. Canby, who had temporarily replaced General Reynolds as commander in Texas, issued an order requiring all civil officeholders to take the "Iron Clad Oath" of 1862. Sheriff S. R. Perry and Tax Assessor/Collector George W. Young, the two major local government officials still in office who had been elected during Presidential Reconstruction in 1866, were disqualified. General J. J. Reynolds, back in command in Texas, appointed their replacements. Leonard C. DeLisle, an ex-Confederate soldier who had become a merchant in Marshall, managed somehow to take the oath as sheriff, and Thomas F. Purnell, a former Union officer, replaced Young. A

[27] Ramsdell, *Reconstruction in Texas*, 232; Rawick (ed.), *American Slave*, IV, Part 1, 131 (first quotation); V, Part 3, 123-124; Captain T. M. K. Smith to General J. J. Reynolds, June 24, 1868 (second and third quotations), Freedmen's Bureau, Records of the Assistant Commissioner for Texas. Captain Smith's conclusion is supported to some extent by an investigation of violence in Texas made by a special committee of the constitutional convention of 1868. The committee found widespread violence in Texas and cited numerous specific examples. None of these examples came from Harrison County. *Report of the Special Committee on Lawlessness and Violence in Texas* (Austin, 1868), reprinted in *Senate Miscellaneous Documents*, No. 109, 40th Congress, 2nd Session.

federal officer became mayor of Marshall. Loughery reported these changes without bothering to become indignant.[28] Perhaps after two years the community had become accustomed to government at the discretion of the military.

Finally, in October, 1869, General Reynolds issued orders for revising the voter registration lists and holding a four-day general election on November 30–December 3 to ratify the new constitution and elect state and local officers under its terms. Registration opened for ten days beginning on November 16. In Harrison County, the total number of voters rose to 3,838, including 2,805 blacks (73.1% of the total) and 1,033 whites. Approval of the constitution was a foregone conclusion, so the real contest was for control of the administration that would finally see Texas back in the Union. The conservative Democrats had no meaningful ticket statewide so the campaign was between moderate Republicans led by former governor Andrew J. Hamilton and radical Republicans supporting Edmund J. Davis. Whites across Texas were unenthusiastic about the election, but blacks tended to support Davis strongly. The radical Republican candidate won by fewer than 900 votes from an official total of more than 79,000.[29]

In Harrison County, the organizational work among black voters begun before the constitutional convention election in 1868 continued to pay off for the Republicans. Jerry Moore, a Freedman in Marshall, remembered how the radicals got their constituency to the polls.

> In the early days they held the election four days. They didn't vote in precincts but at the courthouse. The Democratic Party had no chance to 'timidate the darkies. The 'publican party had a "Loyal League" for to protect the cullud folks. First the Negroes went to the league house to get 'structions and ballots and then marched to the courthouse, double file, to vote.[30]

[28] Ramsdell, *Reconstruction in Texas*, 248, 266-267; Russ, "Radical Disfranchisement in Texas," 49; Marshall *Texas Republican*, April 30, May 4, 1869.

[29] Ramsdell, *Reconstruction in Texas*, 283-287; Moneyhon, *Republicanism in Reconstruction Texas*, 107-122; List of Registered Voters, 1867.

[30] Rawick (ed.), *American Slave*, V, Part 1, 123.

Davis carried Harrison County by 1,277 votes. Only Grimes County among those voting for Davis gave him a larger majority. Charles W. Garland of the *Jefferson Radical* in neighboring Marion County exulted:

> We say three cheers for old Harrison! The oppressed white loyalist and the down-trodden colored man is at last victorious! And it is to be hoped that tyranny and oppression and the reign of the six-shooter and bowie knife is at an end.[31]

George W. Whitmore, the old unionist turned ''scalawag'' in Tyler, won a seat in congress representing the first district. He also received a majority of more than 1,200 votes in Harrison County. In the light of his past, Whitmore's victory must have been almost more than the community's white conservatives could stand. Henry Rawson, a native of England, became Harrison County's state senator. He had lived in Marshall before the war but had no previous political experience. Both of the community's state representatives, Mitchell Kendall and Henry Moore, were Freedmen. According to the census of 1870, Kendall, who had already served as a voter registrar and delegate to the constitutional convention, was a forty-eight-year old native of Georgia. He was literate and worked as a blacksmith when not in public life. Moore was a sixty-year-old native of Alabama who could not read or write and listed no occupation other than state representative. According to his son Jerry, Moore had saved enough money ($800) to buy his freedom in Alabama and then lived with a ''guardian'' until emancipation. It is not clear just where or for how long Henry Moore lived as a free man before 1865, but perhaps this background helps account for his position as a leader.[32]

County government, of course, went under control of Republicans too. Five justices of the peace—Henry D. Smith, J. A. Price, J. P. Lynch, Z. T. Perry, and A. S. Justus—elected by pre-

[31]Jefferson *Radical*, December 11 (quotation), 25, 1869. These 1869 election returns were not preserved in the State Archives at Austin. Harrison County totals were reported in the Galveston *News*, December 17, 1869.

[32]Jefferson *Radical*, February 5, 1870; Eighth Census, 1860, Schedule 1; Ninth Census, 1870, Schedule 1; Rawick (ed.), *American Slave*, V, Part 3, 121-122.

cinct, took over the duties of the commissioners court. None of these men or the new sheriff, E. K. Taylor, or county clerk C. E. Bolles, had previously held office in the community. Six of the seven were natives of southern states, however, and at least four had been present in Harrison County before the Civil War.[33]

Thus, when General Reynolds proclaimed on April 16, 1870, that all civil authority in Texas had been returned to "officers elected by the people," Harrison County had officials notably different from the men elected to state and local government during Presidential Reconstruction.[34] Although the change was not as radical as possible, the traditional domination by white conservative planters had been broken. It remained to be seen how this "new" government would conduct itself and to what extent the transition in political power would be accompanied by alterations in other aspects of life in the community. Some changes were already evident in 1870.

The most important economic development during Congressional Reconstruction was the move from wage labor to sharecropping as a means of combining land and labor. This new practice appeared importantly by 1867. "We understand," the *Texas Republican* said on January 5, "that, in some instances, Negroes have contracted for half of the crop, the planter furnishing everything." The system had numerous variations, but this statement covered the essentials for years to come. A contract, signed by James Tucker of Elysian Fields in 1877 after sharecropping was a settled institution, showed the planter providing land, housing, work animals, and farm implements while blacks furnished labor and their own food, clothing, and medical care. The crop was shared on a fifty-fifty basis. As early as 1868, sharecropping was so widespread that Lieutenant Henry Sweeny of the Freedmen's Bureau attempted to protect Negro workers by ruling that any cropper driven off his land during a contract period would receive his share of the crop anyway.[35]

[33]Election Registers, 1846-1870; Eighth Census, 1860, Schedule 1; Ninth Census, 1870, Schedule 1.

[34]Ramsdell, *Reconstruction in Texas*, 292.

[35]Marshall *Texas Republican*, January 5, 1867 (quotation), September 18, 1868;

Freedmen generally favored sharecropping over wage contracts because it gave greater control over working hours and allowed them to negotiate concerning crops to be planted. In one sense, then, the new system represented an advance for blacks in the community. On the other hand, sharecropping did not affect patterns of landownership, and it had the potential to lock blacks into patterns of debt to planters and merchants that would be extremely limiting in the future. A sharecropper who had no money at the beginning of a crop year and no wages due each month (as wage labor contracts allowed) could obtain necessities only by borrowing. Harrison County had no bank until the 1870s, and even then bankers had little interest in the business of propertyless Negroes. The sharecroppers, therefore, turned to merchants in town and received credit in the form of supplies, usually provided at prices far higher than for cash purchases. There was no property to serve as collateral for these loans so a system of crop liens developed whereby the sharecropper pledged his part of the crop to be produced as security for the credit extended to him. The farmer was then at the mercy of the merchant, the weather, and the market for cotton. Many wound up in a seemingly endless cycle of sharecropping arrangements and crop liens with little or no hope for property ownership and real economic gain.[36]

The Freedmen's Bureau, the agency most concerned with arranging labor contracts for blacks and overseeing the fulfillment of those contracts, expired in Texas at the end of 1868. Lieutenant Edward C. Henshaw, the last sub-assistant commis-

Lawrence D. Rice, *The Negro in Texas, 1874-1900* (Baton Rouge, 1971), 156-157; Diary of James Tucker, Archives, Barker Texas History Center, University of Texas, Austin.

[36]There are not adequate sources to document the rise of the crop-lien system in Harrison County. Undoubtedly conditions there were similar to those across the rural South as explained in Roger L. Ransom and Richard Sutch, *One Kind of Freedom: The Economic Consequences of Emancipation* (New York, 1977), 87-97, 123-131. Banks do not appear in the Dun Mercantile Agency Reference Books for Marshall until the 1870s. See R. G. Dun and Company (comp.), *The Mercantile Agency Reference Book (and Key) Containing Ratings on the Merchants, Manufacturers and Traders Generally, Throughout the United States and Canada: January 1870* (New York, 1870), which shows no bankers. *The Mercantile Agency Reference Book* for 1875 lists "Raguet and Fry — Bankers and Exchange" among the businessmen of Marshall.

sioner to serve in Marshall, felt that local Negroes were by no means secure in any respect, let alone in their relationship to landowners. The Bureau was understaffed, Henshaw said. "It is true," he wrote,

> that by turning over all the complaints and cases for trial, made in this office, to the civil authorities, much labor would be saved, but in so doing much injustice and great expenses would attach to these poor creatures; and I earnestly believe that by so doing I would be defeating the very object for which this Bureau was instituted.

The Freedmen's Bureau had sought to help blacks economically primarily by urging them to sign contracts and labor faithfully and by attempting to see that landowners respected those contracts. After 1868, as black farmers moved into the "no-win" cycle of sharecropping, even this limited form of economic assistance was removed.[37]

The rise of sharecropping as a new method of combining land and labor marked the end of plantation agriculture in Harrison County. Without slaves or wage laborers fully under control, planters simply could not cultivate cotton and other crops on the scale that was common during the 1850s. Plantations were broken into numerous farms, although, as we will see, this did not necessarily mean a change in landownership or the destruction of the economic-social position of the planter class.

While sharecropping became an increasingly important economic arrangement in the community during Congressional Reconstruction, schools remained the critical social institution. Freedmen recognized that public schools provided an opportunity for progress on all fronts. Some whites spoke of the importance of educating blacks too, but many saw that free schools could elevate the Negro and be expensive for white propertyholders at the same time. They were less than enthusiastic about the idea. Nothing came of the legislation passed in 1866 to es-

[37]Elliot, "Freedmen's Bureau of Texas," 16; Lieutenant Edward C. Henshaw to General Charles Griffin, November 25, 1868 (quotation), Freedmen's Bureau, Records of the Assistant Commissioner for Texas.

tablish public schools for white children; certainly no action was taken to benefit Negro children at community expense. Therefore, in the late 1860s, education for blacks in Harrison County continued to be the job of the Freedmen's Bureau.

As we have seen, Owen F. Baker and Mr. and Mrs. C. E. Coleman worked as Bureau teachers in Marshall during 1866-1867. The Colemans closed their school for the summer at the end of June, 1867. C. E. Coleman then became involved in local politics during the early stages of Congressional Reconstruction and was elected to the constitutional convention. To the great glee of Robert Loughery, authorities in Angelina County arrested Coleman for bigamy when he supposedly married a widow there while on his way to Austin for the convention. Mrs. Coleman, who had in the meantime returned to Illinois, wrote a letter to the *Texas Republican* defending her husband. But neither returned to Harrison County.[38]

Without the Colemans' services, Bureau schools in Marshall remained closed until the spring of 1868. Captain T. M. K. Smith, sub-assistant commissioner of the Bureau, reported in April that the community had two teachers and two schoolhouses in poor condition. He needed money to advance the school system in his district (some things never change), but the Freedmen had less than usual due to poor crops in 1867. Local whites, he found, supported the idea of education for blacks but were unwilling to help financially. Poor whites would not attend Bureau schools and regarded any offer of assistance as an insult.[39]

In spite of these difficulties, the teachers, William Massey and Caroline Poe, both of whom were former slaves, continued their schools through 1868 and into early 1869. Their reports for June, 1868, showed 123 students enrolled, and the monthly total remained approximately 100 for the rest of the year. At the end

[38]For the educational work of the Bureau in 1866-1867, see Chapter 10. The story of Coleman's misadventure is found in Marshall *Texas Republican*, May 2, June 12, September 25, 1868.

[39]Monthly Report by Sub-Assistant Commissioner T. M. K. Smith, April, 1868, Freedmen's Bureau, Records of the Texas Superintendent of Education.

of February, 1869, Mrs. Poe quit teaching for the Bureau, leaving only Massey's school with an enrollment of 65 pupils.[40]

The removal of the sub-assistant commissioner from Marshall in December, 1868, left Massey uncertain and concerned about the future. Will the government still support schools for Freedmen, he asked Joseph Welch, the Bureau's state superintendent of education, "or has she left them to weed their own row . . . ?" Massey explained that he thought it an "honor" to teach. I am trying, he wrote, "to make myself useful to my one *[sic]* color by teaching and trying to teach their children. I am not a complete Educated Man. I have been trying to use my talant *[sic]* as to Elevate my people all I can both Temporal and spiritual."[41] His letter is a touching example of the sincerity and dedication of the pioneer teachers of Freedmen in the community. It was at least an uphill fight.

Massey taught through March, 1869, and was replaced on April 1 by L.J. Gallant, a white instructor from Indiana. Gallant insisted that local Freedmen could not pay enough to support his school properly and asked the Bureau for a salary. (Massey and Mrs. Poe had never received one.) Welch finally agreed in June to pay $15 a month, although, he wrote, "permit me to say we had been under the impression that Marshall could sustain a teacher well." Gallant replied: "This place ought to support a teacher well, but it does not do it. The people are less concerned about the education of their children than any place that I have been since the war." However justified, it seems unlikely that this attitude helped the situation. Gallant's last report, for July, showed fifty children registered and an average daily attendance of thirty-eight. Schools did not reopen in Marshall that fall or the following spring, and all educational efforts of the Freedmen's Bureau in Texas were discontinued at the close of 1870.[42] The Bureau's work in providing schools from

[40] Monthly Reports by William Massey and Caroline Poe, June, August, September, December, 1868, January, February, 1869, Monthly Report by Superintendent Joseph Welch, March, 1869, Ibid.

[41] William Massey to Joseph Welch, February 8, 1869, Ibid.

[42] Monthly Report of Assistant Superintendent Louis W. Stevenson, April, 1869,

1866 to 1869 should not be discounted, but obviously only a handful of Harrison County's blacks received any formal education during Presidential or Congressional Reconstruction.

The United States Census of 1870 provides data on economic and social conditions in Harrison County as Congressional Reconstruction ended and Republicans took over local government. Unfortunately, this census was notoriously poor. Some families were enumerated twice while it is probable that many others were missed entirely. The census of Marshall was taken and then re-taken so that officials in Washington had to throw out the first set of forms returned. The published totals showed only 13,241 people in the county, a decline of nearly 2,000 from the 1860 totals with almost all of the loss coming in the white population. Such a decrease seems unlikely, especially since the community had not been devastated by war, and no other source mentions heavy emigration by whites. Perhaps many people, having little love for the federal government, simply refused to cooperate with its census takers.[43]

This under-enumeration notwithstanding, information drawn from the census of 1870 probably gives an essentially correct view of conditions in the community. The population was approximately two-thirds black (8,931 Negroes and 4,310 whites), bearing out the general contention that Freedmen moved into areas where federal troops and Bureau agents were stationed. Each of the county's five justice precincts had a Negro majority; only the town of Marshall with 1,069 whites and 851 blacks did not. There were 4,442 children in the county aged five to eighteen, but only 687 (575 white and 112 black) attended school. Churches were strong, at least on paper. There were twenty-two Baptist congregations, fourteen Methodist, four Presbyterian, and one Episcopalian. These forty-one churches could

Joseph Welch to L. J. Gallant, June 9, 1869 (first quotation), Gallant to Welch, June 18, 1869 (second quotation), Monthly Report of L. J. Gallant, July, 1969, Ibid.

[43] U.S. Bureau of the Census, *Population of the United States (1870)*, 64. Lathrop, *Migration into East Texas*, 14, says that Negroes were grossly undercounted across the South in 1870. Robert W. Loughery contended in 1880 that the census of 1870 had been a disgrace, see Marshall *Tri-Weekly Herald*, January 15, 1880.

seat 11,300 people, almost every man, woman, and child in the community.[44]

These census returns suggest that Harrison County's economy, after several years of reasonable success due in part to high post-war cotton prices, had suffered notably from adjustments in the labor system and several poor crop years. Disruption of the labor system and the move from wage labor to sharecropping was accompanied by too much rain during 1866 and extreme cold in the spring of 1867. The weather improved in 1868 and so did the cotton crop. Nevertheless, statistics on the 1869 crop year, reported in the census of 1870, showed a serious weakening of the agricultural economy since 1860. Harrison County had 381 farms in 1870 as opposed to 695 ten years earlier. Improved farm land declined from 117,847 acres to 76,187, and farm cash value fell from $2,668,809 to $863,851. Production of cotton stood at 8,165 bales in 1870 compared to 21,440 bales reported in 1860. Manufacturing did not take up the slack. The census listed twenty-five establishments in the county producing $124,904 worth of goods. Published census returns for 1860 had reported thirty-two manufacturers turning out products valued at $203,942.[45]

It should be remembered once more that the census of 1870 probably contained serious errors in the direction of underenumeration. Furthermore, economic decline, regardless of its severity, does not necessarily point toward basic change in economic and social structure. A profile of the community based on a sample of individual households drawn from the census will indicate the extent of change in occupational patterns, wealth distributions, and opportunities for education. Moreover, such a sample permits

[44]U.S. Bureau of the Census, *Population of the United States (1870)*, 272, 430, 555, 636.

[45]U.S. Bureau of the Census, *Agriculture of the United States in 1860*, 144-145; U.S. Bureau of the Census, *Manufacturers of the United States in 1860*, 585; United States Bureau of the Census, Ninth Census, *The Statistics of the Wealth and Industry of the United States . . . from the Original Returns of the Ninth Census, 1870* (Washington, 1872), 254-255, 363, 572. Information on weather and crop conditions in 1866, 1867, and 1868 is found in Hugh Perry to Harriet Person Perry, June 5, 1866, Person Family Papers; Marshall *Texas Republican*, May 11, September 7, 1867, October 30, 1868, January 8, 1869.

comparison of the status of whites and blacks to measure the extent to which Freedmen had been elevated since emancipation.

A random sample of 964 households provided 308 white families (32%) and 656 black families as a basis for analysis and comparison (Table 17). Looking first at the white families, we find them, as in 1860, overwhelmingly agricultural. Nearly 60% reported as farmers or farm laborers. Merchants, professionals, and tradesmen comprised roughly the same proportions of all whites in 1870 as in 1860. In short, other than an increase in those reporting no occupation, probably as a result of poor census taking, occupational patterns among whites showed little change over the decade of Civil War and Reconstruction. At a glance, the distribution of wealth among white households appears to have changed drastically in the ten years since 1860 (Table 18). Nearly 29% owned no property in 1870 (compared to 1.8% in 1860). Only 3.9% were worth $10,000 or more whereas more than 20% had owned $20,000 or more ten years earlier. These changes, however, reveal only a decline in total wealth, due primarily to the loss of slave property; they do not show a significant change in distribution patterns. Wealth remained concentrated in the hands of a relatively small number of households. The wealthiest 4.8% in 1860, for example, owned 29.9% of all wealth. Ten years later the top 3.9% (those worth $10,000 or more) held 31.3%. The Gini Index for wealthholding among whites was higher in 1870 (.668) than in 1860 (.638). Finally, educational opportunities for white children appear to have been more limited in 1870 than during the late antebellum years. In the 1860 census sample, 55% of the households with children aged five to seventeen had at least one child in school while in the 1870 sample this proportion was only 44%.[46]

The white population, then, in spite of the economic impact of war and freeing the slaves, showed no major alterations in oc-

[46] Eighth Census, 1860, Schedule 1; Ninth Census, 1870, Schedule 1. Table 17 is based on quantitative data drawn from Ninth Census, 1870, Schedules 1 and 3. Comparisons between 1870 and 1860 are based on this table and Table 1 in Chapter 1. Table 18 is based on quantitative data drawn from Eighth Census, 1860, Schedule 1, and Ninth Census, 1870, Schedule 1. The Gini Index of Concentration is explained in Chapter 1.

TABLE 17

Demographic and Economic Characteristics of the Population of Harrison County, 1870

Characteristic	Whole Sample	Whites	Blacks
Percent of Population	100.0	32.0	68.0
Proportion Male	88.5	89.0	88.3
Mean Age	38.5	39.9	37.8
Birthplace			
Upper South	33.2%	33.5%	33.2%
Lower South	60.7	53.2	64.2
Free States	3.9	7.8	2.0
Foreign Born	2.0	5.5	.3
Unknown	.2	0.0	.3
Occupation			
Farmer	19.9%	54.9%	3.5%
Farm Laborer	52.7	4.5	75.3
Merchant/Professional	3.2	9.4	.3
Trades	4.6	8.8	2.6
Other	7.2	11.3	3.6
Unknown	12.4	11.0	13.1
Mean Real Property	$459	$1,415	$10
Mean Personal Property	$181	$527	$19
Mean Total Wealth	$640	$1,942	$29
Mean Number Dependents	3.7	3.7	3.7
Percentage With At Least One Child Aged Five to Seventeen	61.5	55.2	64.5
Percentage with at Least One Child Aged Five to Seventeen Who Had At Least One Child in School	16.5	44.1	5.4

TABLE 18

Distributions of Wealth among the White Population of Harrison County, 1860 and 1870

Dollar Value of Wealth	0	1–249	250–499	500–999	1,000–4,999	5,000–9,999	10,000–19,999	20,000–49,999	50,000+	Totals
1860										
Percentage of White Population	1.8	8.4	4.4	7.6	28.0	13.4	16.0	15.6	4.8	100.0
Percentage of Total Wealth	0.0	.1	.1	.4	5.6	8.0	17.8	38.0	29.9	100.0
Gini Index = .638										
1870										
Percentage of White Population	28.9	3.6	9.4	14.6	32.8	6.8	3.3	.6	0.0	100.0
Percentage of Total Wealth	0.0	.3	1.7	5.3	38.2	23.1	22.0	9.4	0.0	100.0
Gini Index = .668										

cupational patterns, wealth distributions, or educational opportunities. There was, of course, the drastic social and economic change of emancipation. To what extent had blacks risen from the status of slaves? How did they compare with whites? Table 17 reveals some interesting demographic similarities. White and black household heads were nearly the same age (late 30s), a high proportion were male (approximately 89%), and a majority were native to the lower South. Families averaged 3.7 dependents regardless of race, and a sizable majority depended on agriculture for a living. At this point, however, similarities between whites and blacks end and overwhelming economic-social differences appear.

More than half of the whites gave their primary occupation as farmer while three-quarters of the blacks said they were farm laborers. Of the 108 household heads who reported farm acreage, 102 were white (94.4%) and 6 were black. Approximately 18% of whites were merchants, professionals, and tradesmen; less than 3% of the Negroes fell into these classes. White households averaged $1,942 in total wealth ($1,415 in real property and $527 in personal); mean wealth in black households was $28.49. Indeed only 11.7% of black families reported property in any form. Of the 170 white households having school-aged children, seventy-five (44.1%) sent at least one child to school during the year prior to the census. Among black households in the sample, only twenty-three (5.4%) of the 423 that had children aged five to seventeen managed to send even one child to school.

Had Harrison County been revolutionized by 1870 when Texas returned to the Union? A careful observer might well have answered this question "yes, no, and maybe." The community's black majority had been freed and given the right to vote. White leaders had suffered huge financial losses, seen the plantation system disrupted, and in many cases been disfranchised and barred from public office. The Freedmen's Bureau had worked for nearly four years to aid and educate blacks, and the state was committed to public schools for all. On the other hand, Reconstruction had not fundamentally altered economic relationships or introduced what the *Harrison Flag* called the "horrors of social equality.'' In general, whites still owned the land while blacks provided the labor. There had been no significant redistribution of productive property or alteration of occupational roles. Whites accepted, albeit with considerable difficulty, the facts of black freedom and enfranchisement, but they remained convinced of Negro inferiority and voiced that feeling regularly. Finally, there is the ''maybe.'' Changes had been made, and both state and local government in the early 1870s promised to differ greatly from the traditional. Perhaps local radicals, aided by Republican control in Austin, would bring more basic change to Harrison County after 1870 than had come during all the years of Presidential and Congressional Reconstruction.

12

Republican Government: 1870–1878

MILITARY RECONSTRUCTION in Texas ended officially on April 16, 1870, when General J. J. Reynolds turned over full civil authority to the administration of Governor Edmund J. Davis. Republicans had capitalized on developments between 1867 and 1870 to take control of the state, but clearly they would have great difficulty in maintaining that position for long. The party was divided between the Radicals led by Governor Davis and a moderate faction headed by Andrew J. Hamilton. Moreover, the majority of Texans were white Democrats who intended to vote the Republicans out of office at the first opportunity. The governor had a Republican legislature to work with in 1870, but he had only a few years to build the unity and enact a program that would somehow win enough white as well as black votes to keep his party in power. Otherwise he would face a return to power by the Democratic Party; white conservatives across the South called it "redemption."[1]

Circumstances facing Republicans in Harrison County differed from those confronting their party statewide for one simple reason: the community's black majority. The Davis Administration received solid support there during the early 1870s, and the county remained under radical control well after "redemption" of the government in Austin. The state legislature came under Democratic control by January, 1873, and the governor's office in January, 1874. Local government in Marshall, however, was not "redeemed" until November, 1878, nearly five years after white conservative rule returned statewide. The story of these years of Republican or radical government in Harrison County is best told by first describing the men who held office and then explaining their major policies. In the process, a basis for evaluating the conservatives' claim that they saved the community in 1878 can be established.

The Republicans from Harrison County who took office in 1870 have been identified previously. George W. Whitmore represented Texas's first district in congress. Henry Rawson went to Austin as a state senator while Mitchell Kendall and Henry Moore took seats in the lower house of the legislature. All three were radical supporters of Governor Davis. J. B. Williamson became district judge. C. E. Bolles served as district and county clerk, the two offices being combined under the Constitution of 1869. The commissioners court consisted of Henry D. Smith, J. A. Price, J. P. Lynch, Z. T. Perry, and A. S. Justus. Each of these men was technically a justice of the peace in one of the county's five justice precincts; Smith presided over the court by virtue of being justice of the precinct including Marshall, the county seat. Finally, E. K. Taylor took over the sheriff's office.[2]

[1] Moneyhon, *Republicanism in Reconstruction Texas*, 128-129; Ramsdell, *Reconstruction in Texas*, 292.

[2] The Jefferson *Radical*, January 27, 1870, praised Rawson as a man of "integrity

As noted bove, these men were not typical of those who had traditionally governed Harrison County. Only Whitmore and Williamson had held office there before, and the former had become an outcast for his determined unionism in 1860-1861 while the latter had served only as the result of appointment during Reconstruction. At the same time, these Republican officeholders did not represent the most radical change possible. Only two, Kendall and Moore, were black, and none can be positively identified as "carpetbaggers." Instead, most were southern-born whites who had lived in the community before the war.

The Republican controlled 12th legislature, assembled in special session by Governor Davis in 1870, sought to guarantee its party an extra year in control by passing a law postponing congressional elections due in the fall of 1870 and state elections due in 1871 until November, 1872. Local officials such as the sheriff and county treasurer who had won two-year terms in 1869 also would not face re-election until 1872. Davis had to call the congressional election in 1871, however, because the Forty-first Congress — to which Whitmore and two other Texas Republicans had been elected — expired on March 4, 1871, and the Forty-second Congress was scheduled to meet before November, 1872. The governor set the election for October 3-6, 1871. Democrats in the first district nominated William S. Herndon, a Confederate veteran, to oppose Whitmore and defeated the Republican incumbent by more than 5,000 votes. Harrison County's black voters gave Whitmore a margin of 2,216 to 1,116 for his conservative opponent, but they could not save him from white Democrats districtwide.[3]

and ability" and said Kendall and Moore would well represent the interests of their "colored brethren." *Flake's Bulletin*, May 3, 1870, identifies all three as radicals. Local officeholders are identified in Election Registers, 1870, J. B. Williamson was appointed district judge by Governor Davis in July, 1870. Ibid.

[3]Gammel (comp.), *Laws of Texas*, VI, 302-313; Ramsdell, *Reconstruction in Texas*, 298-299, 310; Paul D. Casdorph, *A History of the Republican Party in Texas, 1865-1965* (Austin, 1965), 20; Moneyhon, *Republicanism in Reconstruction Texas*, 153, 164; Election Returns, Harrison County, 1871; Philip J. Avillo, Jr., "Phanton Radicals: Texas Republicans in Congress, 1870-1873," *Southwestern Historical Quarterly*, LXX-

The recovery of Democratic strength at the polls statewide was revealed in November, 1872, with the election of a new legislature. Republicans turned out 3,000 fewer voters than in 1871 and lost control of both houses. When the 13th Legislature assembled in Austin on January 3, 1873, Governor Davis and his party were unable to go forward with any part of their program, and complete return to Democrat control of state government was only one year away. Harrison County, however, did not share in these developments. Republicans in the community reelected Henry Rawson to the senate and Henry Moore to the lower house. Both had joined Radical Republicans in support of Governor Davis during 1870-1871. Shack Roberts, a Negro Republican, replaced Mitchell Kendall as the county's other state representative. Roberts was a Methodist minister much interested in education for his fellow blacks. Moore and Roberts received 2,349 and 2,103 votes respectively compared to 661 for Robert L. Hightower and 784 for R. H. Cooper, their white Democratic opponents. Stilwell H. Russell, a young Texas-born Republican destined to become a leader of his party in the area, won the office of sheriff by a margin of 2,273 to 884 over W. H. Poland. William Umbdenstock, a German immigrant who had arrived in Marshall as a railroad hand during the 1850s, won the position of county treasurer with 2,278 votes to 860 for his opponent H.J. Nichols. Umbdenstock, who had established a Republican newspaper called the Marshall *Weekly* in 1867, was also on his way to leadership in the party. The treasurer's office was a step on the way.[4]

At the close of 1872, then, while Texas Democrats looked confidently toward a gubernatorial election scheduled for De-

VII (Apr. 1974), 434, 438-439, contends that Whitmore did very little to help Freedmen or promote other radical policies while he was in Washington.

[4]Moneyhon, *Republicanism in Reconstruction Texas*, 181-182. Results of this election locally are found in Election Returns, Harrison County, 1872. Information on Shack Roberts is found in Brewer, *Negro Legislators of Texas*, 61, 67-68. Russell and Umbdenstock may be identified in Ninth Census, 1870, Schedule 1. Umbdenstock also appears in Eighth Census, 1860, Schedule 1. No copies of his newspaper are extant, but the commissioners court minutes contain references to it, and the Marshall *Tri-Weekly Herald*, October 6, 1877, referred to it as a "Radical Republican journal."

cember, 1873, Harrison County conservatives apparently had little hope for "redemption." In fact, they had not even contested the county offices open in 1872. Poland and Nichols, the badly defeated candidates for sheriff and treasurer, were probably more acceptable to Republicans than to Democrats in the community. General Reynolds had appointed Nichols, a native of Vermont, sheriff in 1869, and Governor Davis put Poland, a native of Alabama, in the same office after E. K. Taylor died in 1870. Local political rivalries probably explain why Russell and Umbdenstock were nominated and elected over Poland and Nichols. In any cases, the point is clear; Harrison County Democrats in 1872 were reduced in county elections to choosing between varieties of Republicans. Curiously, so was the national Democratic Party which supported Horace Greeley and the Liberal Republican ticket against President Ulysses S. Grant. The regular Republican incumbent carried Harrison County 2,374 to 775, approximately the margin of victory achieved there by his party's state and local candidates.[5]

The conservative-controlled 13th Legislature assembled in Austin from January until June, 1873, and made life miserable for the Davis Administration. One of its most important acts called for an election in December to choose yet another legislature and, more significantly, new state officials including a new governor. After a strenuous campaign, Richard Coke, the Democratic candidate, decisively defeated Governor Davis's bid for reelection. The transition of power was anything but smooth as the Republicans challenged Coke's victory on the grounds that the election had been held on one day rather than four as directed in the Constitution of 1869. Violence threatened, but Governor Davis soon bowed to the fact that he simply did not have the support, state or federal, to hold his office. Coke's inauguration in January, 1874, marked the final act of "redemption" for the state government of Texas.[6]

[5]Information on Poland and Nichols is found in Ninth Census, 1870, Schedule 1, and Election Registers, 1869-1870. The votes they received in 1872 and the vote in the presidential election that year are found in Election Returns, Harrison County, 1872.

[6]Moneyhon, *Republicanism in Reconstruction Texas*, 185-194; Ramsdell, *Recon-*

Harrison County was not responsible for Davis's defeat. The vote there was 2,313 (70%) for the governor to 997 for Coke. It was one of only twenty-six counties that gave Davis a majority. Moreover, the community continued to support a Republican delegation to the state legislature. Webster Flanagan of neighboring Rusk County, a noted moderate Republican leader whose father was a United States senator, was elected to the state senate. Shack Roberts, the black leader from Harrison County, was re-elected to the lower house where he was joined by Ed Brown, a Negro from Rusk County, as a representative of the two county district. Finally, as might be expected, Republicans remained completely in control of the local government at Marshall. Indeed the new commissioners court elected by overwhelming margins in December, 1873, may have been more radical than its predecessor. Of the five justices, one, L.J. Gallant, was a native of Indiana who had come to the community as a Freedmen's Bureau teacher, and another, Edmund J. Brown, was black. The other three justices, M. T. Hoskins, J. R. Ford, and J. K. Williams, could not be identified in the censuses of 1860, 1870, or 1880. Harrison County apparently came closer to being governed by "carpetbaggers" and Negroes during the mid-1870s than at any time during the whole Reconstruction era. Both sides found something to celebrate in these 1873 elections. Democrats in Marshall held a "jubilee" on December 11 in honor of "redemption" statewide; two days later "the colored people" held one for their victory in the county.[7]

For a variety of reasons the commissioners court elected in 1873 was highly unstable. First, J. P. Lynch, one of the justices

struction in Texas, 313-317. The details of this controversial election are not essential to an explanation of events in Harrison County.

[7] Galveston *News*, December 6, 14 (quotations), 1873; Moneyhon, *Republicanism in Reconstruction Texas*, 190; *Members of the Texas Legislature, 1846-1962* (Austin, 1962), 78-86; Webb, Carroll, and Branda (eds.), *Handbook of Texas*, I, 609; Brewer, *Negro Legislators of Texas*, 65; Election Returns, Harrison County, 1873; Ninth Census, 1870, Schedule 1; M. T. Hoskins may have come to the community also as a teacher. The medical account books of Dr. William W. Perry for July, 1872, contain two entries for service to "Hoskins — Negro Teacher." Perry Family Papers, Property of Mrs. Eudora C. Hodges, Dallas, Texas.

from 1869–1873, challenged the right of his successor, J. R. Ford, to office. The details are unclear, but Lynch, a farmer from Tennessee resident in the county before 1860, replaced Ford during the spring of 1874. Next, in June, 1874, William S. Coleman, a Marshall lawyer, demanded that Justice Edmund J. Brown be removed from office on the grounds that he lived in neighboring Marion County, and that he was "mentally and morally unfit to fill any office whatsoever." Brown, according to the Texas Election Register, "abandoned his office" and "left the county." A special election in September, 1874, put H. L. Berry, a forty-five year old farmer born in South Carolina, in his position. Finally, L. J. Gallant, the "carpetbagger" justice, died in August, 1874. Another special election in October placed W. L. Hailey in his office. The court's membership remained relatively stable through 1875, but even then there were some interesting moments. In December, for example, H. L. Berry's colleagues fined him $10 for being intoxicated and raising a disturbance in court.[8]

Instability in personnel and other difficulties to be explained below, notwithstanding, Harrison County's Republican government continued to enjoy unvarying support from local voters in 1874 and 1875. S. H. Russell, for example, was reelected sheriff over A. G. Adams late in 1874 by a margin of 2,176 to 777. The radical majority seemed so overwhelming that even Robert W. Loughery, back in Marshall as editor of the *Tri-Weekly Herald* after brief stints with the Jefferson *Times* and Galveston *Times,* found the prospects for a Democratic victory hopeless. "We repeat:" he wrote on May 29, 1875, "the political status of this county is settled for years to come; nothing that we can do will change it."[9]

The community's conservative Democrats received another

[8]Harrison County Commissioners Court Minutes, 1874-1875 (first quotation from June, 1874); Election Registers, 1874-1875 (second and third quotations); Ninth Census, 1870, Schedule 1.

[9]Election Returns, Harrison County, 1874; Marshall *Tri-Weekly Herald*, May 29, 1875 (quotation). Loughery's moves to Jefferson and Galveston are noted in Webb, Carroll and Branda (eds.), *Handbook of Texas*, II, 84-85.

demonstration of their weakness in August, 1875. Democrats in Austin called for the election of a constitutional convention to replace the radical Constitution of 1869 with a suitably conservative new frame of government. Statewide, the convention easily won popular approval, and seventy-five of the ninety delegates, elected three each from the state's thirty senatorial districts, were Democrats. In Harrison County, however, the vote was 2,269 to 839 against the convention. Three of the fifteen Republicans elected came from the fifth senatorial district comprised of Harrison and Rusk counties. The Democratic candidates, two of whom, James Tucker and William S. Coleman, were from Harrison County, each received fewer than 850 votes there, while the Republicans all had more than 2,230 votes from the community. Two of the three Republicans, Sheriff S. H. Russell and David Abner, were from Harrison County. The third, State Senator Webster Flanagan, lived in Rusk. Democratic conservatives had insisted that the "true interests" of blacks and whites were the same and urged Negroes to ignore the "color line," but their pleas were in vain.[10]

The constitutional convention met for eleven weeks beginning in September, 1875, and drafted a long, unwieldly frame of government distinguished primarily by its reaction against every aspect of the Constitution of 1869 and the brief period of Republican control. Flanagan, Russell, and Abner were in a hopeless minority at the convention, but they found the "redeemer" majority willing to leave Harrison County as a Republican enclave in a Democratic state. In short, the county would be designated as a separate senatorial and house district and left to its black majority. Loughery fumed over the "Africanization" of the community which left it "to the tender mercies of the Radical vampyres *[sic]* . . ." At least, he said, the convention could have initiated suffrage restriction to help white minorities protect themselves; but male suffrage was the rule. After much

[10]Connor, *Texas*, 226; Marshall *Tri-Weekly Herald*, August 5, 1875. See Brewer, *Negro Legislators of Texas*, 69, on Abner. The campaign "line" of Democratic conservatives is seen in Marshall *Tri-Weekly Herald*, July 5 (first quotation), 22 (second quotation), 1875.

discussion Harrison County Democrats decided to support the new constitution as a choice among evils. Republicans opposed it, in spite of the way it gave them control of the county at the state was well as local level.[11]

On February 15, 1876, Texans overwhelmingly ratified the new constitution and elected state and local officers under its terms. Harrison County's Republican majority was on the losing side in virtually every contest that extended beyond the community's borders. They carried the county against the constitution 2,713 to 1,036 and voted for all of the unsuccessful Republican candidates for state offices. Local radicals even had an opportunity to support one of their own, William Umbdenstock, for state treasurer. Umbdenstock had 2,660 votes there to 1,110 for his opponent, A.J. Dorn, but the latter won easily statewide. In the second judicial district, comprised of Harrison and several other east Texas counties, Democrat A.J. Booty of Panola County was elected district judge in spite of the fact that he lost Harrison to the Republican candidate, J. B. Williamson, by a margin of 1,060 to 2,710. The situation was similar in the contest for the floater seat for the state house of representatives from Harrison, Panola, Rusk, Cherokee, and Shelby counties. William S. Coleman, the Democrat, lost Harrison County to M.W. Wheeler by a margin of 2,744 to 963 but won the seat on the strength of white votes from the rest of the district.[12]

Local Republicans fared much better in races that were only countywide. Walter Ripetoe won the state senate seat, and Shack Roberts returned to the house of representatives. Neither faced more than token opposition. J. B. Williamson, who ran for county judge as well as district judge, was more successful at home, defeating J. M. Hall and J. F. Williams easily. Williamson would head a commissioners court composed of Dr. W. C. Rain, J.E. Floyd, A.E. Snow, and B.R. Bass. The first three

[11] Marshall *Tri-Weekly Herald*, October 12, November 9 (quotation), December 21, 1875, January 1, 1876. Richardson, Wallace, and Anderson, *Texas*, 227-230 contains a good summary of the new constitution.

[12] Election Returns, Harrison County, 1876; Marshall *Tri-Weekly Herald*, February 22, 1876.

constituted a Republican majority, but Bass was a Democrat. He defeated T. S. Buchanan, the radical nominee in precinct 1, by a margin of 304 to 287, a victory made possible by the fact that commissioners were not elected on a countywide basis. Bass was the first of his party to win local office since 1866, but conservatives found nothing to cheer in one isolated success. W. C. Pierce ran unopposed for county clerk. William E. Singleton was elected sheriff; William Umbdenstock, treasurer; S. H. Smothers, tax assessor; and S. H. Russell, tax collector. All these victorious Republican candidates, except the county commissioners who ran in single precincts, received at least 2,600 votes while their opponents had approximately 1,000 or fewer. Three of the victors, Ripetoe, Roberts, and Smothers, were black; the others who could be identified were "scalawags."[13]

The national elections in November, 1876, created considerable political enthusiasm in Harrison County in spite of the fact that any observer could have predicted the outcome there. Republicans would carry the community by a wide margin and then see their party lose any district or state race. Perhaps interest was high because local people were involved prominently and both parties wanted to prove or increase their strength. Democrat F. B. Sexton and Republican S. H. Russell served as delegates to their respective national conventions. Back home, Russell was nominated to run for congress in the First District against David B. Culberson of Marion County. Editor Loughery of the *Tri-Weekly Herald* seemed to waver for a moment, probably because Russell was a local leader. "He is a man of more than ordinary ability," Loughery wrote, "and the best organizer of the party." However, he, a southern man, had turned on his own

[13]Local contest returns are in Marshall *Tri-Weekly Herald*, February 22, 1876. For information on B. R. Bass as a Democrat, see Marshall *Tri-Weekly Herald*, July 5, 1875, January 1, 1876. Identification of blacks and "scalawags" is based on Eighth Census, 1860, Schedule 1 and Ninth Census, 1870, Schedule 1. "Scalawag" was a derogative term of uncertain origin applied to white southerners who cooperated with the Republicans during Reconstruction. It should be noted that the new constitution restored the positions of county judge and county commissioner, replacing the five justices of the peace who had composed the county court under the Constitution of 1869.

people and supported Governor Davis. That could not be forgiven at the polls. Rutherford B. Hayes, the Republican presidential nominee, carried Harrison County by 1,684 votes (2,947 to 1,299), and Russell defeated Culberson there by an even larger margin, 2,966 to 1,277. Of course, the Democratic presidential candidate, Samuel J. Tilden, won statewide, and Culberson went to congress.[14]

Local conservatives believed at first that Tilden had won the presidency in 1876. Loughery's headline on November 11 read: "Emancipation of the White Race of the South." But the election was disputed, thanks to circumstances in Florida, Louisiana, and South Carolina, and Hayes eventually became president. His victory probably had the same effect for the South as a Democratic success would have had in that the last Republican governments were allowed to fall, and, in general, federal power no longer supported radical efforts across the former Confederacy.[15]

Harrison County remained "unredeemed" in 1877 after every southern state had been returned to white Democratic control. But local conservatives, no doubt encouraged by Democratic successes elsewhere, were more willing to fight radical control than they had been during the early 1870s. Any Republican government was objectionable to them in principle, but simple opposition to government by "scalawags" and Negroes was not sufficient basis for a successful campaign. They needed issues, organization, and a way to deal with the black majority. All these ingredients came together by 1878.

Issues the Democrats could use came from the years of Republican control after 1870. Several measures requested by Governor Davis and passed by the radical controlled 12th Legislature upset conservatives for years to come. One act, for example, created a state militia composed of all able-bodied men between the ages of eighteen and forty-five; only volunteers, however

[14]Winkler (ed.), *Platforms of Political Parties in Texas* 173, 176; Marshall *Tri-Weekly Herald*, October 14 (quotation), November 23, 1876; Election Returns, Harrison County, 1876.

[15]Marshall *Tri-Weekly Herald*, November 11, 1876; C. Vann Woodward, *Reunion and Reaction: The Compromise of 1877 and the End of Reconstruction* (Boston, 1951).

were to be armed and drilled regularly. The governor was commander-in-chief of this militia and could call it into active service whenever in his opinion the law was being obstructed in any county by combinations of men too strong to be dealt with by constituted civil authorities. A second measure established a state police force of 258 men headed by a chief of police but also ultimately under control of the governor. The merits of these acts are open to debate. Davis and other Radical Republicans contended that the militia and state police measures were necessary to deal with the disorder and lawlessness rampant across Texas and to protect the civil rights of Freedmen. Democrats felt that the governor was being given dictatorial power in an effort to guarantee his control of the state.[16]

The militia and state police were not of major importance in Harrison County. Davis declared martial law four times during his administration but never in that community. The legislature, shortly after coming under Democratic control in 1873, repealed the State Police Act. Nevertheless, the acts became symbolic of "radical tyranny." The fact that Negroes participated in both armed forces made them that much more obnoxious to conservatives.[17]

Several other measures passed under Davis in 1870 were blatantly political. One gave the governor power to fill by appointment all vacant public offices in Texas. This act allowed Davis to make William Umbdenstock treasurer and W. H. Poland sheriff of Harrison County in October, 1870. Another law empowered the governor to select one newspaper in each judicial district to do public printing and publish all official notices. William Umbdenstock's Republican paper, the Marshall *Weekly,* became the official journal of the sixth judicial district in East Texas.[18]

[16]Passage of the militia bill and the police force bill is discussed in Moneyhon, *Republicanism in Reconstruction Texas*, 135-142. The laws as passed are in Gammel (comp.), *Laws of Texas*, VI, 185-186, 193-195.

[17]Connor, *Texas,* 222; Ramsdell, *Reconstruction in Texas,* 313.

[18]Ramsdell, *Reconstruction in Texas,* 298-299; Election Registers, 1870; Harrison County Commissioners Court Minutes, 1870-1871. "List of Newspapers Published in

Although law and order measures and acts designed to promote the Republican Party drew the most attention, state government during the early 1870s also concerned itself with education and railroads. Laws calling for the creation of public schools and permitting local government support for railroad construction were in reality more significant for Harrison County during the 1870s than, for example, the militia or state police acts. The community might become agitated over the governor's powers, but schools and railroads involved their local government directly and cost more too. ''Redemption'' depended heavily on issues arising from these areas.

The Constitution of 1869 mandated the creation of ''public free schools'' for all children aged six to eighteen in Texas. The system was to be directed by a Superintendent of Public Instruction and financed by a perpetual school fund consisting of all lands and monies previously set aside for education plus all revenues from future sales of public lands, one-quarter of the income from general taxation, and a $1 poll tax on males aged twenty-one to sixty. The 12th Legislatures passed an act pursuant to this constitutional provision on August 13, 1870. Each county was designated a school district with the county court serving as an ex-officio school board. The school fund established under the constitution was to be used primarily for teachers' salaries; school buildings could be paid for with the proceeds of a 1% property tax levied by the county school board. Private schools were not to receive school fund money if a public school existed anywhere in the district. There was compulsory attendance for all children aged six to eighteen at either a public school or a good private school. Nothing was said about racial arrangements either to permit or to outlaw segregation.[19]

Little came of this measure immediately. There is no indication in the commissioners court minutes that the government of Harrison County took any notice of it other than beginning to

Texas,'' in *The Texas Almanac for 1872* (Galveston, 1871), 210, shows a ''W. Umbomstein'' as publisher of the Marshall *Weekly.*

[19]Gammel (comp.), *Laws of Texas*, VI, 287-292; VII, 417-418.

take a scholastic census in the spring of 1871. We can only guess at the reasons for delay and inaction. Perhaps, although the justices were Republicans, they objected, as did many statewide, to the idea of integrated schools. Possibly they were slow to act because they knew that Governor Davis disagreed with and would try to alter the system because it left so much discretion to local authorities. Maybe they simply did not have time to do much before the law was altered.[20] In any case, Governor Davis would soon obtain the changes he desired.

The 12th Legislature assembled again in January, 1871, and on April 24 passed a new free public school law creating what one authority has called the "most imperial system of education known to any American state." The law conformed closely to the original recommendations made by Governor Davis the previous year. Funding and attendance requirements remained the same as in the original law, but the supervisory framework was totally centralized. A state Board of Education composed of the governor, superintendent of public instruction, and attorney general had overall direction and ultimate authority. The superintendent of public instruction appointed supervisors for each state judicial district who in turn divided the counties in their district into school districts and appointed five directors for each. These local directors, answerable ultimately to the state Board of Education, were to be the immediate supervisors in their district. They were empowered to levy a 1% property tax for building and maintaining schools in their localities. Interestingly, this radical law apparently allowed segregation. The state Board of Education, it said, can make no rule "that will prevent the directors of the school districts from making any separation of the students that the peace and success of the school and the good of the whole may require."[21]

[20] Harrison County Commissioners Court Minutes, 1870-1871; Moneyhon, *Republicanism in Reconstruction Texas*, 136-138, 144; Ramsdell, *Reconstruction in Texas*, 299-300.

[21] Eby, *Development of Education in Texas*, 159 (first quotation); Gammel (comp.), *Laws of Texas*, VI, 959, 960-961 (second quotation), 962.

The public school law of 1871 went into effect in Harrison County early that fall. At least twelve teachers opened schools during October. William Massey and Caroline Poe, two of those employed, were familiar faces in the community from their days with the Freedmen's Bureau schools. Walter Ripetoe, the future state senator, also began teaching on October 1. Massey, Poe, and Ripetoe were black, and so, probably, were most of the others. Their pay varied according to the class of certificate held and the number of days taught, but most earned fifty to seventy-five dollars per month. There are no records concerning attendance at the new schools, but given the number of teachers employed, interest among parents and children must have been strong.[22]

William S. Speer, an enthusiastic newcomer, became "principal" of Harrison County's fledgling school system in December, 1871, and expanded it rapidly. "My ambition," he informed the state superintendent of public instruction, "is to excell all others in organizing schools." One glowing report followed another during the first six months of 1872. In mid-January, he reported twenty-nine schools employing thirty-five teachers. Two months later, he wrote (as briefed by a clerk in the superintendent's office), "Sum results, teachers enthusiastic, people confident, Marshall sulky, county friendly, principal strong, April arrangements splendid. . . ." The superintendent's Register of Disbursements supports Speer's reports by listing thirty-five Harrison County teachers receiving payments during the spring of 1872. Speer sought re-appointment but for some reason was unsuccessful and moved to Waco. The community's schools, however, continued to operate into 1873 at the level reached under his direction. At least thirty-one teachers were employed until the end of May that year. The radicals' school system may have

[22]This information on public school activity in Harrison County during 1871 is drawn from Register of Disbursements, Office of the Superintendent of Public Instruction, 1871-1874, Archives Division, Texas State Library, Austin. This volume contains the names of teachers, their periods of service, and amounts paid to them.

been overly centralized, but it was the closest thing to free public instruction that the community had ever had.[23]

The school system established in 1871 quickly pulled on the purse strings of Harrison County propertyholders. The scholastic census cost $4 per day for each justice of the peace doing the enumeration. More importantly, local ad valorem taxes began to reflect the costs of free schools. The Republican controlled county court in May, 1871 ordered the collection of two special school taxes: one-quarter of 1% (25¢ on the $100) for buildings and education and one-eighth of 1% (12.5¢ on the $100) for "school purposes." There was also a special $1 poll tax for school purposes levied on all males aged twenty-one to sixty. School taxes contributed heavily to rising discontent across the state which climaxed in a Taxpayers' Convention held at Austin in late September, 1871. Harrison County was not represented importantly in this meeting, but almost certainly a majority of the community's white population agreed with the angry protest it adopted concerning taxation under the public school law of 1871. Nevertheless, in 1872 school taxes in Harrison County rose to the full 1% allowable under the law. Taxes to support public education were the largest single item in assessments on property holders in the community that year. A taxpayer with $5,500 in property, for example, paid $29.88 in state taxes ($27.50 ad valorem, $1.38 frontier bonds tax, and $1 poll), $28.50 in county taxes ($13.75 ad valorem, $13.75 for roads and bridges, and $1 poll), and at least $55.00 for schools.[24]

The Democratic 13th Legislature elected in 1872 wasted little time in beginning to dismantle the radicals' centralized pub-

[23] William S. Speer to State Superintendent of Public Instruction, February 14 (first quotation), January 18, March 22 (second quotation), 1872, in Letters Received, State Superintendent of Public Instruction, 1871-1873, Archives Division, Texas State Library, Austin; Register of Disbursements, Superintendent of Public Instruction, 1871-1873.

[24] Harrison County Commissioners Court Minutes, 1871; Harrison County Tax Rolls, 1872. Apparently the tax for "buildings and education" was levied under the public school law of 1871 and the tax for school purposes under a general tax law passed in April of that year. See Winkler (ed.), *Platforms of Political Parties in Texas*, 133. (The Taxpayers Convention of 1871 is dealt with on pages 128-140 of Winkler's work.)

lic education system. An act of April 30, 1873, passed over Governor Davis's veto in May, returned control of schools largely to the local level. Each county was to elect a five-man school board that was in turn to divide the county into school districts and see to the election of a board of trustees in each. These local officials defined the course of study, hired teachers, and exercised general supervisory authority. The permanent school fund remained intact, but the state (state treasurer) simply distributed it to the counties (county treasurer) according to their populations of school-aged children. County boards of directors were allowed to levy ad valorem property taxes in their districts if necessary, but for 1873, the law specified a tax of 25¢ per $100 for building and repairing school houses.[25] This was probably still too high to suit every taxpayer, but it was much less of a burden than the $1 per hundred rate of 1872.

Harrison County's Republican officeholders tried to do what they could with this new decentralized system, but as had been the case throughout Reconstruction, changes came so rapidly that a public school system could not get off the ground. The Constitution of 1876 wrecked the whole radical public education system, even as it stood after modification by the 1873 law. The article on education abolished the office of state superintendent of instruction, reduced the free school age to the years from eight to fourteen, eliminated compulsory attendance, and made local taxation for school purposes impossible. At least the school fund was continued, and the legislature was directed to create a free public school system.[26]

The 15th Legislature rewrote the school law in 1876 according to the new constitution, and public education became as decentralized as it had previously been centralized. Parents and guardians in any locality could, on a voluntary basis, form a "school community" and make a list of the children to be instructed. The county judge was then to approve this action, appoint three trustees, and direct the county treasurer to apportion

[25] Gammel (comp.), *Laws of Texas*, VI, 536-547.

[26] Eby, *Development of Education in Texas*, 170-171.

school fund money to the "school community" according to the number of pupils. The entire process had to be repeated each year, and "school community" lines could shift that often. This system amounted to a conservative's dream of local parental control. The only significant state restriction was segregation. "School communities" had to be separated according to race or there would be no money from the school fund.[27]

The public school system established in 1876 was clearly too fragmented to be effective. A newspaper story in 1880 claimed that there were 116 "school communities" in Harrison County, 108 black and 8 white.[28] If this was accurate, or if there were only half that number of "communities," it seems certain that the county was broken up into too many small, inefficient schools wasting school fund money. White and black children alike were little closer to effective free public education than they had been in 1865.

In the meantime, the citizens of Marshall had an opportunity to take advantage of being an urban area and build a better school system than was possible in rural areas. The legislature passed a law in 1875 allowing incorporated towns to take control of schools within their limits and, with voter approval, to levy local taxes for support of those schools. Marshall opened its system in February, 1877 with a school for whites and one for blacks. These schools received state funds, but they were not entirely free; students paid small tuition fees too. These schools did not grow rapidly, enrolling only 367 pupils during the spring of 1877. Marshall had 1,323 children aged six to eighteen at the time. This lack of growth was explained partly by the presence of private schools such as Marshall University, the Marshall Masonic Female Institute, and Wiley College, a black school opened in 1873 by the Freedmen's Aid Society of the Methodist Episcopal Church. But these schools, all of which were essentially elementary and secondary in their courses of instruction, had only 196 students at the time so they were hardly taking up

[27] Ibid., 171-172; Gammel (comp.), *Laws of Texas*, VIII, 205 (quotation), 1035-1046.
[28] Marshall *Tri-Weekly Herald*, September 28, 1880.

all the available students. Perhaps then, a more important reason for small enrollment was the tuition charges. There was a move in August, 1877 to authorize a local property tax of 25¢ on the $100 to support the city school system, but the vote was 129 to 114 against the levy. And a majority of the registered voters did not even participate.[29] Marshall, like the county as a whole, continued without an effective free school system.

In summary, public education remained an issue from 1870 to 1878. Thanks to laws passed by the Democrats once they controlled the state government, Harrison County's white conservatives were less upset by the question than they could have been. School taxes did not really bother them after the early 1870s. Nevertheless, they remembered Davis's school laws as examples of radical tyranny and taxation.

Local government made railroads more expensive than public schools during the later years of radical government in Harrison County. The Constitution of 1869 prohibited land grants to railroad corporations, and Governor Davis generally opposed direct state subsidies in any form. He signed only one subsidy bill, an act granting state bonds to the International Railway company which was to build from the Red River on the Arkansas border to Laredo. Twice the governor vetoed bills offering similar state bond subsidies to the Southern Pacific Railroad, the line begun in Harrison County during the 1850s and put into operation before secession. The second act in 1871 passed over Davis's veto, but no bonds were ever issued.[30] Resourceful railroad promoters were not deterred, however, by momentary difficulties in obtaining direct state aid. They looked elsewhere, and the 12th Legislature helped with their search.

On April 12, 1871, a new law permitted counties to enter the business of subsidizing railroad construction. Upon the re-

[29]Eby, *Development of Education in Texas*, 207, 275-276; Marshal *Tri-Weekly Herald*, February 24, April 3, July 24, August 28, 1877; Lloyd K. Thompson, "The Origins and Development of Black Religious Colleges in East Texas" (Ph.D. Dissertation, North Texas State University, 1976), 20-58.

[30]Ramsdell, *Reconstruction in Texas*, 300-301; Moneyhon, *Republicanism in Reconstruction Texas*, 140-142, 149-150.

quest of fifty registered voters, a county court could order an election on the issuance of local bonds to railroad companies. If approved, the bonds were to be issued by the county court once it had levied a tax bringing in revenue enough to pay the annual interest costs and to retire 2% of the principal amount each year.[31] To communities eager for the progress brought by railroads, this measure meant only opportunity. But if enthusiasm for development overcame caution and good judgment, it could mean overwhelming tax burdens in the future. The radical government of Harrison County fell into this trap.

Harrison County, of course, already had a railroad. The Southern Pacific had survived the Civil War, and in spite of constant financial turmoil, had managed by 1872 to build from the Louisiana line to Longview in Gregg County with a branch extending from Jonesville east of Marshall to Swanson's Landing on Caddo Lake. The company had five locomotives and sixty-three cars of various types. Its main shops were located at Hallsville about thirteen miles west of Marshall.[32] The Southern Pacific, limited as it was, put Harrison County far ahead of most Texas communities in railroad construction, but promoters and many citizens too dreamed of much more. They saw Marshall as a major eastern terminal on the first southern transcontinental railroad line. How much would the community pay to make this dream a reality?

The old Southern Pacific Railroad, chartered in Texas, was not destined to be the vehicle for building across Texas toward California. Instead, the Texas Pacific Railway Company chartered by the United States Congress on March 3, 1871 became the focus of Harrison County's hopes for railroad promotion during the 1870s. In 1872, Texas authorized the Texas Pacific to acquire the rights and franchise of the Southern Pacific, a move that was accomplished on March 21. Then on May

[31] Gammel (comp.), *Laws of Texas*, VI, 931-934.

[32] Muir, "Thirty-Second Parallel Pacific Railroad," 176-195. There is some question as to whether or not the branch from Jonesville to Swanson's Landing, taken up during the Civil War, was ever relaid. Muir says it was, but Max S. Lale, a local authority on Harrison County, has informed the author that it was not.

2, 1872, Congress changed the company's name to the Texas and Pacific Railway Company and directed that it build from Marshall through El Paso to San Diego, California. The railroad was to receive land grants in New Mexico, Arizona, and California, and it was negotiating for similar support in Texas. It had to have one hundred miles of track consecutive from Marshall operative within two years. Thomas A. Scott, a well-known promoter from Pennsylvania, was president, and General Grenville M. Dodge, formerly chief engineer on the Union Pacific, assumed that position on this new transcontinental venture.[33] Harrison County was no longer involved in building a planters' railroad to move cotton; the stakes were much larger.

General Dodge arrived in Marshall during 1872 planning to begin construction within a year. As might be expected, the railroad sought to raise capital from every source possible; a search that soon led to the government of Harrison County. In April, 1872, the commissioners court received a petition signed by nearly 150 citizens of Harrison County requesting an election to approve the issue of $300,000 in bonds to the Texas and Pacific Railroad. In the future, many would blame this bond issue and the resulting taxes on the radicals so it is of importance to note that men of all political views signed the petition. There were white radicals such as J. B. Williamson and William B. Umbdenstock, blacks including Shack Roberts and Edmund Brown, and white conservatives such as former County Judge George Lane and ex-Governor Edward Clark. Party lines did not unite the petitioners; instead it seems that they shared a common interest as townsmen involved in commerce and the professions. Living in Marshall, they worked as merchants (J. H. Van Hook, Isaac Schwartz, George B. Adkins, and others), doctors (William H. Dial, E. P. M. Johnson, Benjamin F. Eads, and others), and lawyers (George Lane, F. B. Sexton, William Stedman,

[33]Reed, *History of Texas Railroads*, 360-361; Webb, Carroll, and Branda (eds.), *Handbook of Texas*, II, 752-753; Stanley P. Hirschon, *Grenville M. Dodge: Soldier, Politician, Railroad Pioneer* (Bloomington, Ind., 1967), 183-185. An amendment to the state constitution was necessary to allow land grants to railroads in Texas, but that came in 1873.

and others). The names of large planters such as William T. Scott, always present in the antebellum promotions, were notably absent from this petition. Apparently then, the town of Marshall, not the radicals as such, initiated the process of community overcommitment to promote railroad building.[34]

The commissioners court ordered a special registration of voters and set the bond-issue election for June 3-5, 1872. The county proposed to give the Texas and Pacific $300,000 in thirty-year bonds bearing 7% interest payable in gold; 2% of the principal amount would be paid off annually. The railroad in return would make Marshall the major eastern terminal on its transcontinental route, establish its Texas offices in the town, and move its main shops there. Technically, the Texas and Pacific was to uphold its part of the bargain first and then receive the bonds.[35]

The bond issue won approval by a vote of 1,866 to 25 in June, 1872. Nearly two years later, on April 10, 1874, representatives of the railroad led by attorney F. B. Sexton appeared before the commissioners court and asked for the bonds. A group of citizens led by former County Judge N. V. Board challenged this request on a variety of grounds. They charged that the railroad had pressured citizens into signing the petition while misrepresenting what it would do for Marshall. Moreover, Board said, the Texas and Pacific forced the special registration, paid the fees for many who registered, and used money to influence the vote. Only those who registered especially for the bond election could vote; other regular voters were disfranchised. And finally, the protestors said, the railroad had demanded and received sixty acres in Marshall worth $30,000; a part of the deal kept secret before the election. The commissioners court heard all of Board's evidence and then ruled that the Texas and Pacific had met the requirements for the bond issue. It was ordered that the $300,000 in bonds be registered with the state comp-

[34]Harrison County Commissioners Court Minutes, 1872; Hirschon, *Dodge*, 184-185.

[35]Harrison County Commissioners Court Minutes, 1872.

troller and turned over to the railroad. The court also levied a special tax of 75¢ on every $100 in assessed property, the largest special tax since the public school assessment of 1872, to pay the interest and 2% of the principal annually.[36]

N. V. Board and a large group of citizens quickly brought suit in the district court seeking a permanent injunction against issuance of the bonds. Their petition, filed on April 20, 1874, recited all the charges of unfair pressure and corruption concerning the election and warned that the Texas and Pacific would immediately negotiate the bonds "into the hands of innocent holders" and thus the county would "sustain a great and irreparable debt." District Judge Matthew D. Ector agreed to issue an injunction as soon as the petitioners filed a bond of $100,000 required by law in such cases. The bond was not given so no injunction was issued. In any case, it appears that the county court had issued the bonds before Board's petition was heard. The Texas and Pacific received its $300,000 in local support, and Harrison County had a railroad debt equal to more than 10% of the value of all property in the community that year. Interest charges would be $21,000 the first year, and $6,000 in bonds had to be retired each year too.[37]

Board and his group of objecting taxpayers did not drop legal action against the commissioners court and railroad when they failed to get an injunction in 1874. Instead, they pursued the matter to the Texas Supreme Court in 1876 asking for an annulment of the bond issue and an injunction against collection of the railroad tax. Arguments on both sides were lengthy and complex, but essentially Hec McKay and W. S. Coleman, lawyers for the taxpayers, claimed that the election and issuance of the bonds had been fraudulent while F. B. Sexton and

[36]Ibid. These minutes did not record all the citizens' complaints; some had to be determined from papers filed in the legal actions that followed (see Note 37 below). The Marshall *News-Messenger*, August 12, 1964, quoted an unnamed source from the 1880s claiming that the sixty acres actually cost $67,500.

[37]*N. V. Board et al.* v. *Texas and Pacific Railway Co. and County Court of Harrison County* (quotations), Civil Case Papers, 1874, District Clerk's Office, Harrison County Courthouse, Marshall; Harrison County Commissioners Court Minutes, 1874; Harrison County Tax Rolls, 1874.

William Stedman replied for the railroad that the county court had acted within its powers and no lawful appeals were possible. Associate Justice George F. Moore ruled against Board's appeal. Third parties, those who had bought the bonds from the Texas and Pacific, were affected by the suit, he said, and yet they were not involved in the case. Even if these bondholders knew that fraud was involved in obtaining the bonds, their interests could not be adversely affected by a case to which they were not parties. An order against collection of the railroad tax would obviously impair the rights of bondholders.[38] The bond issue stood, and Harrison County would have to pay for it.

The *Tri-Weekly Herald* of January 6, 1877, carried a notice from county tax collector S. H. Russell informing propertyholders that the railroad subsidy tax (75¢ on the $100) for 1874, 1875, and 1876 would now be collected. Collection had been delayed due to the recently decided supreme court case. Please come forward and pay, Russell urged, and "save me the annoying and disagreeable duty of enforcing collection by levy and sale." A group of citizens attempted in vain during the early months of 1877 to reach a compromise with the railroad and thereby with the bondholders.[39] That failing, the railroad subsidy tax stood as the major item on each propertyholder's bill in 1877 and 1878 as well as for the three years when it had gone uncollected. There is no way to determine the proportion of citizens who actually paid this tax for any year. But in a sense this does not matter. The debt was there, and although conservative Democrats wanted the railroad as much as anyone else, it provided an excellent basis for attacking the Republicans.

Finally, in addition to the costs of schools and the railroad, Harrison County "redeemers" made an issue of general extravagance on the part of radicals and the indebtedness that resulted. A proper evaluation of these charges is extremely difficult. Even the commissioners court minutes, the best source available, do not consistently provide all the information necessary on county

[38] *T. [sic] V. Board Et Al.* v. *Texas and Pacific R. W. Co. and Others*, 46 *Texas* 316.
[39] Marshall *Tri-Weekly Herald*, January 6 (quotation), February 15, April 5, 1877.

finances. Available evidence, however, suggests that local government did indeed cost more during the years from 1870 to 1878. Whether the extra cost was justified or not is yet another matter.

Harrison County's problems with indebtedness may have begun during Congressional Reconstruction. On October 7, 1867, county treasurer John C. Harris, in his last report before he was removed by General Reynolds, showed a positive balance of $536.98. Through the next two years, the commissioners court under N. V. Board, also a military appointee, did little more than routine business. Road maintenance took more time than any other matter, and it was handled in the old manner by appointing those living along each section of a road to take care of it. No treasurer's reports were recorded in 1868 or 1869. Nevertheless, prior to 1870, the county government did little and taxed less than 50¢ on the $100 property evaluation and, from every indication in the commissioners court minutes, had few debts.[40]

The newly elected Republican officials who took office in May, 1870, soon asked Jacob Foster, the county treasurer since Harris's removal in 1867, for an accounting. Foster's books apparently contained unexpectedly bad news because in September the commissioners court levied a special tax of 50¢ on the $100 to "pay debts." A similar tax was levied in 1871, although the rate dropped to 25¢ on the $100. There is good evidence then, that for some reason, most likely difficulty in collecting taxes, county government was operating at a deficit when the radicals took over. Undismayed, however, the new officials stepped up government activity and spending with most of the pay warrants approved by the justices going to themselves and their friends. For example, they received $4 each per day for taking the school census in 1871 and were also paid for assessing a special tax on dogs levied in 1870. At 12½¢ per dog, H. D. Smith earned $157.25 by early 1871; J. P. Lynch, $122; and Z. T. Perry, $107.

[40]Harrison County Commissioners Court Minutes, 1867-1870; Harrison County Tax Rolls, 1867-1870.

The new position of county road commissioner at $500 per year went to William Umbdenstock in September, 1870, almost simultaneously with his appointment to replace Foster as county treasurer. Bridge construction in the county, authorized by an act of the state legislature in 1870 which permitted special taxes for this purpose, brought sizable contracts to Republicans. In December, 1871, for example, J. B. Stroud was paid $352 for building a bridge, and W. C. Pierce (soon to become county clerk) received $275 for another. The next month, A. S. Justus, a member of the court, received $412.50 for constructing a bridge over Eight Mile Creek on the Jefferson Road. J. P. Lynch earned $300 keeping the county poor house for 150 days in 1872. L. J. Gallant, one of the justices elected in 1873, was paid $273.25 in April, 1874 for taking lunatics to the state asylum in Austin. On the same date, state representative Mitchell Kendall earned $165.50 for working on irons for the sheriff. Throughout the years all the justices regularly received sizable amounts from fees in dismissed cases.[41]

County treasurer Umbdenstock regularly gave accountings to the commissioners court from early 1871 into 1874. The minutes reported no specific balances, but on several occasions, it was noted that the treasurer had paid out more than he had received. Just how far expenditures had exceeded income became clear in July, 1874, when the commissioners court invited all claimants against the county to register their claims. By September 3, when the registration process ended, Harrison County had $41,552.35 in approved debts. The largest claimants were Republican officials including Justices A. S. Justus and J. P. Lynch, Sheriff S. H. Russell, and County Clerk W. C. Pierce. There were many small debts, primarily jury tickets, but it appears that in some cases Republicans had bought up these county obligations too. W. H. Poland, a former Davis appointee as

[41] Harrison County Commissioners Court Minutes, 1870-1874 (quotation). The road commissioner position given to Umbdenstock was newly authorized by the state legislature. Gammel (comp.), *Laws of Texas*, VI, 218-219.

sheriff, for example, registered a huge number of jury tickets originally issued to others.[42]

In spite of owing more than $40,000 and having just recently committed the county to a $300,000 subsidy for the Texas and Pacific Railroad, the justices in January, 1875, decided that the community had to have a new jail. They signed a contract with P.J. Pauley and Brother of St. Louis to handle the construction for $14,800. The jail may well have been necessary and the price not exorbitant; nevertheless, it represented a major addition to the costs of Republican government.[43]

The county's debt, as it mounted during the early 1870s, took a variety of forms. The railroad subsidy consisted of interest-bearing bonds. Many obligations due individuals in the local community were in the form of scrip or temporary paper money issued by the county. Scrip was a negotiable promise to pay which local government eventually had to buy and cancel. The value of scrip reflected the financial condition and credit-rating of the government issuing it. And, as might be expected, Harrison County scrip depreciated; some unfriendly conservatives claimed that its value fell as low as 14¢ on the dollar by the mid-1870s.[44] The radicals appeared on the verge of spending the community into financial ruin.

County government expenditures declined markedly after early 1875. Debts, public criticism, and conservative control of state government probably contributed to a general tightening of the purse strings. By mid-1876, for example, the state legislature had directed that county courts return to the old method of appointing local citizens to oversee sections of road in their neighborhood. There were no more bridge-building contracts.

[42] Harrison County Commissioners Court Minutes, 1871-1874.

[43] Ibid., 1875.

[44] The handling of scrip or "script" in county finances is explained in Marshall *Tri-Weekly Herald*, February 17, 1880. The claim that Harrison County scrip fell to 14¢ on the dollar is found in a letter from R. P. Littlejohn to Ernest Powell (a local historian) on February 7, 1936, Reconstruction File, Harrison County Historical Museum, Marshall. The Reconstruction File at the county museum contains miscellaneous letters, documents, and clippings related to that era of Harrison County history.

Maintaining jail prisoners appears to have been the largest expense approved by the court. It seems too that after 1875 county treasurer Umbdenstock had some success in reducing the debt. From August, 1876, through December, 1877, for example, he reported paying out $20,993.87 from a new indebtedness fund created in 1875. In addition to this fund for handling the registered debt, Umbdenstock maintained a general fund to meet other obligations and a special fund to pay for the new jail. The commissioners court issued a public report at the beginning of 1878 showing large amounts paid from all funds and a total debt of $49,130.26. Three months later, the quarterly report for January-March, 1878, showed a reduction of indebtedness to $37,647.17.[45] Thus by the late 1870s, the Republicans were making an apparently successful effort to get the county's finances under control. It was too late, however, to defuse the issue.

Were the expenditures of the early 1870s necessary, and if the money went for worthwhile purposes, were the charges exorbitant to the point that they smacked of corruption? No one could say for certain, then or now. Bridges, for example, probably improved travel conditions, but it could easily be argued that the gains did not justify the expense. Moreover, said some critics, the contracts approved pay so well that they amount to little more than the radicals allowing each other to steal from the public coffers. Rumors of waste and corruption circulated through the community regularly, but they did not surface as formal charges and no wrong-doing in office was ever proven. Developments in late 1877 provide an example. A local grand jury reported that county officials "are receiving quite a large amount of censure for the misappropriation of the public funds; whether guilty or not we are not prepared to say. . . ." The report recommended an investigation by experts. Judge Williamson indignantly denounced giving voice to "Madame Rumor" without any facts and challenged the grand jury to do an actual

[45] Harrison County Commissioners Court Minutes, 1875-1877; Gammel (comp.), *Laws of Texas*, VIII, 899-906; Marshall *Tri-Weekly Herald*, January 12, April 8, 1878.

investigation. County officials are serving the people well, he said, and financial management has improved to the point that scrip is appreciating in value. Even Robert Loughery, while not prepared to say that the radicals were innocent, criticized the jury for going off "half-cocked."[46]

As would be expected, taxation mounted with spending and debts during the 1870s and continued high even after efforts began to reduce expenditures and indebtedness. There were the new school taxes in 1871 and 1872, and the very threatening railroad subsidy levy beginning in 1874. From 1870 into 1876, the county assessed a roads-and-bridges tax, usually 12.5¢ on each $100 worth of property. The new jail necessitated a special tax in 1876 (16.7¢ per $100), 1877 (12.5¢), and 1878 (12.5¢). Taxes for the payment of debts, applied lightly in 1870 and 1871, became heavy, at least 25¢ on the $100 beginning in 1874 and continuing through 1878. There were, of course, annual taxes for general county purposes, commonly at the rate of 25¢ per $100, and poll taxes on males twenty-one or older. A hypothetical forty-year-old Harrison County male holding $1,000 in taxable real property would have owed $3.75 to the county in 1869, $16.00 in 1872, $15.00 in 1874, $15.32 in 1876, and $16.42 in 1878 (See Table 19). The increase during the years of Republican government amounted to more than 300%. Moreover, there were personal property taxes, special assessments such as the tax on dogs, and state taxes as well.[47]

These taxes were not all collected as levied. Attempts to collect the railroad-subsidy tax, for example, did not begin until 1877. Furthermore, a good many propertyholders simply did not pay their obligations to the county. In the spring of 1877 and again a year later, Sheriff S. H. Russell advertised hundreds of tracts of land that were to be sold for unpaid taxes. The lists

[46]Marshall *Tri-Weekly Herald*, December 6 (first quotation), 8, (second and third quotations), 1877, April 2, 1878.

[47]Harrison County Tax Rolls, 1869-1878. The tax rates in Table 19 were determined from the county tax rolls except in 1876 when, for some reason, local taxes were not recorded. The tax rates for 1876 were taken from the Harrison County Commissioners Court Minutes.

TABLE 19

Rates of Local Taxation per $100 Assessed Value in Harrison County, 1869-1878
(Based on Hypothetical Adult Male Taxpayer with $1,000 in Real Property)

1869—.00075 (½ of state tax rate) + .0025 special county tax + .50 poll tax = .75 + 2.50 + .50 = $3.75.

1872—.0025 (½ of state tax rate) + .0025 roads and bridges tax + .01 school tax + 1.00 poll tax = 2.50 + 2.50 + 10.00 + 1.00 = $16.00

1874—.0025 (½ of state tax rate) + .011 special county tax + .0005 roads and bridges tax + 1.00 poll tax = 2.50 + 11.00 + .50 + 1.00 = $15.00.

1876—.0025 (½ of state tax rate) + .0025 county debt tax + .0075 railroad subsidy tax + .0167 jail tax + .0001 lunatic tax + .00005 roads and bridges tax + 1.00 poll tax = 2.50 + 2.50 + 7.50 + 1.67 + .10 + .05 + 1.00 = $16.42.

1878—.0025 (½ of state tax rate) + .0025 county debt tax + .0075 railroad subsidy tax + .00125 jail tax + .00167 school tax + 1.00 poll tax = 2.50 + 2.50 + 7.50 + 1.25 + 1.67 + 1.00 = $16.42.

included properties belonging to many prominent members of the community. A check of the tax rolls for the years following Russell's "tax sales" shows virtually every one of these individuals still owning the land in question.[48] Apparently, once forced sales were threatened, propertyholders paid the back taxes. It is likely, however, that over the years before the radicals took strong action, there was widespread nonpayment of local taxes.

In summary, an examination of financial policy from 1870 to 1878 in Harrison County supports several generalizations. First, although the local government was not debt-free when the radicals took over, expenditures and indebtedness increased sharply after 1870. Second, most of the county's new business went to Republican officeholders and their allies. Third, al-

[48] Marshall *Tri-Weekly Herald*, April 14, 1877, March 28, April 11, 1878; Harrison County Tax Rolls, 1878-1879.

though radical officials drew extensive direct financial benefits from public office, the charges of waste and corruption were unproven then and cannot be proven today. Fourth, successful efforts to cut spending and reduce the debt began in 1875-1876, several years before "redemption." Finally, property taxes, whether collected or not, rose to unprecedented levels.

Harrison County's conservative Democrats had never really needed issues as a basis for opposition to Republican control of the community. Any government resulting from federal intervention, based on black votes, and run by men other than traditional leaders was unacceptable from the outset. By 1878, however, the conservatives had issues aplenty from radical spending, debts, and taxes. The charges against Republican government were not necessarily just or fair, but political contests are not given to objectivity or balance. It was true that the radicals had sharply increased the costs of local government and benefitted personally in the process. To white Democrats, this was simply the clinching evidence that Harrison County had to be "redeemed."

13

"Redemption": 1878–1880

THE 15TH LEGISLATURE, the first to meet under the "redeemer" Constitution of 1876, scheduled a general election for Tuesday, November 5, 1878.[1] Harrison County Democrats planned an all-out effort to win control of their local government at that time. They had an excellent issue, county finances, but, as mentioned before, they needed to organize and to find a way to deal with the community's black majority. The organization was developed in the early fall of 1878 during the two months or so prior to the election. Republicans then found

[1]Gammel (comp.), *Laws of Texas*, VIII, 1005-1006.

themselves facing a serious challenge to their control of local government for the first time since 1870.

In mid-September, 1878, a handbill circulated in Marshall calling a public meeting at the courthouse "to nominate a Citizens' ticket of good and true men of both colors as candidates for the various county offices." It was signed by James F. Taylor, a former Whig and Constitutional Union Party leader; Amory R. Starr, son of James Harper Starr, famed leader of the Republic of Texas; E. J. Fry and Edmund Key, private bankers in Marshall; John D. Rudd, Democratic Party county chairman; Herman Kretz, an official of the Texas and Pacific Railway; and many others. "We recognize the signers as among our best citizens," commented Loughery's *Tri-Weekly Herald*. This handbill was the first step in forming the Citizens Party, as it happened, the vehicle not only for "redeeming" Harrison County in 1878 but also for maintaining white conservative control of the community until 1952 when it was declared unconstitutional by a federal circuit court.[2]

The first call for nominating a citizens ticket apparently met with the usual apathy among whites. Even Loughery, who had always urged conservatives to vote, was not optimistic about its chances. Republicans held their county convention on September 25 and nominated a slate of candidates for all county offices except the four county commissioner positions. County Judge J. B. Williamson headed the ticket which included two Negroes, John Hudson and S. H. Smothers, running respectively for the state house of representatives and county surveyor. At the same time, conservatives, attempting to get the Citizens Party off the ground and well aware of their probable weakness at the polls, sought an agreement with the Republicans that would assure control of the commissioners court by compromise candidates. Representatives of both sides went so far as to suggest nominees for three of the county's four commissioner pre-

[2]Marshall *Tri-Weekly Herald*, September 17, 1878 (quotations). The role of the Citizens Party in maintaining white control after 1880 is outlined in Rice, *The Negro in Texas*, 114-115, and the Marshall *News-Messenger*, April 6, 1952. It became the vehicle for a white primary. See *Perry et al.* v. *Cyphers et al.*, 186 *Federal Reporter*, 2nd Series, 608.

cincts, but nothing came of this attempt at compromise. The radicals soon nominated their own candidates. Loughery blamed the Republicans for rejecting what he considered a reasonable request that for two years the commissioners be men acceptable to the conservatives.[3] More than likely he was correct. After all, political parties enjoying a more than two to one majority over their opponents rarely feel a pressing need to make concessions.

The Citizens Party then held a nominating meeting on October 12, 1878. Former governor Edward Clark lent his prestige as presiding officer, and William T. Scott, the county's wealthiest antebellum planter and political leader, came out of "retirement" to participate. The Citizens Party ticket was led by Scott, George Lane, Solomon R. Perry, and J. P. Alford. Scott, who had been elected three times to the state senate during the 1850s, ran for the lower house against John Hudson. Lane, three-term county judge before and during the Civil War, sought to return to that office. Perry was certainly familiar with the office he ran for, having been elected sheriff first in 1850. Alford had won the county clerk's office in 1866 and then been removed by General Reynolds. Of the Party's candidates for county commissioner, John D. Rudd and Amory R. Starr were well-known conservatives. The other two, John E. Hooper, a fifty-eight-year-old doctor/farmer from Alabama, and R. T. Hailey, had participated in the county Democratic convention on June 15, 1878. The Citizens Party made no nominations for county attorney, district clerk, tax collector, or county surveyor; an indication that radical nominees for those offices were acceptable. This move left one of the two Negro candidates, S. H. Smothers, unopposed.[4]

Thus, by mid-October, 1878, Harrison County's "redeemers" were organized and in the field. Presenting themselves as a

[3]Marshall *Tri-Weekly Herald*, September 17, 21, 26, 1878. The negotiations between a committee from the Citizens Party headed by Amory R. Starr and the Republicans represented by William Umbdenstock and several others are detailed in two reports by Starr to the "Citizens Club of Harrison County," September, 1878. Henry Raguet Family Papers, Archives, Barker Texas History Center, University of Texas, Austin. Loughery's views are in Marshall *Tri-Weekly Herald*, October 10, 12, 1878.

[4]Marshall *Tri-Weekly Herald*, October 15, 1878; Marshall *Messenger*, October 18, 1878.

non-partisan citizens group seeking to restore good government to a financially ruined community, they avoided all use of major party labels. They were the Citizens Club rather than the Democrats and their opponents were radicals, not Republicans. Anyone could see, however, that the new party represented an attempt by traditional white leaders to resume control of the county. And somehow the ''redeemer'' minority had to persuade the black majority that a change of local government leadership was in their best interests.

The conservatives did not have to originate their appeal to blacks during the campaign. Instead, they used and expanded several arguments common in the community before the fall of 1878. First, there was the promise that southern whites would protect the rights of Negroes just as effectively as Republican ''carpetbaggers'' and ''scalawags.'' There was no reason for black prejudice against whites, the argument went. As the Marshall *Messenger,* the town's second newspaper, put it in July, 1877: ''The white people of the South are pledged to accord them [Negroes] the political rights conferred upon them and will stand by these pledges faithfully.'' A year later the *Messenger* urged a policy of guaranteeing black rights as Wade Hampton had in ''redeeming'' South Carolina. ''Make the same pledge to the Negroes of this county that Hampton did to those of that state, and it will inspire confidence in the Negroes, and they will trust their old masters. . . .'' Resolutions adopted by the nominating meeting of the Citizens Party sounded this theme. All classes must cooperate in government, they said. Blacks have a right to vote, and they must exercise that right with whites for good government.[5]

A second line of argument emphasized how radical government threatened the financial well-being of blacks as well as whites. The county's debts must be paid, said the conservatives, and Negroes will be taxed as heavily as anyone else for that purpose. The Citizens Party platform adopted on October 12 made

[5]Marshall *Messenger*, July 21, 1877 (first quotation), August 23 (second quotation), October 18, 1878.

this same point in several ways. "Bad" government injures all citizens; blacks and whites must unite to save themselves.[6]

The conservatives insisted too that Negroes had been taken advantage of by local white radicals. A few "hacks" run the party from year to year, they said, enjoying the support of black voters while taking virtually all of the offices and income for themselves. Jasper Black, a Negro, published a letter in the *Tri-Weekly Herald* of October 17 saying that Harrison County blacks had made fools of themselves politically. We elected C. E. Coleman to the constitutional convention (1868-1869), Black said, and he took the position and the pay and went home to the North. In my precinct, the letter continued, we elected M. T. Hoskins justice of the peace. He took all the fines and fees possible and left. It is time, Black said, to quit blindly voting Republican.[7]

While attacking local radicals, the conservatives went to great lengths to assure blacks that the Citizens Party did not oppose the Republican Party as such. This is purely a county affair, they said; we have no quarrel with your support for Republicans at the state and national levels. In fact, the argument continued, many white Republicans in the community support the Citizens Party. The *Herald* and *Messenger* both hammered at this last point in virtually every issue. The *Messenger* of October 18 provides a good example.

> There are many prominent gentlemen, connected with the railroad, who are known and respected as honorable Republicans, who have made homes among us, and are identified with the interests of the county, who recognize the fact that this condition of things has been the result of bad government by their own party. These gentlemen, seeing the absolute necessity of a change of affairs, have said to the citizens in their meetings; if you will lay aside all politics and partyism in county elections, and ask the colored people to unite

[6]Ibid., October 18, 1878; Marshall *Tri-Weekly Herald*, September 26, October 15, 1878.

[7]Marshall *Tri-Weekly Herald*, September 26 (quotation), October 17, 1878.

> with you in this work, then we will drop all party issues and join with you.[8]

Finally, in addition to specific promises and arguments involving protection of political rights, financial interests in good government, and nonpartisanship, conservative whites made a general plea for racial harmony. This appeal underlay every part of the Citizens Party's message to black voters, but no one made it more clearly than Robert Loughery in the *Herald* of October 29. Debt and imminent bankruptcy face the county, he wrote,

> But there is another question more important than this to the colored man. It is peace and permanent reconciliation. That the two races should work together as friends instead of enemies. That there should be a cordial and kind understanding between the two races that each will be willing to assist the other.
>
> . . . a house divided against itself cannot stand. . . .[9]

The sincerity of white appeals to black voters is difficult to discover. Certainly men such as Loughery had supported slavery, and they did not believe in Negro equality. For the moment, however, given existing circumstances, they probably convinced themselves that Negroes who would help restore "good" government deserved fair treatment. In any case, they made every effort to take their message to the black majority. Both newspapers, as noted, carried the Citizens Party "line," and leaders campaigned across the county too. James Tucker, a conservative at Elysian Fields, recorded in his diary on October 17 that George Lane, R. L. Hightower, and several blacks had made speeches with the idea of influencing "the nigger vote" in that area. "I have no faith in the movement," Tucker added.[10]

Tucker's reaction was probably common early in the campaign; Loughery of the *Herald* had felt much the same at first. But as the election drew nearer, Citizens Party leaders became more optimistic about their chances. Blacks were responding to

[8] Marshall *Messenger*, October 18, 1878.

[9] Marshall *Tri-Weekly Herald*, October 29, 1878.

[10] James Tucker Diary, October 17, 1878.

conservative appeals, they believed, and deserting the local Republicans in large numbers. There were rumors of radical threats against these Negroes, and somewhat ironically, the Citizens Party wound up as the apparent champion of Negro suffrage in Harrison County. Members of the party in Marshall pledged to sacrifice their time, property, and lives, if necessary, to vindicate "the rights of their colored friends and fellow members." Amory Starr headed a volunteer militia company of eighty men that sought and received arms from the state adjutant general. Some saw Starr's company as a threat to Negroes and radicals, but conservatives insisted that the armed men only meant to prevent unfair pressure by the Republicans. "There must be a free, fair and peaceable election," said the *Messenger.*[11]

Harrison County residents voted on November 5, 1878, at one of ten polling places set by the commissioners court back in April. Rural areas were divided into six precincts; the incorporated town of Marshall, which was wholly within precinct three, into four wards. Voters residing in precinct three but outside the corporate limits of Marshall were to vote at the office of Justice of the Peace William Roy. Some of the election judges were Republicans and some were conservatives as required by law. The presiding officer at precinct three outside the corporation was W. L. Sloan, a Democrat.[12] These election arrangements made in April proved critical in November.

The election passed off calmly enough on November 5. Two days later the *Herald* reported a radical victory in all important contests. Loughery expressed pleasure nevertheless that the usual Republican majority had been cut from approximately 1,500 to 137 votes. Averaging the majorities received by candidates in each precinct, he found the Democrats with an advantage of 476 votes in precincts one, four, five, and six. Republican candidates, however, had majorities totalling 613 votes from precincts two and three and the city of Marshall. Loughery thus

[11] Marshall *Tri-Weekly Herald*, October 26, 1878; Marshall *Messenger*, October 25 (first quotation), November 1 (second quotation), 1878.

[12] Harrison County Commissioners Court Minutes, April, 1878; Marshall *Tri-Weekly Herald*, April 4, 1878.

claimed that a change of sixty-nine votes, one more than half of the average Republican majority overall, would have elected the Citizens Party ticket. He blamed the defeat on a lack of effort in precincts two and six. The *Messenger* also found triumph in the defeat and insisted that the conservative showing would have a beneficial moral and political effect.[13]

It seems clear from the returns that a large number of Negroes voted the Citizens Party ticket in 1878. The number of votes cast was greater than the total in any previous county election during the decade. There were 3,850 votes cast in the county judge race, for example, as opposed to 3,672 in the same contest in 1876. Thus, blacks were not prevented from voting, and yet the election was much closer than any since black enfranchisement. Where Williamson had won by a margin of 2,664 votes to a total of 1,008 for several opponents in 1876, he defeated Lane by only 1,954 votes to 1,896 in 1878. Other races showed similar results. Even if allowances are made for an increase in the white electorate, it appears that more than 500 blacks voted for the Citizens Party.[14]

Why did blacks vote for "redemption"? Were they persuaded by the various appeals made by the Citizens Party, or were they intimidated or cheated? There is evidence that some Negroes were convinced by the conservative arguments. As noted above, blacks joined the Citizens Clubs and campaigned for its ticket. Many years later, Simpson Campbell, a Freedmen who had belonged to W. L. Sloan, recalled the election as follows:

> It was a democratic ticket and control by Southerners. They told us niggers if we'd vote that ticket we'd be rec'nized as white folks, but I didn't 'lieve a word of it. Old man Sloan told all his niggers that and they all voted that ticket but two —that was Charley Tang and Simp Campbell.[15]

[13] Marshall *Tri-Weekly Herald*, November 7, 1878; Marshall *Messenger*, November 8, 1878.

[14] Election Returns, Harrison County, 1876, 1878. There was, of course, the possibility that whites prevented a large number of Negroes from voting and then stuffed the ballot box to make up the difference. It appears, however, from evidence to be presented below that this was not the case.

[15] Rawick (ed.), *American Slave*, IV, Part 1, 192. It is interesting that, according to the statement of age in the narrative, Campbell was only eighteen in 1878.

Thus conservative arguments about common interests and promises of fair treatment were effective in some cases.

Evidence of intimidation, either physical or economic, is very limited. R. P. Littlejohn, one of the Citizens Party leaders, claimed years later that many Negroes were kept from the polls and also told of forcing a black election judge to resign his commission and putting a conservative white in his place.[16] Such stories probably had a basis in fact, but it is doubtful that intimidation kept large numbers of Republican voters from participating. The vote, as noted above, increased over previous totals, and as we will see, the radicals did not charge their opponents with the use of pressure tactics.

Fraud may have been more important than intimidation as a "redeemer" method of dealing with the black majority. There is a legend in Harrison County that white conservatives printed ballots of the same size and on the same color paper as the Republican ticket and then switched the ballots. Unsuspecting Negroes voted for Citizens Party candidates without knowing what they were doing. As in the case of most legends, supporting evidence is confusingly fragmentary, and the precise truth of the matter will never be known. Conservatives themselves told the most complete versions of the story later, probably to show how ignorant the Negroes were. But their accounts do not agree on the particulars. R. P. Littlejohn said that the radical tickets were printed in Jefferson on yellow paper and that Bart Jennings printed the Citizens Party tickets that were switched. He claimed that conservatives went among the Negroes on election day somehow convincing them to trade their ballots for the newly printed imitations. Chesley M. Adams, whose stepfather lived in Marshall during 1878, described radical ballots printed in Shreveport on red paper. "Mr. Adair" printed the Citizens Party copies in Adams's version, and whites simply stuffed ballot boxes with them instead of tricking Negroes.[17]

[16]R. P. Littlejohn to Ernest Powell, February 7, 1936, Reconstruction File.

[17]The ballot switching story is told, without documentation, in Sallie M. Lentz, "Highlights of Early Harrison County," *Southwestern Historical Quarterly*, LXI (October, 1957), 255, and is repeated on the basis of Lentz's statement and with reference to an issue of the *Tri-Weekly Herald* dated October 25, 1878, by Rice, *The Negro in Texas*, 116. (There was no *Tri-Weekly Herald* on October 25, and it is difficult to see

Contemporary evidence on the ballot-switching legend is even less helpful than the accounts given later. One letter to the *Herald* shortly after the election laughed at several radical black leaders for complaining about similarities in the color of the tickets voted. The Citizens Party ticket was voted freely, the writer said, by Negroes who were tired of Republican government. Finally, as we will see, there were several legal actions following the election, and although the matter of colored tickets came up, no one charged the conservatives with tricking Negroes into voting the wrong ballot. There probably is some basis for this color-of-the-ballot legend, but it cannot be said that this decided the election. Several other charges of fraud, although not necessarily proven, have better documentation. William Umbdenstock claimed that 500 voters in precinct one at Elysian Fields were denied an opportunity to cast their ballots because they were printed on the Republican Party's orange/red paper. This charge eventually, as we will see, became part of a federal district court case against the election judges. The defendants admitted delaying a number of voters for two hours due to the complaints of several white citizens about the colored ballots but said the tickets were accepted when no law against them could be produced. The federal jury found them innocent of interfering with the vote. Umbdenstock also charged the election judges at precinct five in Woodlawn with placing the ballot box so high that voters could not see their tickets actually being deposited. The judges then switched 125 ballots from Republican to conservative, Umbdenstock said. Nothing came of this charge. It should be noted that the presiding judge appointed for precinct five in April, 1878 was H. L. Berry, a former white Republican county officeholder.[18]

how a story of ballot switching could have been published before the election.) R. P. Littlejohn to Ernest Powell, February 7, 1936, Reconstruction File; Chesley M. Adams, "Reconstruction in Harrison County," Unpublished Oral account narrated to Ernest Powell in 1936, Lentz Collection, East Texas Baptist College Library, Marshall.

[18] Marshall *Tri-Weekly Herald*, November 14, 1878. Umbdenstock's charges are found in his statement in *Reuben Knight* v. *William Umbdenstock*, 1878, Civil Case Papers, District Clerk's Office, Harrison County Courthouse, Marshall. The federal case resulting in part from these charges was styled *United States of America* v. *Dushee McKay et*

Fraud may have helped keep the 1878 election close; it is impossible to say with certainty. One thing, however, is clear: if the "redeemers" hoped to win by cheating, they were disappointed. As noted above, complete returns at first gave the Republicans victories in every contest. The conservatives' opportunity to turn apparent defeat into victory came only from the discovery of a technicality a few days after the election.

"The Battle Not Over Yet" read a headline in the *Messenger* on Friday, November 8. Citizens Party leaders had realized that the polling place for precinct three, Justice William Roy's office, was located in ward three, placing it *within* rather than outside the corporation of Marshall. More than 1,000 voters—at least one quarter of the total countywide—had cast their ballots at this box and given heavy Republican majorities. In the county judge's race, for example, Williamson received 758 votes in precinct three and Lane had 266. Technically, all the votes in Roy's box, as the precinct three box soon became known, had been cast improperly by individuals voting in the wrong precinct. Should these ballots be counted? If they were, the radicals would remain in office; if not, Harrison County would be "redeemed."[19]

On November 15, ten days after the election, Citizens Party leaders sought and received an injunction from State District Judge A.J. Booty ordering County Judge J. B. Williamson not to count the votes from precinct three. Their petition, of course, cited the improper location of the ballot box for that precinct. Williamson reacted by refusing to count the votes without Roy's box, intending, the conservatives believed, to declare the radical candidates victorious on the basis of the first returns and issue

al. Its record is found in the Final Record, United States District Court at Jefferson, Federal Records Center, Fort Worth, Texas. See also the account of this trial in Marshall *Tri-Weekly Herald*, October 23, 25, 1879. Berry's appointment is in Harrison County Commissioners Court Minutes, April, 1874.

[19] Marshall *Messenger*, November 8, 1878. The number of votes cast in precinct three was determined by comparing the returns certified by J. B. Williamson, Election Returns, Harrison County, 1878, and those reported by the conservatives as correct without Roy's box, Marshall *Tri-Weekly Herald*, November 19, 1878. W. S. Coleman to Governor Richard B. Hubbard, November 22, 1878, Governors' Letters, said that there were 1,061 votes in the box.

them certificates of election. The Citizens Party then got a second injunction from Judge Booty on the 18th restraining Williamson from granting the certificates of election. Faced with the county judge's continuing refusal to count the votes "properly," the party appointed William J. Johnston, W. D. McFarland, and C. M. Raguet, all conservatives, to determine the election results. These men could not obtain the original returns which were in Williamson's possession, but they obtained what the *Herald* termed "duplicates properly attested to by returning officers," counted all except the precinct three box, and declared the Citizens Party candidates elected.[20]

The "redeemers" pressed their advantage immediately. In the late afternoon of November 18, armed with the injunctions against Williamson and their own version of the election returns, they simply occupied the critical offices. George Lane was ill so Amory Starr presided as the Citizens Party candidates for county commissioner met and constituted themselves as the commissioners court. Starr, acting as county judge, took control of Williamson's office and of the county seal and issued certificates of election to his conservative cohorts. Joseph P. Alford took over the county clerk's office, and Solomon R. Perry moved into the sheriff's office that same afternoon. Jacob Wolff, the radical incumbent county clerk, refused at first to give up his office whereupon Alford came with "as many men as could conveniently enter the room" and ordered him to leave. Wolff attempted to refuse again but was told that his consent was not expected or necessary. "I then," Wolff wrote later, "of course, vacated the office, protesting against the proceedings." Perry took over from Sheriff William E. Singleton under similar circumstances. The commissioners court met again the next morning, the 19th, with Amory Starr still presiding and ordered J. B. Williamson to give up the county judge's office, William Umbden-

[20]The original petition for an injunction and the petition for a second injunction are found in Election Returns, Harrison County, 1878. (There is a special file on the disputed election containing much of the material cited here. Some of it is very different from that usually found in election returns.) Local developments are explained also in Marshall *Tri-Weekly Herald*, November 16, 19, 1878.

stock to vacate the treasurer's office, and William C. Pierce to retire as tax collector. Starr summarized the situation confidently in a letter to his friend R. H. Irion on the 20th.

> . . . politics have run high, and we have beaten them out. I held county commissioners court yesterday (Lane county judge being sick) and those officers who had not *turned over* to our men, I had posses sent out for and *turned* out. I'll have old Williamson in jail shortly if he don't return some papers he took out of the records. It's good fun but I've had no rest.[21]

Williamson did not give in easily to this combination of legal pressure and direct action. On the afternoon of the 18th, he sent election returns on the state representative race between William T. Scott and John Hudson to Austin. He counted Roy's box and reported Hudson the winner, adding: "I certify that a few hours before these returns were made out, my office and seal were taken possession of by a mob and hence the seal is not attached." The next day, Tuesday, November 19, he began to issue certificates of election to the Republican candidates. On the 20th, he prepared full election returns on all the county races, the total, of course, including the precinct three box, to be sent to the secretary of state in Austin. And finally, on the 21st, he appealed for assistance to Governor Richard B. Hubbard who had final authority in that only he could authorize commissions of office for victorious candidates. Terming the takeover of county offices by a "mob" an "outrage," Williamson suggested no course of action but indicated that he would simply wait for the governor's response. On the 22nd, Williamson sent his version of the election returns to Austin and made a stronger appeal to Governor Hubbard. "We have done nothing to deserve such treatment," he wrote. We have reduced the county debt by $35,000 in the last two years, and local affairs have never been administered so well. The Citizens Party candi-

[21] Harrison County Commissioners Court Minutes, November, 1878; Jake Wolff to Major K. M. Walton, February 4, 1879, Election Returns, Harrison County, 1878; Marshall *Tri-Weekly Herald*, November 19, 1878; Amory R. Starr to R. H. Irion, November 20, 1878, Henry Raguet Family Papers.

dates are acting, Williamson asserted, only from "political *hatred.*" "Now, Governor," he wrote, "we ask your protection. We are able in this county to do as they have done, take the law in our own hands, but will not."[22] Was this a pledge of non-violence or a threat?

The conservatives, of course, made their own appeals to Governor Hubbard. State Representative W. S. Coleman gave his version of events in a letter on November 22 and concluded by asking the governor not to issue commissions to the radicals. George Lane wrote on the same day:

> We have had a terrible time in this county with these radical scoundrels who have robbed the county and mismanaged its affairs. . . . We therefore made a hard pull . . . for the offices and have got on this far and we have full hope our friends will give us truly all the aid we will be entitled in a due administration of the law.[23]

Hubbard, a conservative Democrat, ordered the secretary of state not to issue any commissions of office for Harrison County and wrote to Williamson, Coleman, and Lane promising an investigation. Williamson thanked the governor for his reply and seemed patient. P. E. Coleman, another Harrison County radical, however, wrote angrily denouncing the Citizens Party and warning that "Such flagrant disregard for law and order is calculated to produce serious troubles. . . ." Hubbard acted on November 29 by sending the election returns and letters from Harrison County to Attorney General Hannibal H. Boone and asking for a legal opinion on the situation.[24]

[22]Williamson's actions on the 18th, 19th, and 20th are documented in Election Returns (first quotation), Harrison County, 1878. His letters to Governor Hubbard on November 21 (second quotation) and 22 (third-fifth quotations) are found in the Governors' Letters.

[23]W. S. Coleman to Governor Hubbard, November 22, 1878, George Lane to Governor Hubbard, November 22, 1878 (quotation), Governors' Letters.

[24]Governor R. B. Hubbard to J. B. Williamson, November 23, 1878 (Identical letters sent to Coleman and Lane on the same day), Williamson to Hubbard, November 27, 1878, P. E. Coleman to Hubbard, November 24, 1878 (quotation), Hubbard to Hannibal H. Boone, November 29, 1878, Governors' Letters.

In the meantime, Harrison County's conservatives celebrated their success to an extent that, under the circumstances, must have been especially infuriating to the Republicans. There were public rallies at Marshall, Elysian Fields, and other towns. The *Herald* published a long satirical article entitled "the Salt River Expedition" making fun of the radicals sailing reluctantly away "up Salt River." Loughery even went so far as to poke fun at William Umbdenstock's German accent. The *Messenger's* headline read: "HARRISON COUNTY REDEEMED." The conservative victory, the paper said,

> brings with it a newness of joy and life, that fills every heart with rejoicing, and swells every breast with pride, and loosens every tongue with loud acclamations and praise.
>
> Radicalism is gone glimmering. The Negroes themselves will not shed a tear or heave a sigh of regret, because they now see that intelligence, wealth, and virtue must prevail. . . .[25]

Attorney General Boone sent Governor Hubbard two opinions, one dated November 30 and the second December 11, on the situation in Harrison County. The first, apparently based solely on an examination of the election returns, indicated that the "redeemers'" celebration was premature. Only an incumbent county judge can issue certificates of election, Boone said, so those issued by the conservatives were "without warrant of law." On the other hand, J. B. Williamson's certificates were "warranted by law" and individuals holding them should be commissioned by the governor unless their election was legally contested. Boone's second opinion, dated December 11, was based on a broader study of the situation. He did not change his view on the legality of certifying election winners, but he advised the governor not to issue commissions to anyone immediately. Those in office could perform their duties without commissions, he said, and those who felt that they had been wrongfully denied office could

[25]Marshall *Tri-Weekly Herald*, November 19, 1878; Marshall *Messenger*, November 22, 1878 (quotations).

take legal action. We can only speculate on Boone's reasons for giving a second opinion more favorable to the "redeemers." Perhaps political bias entered the situation; perhaps he was genuinely convinced that the dispute over the precinct three box should be settled by legal action. In any case, both opinions advised leaving a decision to the courts; that of November 30 required the "redeemers" to take the initiative; that of December 11 called on the radicals to originate the suits. Loughery was pleased. "This seems to be a kind of recognition of the value of possession," he wrote on December 14, "and it transfers the controversy at once to the courts."[26]

By mid-December, all of the Citizens Party candidates filed contest of election suits against their Republican opponents. They were acting in light of Attorney General Boone's November 30 opinion that only Judge Williamson could legally certify election winners. They had to file contest suits or face the possibility that Governor Hubbard might commission their radical opponents. The suits, all essentially the same, were filed in state district court at Marshall, and the original case papers on several remain in the district clerk's office there. The conservatives' cases hinged on the argument that the votes in precinct three were improperly cast and could not be counted. The improper location of this particular box within ward three of the town of Marshall was explained again and again. Counsel for the radicals replied that the polling place had been properly established by the commissioners court and that the heavy Republican majorities cast there were entirely legal. The radicals, as noted above, charged the conservatives with fraud at Elysian Fields and Woodlawn. They condemned the procedure by which their opponents had "violently and forcibly" taken control of county offices, pointing out that the vote count by Citizens Party members had been "simply the acts of private citizens." Finally, the Republican defendants pointed out that not counting Roy's box

[26] Attorney General Hannibal H. Boone to Governor R. B. Hubbard, November 30 (first quotation) and December 11, 1878, Election Returns, Harrison County, 1878; Marshall *Tri-Weekly Herald*, December 14, 1878 (second quotation).

would disfranchise nearly one-third of those who had voted. If the votes in precinct three had been cast improperly, their briefs argued, though no fault of the voters, then a new election should be held.[27]

The suit brought by George Lane against J. B. Williamson, the most important of these contest of election cases, came to trial in District Judge A. J. Booty's court on December 31, 1878. It was argued for two days and decided on January 2, 1879. Not too surprisingly, since Booty was a conservative and the judge who had issued the original injunction against counting the precinct three box, the ruling was in favor of Lane. The county judge's office and therefore all the other offices belong to the Citizens Party. Williamson asked for a new trial. When Booty rejected this request, he appealed to the Supreme Court of Texas. Loughery felt that Williamson and his friends had no chance. "The Citizens are in possession of the offices," he informed his readers on January 4, "and are likely to hold them."[28]

As Williamson's appeal went to the Texas Supreme Court in January, 1879, the Harrison County "redeemers" faced several other hurdles in Austin too. First, there was the question of representation in the 16th Legislature. Walter Ripetoe, the black state senator elected in 1876, still had two years to serve on his term, and William S. Coleman, the "floater" state representative had been re-elected. However, both William T. Scott, the conservative, and John Hudson, the Negro Republican, claimed the Harrison County state representative's seat. Their contest, like those for local offices, depended on the precinct three box. The House Committee on Privileges and Elections, controlled by conservative Democrats, agreed on the 20th to seat Scott.

[27] George Lane to Governor R. B. Hubbard, December 19, 1878, Election Returns, Harrison County, 1878. Original case papers on these contest of election suits were filed in Civil Case Papers, District Clerk's Office. The papers on *George Lane* v. *J. B. Williamson* are missing, perhaps because the case was appealed, but those on *Knight* v. *Umbdenstock* and others, all of which are virtually identical, are preserved. The summary of arguments is based on those in the latter case. The quotations are from Umbdenstock's reply to Knight's charges.

[28] Marshall *Tri-Weekly Herald*, January 2, 4 (quotation), 1879; District Court Minutes, Book L, District Clerk's Office, Harrison County Courthouse, Marshall.

Hudson received mileage for his trip to Austin. A second hurdle, or so the conservatives seemed to fear, came in the form of a new governor, Oran M. Roberts, who took office on January 21. The Republicans made new appeals to Roberts, and the conservative leaders were concerned that he might respond with commissions of office. This would be all wrong, George Lane wrote William T. Scott on the 30th in a letter undoubtedly intended for officials in Austin. We have won in the courts, he said, and we intend to stay in office. "We are law abiding people here as you know but the issuance of commissions to the other side may make a handle for them to bring about trouble that may be very unpleasant." Roberts, a Democrat, investigated and left the "redeemers" in office. His decision is hardly surprising, especially in light of the fact that at least one important Republican advised him to leave the situation alone. Shack Roberts, a black leader who had served two terms as a state representative from Harrison County, wrote on February 10 as follows:

> Now I have talked to a great many of the party, and it is the general desire that the officers *now in office* remain there, and most of the citizens are satisfied. And, I would state, that if you can consistantly *[sic]* do so, it will be satisfactory to all *(except the outs)* if you can issue Commissions to the officers *now in office* — . . .

We can only speculate on the motivation of this letter, written on stationery from the county clerk's office, attested to by D.L. Hawley, the deputy county clerk, and signed with Roberts's "mark" since he was illiterate.[29] Perhaps he had fallen out with Williamson and the other Republicans, possibly because Negroes provided the votes and whites took most of the offices. It is possible also that Roberts was simply convinced by the Citizens Party's arguments concerning good government for the community.

Harrison County "redeemers" thus overcame all potential

[29] George Lane to William T. Scott, January 30, 1879 (first quotation); Shack Roberts to Governor Oran M. Roberts, February 10, 1879, Election Returns, Harrison County, 1878. If the precinct three box was counted, Hudson won by a margin of 1,940 to 1,868; if not counted, Scott won 1,621 to 1,170. Election Returns, Harrison County, 1878; Marshall *Tri-Weekly Herald*, January 23, 1879.

political obstacles in 1879. There remained only Williamson's appeal to the Texas Supreme Court. The ruling in *J. B. Williamson* v. *George Lane,* handed down on December 12, 1879, confirmed conservative control of the offices they had already held for more than a year. Chief Justice George F. Moore's lengthy and complicated opinion hinged on the idea that the contesting of an election was a political question rather than a civil suit. State law decreed that while election contests could be heard in district courts, only suits at law could be appealed to the Supreme Court. On this basis, Moore concluded that election contests were not within the appellate jurisdiction of his court and dismissed the case.[30] Judge Booty's original decision in favor of Lane stood. In the "redemption" of Harrison County, possession of office turned out to be not, as the saying goes, "nine-tenths of the law," but "ten-tenths" instead.

Although it did not directly threaten their control of local government, Harrison County conservatives faced one other legal problem arising from the election of 1878. In early December, United States District Attorney Andrew J. Evans arrested five men from the Elysian Fields area for violation of the federal Enforcement Act of 1870 which outlawed any infringement upon the right to vote protected by the Fifteenth Amendment. The men arrested were the three election judges, Dushee McKay, John Cocke, and Anthony Gaines (a Negro), and two private citizens, Dr. H. C. Gray and R. L. Hightower, a lawyer. These five were accused by a number of Negro complainants with combining to refuse the ballots of 320 black citizens, thus infringing the right to vote. Arrested by deputy federal marshall Walter P. Lane, the five were formally charged at the federal district court in Tyler and released on bonds of $400 each. Loughery dismissed the charges as purely political; nevertheless, conviction would cast an additional cloud over the Citizens Party victory.[31]

[30] *J. B. Williamson* v. *George Lane*, 52 *Texas* 335.

[31] Marshall *Tri-Weekly Herald*, December 3, 5, 7, 1878. The Enforcement Act of 1870, is explained briefly in Alfred H. Kelly and Winfred A. Harbison, *The American Constitution, Its Origins and Development* (New York, 1963), 483.

The trial was transferred from Tyler to a new federal district court in Jefferson on the grounds that those involved, especially the government's witnesses, were too poor to pay for travelling to Tyler. This meant that Judge Amos Morrill, a Massachusetts-born unionist who had left Texas during the Civil War and become a Republican during Reconstruction, presided. When the case came before him in October, 1879, Morrill ruled against a seventeen-point demurrer and bill of exceptions filed by the defense lawyers, much to their chagrin, and the matter went to a jury trial. The defendants claimed that they were not charged with denying the right to vote on the basis of race, color, or previous condition of servitude and that therefore they could not have violated the Fifteenth Amendment. They had a precedent for this argument in that the United States Supreme Court in *United States* v. *Reese* (1876) ruled that the amendment did not constitute a positive guarantee of the franchise. The accused also claimed that no one had actually been prevented from voting. McKay, Cocke, and Gaines had refused to accept "colored back tickets" for two hours on complaint of Dr. Gray. But when he could produce no law against such ballots, they were accepted. At the close of the three-day trial on October 23, the jury of eleven whites and one black found the defendants not guilty.[32]

While state and federal court actions were settled in 1879, the "redeemers" governed Harrison County. They had promised "good"—that is, economical—government, and by their own accounting they succeeded. Expenditures were reduced in every way possible The county judge, for example, had his salary slashed from $1,000 to $100 per year. No major county projects were undertaken, and efforts were made to reduce indebtedness. At the close of their first year in office, the commissioners claimed a net reduction of $9,420.34 in the county's debt. They had spent only $11,727.41 while paying $21,147.75 in county obligations, most of these for redeeming scrip. Property

[32]Webb, Carroll, and Branda (eds.) *Handbook of Texas*, II, 237; *United States of America* v. *Dushee McKay et al.* (quotation), Final Record, United States District Court at Jefferson; Kelly and Harbison, *American Constitution*, 483; Marshall *Tri-Weekly Herald*, October 23, 25, 1879.

taxes were reduced only slightly to $1.30 per $100 evaluation in 1879 (down from more than $1.50 per $100 in 1878) and $1.35 in 1880. But the conservatives pointed out that previous debts necessitated many of the county's taxes. The railroad-subsidy tax, for example, accounted for more than half of the assessment rate in 1879 and 1880.[33]

The "redeemers" had more success than the radicals in dealing with the railway subsidy issue; probably as a matter of necessity. Over the years since the railroad tax was first levied in 1874 very little money had actually been collected to pay the interest and 2% of the principal annually. By early 1880, the original $300,000 in bonds amounted to a total obligation of $405,000. Bondholders had been remarkably patient, but finally in January, 1880, at the request of an investor named Alex Davis, District Judge Morrill ordered the commissioners court of Harrison County to levy and collect a special tax to pay $7,000 in past due interest. W. E. Singleton, one-time Republican sheriff and now a federal marshall, served the order on February 2. The community's taxpayers reacted by holding several public meetings and urging the commissioners court to appeal Morrill's ruling while at the same time seeking a compromise with the bondholders to pay the debt at 40¢ on the dollar. At these meetings State Representative W. S. Coleman explained how a compromise was possible under an act passed by the last legislature. He supported such a settlement but strongly urged an appeal in the meantime.[34]

The commissioners' court chose not to appeal Morrill's decision. In mid-February, 1880, they levied a special tax to comply with the court ruling. And at the same time, they set out to develop a compromise with the bondholders. Once more it is not clear how much money was collected under this tax. At least it was a show of good faith on the part of the commissioners and probably helped in working out a compromise. During the spring of 1880, representatives of the county government worked out an

[33] Marshall *Tri-Weekly Herald*, February 17, 1880; Harrison County Tax Rolls, 1879, 1880.

[34] Marshall *Tri-Weekly Herald*, January 22, February 3, 5, 1880.

agreement that most of the bondholders indicated a willingness to accept. The county would issue new twenty year bonds bearing 6% interest and exchange them for the old subsidy bonds at 50¢ on the dollar of principal and accrued interest. This arrangement, it was believed, was fair to the bondholders and would set the financial burden on the county's taxpayers at a bearable level. An election was set for June 15, 1880, to seek voter approval for the compromise.[35]

The issue was more heated than might have been expected. W. S. Coleman favored legal action rather than a scaling down of the county's obligations. He pointed out that, on one hand, Morrill's ruling did not necessarily have to be enforced, while on the other, bondholders were not bound to accept the proposed new arrangement. Coleman's views were attacked by both newspapers, the *Herald* and the *Messenger*, and the difference of opinion ended tragically. Coleman met R. L. Jennings, co-owner of the *Messenger*, on a Marshall street and called the newspaper story a "tissue of lies." Both men drew pistols and fired. Coleman, a lawyer and state representative, was killed.[36]

On June 15, Harrison County's taxpaying voters approved the compromise bond issue by a wide margin. Steps were then taken to reach agreements with the bondholders and issue new bonds. Negotiations were handled by the local bankers, Garret and Key. Two years later the *Herald* reported that the railroad-subsidy tax necessary to pay the court judgment and the compromise bonds stood at 65¢ on the $100 evaluation, a lower rate than was set to meet the original obligation.[37] The "redeemers," largely out of necessity, had moved toward settling the subsidy bond issue. Harrison County's railroad provides an excellent case study in the price of progress.

The conservatives believed that their record in office would be tested at the polls in 1880. Political excitement mounted that

[35] Ibid., February 14, May 20, 29, 1880; Harrison County Commissioners Court Minutes, May, 1880.

[36] Marshall *Tri-Weekly Herald*, June 10, 12, 1880.

[37] Ibid., June 17, 1880, September 21, 1882; Harrison County Commissioners Court Minutes, September, 1880.

year from March into November as Democrats and Republicans prepared for national and state elections while the Citizens Party and radicals faced another contest for control of county government. In July, the Citizens Party decided to hold a primary election to choose most of their candidates for local office. Participation in this primary would be restricted to white men who had supported their party in 1878 or had not been eligible to vote then and to Negroes who were known to have voted for or been in sympathy with the Citizens Party ticket two years earlier. It was not exactly a "white primary," but it is interesting that the "redeemers" felt strong enough in 1880 to risk alienating all black voters who had not been with them two years before. The primary was held on August 14 without any great excitement. William T. Scott again received the conservatives' nomination for state representative, and R. L. Hightower, one of those accused in the Elysian Fields election fraud case in 1878, won the chance to run for the state senate. S. R. Perry and J. P. Alford were unopposed for sheriff and county clerk. Interestingly, George Lane, the sixty-six year old county judge who had long been a favorite of the community's conservative voters, lost the nomination to W. T. S. Keller, a thirty-one year old lawyer with no previous experience in office. For some reason, the party did not nominate candidates for county commissioner until early September. When they did, only one of four incumbents, William P. Blocker, was chosen to run again. The "redeemers" gave no indication of differences within their ranks, but it seems likely that the first county court in dealing with some very difficult issues had not endeared itself to all the voters of their own party.[38]

The Republicans campaigned until mid-October without making formal nominations for local offices. They sought instead to build support for their party among the black majority, hoping that general allegiance to Republican candidates would

[38]Marshall *Tri-Weekly Herald*, July 29, August 10, 17, 24, September 4, 1880; Marshall *Messenger*, July 30, 1880. The three new candidates were R. S. Kelly, T. J. Whaley, and J. D. Cole.

extend to all candidates in November. Finally, the radical party named a ticket led by Henry Moore, a black and former state representative, for the state senate; Peter Choice, another local Negro, for the house of representatives; and J. B. Williamson again seeking the county judge's office. A number of familiar names including ex-treasurer William Umbdenstock and former sheriff W. E. Singleton appeared on the Republican slate too. The *Herald* made much of the fact that Shack Roberts was ignored by the radicals. Perhaps his recommendation to Governor Roberts in 1879 that the "redeemers" be left in office had something to do with this decision.[39]

In contrast to 1878, the Citizens Party went into the campaign of 1880 confident that unity would bring victory. The radicals have weakened, they said, in numbers and in organization while we have gained strength. Their strategy was predictable. Above all, they emphasized their record, as they saw it, of two years of honest and efficient administration. They bombarded the public with statistics to show that county government under their direction had cost less, reduced indebtedness, and lowered taxes. On October 26, a few days before the election, the *Herald* published a report by Amory Starr showing that the average monthly expenditure by the conservative incumbents was $823.04 while the lowest ever recorded by the radicals was $1,144.74. During less than two years from November 17, 1878, to August 18, 1880, Starr claimed, the conservatives had effected a net reduction of $21,604 in the county's indebtedness. "Public finances are a powerful argument . . . ," the newspaper said. How, the *Herald* asked again on November 2, could anyone reject the conservatives' record and vote to place the community again under the yoke of "reckless spend thrifts of the public money"? Secondly, the Citizens Party appealed to black voters as they had in 1878, promising to protect their rights and emphasizing the interests of all in good government. The Marshall *Messenger* summarized this appeal very well on August 27.

[39]Marshall, *Tri-Weekly Herald*, October 21, 23, 1880.

> We must solicit the votes of the colored people, for this is our only hope of success. Get them to join the clubs, under pledge to support the Citizens' ticket; treat them kindly; recognize their rights; gain their confidence, and we will have no trouble in having them vote with us. I deprecate anything like coercion, known as bulldozing. This only drives the colored men farther from us. It is to our interest and the colored man's interest to cultivate a more friendly relation between the blacks and the whites.

To prove that "redeemer" government had been good for the community's Negroes, the Citizens Party argued that the county had far more black than white "community" schools and that much more money was spent monthly on black paupers than on white.[40] Neither point seems especially compelling since "community" schools were created on the initiative of parents and spending on black paupers in a way only indicated who was more impoverished. Nevertheless, some Negroes joined the Citizens Party, and a good many were expected to vote for it.

Harrison County Republicans sought assurance that the election of 1880 would not be stolen from them. A federal judge appointed supervisors for most polling places in the community. Those appointed were drawn from a list compiled by W. E. Singleton, a deputy U.S. Marshall as well as Republican candidate for tax assessor. Loughery of the *Herald* expressed concern that these supervisors would try to influence voters and interfere with legal campaigning.[41]

The election of 1880 marked the final act in the "redemption" of Harrison County. Republican presidential electors carried the community 2,528 to 2,231, but Democrats won a majority in state elections, and Citizens Party candidates swept the local races. R. L. Hightower defeated Henry Moore for the county's state senate seat 3,464 to 1,473, and W. T. Scott returned to the house of representatives, defeating Peter Choice, 3,351 to 1,312. W. T. S. Keller won the county judge's office by a margin

[40] Ibid., July 20, September 28, October 26 (first quotation), November 2, 1880 (second quotation); Marshall *Messenger*, August 27, 1880 (third quotation).

[41] Marshall *Tri-Weekly Herald*, October 30, November 2, 1880.

of 3,538 to 1,393 over J. B. Williamson. Other Citizens Party candidates including S. R. Perry for sheriff, J. P. Alford for county clerk, John D. Rudd for tax assessor, and Walter P. Lane for treasurer were elected by similar margins over their Republican opponents. All four conservative candidates for county commissioner won easily.[42]

Again, as in 1878, it appears that large numbers of Negro voters deserted the radicals. According to the census of 1880, the county's population was nearly two-thirds black. Thus unless there was significant intimidation or fraud, two-thirds or 3,335 of the approximately 5,000 ballots cast should have come from Negroes. Republican candidates generally received about 1,400 votes, suggesting that as many as 1,800 to 2,000 blacks voted for the Citizens Party. Conservative spokesmen gloated that indeed this was the case because the community's Negroes were no longer willing to accept domination by local Republican whites. They voted for the Citizens Party instead and "right nobly did they do their part in the contest for a good county government." These "colored" voters, said the *Herald*, "have proven themselves worthy of the respect and protection of the white people of the county."[43]

Loughery insisted that fraud and intimidation had played no part in the election. The Republican victory in the presidential race proved, he said, that blacks had voted freely and simply had switched to the conservative ticket locally. At least there would be no dispute over the color of the ballots this time. The state legislature had amended the election law on April 19, 1879 to require that all ballots be printed "on plain white paper without any picture, sign, vignette, device or stamp mark" except the names of the candidates and their party.[44]

Republicans, however, believed that they had been cheated again and took a variety of legal actions in the federal district

[42] Ibid., November 18, 1880; Election Returns, Harrison County, 1880.

[43] Marshall *Tri-Weekly Herald*, November 2 (second quotation), 4 (first quotation), 1880.

[44] Ibid., November 4, 1880; Gammel (comp.), *Laws of Texas*, VIII, 1419-1420.

court at Jefferson. First, Williamson and most of the other unsuccessful candidates filed challenges to the election results on the grounds that Negroes had been prevented from voting. Second, action was taken to have many Citizens Party leaders indicted for interfering with the right to vote in nineteen of the county's twenty-three precincts on the basis of color, a violation of the Enforcement Act of 1870. All these actions came before Judge Amos Morrill in Jefferson during February, 1881. The *Herald* claimed that 1,000 Negroes went as witnesses. James Tucker of Elysian Fields commented sourly in his diary: "The Federal persecutions at Jefferson, Texas for alleged election frauds in this county has reached me—even away down here in the backwoods by taking off my hands as witnesses." Forty-five of those indicted pleaded guilty to the violation of United States election laws and were fined one dollar and costs. Similar charges were dismissed against at least twenty other individuals. The contest of election cases were dismissed for want of jurisdiction; no federal offices were involved. The radical leaders may have enjoyed the guilty pleas, but the punishment amounted to nothing, and the election results stood. The Citizens Party remained in control. Loughery told his readers that blacks who testified in Jefferson had been duped again by white Republicans and advised them to leave politics alone in favor of working hard and educating their children.[45]

Reconstruction in Harrison County seems to have been a story without heroes or a happy ending. The white radical leaders, "scalawags" primarily, held office on the basis of black votes. Even if, as appears to have been the case, they were not corrupt, and even if their expenditures, debts, and tax increases were repaid to some extent by social and economic progress, their position was in a sense exploitative. Many of the white Republicans such as S. H. Russell, W. E. Singleton, and William

[45]Marshall *Tri-Weekly Herald*, December 9, 16, 1880, February 3, 8, 15, 17, 19, 1881; James Tucker Diary, February 15, 1881 (quotation). These cases are listed, without any explanatory material, in Final Record, United States District Court at Jefferson, Federal Records Center, Fort Worth, Texas.

Umbdenstock received federal appointments when "redemption" came; their black allies such as David Abner, Shack Roberts, and Henry Moore had to take care of themselves. The mass of Negroes, who were through no fault of their own unprepared for politics, were generally unable to avoid being used by their friends and misled by their enemies. They made few gains under the radicals, and those who cooperated with the "redeemers" would eventually find disfranchisement and segregation as a reward. The white conservatives no doubt genuinely believed that they were saving the county from financial ruin, and only the most hardened cynics among them were completely insincere in their appeals to blacks in 1878 and 1880. Nevertheless, the unwillingness to accept Negroes as equal citizens was always there along with a determination to bring down any Republican government by one means or another.

Fraud played a part in the Citizens Party's initial victory in 1878, but it was not decisive. No matter how many tricks the conservatives boasted of later, their victory hinged on what was for them a lucky technicality concerning the placement of one ballot box. They seized the opportunity to claim victory and take power, and Democrats in the state government and courts allowed their action to stand. In one sense then, "redemption" was accomplished according to the law; in another, it amounted to a virtual *coup d'état* thwarting majority rule through a trifling technicality.

PART FOUR

Threshold of the ''New South''

14

Harrison County in 1880: Change and Continuity Since 1850

"REDEMPTION" MARKED the end of an era in nineteenth-century Harrison County. The years of Civil War and Reconstruction gave way to the "New South" after 1880. As slavery, angry sectionalism, secession, war, emancipation, and Reconstruction slowly receded into the past, obviously the community would never be the same again. Events and developments during the years from 1850 to 1880 had upset basic economic institutions, changed social relationships, and demonstrated the possibility of redistributing political power. And yet many potentially drastic alterations, in landownership and "Negro rule," for example, had not taken place, and "redemption" had returned control to white conservatives. The final step, then, in measuring change and continuity in Harrison County from 1850 to 1880 is to examine the economic, social, and political arrangements in effect as the community emerged from the era of Civil War and Reconstruction and stood on the threshold of the "New South."[1]

Clearly population growth, possibly retarded to some extent by developments during the 1860s, had resumed during the 1870s. The census of 1880 reported 25,172 people resident in Harrison County, an increase of almost exactly two-thirds since 1860. Blacks, who as slaves had constituted nearly 59% of the total at the close of the antebellum period, outnumbered whites by an even greater margin, 68% to 32% in 1880.[2] The "redeemers" were undoubtedly correct when they said that Harrison County's future depended on black as well as white progress. Thus it is especially important when considering change to see if Negroes had risen to a position in 1880 that appeared to promise real economic and social advance.

Interestingly, as the population increased from 1860 to 1880, several demographic characteristics remained very stable (see Table 20 and refer to Table 1 in Chapter 1). The mean age for household heads in 1880 was 40.2 years compared to 40.5 years twenty years earlier. And there was little age difference between whites and blacks. In spite of war and emancipation, there was only a slight decrease (3%) in the proportion of households headed by males. Whites and blacks were identical in this characteristic; so the female-headed household that became common among Negro families in the mid-twentieth century does not appear to have been a product of slavery or Reconstruction. Finally, the vast majority of Harrison County's household heads (more than 90%) were native to the southern states. In

[1]The "New South" era is beyond the scope of this study, and no attempt will be made to deal with it here. For a summary of the "New South" ideal and its historiography, see Paul M. Gaston, "The 'New South,' " in Arthur S. Link and Rembert W. Patrick (eds.), *Writing Southern History: Essays in Historiography in Honor of Fletcher M. Green* (Baton Rouge, 1965), 316-336.

[2]U.S. Bureau of the Census, *Population of the United States at the Tenth Census (1880)*, 373.

TABLE 20

Demographic and Economic Characteristics of the Population of Harrison County, 1880*

Characteristic	Whole Sample	Whites	Blacks
Percent of Population	100.0	34.4	65.6
Proportion Male	86.6	86.6	86.6
Mean Age	40.2	41.0	39.7
Birthplace			
Upper South	28.9%	24.4%	31.2%
Lower South	64.6	57.6	68.3
Free States	2.8	8.1	0.0
Foreign Born	3.4	9.9	0.0
Unknown	.3	0.0	.5
Occupation			
Farmer	54.0%	51.2%	55.5%
Farm Laborer	11.3	2.0	16.2
Merchant/Professional	4.6	10.8	1.4
Trades	6.5	12.2	3.5
Services	16.8	11.6	19.5
Other	6.1	11.7	3.2
Unknown	.7	.6	.8
Literacy			
Read and Write	42.3%	95.6%	14.3%
Read but not Write	3.5	.3	5.2
Not Read or Write	54.2	4.1	80.5
Mean Number Dependents	3.9	3.6	4.0
Percentage With At Least One Child Aged Five to Seventeen	64.9	57.0	69.1
Percentage with at Least One Child Aged Five to Seventeen Who Had At Least One Child in School	30.8	41.8	26.0

* Based on Heads of Households.

this case, however, there was a notable difference between whites and blacks. All of the latter were southern-born while 18% of the former were from free states or foreign nations. There had been a doubling of the proportion of non-southerners among white household heads since 1860, although they still remained a small group in absolute numbers. There were only, for example, 382 foreign-born people in the county, most of whom lived in Marshall.[3]

The level of education, at least the attainment of literacy, and the existence of educational opportunity in Harrison County in 1880 were not very encouraging. The white population was generally literate. According to the census, only 4% of all household heads could not read or write. But among the black majority 81% were illiterate. Progress is difficult in a community where 542 of 1,000 heads of households selected at random cannot read or write. And in spite of considerable talk about education, the schools necessary to teach basic skills to the community's children were not available either. Among white households with school-age children, only 42% had even one of those children attending school in 1879–1880. The situation among blacks was worse. Three of every four Negro households with children aged five to seventeen had had no children in school within the past year. This circumstance may be explained by a variety of factors, but basically there was no adequate free public school system.[4]

The community's population thus seemed little changed in 1880, and conditions in the field of education were not very promising. But perhaps forces for major economic change were at work anyway. What does the census reveal concerning Harrison County's economic structure in 1880? Were there signs of commercialization, industrialization, and urbanization? Did agriculture provide a sound base for development in other areas?

Commercial activity remained relatively limited in the community on the eve of the "New South" era. In 1880, as in

[3]The quantitative data in Table 20 are drawn from Tenth Census, 1880, Schedules 1 and 2. The number of foreign-born in Harrison County is drawn from U.S. Bureau of the Census, *Population of the United States at the Tenth Census (1880)*, 443.

[4]Tenth Census, 1880, Schedule 1.

all previous censuses, very few men, less than 2% of all household heads, reported their primary occupation as merchant, grocer, trader, etc. Another source, the *Reference Book* of the Robert G. Dun Mercantile Agency of New York, also indicates the limits of Harrison County's business development during the 1870s. These books, published at least twice a year, listed merchants, manufacturers, and traders across the United States with an estimate of the "pecuniary strength" of each and a "credit rating." The *Reference Book* for January, 1870, listed sixty-six businessmen with Marshall post office addresses. Their activities were generally small scale and not highly specialized. Only sixteen (24%) had an estimated pecuniary strength of $10,000 or more while seventeen (25%) were worth less than $2,000. General stores and groceries constituted more than half of all the listings. None of these Marshall businessmen had a "high" credit rating, but twenty-nine (44%) were rated "good" and thirty-four (52%) "fair." These appear to have been the ratings generally given merchants in small towns across Texas. Only four businesses were not rated at all and were therefore considered unsatisfactory.[5]

Five years later the *Reference Book* rated eighty-six Marshall businesses, an increase of twenty since 1870 due partly to the inclusion of those rated at less than $1,000. There was much more diversity and specialization than earlier with, for example, several furniture stores, a book store, an "eating house," and a bank joining the general stores and groceries. Estimates of pecuniary strength, however, show that the early 1870s, perhaps in part as a result of the Panic of 1873, had not been especially good for commercial development. The number of merchants estimated to be worth $10,000 or more had declined to twelve (16% of the total) since 1870. Fourteen businessmen received good credit ratings, and fifty were considered fair risks, but twenty-two were judged to be so uncertain financially that they were not given ratings.[6]

[5] Ibid.; Dun & Co. (comps.), *The Mercantile Agency Reference Book*, was arranged by state and therein alphabetically by town. Information presented here is based on Marshall only.

[6] Ibid. (1875 volume).

By January, 1880, the number of Marshall businesses listed in the *Reference Book* had increased by only three to a total of eighty-nine. The trend toward diversification continued. The town now had, for example, a photographer, a dairy operator, a confectioner, and a fruit salesman. There were two banking firms, several land agents, and one "speculator." At the same time, there was a continued decline in the pecuniary strength and credit rating of Marshall businessmen. More than half were worth less than $2,000 or could not be estimated while only eleven (12%) were believed to command $10,000. Only eleven had "good" credit ratings, and twenty-two were considered satisfactory.[7]

In short, Harrison County had not made rapid strides toward commercialization by 1880. This is borne out by the small fraction of its people who depended on buying and selling for their livelihood. Furthermore, the Dun Mercantile Agency *Reference Books* do not show a significant increase in the number or size of businesses located in Marshall during the 1870s.

Harrison County gave little indication of significant industrialization by 1880 either. Even if manufacturing is defined broadly to include trades such as shoemaking and blacksmithing, only 8% of the community's household heads fell into that occupational category. The census reported thirty-nine manufacturers in the county with a total capital investment of $93,275 and a total product valued at $281,111. Only 278 men, women, and children found employment in these establishments. Although there was a foundry, a tin-and-iron works, and several producers of agricultural implements including cotton gins, most Harrison County manufacturers operated grist mills, saw mills, slaughter houses, and similar extractive industries. There were virtually no middle-range manufacturers of consumer items such as sewing machines and washing machines, both of which were heavily advertised in the community at this time. It should also be noted that there had been relatively little industrial advance since 1860. Capital investment had increased less

[7]Ibid. (1880 volume).

than $10,000 (from $84,575 to $92,275); the value of goods produced rose only $77,196. By comparison, Dallas County, nearly 200 miles to the west and barely emerging from frontier conditions at the close of the antebellum period, had more than $450,000 invested and produced $1,459,362 worth of goods in 1880.[8]

Urban growth in the community depended on Marshall. First incorporated in 1844, the town became the county's commercial as well as political center before the Civil War. As late as 1870, however, its population was officially set at less than 2,000. Then during the seventies, there was a spurt of growth pushing the 1880 census total to 5,624. The *Southern and Western Texas Guide for 1878* called Marshall a "rapidly advancing" city and commented on its "first class" schools, elegant Capitol Hotel, "fine" jail, ten churches (six white and four "colored"), and two newspapers (*Tri-Weekly Herald* and *Messenger*). Concluding on a note meant to encourage immigrants, the *Guide* said: "The society is a full average of the very best in the State, and the people have the energy and courage to push forward to competence and prosperity, and they extend a cordial welcome to the same class of people, from whatever clime or country they may come."[9]

According to a Galveston *News* story in 1878, Marshall owed "its growth to the railroad." When the Texas and Pacific located its shops and general offices there, the town soon gained 700 citizens and a monthly payroll estimated in the mid-1870s at $50,000 per month. By 1878, the Jefferson Division of the Texas and Pacific ran from Marshall northward seventy-four miles through Jefferson to Texarkana. There, connections were made with the St. Louis, Iron Mountain & Southern Railway

[8]Eighth Census, 1860, Schedule 5; Tenth Census, 1880, Schedules 1 and 3. Advertisements for consumer goods are found in both the Marshall *Tri-Weekly Herald* and the Marshall *Messenger* for 1880.

[9]U.S. Bureau of the Census, *Population of the United States (1870)*, 272; U.S. Bureau of the Census, *Population of the United States at the Tenth Census (1880)*, 344; James L. Rock and W. I. Smith, *Southern and Western Texas Guide for 1878* (St. Louis, 1878), 157 (first quotation), 158 (second quotation).

and with another division of the Texas and Pacific that ran across North Texas to Sherman in Grayson County. Thus Marshall had rail connections not only on an east-west line from Shreveport to Dallas-Fort Worth but to northeast Texas and the Midwest as well. It was an excellent position for commercial development, and the town did take advantage of it at least to the point of becoming a major cotton-marketing center in East Texas. The Galveston *News* pointed out in 1878: "Marshall shipped 6,553 bales of cotton last season, and will do better with this years crop."[10]

Marshall received a new corporate charter from the state in 1871 and broadened its limits to three square miles around the courthouse. Civic-minded "boosterism" became common during the decade. For example, local leaders incorporated a volunteer "Salamander Fire Company No. 1" for the town in 1871. Robert W. Loughery of the *Herald* published a thousand extra copies of his paper in 1876 for free distribution in neighboring counties to the south and west in an effort to boost trade in Marshall. Local merchants joined Loughery in providing the money for this promotional venture. It might be noted, however, that in 1879 the city government passed an ordinance prohibiting hogs running loose in the streets, alleys, and other public places. Marshall's boosters could talk of brick buildings, elegant hotels, and fine jails, but emergence from rural conditions took time.[11]

In 1880, Marshall appeared to be capable of achieving real importance as an urban center. But even Robert Loughery was uncertain about the future. Our town, he wrote, has reached a point at which it must rise to become a large city or "accept the position of a finished village." He felt the need for greater promotional efforts to gain railroad links with New Orleans and with Sabine Pass on the Gulf Coast in southeastern Texas. Marshall will then, Loughery said, be a center for transportation

[10] Galveston *News* article quoted in Marshall *Messenger*, September 20, 1878. Ransom and Sutch, *One Kind of Freedom*, 118, shows Marshall as a cotton-marketing center.

[11] Gammel (comp.), *Laws of Texas*, VI, 243-244, 1386-1391; Marshall *Tri-Weekly Herald*, November 7, 1876, August 16, 1879.

and for the manufacture of machinery and cotton fabrics.[12] Perhaps he was simply applying more pressure to Marshall's promoters, but if the railroad links already existing by 1880, which were far superior to those enjoyed by most East Texas towns, could not convince a booster like Loughery that the town's future was secure, it is questionable that anything could. Could he sense that Marshall on the threshold of the "New South" was destined to be more of a "finished village" than a large city?

Harrison County remained primarily agricultural in 1880 with self-professed farmers and farm laborers constituting 65% of all household heads (see Table 20). Although a notably higher proportion of blacks than whites worked in agriculture, a majority of both races still lived on the land. The plantation system had largely disappeared with the end of slavery and the failure of wage labor during the 1860s. There were more and smaller farms across the county. For example, where the 1860 census reported 695 landholdings averaging 568 acres each, the 1880 summary listed 2,748 farms with a mean size of 129 acres. Farm ownership, however, was not nearly so widespread as these statistics might suggest. Only 1,090 (40%) of the county's 2,748 farms were owned by the families working them. Sharecroppers lived on 991 farms (36%) and cash renters on 667 (24%).[13]

Summary statistics for 1880 indicate that this relatively new agricultural system, heavily dependent on sharecroppers and renters, had changed patterns of production in the county. First, no important crop reached prewar levels in 1879. The county produced 17,619 bales of cotton in 1879, for example, 3,821 fewer than in 1859. More importantly, it seems clear that farmers placed greater emphasis on cash crop production than ever before. The 1879 cotton crop represented a 17.8% decline from 1859 levels, but the corn crop was 57.7% less and the potato crop 60.3% less, and production of peas and beans was 81.6%

[12] Marshall *Tri-Weekly Herald*, January 20, 1880.

[13] U.S. Bureau of the Census, Tenth Census, 1880, *Report on the Productions of Agriculture as Returned at the Tenth Census, 1880* (Washington, 1883), 135, 90-91. Comparisons here and below are drawn with data in U.S. Bureau of the Census, *Agriculture of the United States in 1860*, 144-147.

lower. Put another way, the community's farmers in 1859 grew thirty-one bushels of corn, six bushels of potatoes, and a bushel of peas and beans for every bale of cotton. Twenty years later they grew sixteen bushels of corn, six of potatoes, and little more than a peck of peas and beans for every bale. The county did not have an appreciable increase in meat-producing livestock over this period either. For example, in the case of hogs, the key animal in the community's meat supply, there was actually a slight decline from 30,832 head in 1860 to 30,686 in 1880. Finally, a comparison of data drawn from the 1860 and 1880 census samples reinforces this picture of changing agricultural production patterns. As Table 21 indicates, the bushels of food crops produced for every person on the sample farms declined from more than sixty in 1859 to slightly more than twenty in 1879. Apparently then, unless cash from cotton sales allowed purchases to make up the difference, Harrison County's farm population existed at a lower level of food consumption in 1880 than in 1860. And it seems unlikely that income from cotton was higher since less was being produced while the price per pound in the late 1870s hovered around ten cents, an amount very comparable to antebellum levels.[14]

Although no evidence is available from Harrison County sources specifically, the reasons for increased emphasis on cotton production there were probably similar to those explaining this situation across the South. Small farmers, especially renters and sharecroppers, generally needed credit to begin a new year, and they could obtain it only by giving a lien on their crops for that year. Those who extended credit, generally merchants in town, insisted on cotton production since it was the crop most readily converted into cash. Many farmers abandoned self-sufficiency in food production, not because they were foolishly trying to get rich and deliberately over-produced cotton, but because they ac-

[14]U.S. Bureau of the Census, *Productions of Agriculture at the Tenth Census (1880)* 170-173, 206, 243, 315. Data in Table 21 are drawn from Eighth Census, 1860, Schedules 1, 2, and 4 and Tenth Census, 1880, Schedules 1 and 2. Cotton prices are cited, for example, in the Marshall *Tri-Weekly Herald*, May 29, 1875, December 2, 1876, January 31, September 21, 1878, September 23, 1879, January 1, April 18, 1880.

tually had no choice. Furthermore, the decline in swine raising, which was typical of the South as a whole, was probably due to the demands of the Civil War on meat supplies and to laws reducing the open range rather than to deliberate bad judgment or management on the part of farmers.[15]

Black farmers who had emerged propertyless from slavery were, as would be expected, in circumstances notably inferior to whites. Table 22, based on a manuscript census sample, summarizes the structure and productivity of Harrison County's agricultural economy in 1880 according to race and land tenure. The great majority of white farmers, 81.3%, owned their land while half, 50.7%, of the Negroes were sharecroppers, and more than a quarter, 29.5%, paid cash rent for their land. It is remarkable in a way that nearly 20% had managed to acquire property. Farms worked by whites, even those rented for cash or cropped

[15]Ransom and Sutch, *One Kind of Freedom*, 151-170; Wright, *Political Economy of the Cotton South*, 164-176; McDonald and McWhiney, "The South from Self-Sufficiency to Peonage; 1095-1118.

TABLE 21

Volume of Food Crops per Farm Resident in Harrison County, 1860 and 1880

	1860	1880
Population on Sample Farms		
Free	1,833	2,920
Slave	3,858	—
Total	5,691	2,920
Bushels of Corn	294,810	58,300
Bushels of Other Grains	24,433	1,129
Bushels of Peas and Potatoes	60,834	10,247
Bushels of Corn Per Person	51.8	20.0
Bushels of Food Crops Per Person	66.8	23.9

TABLE 22

Agricultural Property and Production According to Race and Land Tenure, 1880

	Whites				Blacks			
	All	Land-holder	Cash/Renter	Share-cropper	All	Land-holder	Cash/Renter	Share-cropper
Percentage of All Farmers*	34.7	28.2	3.0	3.5	64.7	12.8	19.1	32.8
Mean Improved Acreage	68	76	37	37	35	46	33	32
Mean Unimproved Acreage	191	222	105	22	23	70	11	11
Mean Cash Value of Farm	$1,141	$1,321	$638	$185	$225	$608	$124	$135
Mean Value of Farm Implements	$52	$62	$8	$15	$17	$36	$14	$11
Mean Value of Livestock	$244	$275	$107	$117	$96	$140	$84	$85
Mean Bushels Of Corn	178	195	104	125	71	102	59	65
Mean Bushels Of Other Grains	5	7	0	0	.4	2	.3	.03
Mean Bales of Cotton	10	12	5	5	6	8	6	5
Mean Bushels of Food Crops	34	38	19	13	11	34	5	6
Mean Pounds of Cheese & Butter	57	63	21	44	15	25	12	13

*Land tenure was not recorded in the case of three farmers (one white and two black) who accounted for .6% of all farmers.

for shares, were larger and more valuable than blacks' farms in corresponding land-tenure categories. Whites also owned more livestock, produced more corn, and grew larger quantities of food crops. Only in the area of cotton production did black sharecroppers and cash renters surpass their white counterparts. And this was actually an indication that Negro farmers were more pressed than whites to abandon self-sufficiency in favor of the cash crop. They paid for their greater cotton crops with lower food production.[16]

In summary, Harrison County's agricultural economy had changed in some ways since 1860 but probably for the worse. This is not an argument for slavery and the plantation system; rather it indicates that the new methods of combining land and labor worked out under post-emancipation conditions were inadequate. It is difficult to imagine a different or better answer, however, without massive and long-term interference in local affairs by enlightened governmental authority. And many oppose such an approach or consider it impossible even today. In any case, agriculture showed no sign of progress during the 1860s and 1870s, and other forms of economic activity did not appear ready to replace farming.

Another approach to the question of basic change in Harrison County during the era of Civil War and Reconstruction is to examine geographical and social persistence among the community's people. What proportion of the county's families remained there for a period of at least ten years from one census to another between 1850 and 1880? Did geographic mobility increase or decrease in the 1860s and 1870s as compared to the relatively calm decade of the 1850s? Rapid turnovers of population do not prove that the community was experiencing great change, economic, social, or political. Men move for many reasons; and some, of course, are unable to move as often as they would prefer. Nevertheless, it seems likely that persistent individuals, those who did not move, were reasonably well satisfied with circumstances in their community and inclined to accept

[16]Table 22 is based on data drawn from Tenth Census, 1880, Schedules 1 and 2.

the status quo. High geographical persistence rates thus suggest stability rather than upheaval.

Second, there are questions of social, as distinct from geographical, mobility. Were members of Harrison County's planter elite highly persistent in that class during the antebellum period? More importantly, did the Civil War and Reconstruction destroy this class and replace it with a new economic-social elite? Did the planter class fall along with the plantation system of agriculture? Their fate is strongly suggestive, also, concerning the extent of change from 1850 to 1880.

Geographical persistence among the population of Harrison County from 1850 to 1880 was measured on the basis of the census samples used throughout this study. These random samples, 500 households drawn from the censuses of 1850 and 1860 and 964 households from 1870, included the names, ages, and birthplaces of each household head, his wife (if any), and his eldest son (if any). Once this information was recorded, each subsequent census through 1880 was searched carefully for the household head, the wife, or the son. If any one of the three was located, the family was deemed persistent for the preceding decade. The results of this procedure are presented in Table 23.

Of the 500 households sampled in 1850, 35.6% (178) were geographically persistent until 1860, 18.6% (93) until 1870, and 11.8% (59) for the whole thirty years until 1880. Persistence rates among the 1860 sample were quite comparable — 34.4% (172) remained in the county in 1870 and 24.2% in 1880. Geographical persistence among the 1870 sample was somewhat lower with only 28.6% (276) of the 964 sample households still present in 1880.

At first glance it might appear that the population of mid-nineteenth-century Harrison County with only about one-third of its households persistent for even ten years was notably unstable. But a look at similar studies for other areas of the United States puts the situation in perspective. Mildred Throne's investigation of Wapello County, Iowa, revealed that 30.6% of employed males in 1850 were persistent until 1860. Susan Jackson determined a 33% persistence rate among adult males in Houston, Texas, during the decade of the 1850s. In Trempealeau County, Wisconsin, only 25% of the gainfully employed remained in the county from 1860 to 1870 and 29% from 1870 to 1880. Stephan Thernstrom's study of Newburyport, Massachusetts, found less than 40% of unskilled laborers persistent from 1850 to 1860; 35% from 1860 to 1870; and 47% from 1870 to

TABLE 23

Geographical Persistence in Harrison County, 1850–1880

Population Samples	Persistent to 1860	Persistent to 1870	Persistent to 1880
1850	178 (35.6%)	93 (18.6%)	59 (11.8%)
1860		172 (34.4%)	121 (24.2%)
1870			276 (28.6%)

1880. In Atlanta, persistence rates among native whites from 1870 to 1880 ranged from a low of 24% for unskilled workers to a high of 64% among the proprietorial class. None of these statistics is precisely comparable to those present for Harrison County. One major difference, for example, lies in the fact that they deal with persistent individuals only while my investigation is based on heads of households, wives, and eldest sons. This should reduce the effect of deaths on the Harrison County persistence rate and, therefore, increase that rate in comparison. Nevertheless, this difference being considered, the extent of geographical persistence in Harrison County from 1850 to 1880 appears to have been closely comparable to that in other areas, especially to rural counties of the Midwest.[17]

[17]Mildred Throne, "A Population Study of an Iowa County in 1850," *Iowa Journal of History*, LVII (Oct., 1959), 309-310; Susan Jackson, "Movin' On: Mobility through Houston in the 1850s," *Southwestern Historical Quarterly*, LXXXI (Jan., 1978), 268; Stephen Thernstrom, *Poverty and Progress: Social Mobility in a Nineteenth-Century City* (Cambridge, Mass., 1964), 85; Richard J. Hopkins, "Occupational and Geographic Mobility in Atlanta, 1870-1896," *Journal of Southern History*, XXXIV (May, 1968), 207.

Although it is not essential in documenting the extent of population turnover, it is interesting to seek an explanation of the degree of persistence in mid-nineteenth century Harrison County. Why did some households remain while others moved on? Obviously these questions cannot be answered with certainty. Too many individual considerations enter in. But a comparison of demographic and economic profiles of the persistent and the non-persistent (Table 24) may offer some clues.

From this perspective, persistence appears to have been influenced most by occupation, real-property holding, and in 1850 and 1860, slave ownership. Farmers, merchants, and professionals were always more persistent than those who were tradesmen, overseers, and the unskilled. In every case those who remained in the county for at least ten years were notably wealthier than their non-persistent counterparts. And two-thirds or more of the persistent group were slaveholders. Marital status and having a son appear to have been important also, but the definition of persistence in terms of wives and/or sons introduces an obvious bias in this area. Age was a minor factor, and race appears to have been relatively unimportant from 1870 to 1880. Only a slightly higher proportion of the persistent than the non-persistent were white.

Another, and perhaps more revealing, method of examining the factors involved in geographical persistence is to study the question on the basis of social classes. The 1850 and 1860 population samples were divided into five classes as follows: large planters owning twenty or more slaves, small planters holding ten to nineteen bondsmen, yeomen farmers including small slaveholders (one to nine slaves) and nonslaveholding landowners, poor white farmers who owned no land and no slaves, and non-farmers who were primarily merchants, professionals, tradesmen, and assorted town dwellers. Table 25 reveals that variations in the persistence rates among these classes were striking, especially in 1850. Planters, both large and small, were highly persistent. In fact, a majority of those present in 1850 were still there in 1860. On the other hand, less than one-quarter of poor white households remained for the ten-year pe-

TABLE 24

Comparison of Demographic and Economic Characteristics of Geographically Persistent and Non-persistent Household Heads: Harrison County, 1850–1880

	1850		1860		1870	
	Persistent	Non-Persistent	Persistent	Non-Persistent	Persistent	Non-Persistent
Percentage of Sample	35.6	64.4	34.4	65.6	28.6	71.4
Mean Age	39.2	37.1	41.1	40.2	38.4	38.5
Percentage Male	92.1	92.5	91.9	88.4	94.9	85.9
Percentage Married	82.6	77.0	86.0	76.8	87.3	75.6
Percentage with Son	76.4	66.1	73.3	65.9	68.5	61.6
Race (Percentages)						
White	100.0	100.0	100.0	100.0	34.1	31.1
Black	—	—	—	—	65.9	68.9
Birthplace (Percentages)						
Upper South	52.8	51.6	48.8	40.5	34.1	32.8
Lower South	40.4	42.9	40.7	50.3	60.5	60.8
Non-South	6.8	5.5	10.5	9.2	5.4	6.4
Occupation (Percentages)						
Farmer	78.7	68.6	75.0	71.6	21.7	19.2
Farm Laborer	—	—	—	—	54.7	51.9
Merchant/Professional	14.0	8.4	12.2	11.0	5.4	4.1
Skilled/Unskilled	7.3	23.0	12.8	17.4	18.1	24.8
Percentage Slaveholders	71.9	49.4	66.3	57.9	—	—
Mean Value of Real Property	$1,965	$1,168	$3,590	$2,979	$503	$441
Mean Value of Personal Property	—	—	$12,215	$8,206	$204	$172

riod. Persistence rates from 1860 to 1870 showed somewhat less disparity, but large planters still held a notable advantage over other classes.[18]

Once emancipation came, the bases for social classes were altered. Planters could no longer be defined in terms of numbers of slaves, and poor whites were joined by many free but poor blacks. For purposes of analysis then, the 1870 sample was divided into four groups that approximate the apparent socioeconomic divisions in the population of postbellum Harrison County. There were farmers who owned farm land, farm laborers and farmers who owned no acreage, townspeople such as merchants, professionals, and tradesmen, and a large group of household heads (43% of whom were females) who gave no occupation or were listed as landladies or housewives. Table 25 indicates that patterns of persistence according to social class did not differ notably during the 1870s from those established before the Civil War and Reconstruction. Landed farmers were far more likely to persist than were families in poorer classes.

To this point, persistence in mid-nineteenth-century Harrison County has been examined strictly in terms of geographical mobility. Questions of social, as distinct from geographical, mobility remain; most importantly, to what extent were members of the planter elite persistent in that class from 1850 to 1860 and from 1860 to 1870 and 1880? Was the planter elite highly stable during the antebellum period and then destroyed by the Civil War and Reconstruction? These questions are more difficult

[18] As we have seen, some sample households did not fall into any of these classes. In 1850, for example, there were forty-five household heads who held slaves and listed their occupation as farmer but who apparently owned no land. These people were not planters or yeomen, but at the same time, they were not poor whites or town dwellers. There were also seventeen overseers in 1850, another group that did not fall into any of the usual classes in antebellum society. The persistence rate for this miscellaneous group in 1850 was 23.6%, notably lower than the rate for all classes except the poor whites. In the 1860 sample, 30.4% of those who did not fit into one of the established classes were persistent for ten years.

It should be noted too that in both 1850 and 1860 the small slaveholders in the yeoman farmer class were slightly more persistent than the nonslaveholders (41.5% to 34.7% in 1850 and 38.2% to 34.8% in 1860). Even at the lowest level then, slaveholding was positively related to persistence.

than those concerning geographical persistence in that it is necessary to define a proper measurement of "planter elite" and then to determine not only if those individuals fitting the definition in 1850 and 1860 remained in the county for at least ten years but also to see if they remained in the same socioeconomic class as well.

As a first step in measuring social persistence, the planter elite was defined as those individuals who ranked among the richest 5% of antebellum Harrison County's population in terms of total taxable property. The procedure was to determine the number of families equal to 5% of the total reported in the United States Censuses of 1850, 1860, 1870, and 1880 and then to select the richest taxpayers up to that number in the tax rolls

TABLE 25

Geographical Persistence According to Economic Classes: Harrison County, 1850–1880

	Large Planters	Small Planters	Yeomen	Poor Whites	Non-Farmers
1850 Sample:					
Percentage Persistent to 1860	62.8	49.1	38.5	18.0	35.8
1860 Sample:					
Percentage Persistent to 1870	42.8	37.5	36.7	21.6	32.6

	Farmers With Farms	Farm Laborers and Farmers Without Farms	No Gainful Occupation	Non-Farmers
1870 Sample:				
Percentage Persistent to 1880	45.4	27.8	21.5	26.5

for the corresponding year. In 1850, for example, there were 977 families in Harrison County. Thus, the forty-nine taxpayers (5% of the 977 families) with the greatest amount of taxable property were considered the planter elite. In order to be considered persistent among the planter elite, these individuals had to rank among the top 5% ten years later.[19]

The planter elite in 1850 consisted of forty-nine individuals whose landholdings ranged from 240 to 4,465 acres with an average of 1,536 acres (Table 26). Slaveholdings ranged from twelve to 104 bondsmen with a mean of thirty-three slaves. Total taxable property values ranged from $12,227 to $57,555 with an average of $19,206. In 1860, the fifty-three members of the planter elite were notably wealthier. The mean landholding was 1,970 acres; slaveholding, forty-seven bondsmen. The value

[19]The definition of persistence employed here is a little broader than that employed in measuring geographical mobility among the census samples. In the latter case, only the eldest son was sought, but in determining persistence in the planter elite, if the wife or *any* son could be positively identified, the family was considered persistent. It should be noted, however, that a family was considered persistent only once regardless of the number of sons who were located.

Reliance on the tax rolls rather than the census to define and locate the planter elite raises a number of questions. It has been argued that size of slaveholding alone is not a sound measure of planter status because the age and sex makeup of slave forces varied so greatly. See James C. Bonner, "Profile of a Late Ante-Bellum Community," *American Historical Review*, XLIX (July, 1944), 670-671, n. 26. On the other hand, landholding or the value of real estate alone seem insufficient because the position of a planter depended on a combination of land and slaves. A. Jane Townes, "The Effect of Emancipation on Large Landholdings, Nelson and Goochland Counties, Virginia," *Journal of Southern History*, XLV (Aug., 1979), 403-412, relies on landholdings alone to define the elite while Jonathan M. Wiener, "Planter Persistence and Social Change: Alabama, 1850-1870," *Journal of Interdisciplinary History*, VII (Aut., 1976), 235-260, depends entirely on the value of real estate given in the census. A reasonably accurate picture of the two may be obtained by combining the valuation of real and personal property in the census of 1860, but the census of 1850 did not record the value of personal property. Therefore, the tax rolls which consistently gave the number of acres owned, the value of that acreage, the number of slaves, and the value of those slaves provide the best source for determining the planter elite during the antebellum period. Moreover, once slavery ended, the tax rolls continued to list landholdings and values so that the fortunes of planters may be traced through the 1860s and 1870s. The format of the census was changed in 1880, and the estimate of real and personal property values was dropped. Finally, it seems likely that because state and county finances depended on them the tax rolls would be more thorough and consistent than the census in locating and evaluating taxable property. And these records are arranged alphabetically, greatly facilitating the search for persistent individuals. One major disadvantage of the tax rolls, of course, is the lack of demographic data which is available only in the census.

of taxable property ranged from $33,015 to $94,638 with a mean of $48,565. A good idea of the elite status of this group may be obtained by noting that while they were 5% of the taxpayers, they controlled 30.9% of the total assessed value of property rendered by Harrison County's citizens in 1850 and 29.1% in 1860.[20]

Table 26 also reveals the impact of the Civil War and Reconstruction on the absolute position of the planter elite. Emancipation meant a tremendous loss of property; the slaves owned by the fifty-three members of the planter elite in 1860 had been valued at $1,755,110. Landholdings decreased in size too from a mean of 1,970 acres in 1860 to 1,537 acres in 1870 to 1,258 acres by 1880. And there was a general decline in land values also, at least in the eyes of the tax assessor. Land owned by the planter elite which was assessed at $3.24 per acre in 1850 and $5.39 in 1860 fell to $4.02 an acre in 1870 and $2.08 by 1880. Under these circumstances, the lower boundaries for total taxable property necessary to be included in the wealthiest 5% fell from $33,015 in 1860 to $4,450 in 1870 and $2,000 in 1880. And with the end of slavery and the decline of property values in the postbellum years, not every member of the top 5% of taxpayers was a planter. In 1870, twenty of the wealthiest taxpayers were merchants and ten others owned town lots and money at interest rather than farm property. Ten years later 100 of the 244 taxpayers who constituted the wealthiest 5% did not own significant acreage and did not depend on agriculture as a primary means of support. Thus planters were being joined to some extent by merchants and townspeople in the wealthholding elite.[21]

Clearly then, Harrison County's planter elite suffered heavy economic losses during the decades of Civil War and Reconstruction and lost their monopoly on positions at the top of the economic-social ladder. Absolute losses are one thing, how-

[20] Harrison County Tax Rolls, 1850, 1860; Seventh Census, 1850, Schedules 1, 2, and 4; Eighth Census, 1860, Schedules 1, 2, and 4. Interestingly, Wiener, "Planter Persistence and Social Change," 240-241, found a similar decline in the percentage of all wealth held by the elite class between 1850 and 1860.

[21] Harrison County Tax Rolls, 1860, 1870, 1880.

TABLE 26

Taxable Property of the Planter Elite, 1850–1880

	1850 (49 Cases)	1860 (53 Cases)	1870 (140 Cases)*	1880 (244 Cases)**
Land				
Maximum Acreage	4,465	6,073	5,772	3,722
Maximum Assessed Value	$16,000	$26,418	$22,678	$11,020
Minimum Acreage	240	780	97	100
Minimum Assessed Value	$400	$4,000	$1,200	$200
Mean Acreage	1,536	1,970	1,537	1,258
Mean Assessed Value	$4,971	$10,623	$5,974	$2,613
Slaves				
Maximum Number	104	102	—	—
Maximum Assessed Value	$44,200	$71,400	—	—
Minimum Number	12	16	—	—
Minimum Assessed Value	$3,900	$13,600	—	—
Mean Number	33	47	—	—
Mean Assessed Value	$11,886	$33,116	—	—
Total Property				
Maximum Assessed Value	$57,555	$94,638	$37,895	$22,912
Minimum Assessed Value	$12,227	$33,015	$4,458	$2,002
Mean Assessed Value	$19,206	$48,565	$9,003	$4,584

*Thirty of these cases owned no farm land and were not included in the calculations on landholding.

**One hundred of these cases owned no significant amount of farm land and were not included in the calculations on landholding.

ever, and relative circumstances are another. Emancipation, reduced landholdings, and lower land values notwithstanding, the wealthiest 5% of taxpayers in 1880, the majority of whom still were planters, owned 34.8% of all the property assessed for taxation in Harrison County. This was a higher proportion of all taxed property than had been reported by the planter elites of 1850 and 1860. The wealthholding elite had actually improved their position relative to other taxpayers in the community between 1860 and 1880.[22] To what extent were these the same families who had constituted the antebellum planter elite?

Table 27 summarizes the persistence rates, both social and geographical, among the planter elite in 1850 and 1860. Of the forty-nine members of the elite at mid-century, twenty-seven (55.1%) were persistent in the wealthiest 5% of Harrison County's taxpayers in 1860. Ten others (20.4%) were persistent in the county but not in the planter elite. Twelve (24.5%) had either moved from the county, died without leaving a wife or son there, or died leaving heirs who could not positively be identified as such. In 1870, more than one-quarter of the 1850 planter elite remained in the richest 5% of taxpayers and another one-tenth still resided in the county. Even in 1880, at least a generation later, 16.3% of the 1850 planter elite remained among the county's wealthiest citizens.[23]

Members of the 1860 planter elite were also highly persistent geographically and socially. Even after the Civil War and several years of Reconstruction, 52.8% of this class remained in the wealthiest 5% of the population and an additional 11.3% still lived in the county.[24] Slightly more than one-third were not

[22] Ibid., 1880. The proportion of taxable property owned by the wealthholding elite in 1880 was actually even greater in comparison to 1850 and 1860 because percentages for those years were calculated on the basis of property owned and rendered for taxation by Harrison County residents while the 1880 percentage was calculated on the total value not only of property rendered by residents but of unrendered and nonresident owned property too. The wealthiest 5% owned more than 50% of the property rendered by residents of the county in 1880.

[23] Ibid., 1850, 1860, 1870, 1880.

[24] Ibid. Nearly one-half of those persistent from 1860 to 1870 (13 of 28) not only remained in the wealthiest 5% but increased their landholdings by an average of 749

geographically persistent. Ten years later, 30.2% remained in the wealthiest class, and nearly one-half continued to live in the county.

These statistics suggest several conclusions. First, the extent of social persistence among the planter elite during the decade of Civil War and Reconstruction (52.8%) was almost identical to that for the last antebellum decade (55.1%). And the rate of social persistence for the planter elite among the wealthiest 5% over the twenty years from 1860 to 1880 (30.2%) was greater than the rate of geographical persistence among the population as a whole (24.2%) over those years. Thus, the planter elite was nearly as successful in maintaining its position in society after 1860 as during the decade prior to disunion and war, and the wealthholding

acres. Four remained constant in the amount of acreage held, and eleven saw their landholdings decrease by an average of 611 acres. (The statement that members of the planter elite were "highly persistent" geographically and socially is based on comparisons with similar studies of Alabama and Virginia counties. See below, Note 30.)

TABLE 27

Persistence among the Planter Elite in Harrison County, 1850–1880

1850 Planter Elite	to 1860	to 1870	to 1880
Percentage Persistent in the Planter Elite	55.1	28.6	16.3
Percentage Persistent — Not in the Planter Elite	20.4	10.2	4.1
Percentage Non-persistent	24.5	61.2	79.6
1860 Planter Elite	**to 1870**	**to 1880**	
Percentage Persistent in the Planter Elite	52.8	30.2	
Percentage Persistent — Not in the Planter Elite	11.3	13.2	
Percentage Non-persistent	35.8	56.6	

elite in 1880 had a relatively high proportion of individuals and families who had enjoyed that status in 1860. Second, the proportion of "skidders," individuals who remained in Harrison County but did not have enough taxable property to stay in the top 5%, was greater from 1850 to 1860 (20.4%) than from 1860 to 1870 (11.0%). Put another way, among those who were geographically persistent to 1860, 27% "skidded" socially while for the 1860-1870 decade only 17.6% were "skidders." We do not know what happened to the status of those elite families who moved or who lost parents and/or sons during the 1860s. Perhaps they "skidded" also. Moreover, most of those who "skidded" during the 1850s did not fall very far on the socioeconomic scale. They were still large property holders; they simply had not quite maintained planter elite status as the lower boundary of that class rose from $12,227 to $33,015 in ten years. Nevertheless, all these things considered, the smaller proportion of "skidders" during the 1860s also suggests that the decades of Civil War and Reconstruction did not destroy the position of the planter elite relative to the community's general population. Finally, the degrees of geographical persistence among the planter elite from 1850 to 1860 (75.5%) and from 1860 to 1870 (64.1%) bear out the observation based on the census samples that Harrison County planters were far more stable than the population in general. The decline in planter persistence after 1860 noted in the census samples also appears here, but it is less severe. This suggests that the planter elite weathered the storms of the 1860s and 1870s more successfully than did members of the planter class in general.[25]

What factors explain the geographic and social persistence of this planter elite through the period of Civil War and Reconstruction? For one thing northeastern Texas was not invaded so there was no major dislocation of population or destruction of property. General Nathaniel P. Banks's Red River campaign came close to Harrison County in 1864, but as we have seen, it was stopped by

[25]Wiener, "Planter Persistence and Social Change," 248-249, found that "the greater the landed wealth, the longer the planter family was likely to persist." When the Harrison County planter elite of 1860 is divided into thirds according to the value of taxable property, households in the top third persisted in the 1870 elite at a rate of 56%

the Confederates just southeast of Shreveport. Secondly, the planter elite apparently was not decimated by battle casualties. Harrison County raised all or a large part of thirteen volunteer companies, and deaths were high in some of them. A few of the planter elite themselves volunteered; many of their sons fought. There were no casualties among the family heads, but they did lose sons, in some cases more than one. Nevertheless, the majority of the heads of planter elite families remained at home, and many of their soldier sons survived. Moreover, many had more than one male heir so that the loss of one son or even two did not destroy the family.[26] Finally, and most importantly, the wealthiest class persisted because while the loss of the Civil War led to the end of slavery, it did not mean confiscation and redistribution of real property. The planter elite had owned more slaves *and* land than anyone else in 1860. Eliminate property in slaves but leave landed property largely untouched, and there would be no socioeconomic revolution.[27]

while those in the bottom third persisted at a 50% rate. Households in the top third persisted in the 1880 wealthholding elite at a rate of 38.9% while those in the lower third persisted at a 33.3% rate. Thus, within the planter elite, greater wealth had only a small effect on social persistence.

[26] There were members of the planter elite who volunteered almost as soon as the war began. For example, Thomas W. Winston who owned 1,284 acres of land and thirty-one slaves in 1860 became the captain of the "Texas Hunters" in June, 1861. Marshall *Texas Republican*, June 8, 1861. The great majority of the planter elite, however, do not appear on the rosters of volunteer regiments. Planters' sons do appear with regularity, and as mentioned above, some died. Dr. Harwood P. Perry, owner of seventy-two slaves and 2,238 acres in 1860, had one son killed at Antietam in 1862 and another at the Wilderness in 1864. Simpson, *Marshall Guards*, 22.

As we have seen, the Confederacy passed conscription laws as early as April, 1862, but an exemption was granted for planters or overseers who supervised as many as twenty slaves. In 1864, this "twenty Negro law" was changed to a "fifteen Negro law." Thus, conscription could not force the planter elite into the army. Eaton, *History of the Southern Confederacy*, 89-92. Much has been made of this exemption as a protection for the rich men, but most of the planters were beyond the prime age for soldiering anyhow. And it only made sense for them to manage production at home.

It should be noted too that the proportion of females among the wealthiest 5% of taxpayers did not differ greatly from 1860 (11.3%) to 1870 (12.9%), suggesting that the war did not produce an inordinately large number of wealthy widows.

[27] The critical importance of redistributing landed property in order to achieve basic social-economic change in the South during Reconstruction was argued by contemporary Radical Republicans such as Thaddeus Stevens and George W. Julian. And it has received much attention from revisionist historians since the 1950s. See, for example Fawn Brodie, *Thaddeus Stevens: Scourge of the South* (New York, 1959), 232-233, and

Interestingly, as we have seen, at least one member of the Harrison County planter elite predicted the impact of the war on his class's property with remarkable foresight. Theophilus Perry, in letter after letter written during 1864, urged his wife and father to purchase land, a "little place" of five or six hundred acres. He hoped to buy with Confederate money, but he was willing to trade slaves if necessary. His reasoning was as follows:

> I do not believe that landed property is in as much danger as many think. In Republics there is always a relenting and moderation of sentiments after victory.
>
> I know that Papa thinks landed property is insecure, and worthless as any other kind in the event of our subjugation. I do not think so and cannot. . . . whatever our fortunes may be I think that our money will be worthless in all likelihood, and that our Negro property will be rendered very insecure and precarious.
>
> In revolutions like this landed property is far safer than any other. It behooves every man to procure a little home for his family.[28]

If Perry's view of the future was correct, and to a large extent it was, not only those who had "little homes" but those who had thousands of acres would be equally secure in their real property.

One further indication of the limited extent of change in the wealthiest class during the 1860s is found in a brief examination of those who were new among the top 5% of taxpayers in 1870. More than half of these new members of the elite (57%) had been present in Harrison County in 1860. Most were farmers and slaveholders, and the overwhelming majority were southern-born. Perhaps the greatest change was in the appearance of merchants and mercantile firms among the top 5%. The planter elite was being joined to some extent by a non-agricultural elite in postbellum Harrison County, but large landholders remained predominant, and they were the same people or the same kind of

LaWanda Cox, "The Promise of Land for the Freedmen," *Mississippi Valley Historical Review*, XLV (Dec., 1958), 431.

[28]Theophilus Perry to Harriet P. Perry, January 8, 12 (first quotation), 18 (second and third quotations), 1864, Person Family Papers.

people as those who composed the wealthiest class before the war.[29]

How did the planter elite of Harrison County compare to similar groups in other areas of the mid-nineteenth-century United States in terms of geographical and social persistence? In one Alabama black belt county, Jonathan Wiener found 61% of the planter elite of 1850 still present in 1860 and 63% of the elite group of 1860 still present in 1870. A. Jane Townes found that in Nelson and Goochland counties, Virginia, the geographical persistence until 1870 of individuals with 500 or more acres of land in 1860 was 83% and 87% respectively. The Harrison County planter elite with an 1850-1860 rate of 75.5% and an 1860-1870 rate of 64.1% fell between the experience of the planter class in those areas of Alabama and Virginia. Where social persistence was concerned, Wiener found that in five Alabama black belt counties 47% of the planter elite of 1850 remained in that class in 1860. The comparable figure for those counties from 1860 to 1870 was 43%. Townes discovered persistence rates among those who held 500 or more acres of land from 1860 to 1870 of 67% for Nelson County and 75% for Goochland County. In Harrison County, as noted above, the rates of social persistence were 55.1% from 1850 to 1860 and 52.8% from 1860 to 1870.[30]

These studies are not perfectly comparable. Wiener's is based on the 236 richest planters in terms of real-estate value reported in the census; Townes's is based on planters who paid taxes on 500 or more acres of land; and this study relies on total value of taxable property. Persistence is not defined in precisely the same way in each study either. Nevertheless, the investigations of central Virginia, the Alabama black belt, and East Texas all point toward the same general conclusions. Elite landholding-slaveholding groups in plantation areas of the antebellum South

[29] Harrison County Tax Rolls, 1850, 1860, 1870; Eighth Census, 1860, Schedules 1, 2, and 4.

[30] Wiener, "Planter Persistence and Social Change," 238, 254; Townes, "Effect of Emancipation on Large Landholdings," 409-410.

such as Harrison County were highly stable geographically and socially during the years from 1850 to 1870 and beyond.

In summary, about one-third of the general population of Harrison County persisted geographically from one census year to the next during the period from 1850 to 1880. At first glance this may seem low, but studies of other rural areas during those years have produced similar results. Thus, the community may have been as stable and as satisfactory to its population as most others were at the time. Clearly, however, upper-class families in Harrison County were much more persistent geographically than were families among the population in general. And they were remarkably persistent socially as well. Even in 1880 nearly one-third of the planter elite of 1860 still ranked among the wealthiest 5% of the county's taxpayers. Their rate of social persistence over twenty years was nearly as great as the rate of geographical persistence for the general population over a single decade. The Civil War and Reconstruction did not bring a "revolution in land titles" that ruined the planter class.

How, then, did the Harrison County of 1880 compare to the community of the late antebellum years? Most importantly, slavery was gone and with it the plantation economy. But blacks continued at the bottom of the social ladder, providing much of the labor in an economy that remained essentially agricultural. The planter elite no longer owned human property, but they still held most of the land and dominated socially. Politically, local government rested in the hands of the "redeemers" who were highly similar to, and in some cases the same individuals as, those who held office before secession. In short, the majority of the community's white population had supported the Confederate revolution primarily to keep things the same and failure on the battlefield did not destroy their purpose. Continuity matched change in Harrison County from 1850 to 1880; the Old South had not and would not change its ways easily.

APPENDICES

Appendix 1:

The Census Samples of 1850, 1860, 1870, and 1880

MUCH OF THE quantitative information and nearly all of the statistical analysis in this study is based on samples from the United States censuses of 1850 through 1880. The census of 1850, due to a revision in congressional requirements, was the first to enumerate extensive personal information on all individuals in the community. Schedule 1 (Free Inhabitants) listed the names, ages, sex, birthplaces, and, when appropriate, occupations of every person in each household. It also reported the dollar value of real property owned by each person (usually the household head) and indicated which children, if any, had attended school within the past year. Schedule 2 (Slave Inhabitants) recorded the number of slaves held by each slaveowner and gave the age, sex, and color of each bondsman. Schedule 4 (Productions of Agriculture) listed every farm by the name of its owner and reported in detail on its size and productivity including the number of improved and unimproved acres, cash value of the land and buildings, kinds and total value of livestock, and bushels of corn and bales of cotton grown during the past year. Thus, the manuscript census of 1850 permits the researcher to develop a detailed profile of any free family in the community by linking demographic information from Schedule 1 with data on slaveholding from the second schedule and on farming from the agricultural schedule.

The census of 1860 was virtually identical to that for 1850 except for the addition of a column for the value of personal property to Schedule 1. No important changes were made in 1870 either, although there was, of course, no slave schedule. Before the census of 1880, congress again made important revisions in the law. The population schedule no longer recorded the value of real and personal property; it did, however, add information on the relationship of each person in a household to the head of that household. Valuable information on land tenure was added to the agricultural schedule by identifying each farm operator as a landowner, a cash renter, or a sharecropper.

The sampling procedure began by determining how many households were in the county at each census. There were 972 in 1850, 1,069 in 1860, 2,612 in 1870, and 4,629 in 1880. It was then decided that the samples should consist of 500 households from 1850 and 1860 each and, because the free population more than doubled with emancipation, 1,000 from 1870 and from 1880. Next, computer-generated lists of random numbers (500 for 1850 and 1860, 1,000 for 1870 and 1880) ranging from one up to the total number of households reported each year were used as a basis for choosing those to be included in the sample. This sampling procedure encountered only one major problem. The census of 1870 was so poorly taken in Harrison County that a number of the same households were reported twice, and the final sample had to be reduced to 964. All four of these census samples were genuinely random, and the numbers of households involved were large enough to produce both little sampling error and representative sub-groups.

Once the samples were taken, one important question remained. Were the census samples truly representative of Harrison County as a whole at the date of each census? Put another way, were there statistically significant differences between the sample populations and the entire populations from which they were drawn?

One method of testing the representative nature of the sample populations was to examine them for proportional consistency with the county's total population. For example, if the sample included half of the community's households, it should then contain a comparable percentage of all slaveholders in the county. If it included 50 percent of the county's farms, then those farmers should own approximately 50 percent of all farm property and production reported by the total population. There are a number of difficulties inherent in such a comparison. First, information on the whole community must be drawn from the published census summaries, and there will always be minor discrepancies when dealing with large numbers compiled more than one hundred years ago. Second, some of the statistical categories are not perfectly comparable. The published returns on slaveholding, for example, include *all* slaveholders in the county, while my samples deal only with slaveholders who headed households. Nevertheless, a look at the sample populations as proportions of the whole gives some idea of their validity.

Table 28 indicates that with only a few exceptions, most of which appear in the notoriously poor census of 1870, the samples contained percentages of slaveholders, slaves, farms, and farm property and production reasonably comparable (generally within 5%) to the proportions of the total populations included in the samples. In 1850, for example, the sample included 51.4% of all households, 49.6% of all household heads who were slaveholders, 51.2% of the slaves owned by heads of households, 51.2% of all farms, 51.4% of all corn produced, and 52.5% of all cotton grown in the county.

Another, more technical, method of testing the representa-

TABLE 28

The Census Samples as Proportions of the Total Population of Harrison County, 1850–1880

	1850	1860	1870	1880
Total Households	51.4%	46.8%	36.9%	21.6%
Slaveholding Households*	49.6	46.6	—	—
Total Slaves*	51.1	48.6	—	—
Real Property	(na)	45.6	(na)	(na)
Personal Property	—	46.1	(na)	—
Total Farms	51.2	46.9	28.3	19.6
Improved Acreage	52.9	50.9	27.3	19.4
Unimproved Acreage	50.7	50.2	23.8	19.5
Cash Value of Farm & Equipment	51.9	42.8	27.0	17.2
Corn	51.4	44.7	27.6	20.9
Other Grains	43.3	33.2	(na)	14.1
Cotton	52.5	49.3	25.4	22.9
Food Crops	50.3	39.2	27.1	18.1
Cheese and Butter	48.1	45.7	19.8	(na)
Value/Animals Slaughtered	52.3	44.8	16.7	(na)
Value/Home Manufactures	48.1	50.4	21.5	(na)
Value/Livestock	(na)	46.8	27.8	20.2

*Published statistics on slaveholding are based on all slaveholders regardless of whether or not they headed households. For purposes of testing the sample, I went through the manuscript census and counted the number of slaveholders who were household heads and counted their slaves. The notation (na) is used in other cases where no summary data was available and it was not thought necessary to make a count from the manuscript returns.

tive nature of these census samples is to apply a statistical tool known as the t-test. This measurement involves comparing the means for variables such as improved acreage or bushels of corn for the total population with the means for those items among the sample populations. Obviously then, it can be applied only to those variables for which the published census summaries provide the data necessary to calculate means for the entire population. For the 1850 sample, the t-test was applied to improved acreage, unimproved acreage, corn, other grains, cotton, food crops, cheese and butter, the value of animals slaughtered, and the value of home manufactures. In 1860, all of these were again tested, and the cash value of farms and the value of farm implements were added. (These two variables could not be tested in 1850 because the census summary that year, unlike 1860, lumped them together, preventing the calculating of means for each separately.) The tests for 1870 covered the same items as those for 1860. In 1880, no summary statistics were available for cheese and butter, the value of animals slaughtered, and the value of home manufacturers, but other agricultural products could be tested. In every category in each census year, except for the value of animals slaughtered in 1870, there was no statistically significant difference between the sample means and those for the whole county. Put another way, 99 of 100 samples drawn from the Harrison County census returns for those years would have produced means comparable to those found in my samples.

It seems reasonably certain then that the census samples employed in this study are representative of the entire population of Harrison County. In the first place, the number of households included in each sample is large enough to reduce the chance for error to a low level. Second, the samples were consistent as proportions of the whole county's population and of the variables being measured. And third, the means for agricultural variables such as improved acreage for the samples and the whole population had no statistically significant differences. A study based on every household rather than on samples would not have produced significantly different results.

Appendix 2

Non-Heads of Households in the Population Samples

AS EXPLAINED IN THE preface, the procedure used in drawing samples from the censuses of 1850-1880 resulted in a secondary sample of individuals best described as non-heads of households. These members of the community were eighteen years of age or older, reported an occupation in the census, and had no obvious dependent relationship to the head of household and his family. Although they were, with notable exceptions, not an especially influential part of the county's population, this group deserves at least brief consideration.

There were 160 non-heads of household in the 500 households in the 1850 sample, 183 in 1860, 155 in the 964 households sampled in 1870, and 338 in the 1,000 households that made up the 1880 sample. The great majority of these individuals, especially during the antebellum years, were young unmarried males. In 1850, for example, 97% of the non-heads of household were male, and only 10% were married. By 1880, a good many unmarried females, usually domestic servants, began to appear in the households sampled. Thus, throughout this era, most non-heads of household did not have families and did not have quite the same stake in the community as did the typical head of household.

Although as explained in Chapter 1, it was common in 1850 and 1860 to find overseers as non-heads of household, most individuals in this group had non-agricultural occupations. The majority lived in town and worked in professions, skilled trades, and unskilled service jobs. In 1850, for example, while 12% were overseers, 21% were professionals such as lawyers, 28% were tradesmen such as blacksmiths, and 11% worked in service jobs such as laborers and clerks. By 1880, workers in the older occupations were joined by railroad agents, telegraph operators, and mill workers who did not head their own households. Most of these individuals too lived in Marshall.

Non-heads of household generally had little or no property. Less than 10% owned any real property in 1850. Only about 5% owned slaves. This situation, like their marital status, probably lessened their stake in the community and reduced their influence too.

A survey of the non-heads of household found in those households sampled from 1850 to 1880 reveals few outstanding members of the community. But, there were exceptions. In 1850, for example, J. M. Clough, a thirty-one-year-old lawyer from New Hampshire, appears in the household of Mrs. F. C. Van Zandt, widow of Isaac Van Zandt. Clough had recently married a sixteen-year-old daughter of the Van Zandt family and had not yet established his own home. He was at the time, however, one of the community's state representatives in Austin. Later, he would serve as a lieutenant colonel in the Confederate army before his death at Fort Donelson in 1862 (see Chapter 8).

In 1860, Walter P. Lane was found as a merchant living in the home of his brother, County Judge George Lane. This must have been a very dull existence for one of the most active military men ever to live in Harrison County. Lane had fought at San Jacinto in 1836, winning a promotion for bravery, and in the battles of Monterrey and Buena Vista during the Mexican War. After volunteering as a private with the "Texas Hunters" in 1861, he fought at Oak Hills, Pea Ridge, and with Beauregard's army in Mississippi before returning to Texas and participating in the Red River campaign in 1864. At the close of the war, he was a brigadier general (see Chapter 8).

In summary then, the reader should be aware that a group of people in the community did not head households and are therefore not included in the primary census samples on which this study is based. Although it included some notable individuals, this group as a whole did not constitute a large or especially influential part of Harrison County's population.

BIBLIOGRAPHY

Manuscript Sources

Abner Family File. Harrison County Historical Museum, Marshall, Texas

Blocker, William J. Family Bible. Property of Mrs. Robert M. Claypool, Bellaire, Texas.

Bruckmuller, Peter Joseph. Papers. (Letters and "Description of the Family and Life of Joseph Bruckmuller"), Archives, University of Texas, Austin, Texas.

Hall, Montreville J. Ledger Books, 1860-1874. Property of Mrs. Margaret G. Hudson, Gainesville, Florida.

Hope Family File. Harrison County Historical Museum, Marshall, Texas.

Key Family Papers. (Letters of Hobart Key and "Memoranda for my Children" by his son, Edmund Key), Property of Hobart Key, Jr., Marshall, Texas.

McCarty Family File. Harrison County Historical Museum, Marshall, Texas.

Perry Family Papers. (Miscellaneous Papers of Dr. Harwood P. Perry Family), Property of Mrs. Eudora C. Hodges, Dallas, Texas.

Person Family Papers. Duke University Library, Durham, North Carolina.

Quillin Family File. Harrison County Historical Museum, Marshall, Texas.

Raguet, Henry. Family Papers. Archives, University of Texas, Austin, Texas.

Reagan, John H. Papers. Archives, University of Texas, Austin, Texas.

Reconstruction File. Harrison County Historical Museum, Marshall, Texas.

Rogers Family File. Harrison County Historical Museum, Marshall, Texas.

Rose, Preston R. Family Papers. Archives, University of Texas, Austin, Texas.

Tucker, James. Diary. Archives, University of Texas, Austin, Texas.

Vickers, Pleasant N. Diary (June 16, 1853-July 20, 1856). Harrison County Historical Museum, Marshall, Texas.

Webster, John B. Plantation Journal (February 17, 1858-November 5, 1859). Property of Douglass V. Blocker, Marshall, Texas. A typescript of the Plantation Journal is available at the East Texas Baptist College Library, Marshall, Texas.

Unpublished Government Records: National

Seventh Census of the United States, 1850. Schedule 1 (Free Inhabitants), Schedule 2 (Slave Inhabitants), Schedule 4 (Productions of Agriculture), Schedule 5 (Products of Industry), and Schedule 6 (Social Statistics). Schedules 1 and 2 are housed in the National Archives, Washington, D. C. Schedules 4-6 are in the Archives Division, Texas State Library, Austin, Texas. All of these schedules are available on microfilm.

Eighth Census of the United States, 1860. Schedule 1 (Free Inhabitants), Schedule 2 (Slave Inhabitants), Schedule 4 (Productions of Agriculture), Schedule 5 (Products of Industry), and Schedule 6 (Social Statistics). Schedules 1 and 2 are housed in the National Archives, Washington, D.C. Schedules 4-6 are in the Archives Division, Texas State Library, Austin, Texas. All of these schedules are available on microfilm.

Ninth Census of the United States, 1870. Schedule 1 (Inhabitants), Schedule 3 (Productions of Agriculture), Schedule 4 (Products of Industry), and Schedule 5 (Social Statistics). Schedule 1 is housed in the National Archives, Washington, D.C. Schedules 3-5 are in the Archives Division, Texas State Library, Austin, Texas. All schedules are available on microfilm.

Tenth Census of the United States, 1880. Schedule 1 (Inhabitants), Schedule 2 (Productions of Agriculture), and Schedule 3 (Products of Industry). Schedule 1 is housed in the National Archives, Washington, D.C. Schedules 2 and 3 are in the Archives Division, Texas State Library, Austin, Texas. Available on microfilm.

United States Bureau of Refugees, Freedmen, and Abandoned Lands, 1865-1869. Records of the Assistant Commissioner for the State of Texas. National Archives, Washington, D.C. These materials, part of Record Group 105, are available on microfilm.

____________. Records of the Superintendent of Education for the State of Texas. National Archives, Washington, D.C. These materials, part of Record Group 105, are available on microfilm.

Final Record, United States District Court at Jefferson, Texas (1879-1881). Federal Records Center, Fort Worth, Texas.

Unpublished Government Records: State

Executive Record Book (Governors' Outgoing Letters). Archives Division, Texas State Library, Austin, Texas.

Governors' Letters (Governors Hamilton, Throckmorton, Pease, Davis, Hubbard, and Roberts), Archives Division, Texas State Library, Austin.

List of Registered Voters in Texas, 1867. Archives Division, Texas State Library, Austin, Texas.

Records of the Comptroller of Public Accounts, Ad Valorem Tax Division, County Real and Personal Property Tax Rolls, 1850-1880. Archives Division, Texas State Library, Austin, Texas. The tax rolls are available on microfilm.

Records of the Secretary of State. Election Registers, 1848-1880. Archives Division, Texas State Library, Austin, Texas.

____________. Election Returns, 1836-1900. Archives Division, Texas State Library, Austin, Texas.

Texas Department of Education. Letters Received, 1871-1873. Archives Division, Texas State Library, Austin, Texas.

____________. Register of Disbursements; Office of the Superintendent of Public Instruction, 1871-1874. Archives Division, Texas State Library, Austin, Texas.

____________. Scholastic Census, 1854-1874. Archives Division, Texas State Library, Austin, Texas.

Unpublished Government Records: Local

Civil Case Papers. Sixth District Court (1848-1875) and Second District Court (1875-1884). District Clerk's Office, Harrison County Courthouse, Marshall, Texas.

Civil Minutes. Second District Court (1875-1884). District Clerk's Office, Harrison County Courthouse, Marshall, Texas.

Commissioners Court Minutes. County Clerk's Office, Harrison County Courthouse, Marshall, Texas.

Deed Records. County Clerk's Office, Harrison County Courthouse, Marshall, Texas.

Medical Register. District Clerk's Office, Harrison County Courthouse, Marshall, Texas.

Probate Papers. County Clerk's Office, Harrison County Courthouse, Marshall, Texas.

Published Documents and Source Materials

DeBow, James D. B. (editor). *Statistical View of the United States . . . Being a Compendium of the Seventh Census . . .* Washington, D.C.: Beverley Tucker, Senate Printer, 1854.

The Federal Reporter. Second Series, Cases Argued and Determined in the United States Courts of Appeals, United States Courts of Claims and United States Court of Customs and Patent Appeals. St. Paul, Minnesota: West Publishing Co., 1925.

Gammel, H. P. N. (compiler). *The Laws of Texas, 1822-1897*. 10 volumes. Austin: Gammel Book Co., 1898-1902.

Members of the Texas Legislature, 1846-1962. Austin: Texas State Legislature, 1962.

Oldham, Williamson S., and George W. White (compilers). *A Digest of the General Statute Laws of the State of Texas . . .* Austin: J. Marshall & Co., 1859.

Reports of Cases Argued and Decided in the Supreme Court of the State of Texas. 65 volumes. St. Louis: Gilbert Book Co., 1848-1886.

Report of Special Committee on Lawlessness and Violence in Texas (Austin, 1868), Reprinted in *Senate Miscellaneous Documents*, No. 109, 40th Congress, 2nd Session.

Scott, Robert N. (compiler). *The War of the Rebellion: A Compilation of the Official Records of the Union and Confederate Armies*. 70 vols. in 128. Washington, D.C.: Government Printing Office, 1880-1901.

United States Bureau of the Census, Eighth Census. *Population of the United States in 1860; Compiled from the Original Returns of the Eighth Census*. Washington, D.C.: Government Printing Office, 1864.

United States Bureau of the Census, Eighth Census. *Agriculture of the United States in 1860; Compiled from the Original Returns of the Eighth Census*. Washington, D.C.: Government Printing Office, 1864.

United States Bureau of the Census, Eighth Census. *Manufactures of the United States in 1860; Compiled from the Original Returns of the Eighth Census*. Washington, D.C.: Government Printing Office, 1865.

United States Bureau of the Census, Ninth Census. *The Statistics of the Population of the United States; Compiled from the Original Returns of the Ninth Census (June 1, 1870)*. Washington, D.C.: Government Printing Office, 1872.

United States Bureau of the Census, Ninth Census. *The Statistics of the Wealth and Industry of the United States . . . from the Original Returns of the Ninth Census, 1870*. Washington, D.C.: Government Printing Office, 1872.

United States Bureau of the Census, Tenth Census. *Statistics of the Population of the United States at the Tenth Census (June 1, 1880)*. Washington, D.C.: Government Printing Office, 1883.

United States Bureau of the Census, Tenth Census. *Report on the Productions of Agriculture as Returned at the Tenth Census, 1880*. Washington, D.C.: Government Printing Office, 1883.

United States House of Representatives. *The Reports of the Committees of the House of Representatives made during the First Session Thirty-Ninth Congress, 1865-1866*. 3 volumes. Washington, D.C.: Government Printing Office, 1866.

Wallace, Ernest, and David M. Vigness (editors). *Documents of Texas History*. Austin: Steck Company, 1963.

Winkler, Ernest William (editor). *Platforms of Political Parties in Texas*. Austin: University of Texas, 1916.

Newspapers

Clarksville *Northern Standard.*

Galveston *News.*

Flake's Bulletin [Galveston].

Marshall *Harrison Flag.*

Jefferson *Radical.*

Marshall *News-Messenger.*

Marshall *Star State Patriot.*

Marshall *Tri-Weekly Herald.*

Marshall *Messenger.*

Marshall *Texas Republican.*

Books

Bailyn, Bernard. *The Ideological Origins of the American Revolution.* Cambridge, Massachusetts: Harvard University Press, 1967.

Bateman, Fred, and Thomas Weiss. *A Deplorable Scarcity: The Failure of Industrialization in the Slave Economy.* Chapel Hill, North Carolina: University of North Carolina Press, 1981.

Battle, Kemp B. *History of the University of North Carolina.* 2 volumes. Raleigh, North Carolina: Edwards and Broughton, 1912.

Billington, Monroe Lee. *The American South: A Brief History.* New York: Scribner, 1971.

The Black Citizen and American Democracy: Black Culture in Harrison County, Past, Present, and Future. Marshall, Texas: Marshall Public Library, 1976.

Blassingame, John W. *The Slave Community; Plantation Life in the Antebellum South.* New York: Oxford, 1972.

Bonner, James C. *Georgia's Last Frontier: The Development of Carroll County.* Athens, Georgia: University of Georgia Press, 1971.

Branda, Eldon S. See Webb, Walter P., H. Bailey Carroll, and Eldon S. Branda.

Brewer, J. Mason. *Negro Legislators of Texas and Their Descendants*. Dallas: Mathis Publishing Co., 1935.

Brodie, Fawn. *Thaddeus Stevens: Scourge of the South*. New York: Norton, 1959.

Burnham, W. Dean. *Presidential Ballots, 1836-1892*. Baltimore: Johns Hopkins Press, 1955.

Cairnes, John E. *The Slave Power: Its Character, Career and Probable Designs. . . .* 2nd edition. London: Macmillan, 1863.

Campbell, Randolph B., and Richard G. Lowe. *Wealth and Power in Antebellum Texas*. College Station, Texas: Texas A&M University Press, 1977.

Campbell, Thomas H. *History of the Cumberland Presbyterian Church in Texas*. Nashville: Cumberland Presbyterian Publishing House, 1936.

Capers, Gerald M. *John C. Calhoun: Opportunist, a Reappraisal.* Gainesville, Florida: University of Florida Press, 1960.

______________. *Stephen A. Douglas: Defender of the Union*. Boston: Little, Brown, 1959.

Carlson, Avery Luvere. *A Monetary and Banking History of Texas . . . 1821-1929*. Fort Worth: Fort Worth National Bank, 1930.

Casdorph, Paul D. *A History of the Republican Party of Texas, 1865-1965*. Austin: Pemberton Press, 1965.

Coit, Margaret L. *John C. Calhoun: American Portrait*. Boston: Houghton Mifflin, 1950.

Connor, Seymour V. *Texas: A History*. New York: Crowell, 1971.

Current, Richard N. *The Lincoln Nobody Knows*. New York: McGraw-Hill, 1958.

______________. *Lincoln and the First Shot*. Philadelphia: Lippincott, 1963.

Curti, Merle. *The Making of an American Community: A Case Study of Democracy in a Frontier County*. Stanford, California: Stanford University Press, 1959.

David, Paul A., et al. *Reckoning With Slavery: A Critical Study in the Quantitative History of American Negro Slavery*. New York: Oxford, 1976.

Degler, Carl N. *The Other South: Southern Dissenters in the Nineteenth Century*. New York: Harper, 1974.

Dun, R. G. & Co. (compilers). *The Mercantile Agency Reference Book (and Key) Containing Ratings on the Merchants, Manufacturers, and Traders Generally, Throughout the United States and Canada*. 99 volumes. New York: R. G. Dun & Co., 1867-1905.

Eaton, Clement. *The Freedom-of-Thought Struggle in the Old South*. New York: Harper, 1964.

____________. *A History of the Old South*. 2nd edition. New York: Macmillan, 1966.

____________. *A History of the Southern Confederacy*. New York: Collier-Macmillan, 1961.

Eby, Frederick. *The Development of Education in Texas*. New York: Macmillan, 1925.

An Economic Survey of Harrison County, Prepared for the Texas and Pacific Railway Company. Austin: University of Texas, College of Business Administration, 1949.

Elkins, Stanley M. *Slavery: A Problem in American Institutional and Intellectual Life*. Chicago: University of Chicago Press, 1959.

Escott, Paul D. *Slavery Remembered: A Record of Twentieth Century Slave Narratives*. Chapel Hill, North Carolina: University of North Carolina Press, 1978.

Fogel, Robert William, and Stanley L. Engerman. *Time on the Cross: The Economics of American Negro Slavery*. 2 volumes. Boston: Little, Brown, 1974.

Fornell, Earl Wesley. *The Galveston Era: The Texas Crescent on the Eve of Secession*. Austin: University of Texas Press, 1961.

Franklin, John Hope. *Reconstruction After the Civil War.* Chicago: University of Chicago Press, 1961.

Friend, Llerena. *Sam Houston, The Great Designer.* Austin: University of Texas Press, 1954.

Garraty, John A. *The Nature of Biography.* New York: Knopf, 1957.

Genovese, Eugene D. *From Rebellion to Revolution: Afro-American Slave Revolts in the Making of the New World.* Baton Rouge: Louisiana State University Press, 1979.

____________. *The Political Economy of Slavery: Studies in the Economy and Society of the Slave South.* New York: Pantheon Books, 1965.

____________. *Roll, Jordan, Roll: The World the Slaves Made.* New York: Pantheon Books, 1974.

____________. *The World the Slaveholders Made: Two Essays in Interpretation.* New York: Random House, 1971.

Gray, Lewis Cecil. *History of Agriculture in the Southern United States to 1860.* 2 volumes. Washington: Carnegie Institution of Washington, 1933.

Gutman, Herbert G. *The Black Family in Slavery and Freedom, 1750-1925.* New York: Pantheon Books, 1976.

Hamilton, Holman. *Prologue to Conflict: The Crisis and Compromise of 1850.* Lexington, Kentucky: University of Kentucky Press, 1964.

Heartsill, William W. *One Thousand Four Hundred and Ninety-One Days in the Confederate Army: A Journal Kept by W. W. Heartsill. . .* Edited by Bell I. Wiley. Jackson, Tennessee: McCowat-Mercer Press, 1953.

Hilliard, Sam Bowers. *Hog Meat and Hoecake: Food Supply in the Old South, 1840-1860.* Carbondale, Illinois: Southern Illinois University Press, 1972.

Hirschon, Stanley P. *Grenville M. Dodge: Soldier, Politician, Railroad Pioneer.* Bloomington, Indiana: Indiana University Press, 1967.

Johnson, Ludwell H. *Red River Campaign: Politics and Cotton in the Civil War.* Baltimore: Johns Hopkins Press, 1958.

Johnson, Michael P. *Toward a Patriarchal Republic: The Secession of Georgia.* Baton Rouge: Louisiana State University Press, 1977.

Jordan, Terry G. *German Seed in Texas Soil: Immigrant Farmers in Nineteenth Century Texas.* Austin: University of Texas Press, 1966.

Kelly, Alfred H., and Winfred A. Harbison. *The American Constitution, Its Origin and Development.* 3rd edition. New York: Norton, 1963.

Kerby, Robert L. *Kirby Smith's Confederacy: The Trans-Mississippi South, 1863-1865.* New York: Columbia University Press, 1972.

King, Alvy L. *Louis T. Wigfall, Southern Fire-eater.* Baton Rouge: Louisiana State University Press, 1970.

Lale, Max S. *As It Was in the Beginning* [History of Trinity Episcopal Church]. Marshall, Texas: Demmer Co., 1950.

Lane, Walter P. *The Adventures and Recollections of General Walter P. Lane, A San Jacinto Veteran. . .* Marshall, Texas: News Messenger Publishing Co., 1928.

Lathrop, Barnes F. *Migration into East Texas, 1835-1860: A Study from the Unites States Census.* Austin: Texas State Historical Association, 1949.

Link, Arthur S., and Rembert W. Patrick (editors). *Writing Southern History: Essays in Historiography in Honor of Fletcher M. Green.* Baton Rouge: Louisiana State University Press, 1965.

Luke, Clive J. *The Marshall Powder Mill Site; The 1973-1974 Excavation.* Austin: State Department of Highways and Public Transportation, 1978.

McLean, John H. *Reminiscences of Reverend Jno. H. McLean.* Dallas: Smith and Lamar, 1918.

Moneyhon, Carl H. *Republicanism in Reconstruction Texas.* Austin: University of Texas Press, 1980.

Moore, Albert Burton. *Conscription and Conflict in the Con-*

federacy. New York: Macmillan, 1924.

Nevins, Allan. *The Gateway to History*. Garden City, New York: Doubleday, 1962.

Nichols, James Lynn. *The Confederate Quartermaster in the Trans-Mississippi Department*. Austin: University of Texas Press, 1964.

Nixon, Pat Ireland. *A History of the Texas Medical Association, 1853-1953*. Austin: University of Texas Press, 1954.

North, Douglass C. *The Economic Growth of the United States, 1790-1860*. New York: Norton, 1966.

Oates, Stephen B. *With Malice Toward None: The Life of Abraham Lincoln*. New York: Harper, 1977.

Owens, Leslie Howard. *This Species of Property: Slave Life and Culture in the Old South*. New York: Oxford University Press, 1976.

Owsley, Frank Lawrence. *Plain Folk of the Old South*. Baton Rouge: Louisiana State University Press, 1949.

Phillips, Ulrich B. *American Negro Slavery: A Survey of the Supply, Employment and Control of Negro Labor as Determined by the Plantation Regime*. New York: D. Appleton and Co., 1918.

Pierce, George Foster. *Incidents of Western Travel: in a Series of Letters*. Edited by Thomas O. Summers. Nashville, Tennessee: Southern Methodist Publishing House, 1859 edition.

Potter, David M. *The Impending Crisis, 1848-1861*. New York: Harper, 1976.

Procter, Ben H. *Not Without Honor: The Life of John H. Reagan*. Austin: University of Texas Press, 1962.

Ramsdell, Charles William. *Reconstruction in Texas*. Austin: University of Texas Press, 1970.

Randall, James G., and David Donald. *The Civil War and Reconstruction*. Boston: D.C. Heath, 1961.

Ransom, Roger L., and Richard Sutch. *One Kind of Freedom: The Economic Consequences of Emancipation*. New York:

Cambridge University Press, 1977.

Rawick, George P. (editor). *The American Slave: A Composite Autobiography*. 19 volumes. Westport, Connecticut: Greenwood, 1972.

Redfield, Robert. *The Little Community*. Chicago: University of Chicago Press, 1956.

Reed, St. Clair Griffin. *A History of the Texas Railroads and of Transportation Conditions under Spain and Mexico and the Republic and the State*. Houston: St. Clair Publishing Co., 1941.

Rice, Lawrence D. *The Negro in Texas, 1874-1900*. Baton Rouge: Louisiana State University Press, 1971.

Richardson, Rupert N., Ernest Wallace, and Adrian Anderson. *Texas: The Lone Star State*. 3rd edition. Englewood Cliffs, New Jersey: Prentice-Hall, 1970.

Robinson, Donald L. *Slavery in the Structure of American Politics, 1765-1820*. New York: Harcourt Brace, 1971.

Rock, James L., and W. I. Smith. *Southern and Western Texas Guide for 1878*. St. Louis: A. H. Granger, 1878.

Russo, David J. *Families and Communities: A New View of American History*. Nashville, Tennessee: American Association for State and Local History, 1975.

Scarborough, William Kauffman. *The Overseer: Plantation Management in the Old South*. Baton Rouge: Louisiana University Press, 1966.

Simkins, Francis Butler, and Charles Pierce Roland. *A History of the South*. 4th edition. New York: Knopf, 1972.

Simpson, Harold B. *The Marshall Guards: Harrison County's Contribution to Hood's Texas Brigade*. Marshall, Texas: Port Caddo Press, 1967.

Smith, Edward. *Account of a Journey Through Northeastern Texas. . . .* London: Hamilton, Adams & Co., 1849.

Stampp, Kenneth M. *The Era of Reconstruction, 1865-1877*. New York: Knopf, 1965.

______________. *The Peculiar Institution: Slavery in the Ante-Bellum South.* New York: Random House, 1956.

Sternsher, Bernard. *Consensus, Conflict, and American Historians.* Bloomington, Indiana: Indiana University Press, 1975.

Sutter, Ruth E. *The Next Place You Come To: A Historical Introduction to Communities in North America.* Englewood Cliffs, New Jersey: Prentice-Hall, 1973.

Texas Newspapers, 1813-1939; A Union List of Newspaper Files Available in Offices of Publishers, Libraries, and a Number of Private Collections. Houston: San Jacinto Museum of History, 1941.

Thernstrom, Stephan. *The Other Bostonians: Poverty and Progress in the American Metropolis, 1880-1970.* Cambridge, Massachusetts: Harvard University Press, 1973.

______________. *Poverty and Progress: Social Mobility in a Nineteenth-Century City.* Cambridge, Massachusetts: Harvard University Press, 1964.

Thomas, Emory M. *The Confederate Nation, 1861-1865.* New York: Harper, 1979.

Thornton, J. Mills, III. *Politics and Power in a Slave Society: Alabama, 1800-1860.* Baton Rouge: Louisiana State University Press, 1978.

Van Zandt, Khleber M. *Force Without Fanfare; The Autobiography of K. M. Van Zandt.* Edited by Sandra L. Myres. Fort Worth: Texas Christian University Press, 1968.

Walton, Seth, et al. (compilers). *Inventory of County Records: Harrison County.* Austin: Texas State Library, 1979.

Webb, Walter P., H. Bailey Carroll and Eldon S. Branda (editors). *The Handbook of Texas.* 3 volumes. Austin: Texas State Historical Association, 1952, 1976.

Webber, Thomas L. *Deep Like the Rivers: Education in the Slave Quarter Community, 1831-1865.* New York: Norton, 1978.

Woodman, Harold D. *King Cotton and His Retainers: Financing and Marketing the Cotton Crop of the South, 1800-1925.* Lexington, Kentucky: University of Kentucky Press, 1968.

Woodward, C. Vann. *Reunion and Reaction: The Compromise of 1877 and the End of Reconstruction*. Boston: Little, Brown, 1951.

Wooster, Ralph A. *The People in Power: Courthouse and Statehouse in the Lower South, 1850-1860*. Knoxville, Tennessee: University of Tennessee Press, 1969.

____________. *Politicians, Planters, and Plain Folk: Courthouse and Statehouse in the Upper South, 1850-1860*. Knoxville, Tennessee: University of Tennessee Press, 1975.

Wright, Carroll D. *The History and Growth of the United States Census*. Washington: Government Printing Office, 1900.

Wright, Gavin. *The Political Economy of the Cotton South: Households, Markets, and Wealth in the Nineteenth Century*. New York: Norton, 1978.

Wright, Louise Wigfall. *A Southern Girl in '61*. New York: Doubleday, Page & Co., 1905.

Wright, Marcus J. (compiler). *Texas in the War, 1861-1865*. Edited by Harold B. Simpson. Hillsboro, Texas: Hill Junior College Press, 1965.

Articles

Avillo, Philip J., Jr. "Phantom Radicals: Texas Republicans in Congress, 1870-1873." *Southwestern Historical Quarterly*, LXXVII (April, 1974), 431-444.

Bailey, David Thomas. "A Divided Prism: Two Sources of Black Testimony on Slavery." *Journal of Southern History*, XLVI (August, 1980), 381-404.

Blassingame, John W. "Using the Testimony of Ex-Slaves: Approaches and Problems." *Journal of Southern History*, XLI (November, 1975), 473-492.

Blocker, Albert B. "The Boy-Bugler of the Third Texas Cavalry: The A. B. Blocker Narrative." Edited by Max S. Lale. *Military History of Texas and the Southwest*, XIV [1978] (#2), 71-92; (#3), 147-167; (#4), 215-227; XV [1979] (#1), 21-34.

Bonner, James C. "Profile of a Late Ante-Bellum Community." *American Historical Review*, XLIX (July, 1944), 663-680.

Campbell, Randolph B. "Family History from Local Records: A Case Study from Nineteenth Century Texas." *East Texas Historical Journal*, XIX (Fall, 1981), 13-26.

____________. "Local Archives as a Source of Slave Prices: Harrison County, Texas as a Test Case." *The Historian*, XXXVI (August, 1974), 660-669.

____________. "Planters and Plain Folk: Harrison County, Texas, as a Test Case, 1850-1860." *Journal of Southern History*, XL (August, 1974), 369-398.

____________. "Texas and the Nashville Convention of 1850." *Southwestern Historical Quarterly*, LXXVI (July, 1972), 1-14.

____________. "The Whig Party of Texas in the Elections of 1848 and 1852." *Southwestern Historical Quarterly*, LXXIII (July, 1969), 17-34.

Campbell, Randolph B., and Donald K. Pickens (editors). " 'My Dear Husband': A Texas Slave's Love Letter, 1862." *Journal of Negro History*, LXV (Fall, 1980), 361-364.

"Census of the State of Texas for 1858." *The Texas Almanac for 1859*. Galveston: Richardson & Co., 1858, 208-211.

Conrad, Alfred H., and John R. Meyer, "The Economics of Slavery in the Ante-Bellum South." *Journal of Political Economy*, LXVI (April, 1958), 95-130.

Cox, LaWanda. "The Promise of Land for the Freedmen." *Mississippi Valley Historical Review*, XLV (December, 1958), 414-440.

Crouch, Barry A., and L. J. Schultz. "Crisis in Color: Racial Separation in Texas During Reconstruction." *Civil War History*, XVI (March, 1970), 37-49.

Dimick, Howard T. "The Bonfoey Case at Marshall." *Southwestern Historical Quarterly*, XLVIII (April, 1945), 471-483.

"East Texas Immigration Society, Elysian Fields, Texas." *The*

Texas Almanac for 1872. Galveston: Richardson, Belo & Co., nd, 98-101.

Elliot, Claude. "The Freedmen's Bureau in Texas." *Southwestern Historical Quarterly*, LVI (July, 1952), 1-24.

Folsom, Burton W., II. "The Politics of Elites: Prominence and Party in Davidson County, Tennessee, 1835-1861." *Journal of Southern History*, XXXIX (August, 1973), 359-378.

Foust, James D., and Dale E. Swan. "Productivity and Profitability of Antebellum Slave Labor: A Micro-Approach." *Agricultural History*, XLIV (January, 1970), 39-62.

Fox, Henry. "Fluctuations of Confederate Currency in the State of Texas from . . . 1861 to . . . 1865." *The Texas Almanac for 1867*. Galveston: Richardson & Co., 1866, 213-214.

Franklin, John Hope. "The Great Confrontation: The South and the Problem of Change." *Journal of Southern History*, XXXVIII (February, 1972), 3-20.

Friedberger, Mark, and Janice R. Webster. "Social Structure and State and Local History." *Western Historical Quarterly*, IX (July, 1978), 297-314.

Gallman, Robert E. "Slavery and Southern Economic Growth." *Southern Economic Journal*, XLV (April, 1979), 1007-1022.

Hopkins, Richard J. "Occupational and Geographic Mobility in Atlanta, 1870-1896." *Journal of Southern History*, XXXIV (May, 1968), 200-213.

"Horticulture." *The Texas Almanac for 1857*. Galveston: Richardson & Co., 1856, 5-29.

Jackson, Susan. "Movin' On: Mobility Through Houston in the 1850s." *Southwestern Historical Quarterly*, LXXXI (January, 1978), 251-282.

Lale, Max S. "Stagecoach Roads to Marshall." *East Texas Historical Journal*, XVII (Fall, 1979), 18-32.

Lale, Max S., and Randolph B. Campbell (editors). "The Plantation Journal of John B. Webster, February 17, 1858-November 5, 1859." *Southwestern Historical Quarterly*, LXXXIV (July, 1980), 49-79.

Lentz, Sallie M. "Highlights of Early Harrison County." *Southwestern Historical Quarterly*, LXI (October, 1957), 240-256.

"List of Newspapers Published in Texas." *The Texas Almanac for 1872*. Galveston: Richardson & Co., 1871, 209-210.

McDonald, Forrest and Grady McWhiney. "The South from Self-Sufficiency to Peonage: An Interpretation." *American Historical Review*, LXXXV (December, 1980), 1095-1118.

Middleton, Annie. "The Texas Convention of 1845." *Southwestern Historical Quarterly*, XXV (July, 1921), 26-62.

Owsley, Frank L. "The Pattern of Migration and Settlement on the Southern Frontier." *Journal of Southern History*, XI (May, 1945), 147-176.

Richardson, S. J. "Harrison County." *The Texas Almanac for 1867*. Galveston: Richardson & Co., 1866, 114-116.

Russ, William A., Jr. "Radical Disfranchisement in Texas, 1867-1870." *Southwestern Historical Quarterly*, XXXVIII (July, 1934), 40-52.

Schoonover, Thomas (editor). "Documents Concerning Lemuel Dale Evans' Plan to Keep Texas in the Union in 1861." *East Texas Historical Journal*, XII (Spring, 1974), 35-38.

Smith, Thomas H. "The Renascence of Local History." *The Historian*, XXXV (November, 1972), 1-17.

Smyrl, Frank. "Unionism in Texas, 1856-1861." *Southwestern Historical Quarterly*, LXVIII (October, 1964), 172-195.

Stampp, Kenneth M. "Rebels and Sambos: The Search for the Negro Personality in Slavery." *Journal of Southern History*, XXXVII (August, 1971), 367-392.

Throne, Mildred. "A Population Study of an Iowa County in 1850." *Iowa Journal of History*, LVII (October, 1959), 305-330.

Townes, A. Jane. "The Effect of Emancipation on Large Landholdings, Nelson and Goochland Counties, Virginia." *Journal of Southern History*, XLV (August, 1979), 403-412.

White, Raymond E. "Cotton Ginning in Texas to 1861." *Southwestern Historical Quarterly*, LXI (October, 1957), 255-269.

Wiener, Jonathan M. "Planter Persistence and Social Change: Alabama, 1850-1870." *Journal of Interdisciplinary History*, VII (Autumn, 1976), 235-260.

Woolfolk, George R. "Cotton Capitalism and Slave Labor in Texas." *Southwestern Social Science Quarterly*, XXXVII (June, 1956), 43-52.

Wooster, Ralph A. "An Analysis of the Texas Know-Nothings." *Southwestern Historical Quarterly,* LXX (January, 1967), 414-423.

Theses, Dissertations, and Unpublished Papers

Adams, Chesley M. "Reconstruction in Harrison County." Unpublished oral account (narrated to Ernest Powell in 1936), Lentz Collection, East Texas Baptist College Library, Marshall, Texas.

Armstrong, James C. "History of Harrison County, Texas, 1839-1880." M. A. Thesis, University of Colorado, 1930.

Curlee, Abigail. "A Study of Texas Slave Plantations, 1822-1865." Ph.D. Dissertation, University of Texas, 1932.

Dart, Justin Whitlock, Jr. "Edward Clark, Governor of Texas," M.A. Thesis, University of Houston, 1964.

Edwards, Mary Jo. "Texas Agriculture as Reflected in Letters to the *Southern Cultivator* Prior to 1861." M.A. Thesis, East Texas State Teachers College, 1948.

Fitch, Rebecca Fortson. "The Use of Native Materials in the Antebellum Buildings of Harrison County, Texas." M.A. Thesis, North Texas State University, 1952.

Finnel, Woolsey, Sr. (compiler). "The Reverend Daniel Brown of Culpepper County, Virginia, and Allied Families. . . . Compiled . . . during the Period, 1948-1954." Unpublished and unpaginated genealogical booklet, property of Douglass V. Blocker, Marshall, Texas.

Hargrove, Dr. C. R. "Memoir on Reconstruction." Unpublished

paper, Lentz Collection, East Texas Baptist College Library, Marshall, Texas.

Lentz, Sallie M. "Bonfoey." Unpublished paper, Lentz Collection, East Texas Baptist College Library, Marshall, Texas.

____________. "The Use of Scrip to Pay for County Government." Unpublished paper, Lentz Collection, East Texas Baptist College Library, Marshall, Texas.

Lothrop, Mrs. Milton. "The Organization and History of the Presbyterian Church." Unpublished paper, Lentz Collection, East Texas Baptist College Library, Marshall, Texas.

McGee, Mrs. M. P. "A Brief History of the First Baptist Church, Marshall, Texas." Unpublished paper, Lentz Collection, East Texas Baptist College Library, Marshall, Texas.

Muir, Andrew Forest. "The Thirty-Second Parallel Pacific Railroad in Texas to 1872." Ph.D. Dissertation, University of Texas, 1949.

Thompson, Lloyd K. "The Origins and Development of Black Religious Colleges in East Texas." Ph.D. Dissertation, North Texas State University, 1976.

INDEX

A

B

C

D

E

Q

R

S

T

Y